D0931135

Inclusive Leisure Services: Responding to the Rights of People with Disabilities

Second Edition

Inclusive Leisure Services: Responding to the Rights of People with Disabilities

Second Edition

John Dattilo, Ph.D.

University of Georgia

Venture Publishing, Inc.
State College, PA

Production Manager: Richard Yocum
Manuscript Editing: Valerie Paukovits
Additional Editing: Richard Yocum
Cover Design: Venture Publishing, Inc.
Cover Photograph: © 2001, The Art Institute of Chicago, All Rights Reserved.

Library of Congress Catalogue Card Number 2001097303
ISBN 1-892132-27-3

For Dad

Acknowledgments

My appreciation extends to the many people I have come to know in my personal and professional life. I am especially indebted to those, who among many other characteristics, happen to have a disability. Their comments have enriched this book and have greatly influenced my ideas. This book has evolved over the past two decades while I taught and conducted research on leisure for people with disabilities. Students enrolled in my courses on inclusive leisure services have influenced what I have included in the book. Their suggestions and feedback concerning the material I presented in class helped shape the content of this text. I am pleased that I received the support to complete a second edition of the book.

I would like to thank my father, who has given me so much support and whose memories continue to inspire me. He taught me through his example to have a strong commitment to family and compassion for others. My mother continues to motivate me with her positive ways—to her, as well, I am indebted. Thanks goes to David and Steven who have kept me focused on what is important in life and Anne who unselfishly continues to encourage me to write books and helps me keep a positive perspective on life.

I would also like to thank Douglas Kleiber for his contributions and for helping me to better understand leisure behavior. I am grateful for his continuous professional and personal support. Several people helped me in developing the first and second editions of the book who deserve recognition: George Alderson, Brenda Arnold, Michele L. Barbin, Leslie Black, Sarah Brownlee, Amanda Darley, Mary Ann Devine, Bonnie Godbey, Lynda Greer, Diane Groff, John McGovern, William Murphy, Roger Nielsen, Valerie Paukovits, Susan St. Peter, Kathleen Sheldon, Ralph Smith, Marlee Stewart, Mary Ulrich, Brent Wolfe, Robin Yaffe, Richard Yocum, and the entire Venture staff.

My goal is that this text will assist readers in understanding the importance of inclusive leisure services. I hope that this knowledge will be applied to systematic service delivery so that people—who among many other characteristics happen to have a disability—can experience enjoyment and leisure.

J. D.

Table of Contents

List of Tables and Figures

Section A

Develop an Awareness

Chapter 1

Become Oriented

If we are to achieve a culture rich in contrasting values,
we must recognize the whole gamut of human potentialities.
And so we are a less arbitrary social fabric,
one in which each diverse human gift will find a fitting place.
-Margaret Mead

Orientation Activity: Think about Leisure

Directions Alone: Next to each item, indicate if it is most associated with free time, recreation, or leisure.

Directions with Others: Move about the room and compare your list with other people, discussing the differences.

1. Activity that may or may not be fun
2. Associated with intrinsic motivations
3. Depends on the perspective of the person
4. Periods in the absence of work
5. Transcends time, environments, and situations
6. Not busy with requirements of daily living
7. Emphasizes a person's perception
8. Involves self-determination
9. Activity designed to be fun

Debriefing: Free time exists when people are not consumed by requirements associated with work or requirements of daily living; therefore, items four and six reflect free time. Recreation is typically associated with activity designed to be fun but might not result in people experiencing positive emotions; therefore, items one and nine relate to recreation. Finally, leisure depends on and emphasizes the perspective of the individual and is associated with intrinsic motivation and self-determination. In addition, leisure transcends time, environments, and situation; therefore, items two, three, five, seven, and eight connect to leisure. Consider the following questions when reflecting on the activity you have recently completed:

- What is the primary purpose of leisure services?
- Who are people with disabilities?
- How can we facilitate leisure for people with disabilities?

Introduction

This book intends to encourage leisure services providers to promote inclusion of people with disabilities in their programs. Throughout the book information is provided to create opportunities for people with and without disabilities to engage in leisure pursuits together. Hopefully, this book will help all of us to become more relaxed in our interactions with people with disabilities. There is value in coming into contact with people with disabilities and getting to know them. Karen Mihalyi stated:

> It's difficult at first when you are not familiar with a group you have a stereotype about. If you are not used to relating to people with disabilities, you are not sure how to. You don't want to make a mistake, do something that might offend them. So you hold back. Now I dive right in and hope that people know I am trying my hardest. I am really losing my self-consciousness around people with disabilities. At first I think I listened mostly. I listened to people and read some—mainly by people who had disabilities. But my ease mostly came by getting close with people, hearing their stories and loving them. (Bogdan and Taylor, 1992, p. 6)

What is the value of reading this book?

With each day that passes, communities are becoming more diverse. While many of us would hail this increasing diversity as a sign of the health and vigor of American culture, the broadened spectrum of linguistic, cultural, ethnic, and ability differences challenges today's human services professionals (Ryndak & Kennedy, 2000). As a result, leisure services professionals provide programs to individuals with a variety of interests and characteristics. Holland (1997) observed that leisure services professionals are expected to work with, and have significant knowledge and understanding of, individuals from many cultural, racial, and ethnic backgrounds.

To facilitate inclusion we must develop an awareness of and appreciation for diversity and an interest in involving all citizens in our programs.

According to Smith and Hilton (1997, p. 3), experiences designed to educate people about inclusion should include knowledge of disabilities and relevant legislation and encouragement of appropriate attitudes and skills needed to promote inclusion.

Leisure services professionals have identified a need to train staff on issues related to disability awareness, sensitivity toward people with disabilities, and methods for modifying programs so that they can be inclusive (Devine, McGovern & Hermann, 1998). Seventy-three percent of the 369 park and recreation agencies surveyed by Devine and Kotowski (1999) identified a need for teaching disability awareness and sensitivity. These findings support observations that leisure service personnel are perceived as not being equipped to conduct inclusive programs, both in terms of staff-to-participant ratios and knowledge regarding activity adaptations and programming techniques.

After surveying over 300 professionals affiliated with therapeutic adventure programs in the United States, Herbert (2000) concluded that staff should acquire greater knowledge of inclusive practices. In addition, Kozub and Porretta (1998) surveyed 295 coaches and reported that the coaches felt inadequately trained to address needs of individuals with disabilities in inclusive contexts, specifically sports settings. Anderson and Heyne (2000) interviewed six focus groups containing a total of 65 individuals with disabilities and leisure services professionals. They concluded that persistent constraints exist for people with disabilities and service providers, including a lack of awareness, acceptance, information, prepared recreation staff, social inclusion, physical access, communication, and networking between agencies and consumers.

Clearly, more information is needed to further inform leisure service providers about models for inclusive leisure service provision and strategies used to enhance inclusive leisure services (Devine, 1999). After interviewing and observing teachers, LaMaster, Gall, Kinchin, and Siedentop (1998, p. 78) concluded that regardless of the experience of teachers, they were inadequately prepared to cope with the challenges of inclusion, and they understood and felt that lack of preparation.

As leisure services providers we are in an excellent position to enhance the lives of people with disabilities. Services we design enhance participants' sense of competence and self-determination. The ability to make choices and take control of one's life can permit all individuals to match their skills to the challenges presented in community recreation opportunities.

Once we recognize our ability to enhance the quality of life for people with disabilities we can develop strategies to promote inclusive leisure services. We can build on people's talents and opportunities and know that all people bring important gifts to community life.

What is leisure?

Although some debate exists over the definitions of the terms "recreation," "free time," and "leisure," there appears to be consensus among consumers, practitioners, researchers, and theorists about their meanings.

Typically, *recreation* is defined as an activity developed by a society and designed primarily for fun, enjoyment, and satisfaction (e.g., swimming, table games, dance). The notion of recreation, therefore, relates directly to the activity and is independent of the participant's feelings and experiences. People who participate in recreational activities may experience enjoyment and satisfaction or may encounter failure, rejection, and feelings of helplessness.

Free time often describes time that is not obligated—time when daily tasks, such as responsibilities associated with family, work, or home maintenance, are not being attended to. When people are not busy performing specific required tasks, they possess free time. Although many people experience enjoyment and satisfaction during their free time, this free time may trigger feelings of boredom, anxiety, and despair in others.

Leisure integrates elements of activity and time, but more importantly emphasizes the person's perception that he or she is free to choose to participate in meaningful, enjoyable, and satisfying experiences. As individuals get in touch with the positive feelings, control, competence, relaxation, and excitement associated with the leisure experience, they will be intrinsically motivated to participate. That is, they will participate in leisure simply to be involved in the experience, not for some tangible outcome or external reward. Leisure, then, is an experience, a process, and a subjective state of mind. As a state of mind, leisure transcends time, environments, and situations. To fully partake in leisure is to express talents, demonstrate capabilities, achieve one's potential, and experience a variety of positive emotions.

The practical value of knowing what contributes to experiencing leisure is clear and direct. It leads us to concentrate on facilitating the leisure experience. In turn, learning how to facilitate leisure makes it possible for us to reduce or eliminate constraints and barriers to leisure participation.

Many people have identified that the key to leisure is the state of mind the person has at the time of the experience. Goodale (1992) reported two principal components of a subjective state of leisure: people perceive themselves to have freely chosen the activity and they engage in the activity purely because doing so is meaningful and enjoyable. Shamir (1992) described these two related aspects of leisure as intrinsic motivation and perceived freedom. *Intrinsic motivation* refers to the motivation one has for doing the activity because of the expected pleasure of participation in the activity itself, not because of expected results or external rewards. *Perceived freedom* refers to the feeling of self-determination that results from being able to choose the activity. Some people regard self-determination as the basis of intrinsic motivation. Russell (1996, p. 48) provided the following illustrations to help us to better understand the notion of the leisure experience:

> Leisure gives us a sense of living for its own sake. Cross-country skiers often exclaim about the sensations of peacefulness and physical exertion while gliding along. Artisans may explain their interest in working with clay on the potter's wheel because of the elastic, smooth substance responding to their hands. Dancing could be described as moving to a rhythm. Hikers often stress the experience of being a part of the beauty of the natural environment. These are all intrinsic rewards.

Perceived freedom to choose to participate is an important element of leisure. A feeling of perceived control over the activity (as opposed to being controlled or being restricted in the activity) is important to the leisure experience. In addition, it is important for individuals to feel that they are free to discontinue participation when they desire to do so.

According to Murphy (1975), the fundamental consideration for all human beings is that individuals should have a measure of freedom, autonomy, choice, and self-determination. When considering Bregha's (1985) position that leisure is the most precious expression of our freedom, it becomes clear that leisure is an inalienable human right. Therefore, we must make every effort to help people with disabilities become involved in active leisure participation. The challenge lies in finding ways to remove barriers to participation while providing opportunities to develop the skills, awareness, and understanding needed to freely choose participation in various leisure experiences. The goal in providing leisure services to people with disabilities, then, is to help individuals develop the skills and opportunities needed to feel free to participate in such chosen experiences.

Leisure also affects our sense of identity. Positive leisure involvement should positively influence our perceptions of ourselves. In discussing positive ways to view ourselves and others. Fulghum (1989) illustrated the role leisure can play in defining our identities:

> Making a living and having a life are not the same thing. Making a living and making a life that's worthwhile are not the same thing. Living *the* good life and living *a* good life are not the same thing.

A job title doesn't even come close to answering the question "What do you do?" But suppose that instead of answering that question with what we do to get money, we replied with what we do that gives us great pleasure or makes us feel useful to the human enterprise? (p. 65)

Leisure is important to the well-being of people, as it provides the opportunity to make personal choices, the opportunity to interact with others, and the emotional value of enjoyment. A mission statement developed by the Community Recreation Department of Nova Scotia entitled "Recreation for People with a Disability: The Value of Leisure," illustrates the value of leisure for all people, including people with disabilities:

The value of leisure experience in enhancing the quality of life for people with a disability should not be underestimated. Recreation offers most people with a disability the same fun and challenge it does all participants. For some people, the recreation environment is a safe, nonthreatening setting in which to experience decision making, risk taking, and community involvement. It can also provide an ideal opportunity for people with a disability to develop basic social and motor skills. The chance to independently choose activities in which to become involved, or even to decide whether or not to participate, can be a significant learning experience. Satisfying leisure experiences can contribute to a sense of self-worth, contribution, and belonging to the community that may otherwise be missing.

What is a disability?

To understand issues surrounding people with disabilities and actions that can be taken to promote inclusion, it is useful to clarify the identification of people with disabilities. According to the Americans with Disabilities Act (ADA, 1990), a person with a disability is anyone who has a physical or mental impairment that substantially limits one or more major life activity. Major life activities include seeing, hearing, speaking, walking, dressing, feeding oneself, working, learning, recreating, and other daily physical or mental activities. This broad definition incorporates many people, including individuals with:

- sensory impairments such as visual and hearing impairments,
- communication disorders such as speech impairments,

- cognitive disabilities such as mental retardation or brain injury,
- physical disabilities such as cerebral palsy or multiple sclerosis,
- chronic health disorders such as cardiac or pulmonary disease,
- impaired mental health such as depression or schizophrenia,
- chemical dependence, and
- HIV infection.

Some people currently free of disease or impairment and not limited in major life activities may also be covered by the ADA. This includes people who have a record of a disability, such as a history of alcoholism or chemical dependence, mental or emotional illness, heart disease, or cancer. Other examples include people who have been misclassified as having a disability (e.g., mental retardation or mental illness) when they did not. In addition, the ADA covers people who are regarded as having a disability. An example of a person regarded as having a disability is an individual who has a significant facial deformity that does not limit major life activities. While the person is not physically or mentally restricted in his or her activities, public reaction to the person's appearance may result in discrimination. Another example is a person rumored to be, but who is not, infected with HIV. In summary, a person with a disability is anyone who:

- has a physical or mental impairment substantially limiting one or more major life activities,
- has a record of such impairment, or
- is regarded as having such impairment.

The U.S. Supreme Court continually interprets the definition of disability stipulated in the ADA. Deciding who qualifies as an individual with disabilities is a challenging task that will require considerable effort in the future. For example, Fawley (1999, p. 12) reported that on June 22, 1999 the U.S. Supreme Court ruled that the ADA:

> does not cover people who can use eyeglasses, medication or other treatments to correct their disabilities. Because people with diabetes can control their disease with insulin, they are not covered in the new version of the law. According to Joseph LaMountain, national director for the American Diabetes Association "The bottom line is that a person with diabetes will first have to show that, even with treatment, he or she is substantially limited in a major life activity. Once that is shown, the person will then have to turn around and prove that with reasonable accommodation, he or she can do the job in question.

There are many characteristics associated with disabling conditions that influence the ability of individuals to enjoy meaningful leisure. For example, people who have conditions that result in sporadic performance (e.g., multiple sclerosis) have different concerns than people whose condition is continuous (e.g., cerebral palsy). The age of onset that the disability occurs will influence a person's approach to leisure such as a person who is congenitally blind (blind at birth) as compared to someone who is adventitiously blinded (acquired the blindness) as an adult. The length of time the person has the disability can also be an important consideration, such as the difference between someone who has recently recovered from a spinal cord injury as compared to someone who sustained the injury many years ago. The prognosis of the condition that causes the disability can affect people's leisure such as the difference between someone who has a static condition such as a hearing loss caused by medication taken as a child compared to a hearing loss that is progressively deteriorating. The severity of the condition also influences a person's participation such a person with mental retardation who requires intermittent supports as compared to someone who needs pervasive supports.

When considering these many factors that influence an individual's leisure participation it becomes apparent that each person will have unique leisure needs and require different types of accommodations. Shapiro (1993, p. 5) identified the diversity associated with people who have disabilities with the following description:

> There are hundreds of different disabilities. Some are congenital; most come later in life. Some are progressive, like muscular dystrophy, cystic fibrosis, and some forms of vision and hearing loss. Others, like seizure conditions, are episodic. Multiple sclerosis is episodic and progressive. Some conditions are static, like the loss of a limb. Still others, like cancer and occasionally paralysis, can even go away. Some disabilities are "hidden," like epilepsy or diabetes. Disability law also applies to people with perceived disabilities such as obesity or stuttering, which are not disabling but create prejudice and discrimination. Each disability comes in differing degrees of severity. Hearing aids can amplify sounds for most deaf and hard-of-hearing people but do nothing for others. Some people with autism spend their lives in institutions; others graduate from Ivy League schools or reach the top of their professions.

There are indeed a variety of disabling conditions; however, a person with a particular disability may be very different from another individual with the same disabling condition. For example, the National Office of

Disability/Harris Survey of Americans with Disabilities (2000) reported that it is misleading to think of people with disabilities as a homogeneous group because disabilities vary in type and severity.

Although the information presented in this section identifies how disability is defined by the ADA, it is helpful for us to focus on environmental and attitudinal barriers experienced by individuals that we can minimize as opposed to focusing on limitations within a person. Similarly, Bleecker (2000) stated that a person with a disability should no longer be viewed as someone who cannot function because of an impairment, but rather as someone who needs an accommodation to function.

What is the problem?

Some 43 million Americans have one or more physical or mental disabilities, and this number is increasing as the population as a whole is growing older. The 1991 Institute of Medicine ranked disability as the largest public health problem in the United States.

Historically, society has tended to isolate and segregate individuals with disabilities. Despite some improvements discrimination against individuals with disabilities continues to be a serious and pervasive social problem. In his moving story of Franklin Delano Roosevelt's disability and the intense efforts to conceal if from the public, Gallaher (1994, p. 32, 29) described the injustices people with disabilities have experienced throughout the years:

> Throughout history—with specific, glorious exceptions—the crippled have been cursed, tormented, abandoned, imprisoned, and killed. The Spartans hurled their disabled citizens off a cliff to their death. Martin Luther believed deformed children were fathered by the devil and killing them was no sin. The Jews banished their cripples, forcing them to beg along the roadside. American Indians took their deformed newborns and buried them alive. In the 18th century, the handicapped were confined to asylums—to be cared for, perhaps, but also to remove their appearance, offensive to sensitive persons, from the streets. [In the U.S. in the 20th century] the handicapped were kept at home, out of sight, in back bedrooms by families who felt a mixture of embarrassment and shame about their presence. The well-to-do were able to afford custodial nursing care for their handicapped family members, and the loving family was able to care at home for its crippled loved ones. Many of the handicapped, however, were simply ignored by their families and society.

Discrimination against individuals with disabilities persists today in critical areas, such as recreation. Unlike individuals who have experienced discrimination on the basis of race, color, sex, national origin, religion, or age, individuals who have experienced discrimination on the basis of disability have often had no legal recourse to redress such discrimination. Individuals with disabilities continually encounter various forms of discrimination, including outright intentional exclusion, the discriminatory effects of architectural, transportation, and communication barriers, over-protective rules and policies, failure to make modifications to existing facilities and practices, exclusionary qualification standards and criteria, segregation, and relegation to lesser services, programs, activities, benefits, jobs, or opportunities.

Census data, national polls, and other studies have documented that people with disabilities, as a group, occupy an inferior status in our society and are severely disadvantaged socially, vocationally, economically, and educationally. The nation's goals regarding individuals with disabilities are to assure equality of opportunity, full participation, independent living, and economic self-sufficiency. The continuing existence of discrimination and prejudice denies people with disabilities the opportunity to compete on an equal basis and to pursue those opportunities for which our free society is justifiably famous, and costs billions of dollars in unnecessary expenses resulting from dependency and a lack of productivity.

A total of 997 adults with disabilities and 953 adults without disabilities were included in The 2000 National Office of Disability/Harris Survey of Americans with Disabilities. The survey showed that although there have been improvements in the lives of people with disabilities, they lag behind their peers without disabilities in employment and income. People who have disabilities are almost three times as likely to live in poverty. Since having discretionary income often enables people to enjoy themselves and take advantage of recreation activities (e.g., eating at restaurants, going to movies, and attending sporting events), it is not surprising that people with disabilities report far fewer experiences associated with accessing entertainment, socializing, and going shopping. The survey revealed that when comparing people of similar ages and incomes, significant gaps still exist between people with and without disabilities, implying that factors such as lack of accessibility, negative public attitudes, and discomfort may be inhibiting people with disabilities from participating in these recreation activities.

What can we do?

Hopefully as you read this book you will become concerned about the importance of including people with disabilities in community leisure services. Perhaps to better understand the need for inclusion we may consider that even at the lowest estimate, people with disabilities could be the nation's largest minority. Disability, however, is the one minority that anyone can join at any time—as a result of a sudden automobile accident, a fall down a flight of stairs, cancer, or disease. Less than 15% of Americans with disabilities were born with their disabilities (Shapiro, 1993).

Although many suggestions are presented in this text on how to relate to people, I have found one idea that helps guide my interactions with all people, including those who happen to have a disability. When I encounter a man older than me, I think to myself, if that were my father, how would I want others to behave toward him? When I encounter a woman older than me, I think to myself, if that were my mother, how would I want others to behave toward her? When I encounter a child, I think to myself, if that were my child, how would I want others to behave toward him or her? When I encounter a woman about my age, I think to myself, if that were my wife, how would I want others to behave toward her? When I encounter a man my age, I think to myself, if that were I, how would I want others to behave toward me? I use my answers to these questions to help determine my actions toward all individuals. When I do this, I am then more likely to act toward people with kindness, dignity, and respect.

Although this text describes various disabling conditions, it is important for us to focus on the principles that facilitate individuals' inclusion into community leisure services. Hutchison and McGill (1992) suggested that leisure services professionals resist the temptation to view a diagnosis as the only important truth and begin to look for other ways to determine people's interests and abilities, such as by building relationships with people and providing supports.

Inherent at any level leisure service delivery is the need to communicate to potential consumers the availability of services. Therefore, as attempts at marketing are made, it may be helpful to consider that, although people with disabilities are a minority, they are many in number. People with disabilities have clearly emerged as a consumer group with money to spend on leisure pursuits. Shapiro (1993) described an incident that identified people with disabilities as a market to be targeted:

> The Minneapolis-based Target department store chain put its first model with mental retardation, a young girl with Down syndrome,

in a Sunday newspaper advertising insert in 1990. "That ad hit doorsteps at six a.m. Sunday and a half hour later my phone was ringing," recalls George Hite, the company's vice president for marketing. "It was the mother of a girl with Down syndrome thanking me for having a kid with Down syndrome in our ad. It's so important to my daughter's self-image," she said. That ad, one small picture among dozens in the circular, generated over two thousand letters of thanks to stunned Target executives. (p. 36)

Since I have spent some of my life interacting with, befriending, and providing services to people with some very severe disabilities, I have been asked: "How do you know if a person will respond to you or even knows you are there?" My response to this question is always the same. I tell people that sometimes I am not sure whether a person is aware I am there; however, I always assume that the person is aware of me and that the person benefits from my contact. I would much prefer to assume that a person is benefiting by my actions and be wrong, than to assume that they could not, and not give them the chance. As I explain this concept I often share the quote by Baer (1981) when he responded to the question "Why should we proceed as if all people are capable of learning under instruction?"

If I proceed in this way, sometimes—perhaps often—I will be right, and that will be good. What will be good is not that I will have been right (much as I enjoy that), but rather that some children who we otherwise might have thought could not learn will learn at least something useful to them. (p. 93)

As you read this text you may notice that the chapter titles and the various headings used throughout the book begin with action verbs. I intentionally included these words to encourage readers to take action and implement what we have learned. As we gain knowledge about inclusion we have a responsibility to advocate for people with disabilities, to promote their inclusion into community in general, and to promote inclusion in recreation and leisure opportunities within communities. To help emphasize this point, Fulghum (1989) stated:

I do not want to talk about what you understand about this world. I want to know what you will do about it. I do not want to know what you *hope*. I want to know what you will *work for*. I do not want your sympathy for the needs of humanity. I want your muscle. As the wagon driver said when they came to a long, hard hill, "Them that's going on with us, get out and push. Them that ain't, get out of the way." (p. 107)

What is in this book?

Just as Terrill (1992, p. 8) identified the Americans with Disabilities Act as a springboard for "inclusion, independence, and the recognition that all people have the opportunity to be contributing members of society," this book is designed to bring the spirit of the ADA to the field of recreation and leisure. All leisure services professionals need information necessary to work with people with disabilities. This book will educate future and current leisure services professionals about attitude development and actions that promote positive attitudes about people who have experienced discrimination and segregation. Galambos, Lee, Rahn, and Williams (1994, p. 70) expressed the importance of including education that addresses attitudes, which can be one of the most difficult barriers to overcome, because if attitudes are not properly addressed, it can sabotage the program.

Devine (1999) reported on the results of surveys from 226 recreation agencies throughout the United States. One of the main purposes of these surveys was to determine training needs of park and recreation agencies related to inclusion. The training needs indicated were disability awareness, sensitivity training, program modifications, policy and procedure revision strategies, and updates on the ADA regulations.

This book attempts to provide current and future professionals with strategies that will facilitate meaningful leisure participation by all participants, while respecting the rights of people with disabilities (see **Figure 1.1**, p. 16). The first section is devoted to awareness of important concepts. In response to the conclusion that training is needed for leisure service providers on ways to include people with disabilities in community recreation programs (Anderson & Heyne, 2000), the second section presents readers with the Americans with Disabilities Act and specific strategies to facilitate participation within the spirit of the act. The final section introduces readers to people with disabilities, their characteristics, and methods for including them in community leisure services.

This chapter begins the first section of the book, designed to increase awareness of various issues and ideas associated with inclusive leisure services. Chapter 2 provides a description of inclusion, discusses it as a civil rights issue, and identifies who is responsible for providing inclusive leisure services. Chapter 3 provides information to increase awareness of attitude formation and to clarify the impact of negative attitudes. Chapter 4 supplies readers with information and opportunities on how to explore their attitudes. Strategies for enhancing positive attitude formation are presented in Chapter 5. Chapters 6 and 7 encourage sensitivity to appropriate terminology and family issues. Chapter 8 concludes the awareness section by identifying barriers to leisure participation experienced by people with disabilities.

The second section of the book identifies and describes specific methods and procedures that can be used to help promote inclusion. Specifically, Chapter 9 provides information on the Americans with Disabilities Act and sets the tone for this section. The following six chapters provide specific suggestions to help professionals provide inclusive leisure services. Chapter 10 addresses universal design issues. Suggestions to encourage enhancement of self-determination are provided in Chapter 11. Chapter 12 presents guidelines for the development of comprehensive leisure education programs. Chapter 13 is devoted to procedures for increasing social interactions and the development of friendships. Chapter 14 presents recommendations for making necessary accommodations, and Chapter 15 presents suggestions for advocacy.

The final section of the book introduces the reader to several people with disabilities. The information presented in Chapters 16–19 intends to have the reader meet people with disabilities through pictures and written

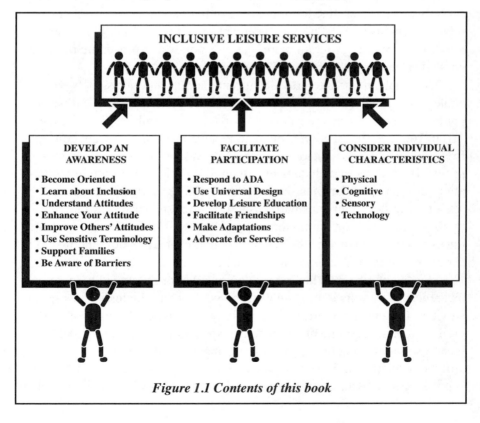

INCLUSIVE LEISURE SERVICES

DEVELOP AN AWARENESS	FACILITATE PARTICIPATION	CONSIDER INDIVIDUAL CHARACTERISTICS
• Become Oriented • Learn about Inclusion • Understand Attitudes • Enhance Your Attitude • Improve Others' Attitudes • Use Sensitive Terminology • Support Families • Be Aware of Barriers	• Respond to ADA • Use Universal Design • Develop Leisure Education • Facilitate Friendships • Make Adaptations • Advocate for Services	• Physical • Cognitive • Sensory • Technology

Figure 1.1 Contents of this book

text, and to have the reader develop an appreciation for the need for leisure in their lives. The specific descriptions and pictures of the people were chosen to provide a diverse introduction to people with disabilities who are living within their communities. However, after examining the broad definition of disability as defined by ADA, it became clear that an overview of each disabling condition presented within the confines of this text would be an unmanageable task. Therefore, a sampling of disabilities was chosen, including physical limitations, cognitive limitations, and sensory limitations. The final chapter of the book provides an introduction to some people with disabilities who use assistive technology.

The chapters are organized in a similar manner and contain segments designed to enhance learning. Each chapter begins with an orientation activity to familiarize the reader with the content presented in the chapter and to provide an opportunity to interact with others about the topic. The orientation activities provide an experiential preview of what is to come in the chapter and set the educational climate. These orientation activities are immediately followed by debriefings to maximize learning associated with the activities. The debriefings consist of a brief discussion about the orientation activity and a few questions requiring the reader to reflect on the activity. Next, each chapter contains an introduction designed to briefly acquaint the reader with the topics to be covered in the chapter. The content of each chapter follows the introduction and comprises the majority of the chapter. A variety of questions and possible responses are posed throughout each chapter. Concluding sections of final thoughts offer readers additional examples and a chance to reflect on the information presented in each chapter. The chapters finish with several discussion questions to encourage the reader to review the material, identify important aspects of the content, and engage in problem solving.

Final Thoughts

Although there is tremendous potential for leisure to enhance the inclusion of individuals with disabilities, this potential is not being fully realized in the lives of many people with disabilities (Mahon, Mactavish & Bockstael, 2000). One solution is to educate leisure services professionals on ways to promote inclusion. This book contains information to help us:

- develop an awareness of inclusion, diversity, disability, attitudes, family issues and common barriers to leisure participation;
- facilitate participation by responding to the ADA, promoting self-determination, developing leisure education, facilitating access;

    encouraging integration, making adaptations, and advocating; and
- consider individual characteristics of participants when developing and implementing leisure services.

People associated with the disability rights movement believe that people with disabilities are not helpless "cripples," nor are they courageous or heroic "superachievers." Most people with disabilities are just regular people trying to lead meaningful lives, not to inspire, nor to be pitied. Hopefully, by getting to know some people with disabilities through this book, we can avoid creating stereotypes and we will see the value in providing inclusive leisure services.

Discussion Questions

1. What are some reasons why it might be helpful to read this book?
2. What is meant by the words "recreation," "free time," and "leisure?"
3. What is intrinsic motivation?
4. What is a disability according to the U. S. Americans with Disabilities Act?
5. What are examples of disabling conditions?
6. What are some characteristics associated with disabling conditions that can influence an individual's ability to experience leisure?
7. Why are some people with disabilities experiencing problems?
8. What are some goals of the U. S. government regarding people with disabilities?
9. Why is poverty a consideration when providing leisure services for people with disabilities?
10. What can leisure services providers do to help people with disabilities?

Chapter 2

Learn about Inclusion

. . . "I know you, you know me,"
one thing I can tell you is you got to be free.
Come together, right now, over me.
Come together, yeah!
–John Lennon

Orientation Activity: Consider Inclusion

Directions Alone: Read the statement presented below and write a paragraph describing what you think the person meant when he wrote it.

Inclusion is recognizing that we are one even though we are not the same.
- Shafik Abu-Tahir

Directions with Others: Divide into small groups and discuss your interpretation of the statement with other members. After a specified time, share your responses with the entire group.

Debriefing: Inclusion does not mean we are all the same or we all agree; rather, inclusion means that we celebrate our diversity and differences with respect and gratitude. Inclusion does not mean that people are oblivious to individual differences. This sentiment is similar to the notion of "color blindness" that infers that all people are the same and we do not notice differences. Inclusion develops a community in which all people are knowledgeable about and supportive of other people. That goal is not achieved by some false image of homogeneity in the name of inclusion. Consider the following questions when reflecting on the activity you have recently completed:

- How do you define inclusion?
- How does the statement by Shafik Abu-Tahir relate to your definition of inclusion?
- What did you learn by doing this activity?

Introduction

The lyrics presented at the beginning of this chapter provide a place to begin to discuss the idea of inclusion. Inclusion is a way of looking at the world and helping people come together. As people come together they get to know one another, begin to understand one another, and develop an appreciation for one another. The use of metaphors can be a way for us to learn about inclusion. For example:

> A walk through a garden reveals a panoply of lovely plants — all varied in form, blossoms, and size. All share such basic needs as soil, water, and sunlight; yet each plant may have different needs as to the type of soil, the amount of water, and the degree of sunlight required for life and growth. Each type of plant is of interest to the observer and offers its own beauty and special characteristics. Seen together, as a whole, the plants form a wondrous garden to behold. (Hanson, 1998, p. 3)

After presenting this description, Marci Hanson (p. 3) identified the metaphor she considered when describing the garden.

> Like the garden, communities are made up of individuals, all of whom contribute their own unique characteristics to the sense of place in which we live. Just as plants share certain common needs for survival, so too do the individuals within communities. Each of the members of the community, similar to the garden plants, has different needs and avenues for growth that are essential if these individuals are to express their full potential.

Similarly, Eileen Szychowsky (Wheat, 2000) a woman participating in a rafting trip, made the following observation:

> In this perfect setting, the beauty, power, and fragility of the Grand Canyon reflect who we are as a society. Each rock layer within the canyon is a thing of unique beauty. However, it is the contrast of colors, shapes, and textures, which only in unity become the Grand Canyon. Likewise, when individuals within our society, regardless of color, nationality, sexual orientation, ability, or disability work in unity, we too, become things of beauty and wonder. (p. 78)

These metaphors of a garden and the Grand Canyon may be helpful to consider when we attempt to develop inclusive leisure services. To address the topic of inclusion, several questions are discussed in this lesson:

- What is a community?
- What do people want from their communities?
- Why are some people with disabilities not included?
- What does inclusion mean?
- How does integration differ from inclusion?
- Whose responsibility is it to create inclusive communities?

What is a community?

After reviewing many definitions, Walker (1999) characterized three interrelated components associated with the idea of *community*: a sense of place, people, and membership or belonging.

In a community, there are varied tasks to be performed. Members of the community engage in interesting and satisfying roles that also benefit the group as a whole. Community members are given respect and they enrich the community with their variety. A community flourishes when its members continually develop and apply their talents in mutually enriching ways (Tomlinson et al., 1997). Amado (2000, p. 5) noted that: "For almost all of us, our sense of community comes from the people we know, not the places we go."

Our sense of community is shaped by where we are and whom we know; however, the essence of community comes from how we feel. If we feel a sense of membership and a sense of belonging, we will then have a sense of community.

What do people want from their communities?

"When a well-known and respected Black woman, Rosa Parks, refused to surrender her bus seat to a White man on the afternoon of December 1, 1955, she was arrested and taken to jail" (Adam Fairclough, 1995, p. 16). Why did Ms. Parks choose such a decision that would result in her incarceration? What did she want from her community? Well, Rosa Parks (1992, p. 116) wrote of the fateful day:

> People always say that I didn't give up my seat because I was tired, but that isn't true. I was not tired physically, or no more tired than I usually was at the end of a working day. I was not old, although

some people have an image of me as being old then. I was forty-two. No, the only tired I was, was tired of giving in.

So what did Rosa Parks want from her community? For that matter, what do all people who differ relative to age, gender, ability, socioeconomic status, race, religion, ethnic background, sexual orientation, education level, political affiliation, and language want? Frankly stated by Marsha Forest and Jack Pearpoint (1995, p. 1), individuals say:

> "I want to be included!" This simple statement is being spoken, signed, key-boarded, whispered, and shouted by people of all ages, shapes, sizes, colors, and cultures. Many are making the request for themselves while others are asking for their friends or aging relatives. It is a simple request and the answer is equally easy: Welcome!

When people want to be included in their communities, what do they mean? Based on a study exploring experiences of adults with disabilities residing in their communities, Walker (1999) concluded that when these adults had positive community experiences they described their community as providing a sense of safety, a feeling of being known, a sense of identity, familiarity with people and places, a feeling of being liked or accepted, and a sense of accommodation.

Therefore, an important way to determine the success of a program is if it encourages an individual to be included in community-based activities. It is helpful for us to work for inclusion of people with disabilities, with all its implications of being socially connected, exchanging and sharing responsibilities. Inclusion means that people with disabilities become full, active, learning members of the community.

Ward and Meyer (1999) explained that people with disabilities have been influenced by the social and political upheaval created by the civil rights movement, and they have identified with the struggles of other disenfranchised groups to achieve inclusion and meaningful equality of opportunity. According to MacNeil and Anderson (1999), inclusive leisure opportunities should be considered a basic civil right for all human beings because people, regardless of ability, deserve the opportunity to experience meaningful leisure.

Why are some people with disabilities not included?

Senator Lowell Weicker (1988) summarized the plight of people with disabilities by stating that the history of the way society has dealt with people with disabilities can be summed up in two words—segregation and inequality. We have treated people with disabilities as inferiors and made them unwelcome in many activities and opportunities generally available to other Americans.

The same excuses being used to exclude children with disabilities were used to segregate children of color. The decision resulting from Brown versus the Board of Education (1954) sent a clear message to U.S. citizens that separate is not equal. According to Berger (1994), any system that says some people must be segregated because they are different is an oppressive system and a civil rights issue. It is simply discriminatory that people labeled "disabled" must earn the right to become ready to be included in their communities (Karagiannis, Stainback & Stainback, 1996).

"Separation is repugnant to our constitutional tradition." These are words of Gilhool (1976, p. 8) as he identified inclusion as a central constitutional value; however, it is clear that Gilhool did not mean that inclusion denies difference, but rather, inclusion accommodates difference, appreciates it, and celebrates it.

Karagiannis et al. (1996) presented a historical review of the treatment of people with disabilities. They concluded that segregation of people with disabilities has been practiced for centuries, and there are entrenched attitudes, laws, policies, and structures that work against achieving inclusion. However, Stainback, Stainback, East, and Sapon-Shevin (1996) warned that the alternative to segregation is not dumping individuals into heterogeneous groups and ignoring their individual differences, rather, inclusion involves developing ways to build inclusive communities that acknowledge individual differences.

Consider the words of Martin Luther King, Jr. (Carson, 1998, pp. 8, 12):

> For a long, long time I could not go swimming until there was a Negro YMCA. A Negro child in Atlanta could not go to any public park. In many of the stores downtown I couldn't go to a lunch counter to buy a hamburger or a cup of coffee. I could not attend any of the theaters . . . I could never adjust to the separate waiting rooms, separate eating places, separate rest rooms, partly because the separate was always unequal and partly because the very idea of separation did something to my sense of dignity and self-respect.

What does inclusion mean?

The following are characteristics of inclusion (see **Figure 2.1**, p. 26) that can be embraced by leisure service providers:

- recognize we are one yet we are different,
- create chances for others to experience freedom to participate,
- value each person and value diversity, and
- support participation.

Recognize We Are One Yet We Are Different

As presented in the orientation activity, Shafik Abu-Tahir (1995, p. 1) stated: "Inclusion is recognizing that we are one even though we are not the same." Inclusion allows people to value differences in each other by recognizing that each person has an important contribution to make to our society. An inclusive philosophy means that the greater the diversity in a given community the richer its capacity is to create new visions. According to Bogdan (2000, p. 5):

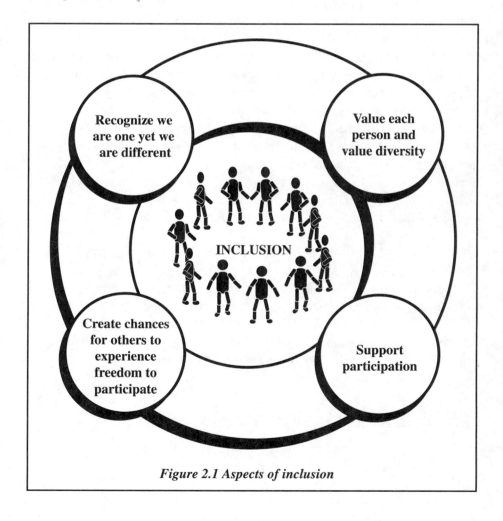

Figure 2.1 Aspects of inclusion

When we move from a state of passive tolerance to a state of celebrating diversity, we then will have arrived at a New Millennium where gender, country of origin, economic status, worldly condition, age, ability level, ethnic or linguistic heritage, religious belief or sexual orientation become fully appreciated. At that point, there will exist an open appreciation for what we each bring to the rich fabric of our plural society.

Sayeed (1999, p. 14) stated: "Inclusion—the word itself conjures a picture of belonging, of being part of woven threads of colorful fabric which are the communities we live in." Similar to the metaphors of a garden or the Grand Canyon, the image of colorful fabric helps to capture the spirit of inclusion.

A man that devoted much of this life promoting the inclusion of all people was Dr. Martin Luther King, Jr. Gardner (1995) reported that Dr. King asked Americans to put aside the clashes among groups and endorse a more inclusionary view of their society. By developing leisure services that are inclusive, we promote ideals expressed by Dr. King.

Create Chances for Others to Experience Freedom to Participate

An important aspect of inclusion involves the creation of opportunities for all people. Inclusion does not mean, however, that people must participate in groups characterized by being diverse. What inclusion does mean is that all people should feel welcome and supported to participate in community programs of their choosing. Some people may choose to participate in groups that are homogeneous, such as a women's bowling league, an evening social sponsored by Alcoholics Anonymous, a luncheon for the Sons and Daughters of Italy, or a wheelchair basketball tournament. The important point to remember is that they do so because they freely choose to participate rather than because they feel they have few or no other options.

Leisure research about people associated with one particular ethnic group supports the conclusion that some people participate in recreation activities sponsored by ethnic organizations designed to attract a homogenous group in an attempt to preserve their ethnic culture in our pluralistic society (Karlis & Kartakoullis, 1996). Subsequently, Karlis (1998) stated that while ethnic-oriented recreation activities allow immigrants and their descendants to come together and preserve their culture, an obstruction to their freedom would exist if these individuals only felt welcome in activities sponsored by their ethnic organizations. Inclusion, then, intends to empower people to participate in recreation activities of their choosing rather than constrain them by limiting their opportunities.

Value Each Person and Value Diversity

In inclusive communities, each person's talents are recognized, encouraged, and supported to the fullest extent possible. Inclusive communities view each person as an important and worthwhile member with responsibilities and a role to play in supporting others; all individuals have a mutually valued presence (Ryndak & Kennedy, 2000).

"Diversity is valuable, not just a reality to be tolerated, accepted, or accommodated, but a reality to be valued" (York, 1994, p. 11). Focus on capacities of people, recognize there is an array of contributions to be made, believe that all people are inherently worthy, and understand that doing one's best and helping others do the same is what is most important. Therefore, "valuing diversity means not only being aware of differences, but also accepting and respecting differences" (Ford, 2001, p. 3).

By assisting all people to feel they are valued members of a community, we can develop more effective services (Grenot-Scheyer, Schwartz & Meyer, 1997). To help illustrate what is meant by inclusion, Bricker (1995, p. 182) provided the following description of what she termed "genuine inclusion."

Genuine inclusion means that during large circle time, the child with disabilities sits next to the other children, sings the songs, and participates in planned activities to the fullest extent possible. Children with disabilities may not perform at the same level as the other children but they are respected and included for their contributions. So, too, in small group and play activities, the child with disabilities is a participating member. If the children go for a walk, the child in a wheelchair goes also. At story time, the child with the augmentative communication system contributes using his or her nonvocal mode of communication.

Support Participation

Fundamental to inclusion is the belief that everyone can benefit and participate in community leisure programs. Therefore, Grenot-Scheyer and colleagues (1997, p. 9) stated that rather than providing "special" services, professionals work within the context of ongoing activities to facilitate participation and interdependence. Based on the belief that everyone belongs and everyone is welcome, an inclusive community views a problem as a sign that help is needed, not that a person must go elsewhere to solve the problem. Once we accept the premise that people are by their very nature different from one another, we can dispose of the notion that a person must earn his or her way into a program by being like everyone else (Meyer, 1994, p. 19).

Inclusion is about ensuring choices, having support, having connections, and being valued. People can make many choices because they have friends, family, and community to support them. The need for connections becomes obvious when you consider that every reference ever given for a job, credit application, or housing application has been a person with whom we have connected. People have connections and support from others because they are valued. Though people may lack many talents, people who know them have found qualities in them they like. To illustrate these characteristics, Moss (1993) presented the following example:

Diane values Larry because she can tell him anything and knows that Larry will not share the information with others. Maria values Erica because she will not quit working at something until it is done. Others value Marty because he is an optimist. None of these traits are dependent on a high intelligence or great physical ability.

How does integration differ from inclusion?

Inclusion implies that everyone deserves to be given a chance to be a part of a community from the beginning of their life. Therefore, the phrase "a part from the start" is central to the notion of inclusion. Some people are abandoning the term *integration* since it implies that the goal is to integrate someone back into the mainstream of school and community life who has been excluded.

Inclusion, unlike integration, does not depend on being segregated in the first place; rather, all individuals have the right to be included in opportunities and responsibilities available in their communities. According to Bricker (1995), this distinction is important because it moves the concept of inclusion of people with disabilities into community-based programs from preferred best practices to a legal and moral mandate.

The question for those delivering leisure services is no longer, "How do we integrate some people who were previously excluded?" but rather, "How do we develop a sense of community and mutual support that fosters success among all members of our community?" If we can develop a sense of community and support within our leisure services our participants will succeed and the goal of inclusion will be achieved.

Whose responsibility is it to create inclusive communities?

Thousand, Villa, and Falvey (1995, p. 1) identified that although children and adults with disabilities have greater possibilities to be welcomed into their communities than past generations, thousands of children and adults with disabilities are still forced into segregated services. The responsibility for advocating for and facilitating inclusion must shift from parents to leisure service providers.

Although segregated recreation programs may have served an important purpose in the past, many parents and professionals believe individuals with disabilities should now have the option of participating in leisure activities with their peers who do not have disabilities. After conducting group interviews with 65 service providers, people with disabilities and their families, Anderson and Heyne (2000) noted that most of the participants reported that specialized, segregated programs were available for people with disabilities in their communities, but that alternatives for more inclusive leisure services was desired. One parent stated (p. 25):

> We try to keep her [our daughter] out of segregated programs as much as possible. There's a Saturday afternoon thing for people who are disabled, but we haven't taken her to those. We would prefer to have her go to the Y and be a part of the rest of the gang.

Block and Malloy (1998) observed that parents who have seen the success of inclusion during school hours want to see their children continue to participate in regular recreation programs after school. Kyle Glozier (2000, p. 14), an eighth-grade boy who happens to have cerebral palsy, made the following comments about inclusion:

> Including kids with disabilities from the very beginning will begin to change society as a whole. Together we can teach society to not push people with disabilities out of the way, forgetting that we deserve our rights as citizens of the United States . . . When I ask my brother, Nigel, "How do you feel having me as your brother?" he answers, "Good. I like you. You're nice." And when I asked my brother Jason, the same question, he says, "You're okay, but you're really scary when you're mad" . . . If all people are exposed to people with disabilities at an early age, the disability makes no difference at all. They see just another person. They see past the disability. This is how we need to see society change.

We are encouraged to develop inclusive services that reflect the values and norms of a host of diverse groups (Minors, 1996). Agencies that are truly inclusive not only tolerate difference but also embrace and celebrate differences. In making the case for inclusive leisure services, Jack Kemp (1994, p. 26–27) stated:

> In the summer, I played on a Little League baseball team and had a great time. They would just choose up sides, and we would get assigned to a team and be in a league for something like six weeks. I was always the last guy picked because I was the worst player, but they always let me play. I got to bat my regular turn and I got to play the field. I don't remember if I ever made a hit or caught the ball. I just remember that I was included. Even though they chose up sides on the basis of skill, they never denied me the opportunity to play.

We are in an excellent position to facilitate and enhance the leisure experience of others. We must provide leisure services that reach all members of the community, that treat everyone fairly, and that help to eliminate any form of discrimination. Schleien (1993, p. 67) challenged leisure service providers when he said:

> The time has come to adopt a new way of thinking, one founded on the premise that the community belongs to everyone, and everyone regardless of level and type of ability belongs to the community. Inclusive community leisure services can be powerful vehicles for promoting this ideal.

Final Thoughts

Martin Luther King, Jr. and many others have shared a vision of inclusion. For leisure services professionals this vision is a daily journey that may be assisted by the following actions:

- welcome all people to our programs,
- provide all people with meaningful choices,
- be knowledgeable about and supportive of others,
- encourage interactions among people,
- celebrate diversity and difference with respect and gratitude,
- recognize and encourage each individual talents,
- view inclusion as a legal and moral mandate, and
- know that inclusion enriches the lives of people who differ in age, gender, ability, socioeconomics, race, religion, ethnic background, sexual orientation, education level, political affiliation, and language.

Discussion Questions

1. What is a community and what do people want from their communities?
2. Why are some people with disabilities not included in their communities?
3. What does inclusion mean?
4. What are some things we can do to value diversity?
5. How does the notion of "freedom of choice" relate to providing inclusive leisure services?
6. How are a garden, the Grand Canyon, and a colorful fabric all metaphors for inclusion?
7. Why is the word "inclusion" used more than the word "integration" to describe the focus of leisure services for people with disabilities?
8. How does the phrase "a part from the start" relate to inclusion?
9. Whose responsibility is it to create inclusive communities?
10. What can we do to create inclusive leisure services?

Chapter 3

Understand Attitude Development

Injustice anywhere is a threat to justice everywhere.
-Martin Luther King, Jr.

Orientation Activity: Examine Differences and Similarities

Directions Alone: Record the following headings at the top of the page: name, difference, and similarity. Think of several people you know and list their names in the first column. Try to identify something about you and that person that is different. Once you have determined a difference, identify something that you and the person share or have in common.

Directions with Others: Move about the room and talk with each person. Identify something about the two of you that is different and record this characteristic. Once you have determined one difference, identify something the two of you have in common. Continue moving about the room finding new people to interview.

Debriefing: The individual qualities of people make them interesting. Why we like some people or why we respect other people is not necessarily due to our similarities, but frequently because they possess unique characteristics. However, it is helpful to begin relationships with the belief that we share common characteristics. When we develop a bond with people we can accept their differences. Therefore, if we encounter people who happen to have a disability or are different from us in some way and we are able to identify and focus on similarities with those individuals, we will increase the likelihood that we will include that person and accept his or her differences. Respond to the following questions related to the orientation activity:

- What was the most difficult aspect of the orientation activity for you?
- How did you feel when you talked about similarities with another person as compared with differences?
- How do you feel when you meet people and they primarily focus their attention on how you are different from them?

Introduction

According to Dunn (1994), a person with a disability has two barriers to face—the inconvenience of the disability and (probably the larger barrier) the negative attitudes of society. These negative attitudes toward people with disabilities represent a major obstacle to successful adjustment. In his remarks regarding the Americans with Disabilities Act, Al Gore (1999, p. 15) said: "Let's face it: for people with disabilities, the biggest obstacles aren't their own limitations, but the roadblocks set up by society—attitudes that equate disable with unable."

Throughout the world various groups—older adults, ethnic and racial minorities, and individuals with physical and mental disabilities—are either not fully accepted or are discriminated against and devalued by those sharing the mainstream cultural perspective (Karnilowicz, Sparrow & Shinkfield, 1994). Unfortunately, negative attitudes of members of a community toward these individuals may halt the progress of inclusion efforts or deprive them of assistance necessary to assure success (Henry, Keys, Jopp & Balcazar, 1996). It is not the actual disability as much as society's perception of the disability that poses the greatest barrier to leisure pursuits for people with disabilities (Bedini, 2000).

Since one goal of this book is to encourage an acceptance of diversity, especially in relationship to individuals with disabilities, examples that promote positive attitudes of acceptance are provided. Our attitudes play a critical role in supporting equal access to leisure services. Attitudes can create positive forces for change or can create major barriers. While the focus of this chapter and the entire book is on people with disabilities, the principles presented here apply to other people who are perceived as being different from those who are in power within our society. Therefore, this chapter encourages us to remove barriers to leisure and stimulate development of approaches that facilitate meaningful leisure participation for all people.

Whose attitude matters?

The attitudes held by leisure services professionals greatly influences community inclusion of people with disabilities. A willingness to include individuals with disabilities into leisure programs is critical if inclusion is to work. Unfortunately, attitudes of some professionals are not very supportive of inclusion. After interviewing professionals working for 13 different leisure service agencies, Germ and Schleien (1997) reported that respondents identified negative staff attitudes as the number one barrier to inclusive community recreation:

> One administrator suggested, "My staff have a resistance to learning about people with disabilities. They fear the inclusion experience." Supervisors also agreed with them, " My instructors are afraid. They have high expectations for themselves and they don't want to feel like failures." Administrators, supervisors and program instructors acknowledge "fear" to be the major attitudinal barrier for staff. Fear of the experience in terms of shouldering responsibility for persons with disabilities, failing to provide an enjoyable program for all participants, and addressing one's own internal feelings and misgivings about disabilities were prominent stumbling blocks. (pp. 32–33)

Block and Malloy (1998) examined attitudes of 88 girls without disabilities, 28 parents, and 9 coaches toward inclusion of a child with disabilities in a fast-pitch softball league and found that although players and parents had a favorable attitude toward inclusion and towards modifying the game rules to enable this player to have a safe and successful experience, the coaches were undecided about inclusion and rule modification.

Devine and Kotowski (1998) provided the following description that may be useful when considering the influence leisure service professionals might have on a person's life:

> Mrs. K., a woman with gray hair who is somewhat stooped over and carrying an oxygen bottle, enters your pool. She stops to rest on the bench outside the pool entrance. After resting, Mrs. K. enters and approaches the reception desk. She sits down again and raises her voice to get your attention. Mrs. K. asks if someone can come out from behind the desk and get her money as there is a long line of patrons waiting to pay and she can't stand for long periods of time. She also asks for assistance with opening the

locker room door because it is too heavy to open by herself. Mrs. K. has emphysema and goes to her local pool several times a week to swim, one of the few activities in which she is still able to participate. Your attitude toward this woman, and others like her who have disabilities, contributes to their interest and willingness to continue participation in activities. In other words, your attitude matters when it comes to welcoming and including people with disabilities in recreation programs.

How are attitudes formed and expressed?

To consider the impact of attitudes on our interactions with others, it may be helpful to examine how attitudes relate to our beliefs, our intentions, and our behaviors. Fishbein and Ajzen (1975) provide a frequently cited description of the relationship among:

- antecedents,
- beliefs,
- attitudes,
- intentions, and
- behaviors.

Antecedents

Antecedents "set the stage" for beliefs to develop. A variety of circumstances can influence development of people's beliefs, such as their communities, past experiences, families, friends, and individual characteristics. These various conditions are considered antecedents to the development of beliefs.

Beliefs

People's *beliefs* involve what they perceive to be true. These beliefs are composed of an individual's perception of information that has been available. Beliefs that are acquired may or may not be correct. Convictions people have based on their beliefs influence development of their attitudes. Beliefs often refer to generally accepted tenets of society. In our society beliefs about people with disabilities are often associated with thoughts that somehow these individuals are less able than people who are not disabled.

Attitudes

Ingstad (1995) defined an attitude as a concept comprising emotion, behavior, and beliefs. He suggested that the word *attitude* be defined as "a statement about disposition to act toward a person, group, or object" (p. 260). Fishbein and Ajzen (1975) described an attitude as a learned predisposition to respond in a consistently favorable or unfavorable manner with respect to a given object. That is, once people develop an attitude about a group of people, when they encounter a person affiliated with this group they will tend to respond to this person in a similar manner. Therefore, attitudes result in positive or negative feelings about some person, object, or issue.

Intentions

Intentions indicate how much effort a person plans to exert to perform a behavior. People anticipate behaving a given way based on the information they have acquired throughout their lives and the attitudes they have formed. However, what people *intend* to do is not always what they *actually* do.

Behaviors

Attitudes impact behaviors. A *behavior* is any observable and measurable act, response, or movement by an individual that can be detected with at least one of the five senses. When clearly described, behaviors generally mean the same thing to different people.

As seen in **Figure 3.1** (p. 38) antecedents, beliefs, attitudes, intentions, and behaviors are interrelated in a dynamic process of attitude development and expression. Each component of the process influences and is influenced by another. Therefore, when one component of the process is altered, the other components change accordingly.

Many individuals within our society possess negative attitudes toward people with disabilities. As stated in the Americans with Disabilities Act of 1990:

Individuals with disabilities are a discrete and insular minority who have been faced with restrictions and limitations, subjected to a history of purposeful unequal treatment, and relegated to a position of political powerlessness in our society, based on characteristics that are beyond the control of such individuals and resulting from stereotypic assumptions not truly indicative of the individual ability of such individuals to participate in, and contribute to, society.

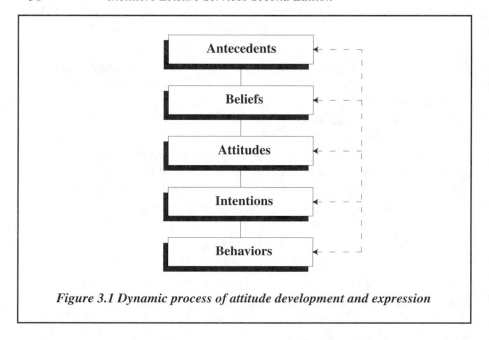

Figure 3.1 Dynamic process of attitude development and expression

Why do negative attitudes develop?

People with and without disabilities can experience stress when interacting with one another. Makas (1988) noted that people without disabilities reported greater emotional distress (exhibited higher physiological arousal), showed less motor activity, displayed less variability in their verbal behavior, expressed opinions less representative of previously reported beliefs, and terminated interactions sooner when interacting with a person who appeared disabled than when interacting with a person without disabilities.

Goffman (1963) suggested that tension between two different people might occur because neither person knows what the other expects. The perception of a person with a disability as being "different" results in personal stress, which can cause a strain in interactions as well as fear, anxiety, avoidance, and segregation (Howe-Murphy & Charboneau, 1987). Wanda, who has a physical disability, illustrated this point when she said:

> People don't talk to me because of the way I am . . . they just kind of look at me and not really know what to say because they feel uncomfortable maybe, but I don't feel uncomfortable.

According to Stern-Larosa and Bettmann (2000, p. 14):

> All of us are born with the ability to identify differences in our
> environments. As we grow, we learn to classify the differences in
> everything we perceive—sounds, colors, shapes, sizes. So children
> naturally notice that people come in all different shapes and sizes
> and colors. Noticing differences is biological. Forming attitudes about
> them is social. The good news is that we can shape how children
> value the differences they perceive.

What happens when we focus on differences?

According to Minow (1990) when we respond to people's traits rather than
their conduct, we may treat a given trait as a justification for excluding
someone we think is different. We feel no need for further justification
because we attribute the consequences to the differences we see. We neglect
the other traits that may be shared and how each of us may be different.

Some of the problems we experience interacting with other people are
based on the way we see these people. Often, if we see the similarities we
share with other people, there is a good chance that the interactions we
have with them will be positive. However, if we focus solely on the
differences that exist between us, interactions can be strained. For example,
when talking with his friend and student, Mitch Bloom, Morrie Schwartz
stated (Bloom, 1997, p. 156):

> The problem, Mitch, is that we don't believe we are as much alike
> as we are. Whites and Blacks, Catholics and Protestants, men and
> women. If we saw each other as more alike, we might be very
> eager to join in one big family in the world, and to care about that
> family the way we care about our own.

The stress many people without disabilities experience when interacting with people with disabilities can be traced to perceptions of people with
disabilities as being different. To clarify what occurs when a person is
viewed as different, the following terms are described:

- stigma,
- stereotype,
- discrimination, and
- segregation.

Stigma

Goffman (1963) defined *stigma* as an undesired "differentness" that separates the person from others in society—not merely a difference, but a characteristic that deeply discredits a person's moral character. Later, Goffman (1974) reported that the person with a stigma is perceived as not quite human. A disabling condition may be so negatively valued that an individual is defined by that single attribute and devalued.

Personal and social identity of a person comes into question because of a disability. Goffman (1963) illustrated how the marginal social position of people who have devalued physical characteristics spreads through everyday life. Living with stigmatized characteristics can transform ordinary social concerns such as shopping and meeting strangers into socially demanding tasks.

Tripp and Sherrill (1991) stated that stigma involves a negative valuation of a person because the individual possesses an attribute that deviates from the norm. An attribute perceived as negative interferes with people's perceptions of positive attributes and creates a perception of undesired difference from what was anticipated. Once people with disabilities become aware of their stigmatized label, their self-perceptions are affected (Eisenberg, 1982).

Stereotype

Most professionals and people with disabilities agree that one of the biggest problems facing people with disabilities is being stereotyped. A *stereotype* is a standardized mental picture of members of a group that represents an oversimplified opinion, attitude, or judgment. For example, some people believe that individuals receiving psychiatric services are a threat to society. This response is based on a stereotype frequently presented in the media. In truth, very few people experiencing mental health problems pose a threat to anyone.

Stereotypes of people with disabilities can result in evaluating them as a category, rather than as individuals. In an effort to explain why stereotypes exist, Allport (1954, pp. 20–21) reported the following:

> We like to solve problems easily. We can do this best if we can fit them rapidly into a satisfactory category and use this category as a means of prejudicing the solution. So long as we can get away with coarse overgeneralizations, we tend to do so.

Although it may be convenient to apply a stereotype to a group of people, it is fundamentally inaccurate. Schuman and Olufs (1995, p. 300) stated:

> We know that any group stereotype, in any particular case, is wrong. That includes good and bad stereotypes. Every person in every group is not identical. But what has never been at issue is the question of individual identity: Each of us is unique. No matter what color we are, what sex we are, what religion we are.

Discrimination

Discrimination involves a person making a distinction categorically rather than individually about another person, then acting differently toward that person. Lott and Maluso (1995a) used the word "discrimination" to refer to the distancing from and avoidance and exclusion of people in low-status social categories by people with greater power.

Title III of the ADA stipulates that discrimination includes failure to make reasonable modification in policies, practices, or procedures when such modifications are necessary to afford goods, services, facilities, privileges, advantages, or accommodations to individuals with disabilities unless the entity can demonstrate that making such modifications would fundamentally alter their nature. Kyle Glozier (2000, p. 14), who has been attending inclusive schools since kindergarten, made the following comments about discrimination:

> Discrimination is when people don't allow people of other races, religions, sexual orientations or abilities to go all the places they want. When people with disabilities can't get on the bus, they get angry.

Toby, an adolescent who is deaf, is interested in signing up for some instructional leisure classes. We may automatically think that Toby does not like to dance. The inaccurate distinction was based on the category of deafness rather than on Toby's individual abilities. Following that inaccurate distinction, we may not offer programs that involve dance to Toby.

Gloria, who is blind, went to an amusement park with a group of friends. Although her friends were required to pay admission, she was given free admission to the park. When stopping for lunch, a waitress asked her friends what Gloria wanted to eat. Ride attendants asked her friends if they thought she was capable of holding on properly during the ride. Gloria was refused admittance to the merry-go-round because the attendants were concerned that she might injure herself when riding alone. The attitudes that Gloria experienced occurred, in part, because people focused on her disability rather than her ability. Gloria's enjoyment and fun was reduced by the attitudes of the park personnel. She was treated "differently" by being given free admission, not being spoken to directly, and the park employess assuming that she was not capable of riding alone. By being overly protected, much of Gloria's excitement associated with park rides was lost.

Shapiro (1993, p. 25) clearly described the problems people with disabilities experience as a result of the many forms of discrimination in the following statement:

> Often the discrimination is crude bigotry, such as that of a private New Jersey zoo owner who refused to admit children with retardation to the monkey house, claiming they scared his chimpanzees. It may be intolerance that caused a New Jersey restaurant owner to ask a woman with cerebral palsy to leave because her different appearance was disturbing other diners. Resentment may have led an airline employee in New York to throw a 66-year-old double amputee on a baggage dolly—"like a sack of potatoes"—his daughter complained, rather than help him into a wheelchair and aid him in boarding a jetliner. Others may feel that disabled people are somewhat less than human and therefore fair game for victimization, as when a gang of New Jersey high school athletes raped a mildly retarded classmate with a baseball bat in 1989.

The consequences of discrimination—limited access to resources, restricted movement, and fewer opportunities—are also characteristic of persons without social or financial power (Lott & Maluso, 1995b). Discrimination can lead to exclusion of people from community life. For example, O'Brien and O'Brien (1992) summarized their research on social support of people with disabilities by identifying that many people leave out those with disabilities when they count who belongs with them in their neighborhoods, schools, work places, and cultural, political, and leisure activities. This unfortunate exclusion decreases the human diversity that can energize a community, with obvious cost to people with disabilities and their families.

If people have experienced discrimination at some point in their lives within a particular context such as recreation, they may anticipate that they will be discriminated against in the future. Anticipation of discrimination may substantially influence an individual's leisure decisions, including the selection of activities and the choice of where and with whom to participate. This could result in their confinement to groups only composed of individuals possessing similar characteristics (Stodolska & Jackson, 1998). When people elect to participate in segregated programs (even when their motivation is to avoid discrimination) members of society may view these groups as alien and undesirable and can even believe that participants' activities reflect hostility and contempt for accepted norms.

Segregation

Segregation occurs when an individual or group is isolated in a restricted area because of discrimination. People who are stigmatized, stereotyped, or identified as deviant may experience segregation. Segregation results in individuals receiving treatment that is different from other people. Hutchison and McGill (1992) reported that segregation is based on the belief that people who have been given similar labels have the same needs and that they can best be served together in a congregated environment that leads to further stigmatization and ostracization.

Segregation has been practiced for centuries, and there are entrenched attitudes, laws, policies, and structures that work against achieving inclusion (Stainback, & Stainback, 1996). According to Stainback, Stainback, and Stefanich (1996) the previously accepted way of dealing with differences among people was segregation, which communicates the message that we do not want to accept everyone or that some people are not worth the effort to make the accommodations necessary to include them.

Some brief history about segregation in the United States may be helpful. Kunen (1996, p. 40) stated:

In its ruling on Plessy v. Ferguson, announced May 18, 1896, the Supreme Court declared laws mandating that "equal but separate" treatment of the races "do not necessarily imply the inferiority of either race" and cited the widely accepted propriety of separate schools for white and colored children. In dissent, Justice John Harlan remarked, "The thin disguise of 'equal' accommodations . . . will not mislead any one, nor atone for the wrong this day done." But the thin disguise endured for a half-century, until a series of school-segregation cases culminating in Brown v. Board of Education of Topeka. "Separate educational facilities are inherently unequal" and violate the Constitution's equal protection guarantee, a unanimous Supreme Court ruled on May 17, 1954. A year later, the court ruled that school districts must admit Black students on a nondiscriminatory basis "with deliberate speed" and instructed the federal courts to retain jurisdiction "during this period of transition."

Segregation separates people from their own culture and denies them the right to participate in the complex, ever-changing realities of their society (Kliewer, 1998). Segregation increases physical and social distance, which results in constructing the world as "us and them." (Sobsey, 1998, p. 8) In his autobiography (Carson, 1998) Dr. Martin Luther King, Jr. wrote about segregation:

> The underlying philosophy of democracy is diametrically opposed to the underlying philosophy of segregation, and all the dialectics of the logicians cannot make them lie down together. Segregation is an evil; segregation is a cancer in the body politic, which must be removed before our democratic health can be realized. There was a time that we attempted to live with segregation. There were those who felt that we could live by a doctrine of separate but equal and so back in 1896, the Supreme Court of this nation through the Plessy v. Ferguson decision established a doctrine of separate but equal as the law of the land. But we all know what happened as a result of the doctrine; there was always a strict enforcement of the separate without the slightest intention to abide by the equal. (p. 90)

As the civil rights movement has shown us, we are aware that different services resulting from segregation are clearly not equal. When people with disabilities are segregated from their peers who do not have disabilities, they may not learn a full range of behaviors. Instead they may only model those behaviors exhibited by people with whom they have the most contact, other people with similar disabilities.

Anderson (1981) related segregation to *exclusion*, which she defined as barring another person from contact with others, resulting in the disregard of him or her as human. Exclusion can hinder the quantity and quality of interpersonal relationships as well as affect a person's development. It involves ignoring someone's physical and social presence. *Seclusion*, on the other hand, involves individuals being removed from social contact while still maintaining a sense of value (Howe-Murphy & Charboneau, 1987).

Hutchison and McGill (1992) reported that when people with disabilities congregate it is difficult, if not impossible, for each person to be treated as an individual because of the tendency of people to generalize and stereotype them. Wolfensberger and Thomas (1983) also commented on congregation when they described the occurrence of deviancy transference. The authors stated that when people with physical disabilities are grouped together with people with mental disabilities it is likely that all the individuals will be suspected of having both mental and physical limitations.

Societal behaviors motivated by negative attitudes have resulted in the isolation of people with disabilities from the social mainstream and the denial of benefits and opportunities available to people without disabilities (Ward & Meyer, 1999). In spite of advances toward inclusion, Miller and Sammons (1999) noted that segregated recreation programs continue to exist. In addition to these segregated programs, people with disabilities are excluded from community recreation programs in subtle ways. Subtle actions that encourage segregation include avoiding social contacts with people with disabilities because interactions may be uncomfortable or inconvenient and people not wanting their children to play with children that happen to have a disability. Perceptions of "differentness" can stem from people being stigmatized. Once people are stigmatized negative stereotypes can develop. If negative stereotypes exist then actions such as segregation and discrimination follow (see **Figure 3.2**).

How can labels influence expectations?

If people develop negative attitudes toward a group of other people, they begin to develop expectations that can be destructive. Three possible reactions can occur that result in the person with a disability or other people who are viewed negatively being stifled:

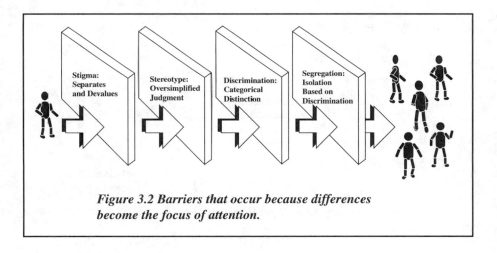

Figure 3.2 Barriers that occur because differences become the focus of attention.

- self-fulfilling prophecy,
- spread phenomenon, and
- overexaggeration assumption.

Self-Fulfilling Prophecy

The *self-fulfilling prophecy* can be described as how a person's expectation for another person's behavior can become an accurate prediction of the person's behaviors simply because it exists. For example, labeling a person "disabled" can reduce many people's expectancy for the person to succeed. Some labels used for people with disabilities imply deficiencies that produce expectations that interfere with the person's development. Although the label of "disability" is the focus here, the idea can be applied to other negative labels such as "homeless."

The self-fulfilling prophecy requires interaction of two people. Initially, a person becomes aware of an expectation of another person. This first individual comprehends this expectation and retains the information. Next, this person must communicate the expectancy to the other person. As indicated in **Figure 3.3**, once this communication has occurred, the other person then must attend to this communication, comprehend, and act upon the expectancy.

Disability labels may generate negative expectations when compared to labels that imply "normalcy" (Algozzine, Mercer & Countermine, 1977).

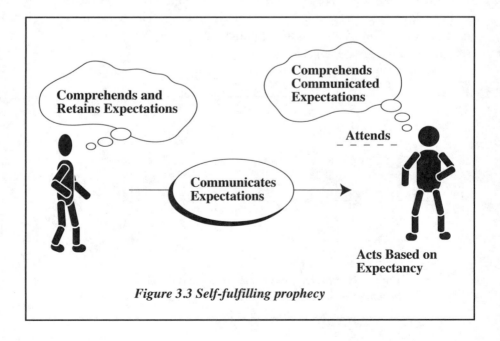

Figure 3.3 Self-fulfilling prophecy

For example, Foster, Ysseldyke, and Reese (1975) reported that children who were labeled "emotionally disturbed" were perceived more negatively than those labeled as "normal" and similar results have been demonstrated for the label "learning disabilities." An individual bearing a deviancy-related label, such as a person with a disability, is expected to behave in a consistent way that is negative. The mere identification of a person who needs assistance from professionals can instill the belief that the person is not quite human (Blatt, 1982).

Although these examples demonstrate how the self-fulfilling prophecy can have negative impacts, positive results are also possible. For example, when Rosenthal and Jacobson (1968) led teachers to believe that randomly selected students would improve substantially during the next school year, the students did achieve more than their classmates. Unfortunately, when the self-fulfilling prophecy is applied to people with disabilities, the results typically involve lowered expectations, reduced participation, and decreased performance. As seen in **Figure 3.4**, this book intends to help us contribute to a self-fulfilling prophecy that raises expectations and performance levels of people with disabilities.

Sometimes we accept as truth what others communicate to us about ourselves. The tendency of individuals to accept negative stereotyping about themselves is often referred to as *internalized oppression.* "Internalized oppression occurs when an individual comes to accept these stereotypical beliefs as truths and acts upon them." (Brown, 1992, p. 27). For

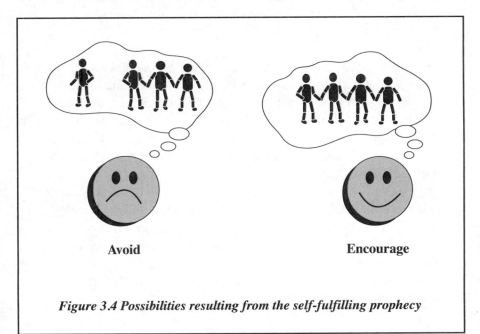

Avoid   Encourage

Figure 3.4 Possibilities resulting from the self-fulfilling prophecy

example, one negative belief held by some members of society is that people with disabilities are not capable of participating in community recreation programs. As a consequence, people with disabilities might not try to enroll in existing integrated programs, or they may feel excessively thankful to be even given a chance to participate. Individuals who feel grateful might not feel comfortable in asking for reasonable accommodations to enable them to participate effectively.

Spread Phenomenon

The tendency to associate an additional disability with a person who has one actual disability is known as the *spread phenomenon*. Tripp and Sherrill (1991) identified the occurrence of the spread phenomenon in relation to people with disabilities. For example, people may speak loudly to an individual who is blind, believe that an individual with a mental impairment lacks physical skills, or assume that an individual with a speech impairment is not mentally alert. Ruth, who uses a communication aid to help her to interact with others, made the following statement about the spread phenomenon:

> People in the community tend to equate one's speaking abilities with one's intelligence. The misconceptions on the part of those around a non-speaking person can be both painful and dangerous to that person, as it usually means he or she will be treated in a sub-human manner. (Crossley, 1999, p. 9)

The spread phenomenon further "handicaps" a person with a disability. Although people with disabilities may be limited in only one aspect of their life, many people believe that these people are handicapped in all situations. This generalization of the disability to all aspects of a person's life (a result of the spread phenomenon) is extremely detrimental. During an interview, Lori, a woman with a spinal cord injury, illustrated the occurrence of the spread phenomenon:

> One thing that really does perturb me is . . . a lot of times people will act like something is wrong with your mind because you're in a chair. They'll come up and they'll ask somebody else "what happened to her?" like I can't talk for myself. They'll talk to whoever I'm with instead of talking to me . . . I don't like that, I don't appreciate that at all.

The following examples illustrate the effect of the spread phenomenon:

Subot approached Maria, a woman who he knew was deaf. Subot handed Maria a note that said: "Can you read?" Maria wrote back: "No!" Maria's sarcastic reply to the note clearly indicates her ability to read. It appears that Subot assumed that her sensory impairment affected Maria's other abilities. Subot may have assumed that because Maria is deaf she also could not read.

Anthony, who uses a wheelchair, is seated in a restaurant with his wife, Sylvia, and a waitress asks Sylvia if she would like to order for him. The waitress may have assumed that because Anthony was in a wheelchair he was helpless, unable to talk, or could not order dinner for himself. If the waitress feels uncomfortable with Anthony and his chair, she may limit communication with him by talking with Sylvia, who does not have an observable disability. In this situation, the waitress's reaction could have created discomfort for Anthony and Sylvia and reduced their enjoyment of the intended leisure experience.

Overexaggeration Assumption

If we overestimate or *overexaggerate* the extent to which being disabled affects the mental status of people with disabilities, they can experience difficulty developing relationships. Some of us assume that people with disabilities think about their disability all the time. Therefore, when we encounter a person with a disability we wrongly assume that the disability should be the focus of the discussion rather than more relevant topics.

Some people may avoid interaction with people with disabilities either to prevent potentially embarrassing situations to avoid having to respond to what they expect are extremes of happiness or despair (Brickman, Coates & Janoff-Bulman, 1978). This tendency for others to reduce interaction can make it more difficult for people with disabilities to develop relationships and necessary supports within their communities. If people become aware that having a disability does not have as great an impact as might be expected, they might find it less threatening to interact with people with disabilities.

Final Thoughts

The development of attitudes is intertwined with antecedents, beliefs, intentions, and behaviors in a dynamic process. Unfortunately, negative attitudes may arise when people make contact with people with disabilities. If having a disability results in the person being perceived as deviant, viewed in a stereotypical way, excluded from participation, discriminated against, or segregated from others, the result can be the devaluation of individuals. Devaluation can result in abuse, neglect, and people receiving far less than their fair share of the things that make life pleasurable (Edgar, 1992).

Benefits people gain in segregated settings can be equaled and exceeded in inclusive surroundings. Involvement with people who do not have disabilities has allowed individuals to upgrade their skills, expand their choices of community activities, and increase their active participation (Laski, 1997).

The music video *Standing Outside the Fire* (Yates & Brooks, 1993) depicts a teenage boy who participates in an inclusive classroom, can drive the family car, and rejects Special Olympics in favor of joining his school track team. At one point in the video the coach sees the youth with Down syndrome looking at the sign-up sheet for a track meet and nudges the boy toward a separate sign-up sheet for Special Olympics. The boy sneers at the Special Olympic poster and defiantly signs his name on the track meet list.

Although behaviors that reflect negative attitudes can limit opportunities for people with disabilities, these negative attitudes (and subsequent behaviors) can be changed. Leisure services professionals can play an important role in changing people's attitudes about people with disabilities.

Discussion Questions

1. How do antecedents and beliefs influence the development of attitudes?
2. What is an attitude?
3. How do cognitive, affective, and behavioral predispositions relate to the expression of attitudes?
4. How do people's intentions relate to their attitudes?
5. How are attitudes manifested in a way that other people are influenced by these attitudes?
6. What is the relationship between stress and the development of negative attitudes toward people with disabilities?
7. What is meant by the words "stigma," "discrimination," "stereotype," and "segregation?"
8. What is the relationship between segregation and exclusion?
9. How does the self-fulfilling prophecy occur and what is its impact on people with disabilities?
10. What is meant by the "spread phenomenon" and how does it influence people's feelings about people with disabilities?

Chapter 4

Enhance Your Attitude

Things do not change, we do.
-Henry David Thoreau

Orientation Activity: Identify Significant Experiences

Directions Alone: Record a brief answer for each of the following questions. Also record any questions you have as you are completing the exercise.

Directions with Others: Divide into small groups and discuss the specific questions assigned. After a specified time, discuss your responses with the entire group.

1. What was your first experience with a person with a disability?
2. How do you feel about the experience?
3. How do the people who raised you view people with disabilities?
4. What events do you think had an impact on their attitudes?
5. In what ways have the attitudes of the people who raised you affected your attitudes?
6. How were their attitudes communicated to you?
7. How do you think your peers view people with disabilities?
8. What events do you think had an impact on their attitudes?
9. In what ways have their attitudes affected yours?
10. How were your peers' attitudes communicated to you?
11. What indirect exposure to people with disabilities have you experienced (e.g., books, films, jokes, television)?
12. Has this exposure been generally positive or negative?
13. How would you describe your reactions to the exposure?
14. What direct contact to people with disabilities have you experienced?
15. Has this contact been generally positive or negative?
16. How would you describe your reactions to the direct contact?
17. How would you summarize your current feelings or attitudes toward people with disabilities in general?

Debriefing: Many attitudes we have today are a result of our earlier experiences related to people with disabilities. At times, we may have directly encountered a person or people with disabilities. The way our parents, siblings, or friends interacted with people with disabilities may have strongly influenced the way we now think. We are also exposed to people with disabilities in indirect ways. The manner in which books, magazines, movies, and television programs present people with disabilities influences our perceptions of people with disabilities. Consider the following questions when reflecting on the orientation activity:

- What are advantages of improving your attitude toward people with disabilities?
- What barriers do you envision as you consider improving your attitude toward people with disabilities?
- Do you anticipate your attitude toward people with disabilities improving?

Introduction

In response to the observation that attitudes of recreation professionals significantly impact the leisure opportunities and lifestyles of individuals with disabilities, strategies that would reduce or eliminate prejudice toward individuals with disabilities have been identified. Development of these strategies has been further encouraged by federal legislation mandating the inclusion of people with disabilities, such as the Americans with Disabilities Act. The outcome of legislation mandating inclusion and equal opportunity will, unfortunately, be unpredictable until people develop positive attitudes toward individuals with disabilities. Therefore, examination of ways to positively influence attitudes of professionals toward individuals with disabilities might be useful.

How can we cultivate a sense of professional competence?

Rizzo and Wright (1987) reported that professionals' perceived ability to work with people with disabilities is related to attitudes. Leisure services professionals who perceive themselves as more competent tend to be more positive in their attitudes toward people with disabilities being integrated into their programs. Bedini (1992) demonstrated that attitudes toward people with disabilities could be improved as a result of exposure to a course on recreation for people with disabilities.

People responsible for professional preparation can play an important role in enhancing positive attitudes and perceived competence in providing leisure services for all people. Rizzo and Vispoel (1991) suggested that academic preparation and experience influence attitudes and perceived competence directly and indirectly. For example, previous exposure to courses about people with disabilities has been linked to the development of favorable attitudes (Rees, Spreen & Harnadek, 1991). More favorable attitudes and greater perceived competence are likely to lead to beneficial learning experiences.

Attitudes toward people with disabilities can be improved through information, persuasion, vicarious experience, and direct contact. The use of multiple methods such as presentations, discussions, simulations, and direct contact have provided significant positive changes in attitudes toward people with disabilities (Jones, Sowell, Jones & Butler, 1981). Rizzo and Vispoel (1992) reported that a planned, systematic intervention using all these procedures had a positive effect on attitudes toward providing services for people with disabilities. In addition, examination of one's own attitudes has also been used as an agent of attitude change. In a study of 88 youth soccer coaches, Rizzo, Bishop, and Tobar (1997) found that as perceived soccer coaching competence increased, attitudes and intentions toward coaching a person with disabilities improved.

After surveying 133 college students, Kowalski and Rizzo (1996) found that the more competent students felt, the more favorable their attitudes toward people with disabilities. The authors concluded that professional preparation programs play a vital role in enhancing both positive attitudes toward individuals with disabilities and perceived competence in providing services to these individuals. Similarly, Soodak, Podell, and Lehman (1998) interviewed 188 professionals trained to provide services to the general public and found that the higher their sense of competence the more likely they were to support inclusion.

This chapter presents information on methods that can influence attitudes and cultivate a sense of professional competence (see **Figure 4.1**, p. 56):

- attend presentations and discussions,
- develop awareness of personal attitudes,
- participate in simulations, and
- make direct contact.

The first strategy focuses on indirect exposure through presentation and discussion of information about people with disabilities and methods that help facilitate their participation in programs. The second technique is the development of awareness of what attitudes people possess and possible

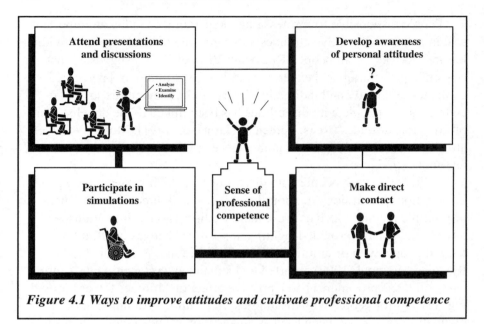

Figure 4.1 Ways to improve attitudes and cultivate professional competence

ways their attitudes were formed. This technique of self-awareness intends to help people become more responsive to information that may improve their attitudes. The third strategy, simulation of disabilities, promotes a vicarious experience of disabling conditions that may enhance development of positive attitudes. Finally, the fourth strategy, direct contact with people with disabilities, can facilitate development of an understanding and appreciation of people's lives and thus improve attitudes.

Attend Presentations and Discussion

Stainback, Stainback, Strathe, and Dedrick (1983) conducted a study to determine whether professionals' attitudes or behavioral intentions toward inclusion of children with disabilities could be modified by having them read and discuss materials on the inclusion of children with disabilities. They reported that the presentation of reading materials and subsequent small group discussions modified attitudes and behavioral intentions of professionals toward the inclusion of children with disabilities. Similarly, Austin, Powell, and Martin (1981) examined the use of class presentations to modify recreation and leisure studies students' attitudes and found that presentations positively influenced participants' attitudes toward people with disabilities. These findings support presenting information to leisure services professionals on methods to facilitate successful inclusion of people with disabilities.

Develop Awareness of Personal Attitudes

An important aspect of developing positive attitudes toward people with disabilities involves examination of one's attitudes and values. Once we become aware of our values, we are more prepared to assume responsibility for making our own decisions (Tinsley & Tinsley, 1982). Valerius, Hodges, and Perez (1997) observed that even the most open-minded people carry with them beliefs and biases. Although we can have much in common with the people we serve, we are often different in many ways relative to ability, racial background, cultural affiliation, ethnic heritage, religion, or sexual orientation. Examining our values might help us avoid making value judgments about others and minimize the extent to which we impose our view of the world in a professional relationship.

Kivell (2000) encouraged leisure service providers to consider the sentiments expressed by Calhoun (1994) who stated that people are not able to really stop thinking at least partially in categories; therefore, they must become seriously self-critical about the inferences made about other people. Acknowledging that various groups of people who have been stigmatized and underserved may begin to sensitize us to address leisure interests and needs of all members of the community (Henderson, 1997).

Beckwith and Matthews (1995) suggested that if professionals want to help facilitate social inclusion they should start by examining their own attitudes. Leisure services providers are encouraged to conduct self-evaluations to help ensure that they are providing inclusive and fully accessible programs (Bedini, 2000). As we examine how we feel about different issues we become more aware of how we think about these issues and more able to improve our actions. With an awareness of oneself comes an ability to take more responsibility for our actions. Barry (1997, pp. 143, 156) spoke to this interaction between awareness and responsibility:

> Certainly there is no more necessary rule for responsible living than to know what we feel, think, and believe; to be aware of factors that contribute to our emotions, thoughts, and beliefs; to know who and what have influenced our attitudes, values, and habits—why we choose one thing instead of another, or follow, perhaps the more rather than the less traveled path . . . The opinions and customs we have absorbed in growing up, the ones we hold and practice, may be rational or irrational, fair or biased, liberating or diminishing. So can our conscience. Being responsible, therefore, is heeding but not hypnotically following the "inner voice" of conscience. It is challenging that voice, critically conversing with it, and always pressing it into discourse with other consciences.

To develop competence in serving diverse groups Dieser and Peregoy (1999) suggested that initially it is helpful for leisure services professionals to gain an awareness of attitudes, beliefs, and knowledge about their own culture as well as an understanding of other cultures. Henderson (1997) warned us that it is easier to acknowledge that diversity exists than to do something about it. The days of mere awareness are over—now is the time for action. Enough is being learned about various aspects of diversity that leisure service providers can apply some of the findings to their programming immediately. Examples of awareness activities are presented in the appendix.

To enhance peoples' attitudes toward individuals with disabilities we can use awareness activities; however, it is helpful if we process these awareness activities. *Processing* is the umbrella term for a set of facilitation techniques designed to assist people in describing, reflecting on, analyzing and communicating about experiences (Hutchison & Dattilo, 2001). Processing helps people to transfer or generalize what they have learned in an activity-based experience to other life contexts such as their home, community, work, or school. Processing involves not only attending to the immediacies of the experience but also relating important aspects of the experience to future issues. Processing can be used to help participants increase awareness of issues prior to an activity; promote change while an experience occurs; reflect on, analyze, or discuss an experience after it ends; and/or promote assimilation into their lives after the experience.

While processing often involves some form of dialogue or discussion in group settings, it can occur through activities such as journal writing, one-on-one conversations, writing activities, drawing, or drama (Luckner & Nadler, 1997). Processing focuses participants' attention from general awareness, to acknowledging responsibility, to making choices, to applying these choices to other life contexts. By processing the experience with participants we can help them see how their experiences might be relevant to their lives. Processing helps people make sense of their experiences.

Participate in Simulations

To alter attitudes toward people with disabilities, distorted ideas supported by deeply felt emotions must be confronted. The first step in the reeducation process must focus on the individual at an emotional level (Tripp & Sherrill, 1991). One strategy that affects people at an emotional level is participation in a simulation of disabling conditions. For example, after a five-hour program that included a disability simulation, children's attitudes toward other children with disabilities were more positive than their attitudes prior to the educational program (Jones et al., 1981). Through disability simulations, participants can develop some sensitivity to the experiences that people with disabilities encounter on a regular basis.

Over the years, many students have returned to my office after working as a leisure services professional. When they talk about the course on inclusion, they typically remember the disability simulation in which they participated and report how it continues to influence the way they deliver services and their sensitivity to the needs of individuals. Sayne (1996, p. 24) provided an interesting description of a special event sponsored by a parks and recreation department that provided the chance for members of the community to participate in an entire day of disability simulations:

> What would drive perfectly healthy, nondisabled boys and girls to partake in recreational activities such as wheelchair basketball, blindfold baseball and chin-ramp bowling. Why would Ed, who doesn't even wear glasses, be writing his name in Braille? And why would Lindsey, whose teacher would be the first to tell you, has no problems talking, be practicing sign language? "Its simple," explains nine-year-old Lindsey, as she eagerly walks with her friends to the next station. "This is a way to learn about people who have different abilities; it's hard to know what people go though unless you try it yourself." . . . Ten-year-old Marianne says it is definitely working. "I have a younger brother who has been diagnosed with CP (Cerebral Palsy)," said Marianne. "This helps me to understand a little better some of the things he's going through at home."

Simulation of disabilities can be effective in changing attitudes; however, the simulation should require participants to observe reactions of other people. Movement through a largely unfamiliar group of people as a single role player may further enhance realism, allowing the person to experience the possible frustrations of the condition but, perhaps more importantly, to experience other people's reactions.

Perlman (1987) suggested that if people would like to become sensitive to the indignities and frustrations experienced by people with disabilities, they should spend a day or two in a wheelchair. Perlman provided the following guidelines for people engaging in a wheelchair simulation:

> Tell yourself that you cannot get up, then try to get into a car. Try to go shopping or use the toilet in a restaurant. See what it feels like to be all dressed up and have to ride to your appointment in a freight elevator with the garbage. I can tell you how that makes me

feel—furious . . . What we need is an attitude that we're all human beings, and as such, we all care about each other. (p. 64)

Many individuals have participated in simulations of a disability while enrolled in introductory courses related to disability. The rationale for the assignments is often to encourage participants to become more sensitive to the requirements placed on an individual with a disability and to develop an awareness of the barriers, both physical and attitudinal, that confront a person who happens to have a disability. Simulations are learning experiences as opposed to recreation activities. The primary intent of a simulation is to develop sensitivity rather than simply provide participants with a "fun" experience. However, it is hoped that participants experience enjoyable and amusing moments during the simulation.

Make Direct Contact

Evans (1976) observed that a strain in social interactions, including uneasiness, inhibition, and uncertainty experienced by people without disabilities in their interactions with people with disabilities appeared to be a strong factor in development and maintenance of negative attitudes. Therefore, the use of structured experiences with people who present positive images of disabilities and are of equally valued status in relation to participants, appears to be effective in attitude modification.

Rowe and Stutts (1987) observed improved attitudes toward people with disabilities when college students participated in a practicum experience requiring them to interact with people with disabilities. Minke, Baer, Deemer, and Griffin (1996) surveyed over 300 teachers and concluded that teachers in inclusive settings reported more positive views of inclusion, higher levels of personal efficacy, and higher ratings of their own competence than did teachers who were not exposed to inclusion. Similarly, after surveying almost 3000 U.S. college students studying physical education, Folsom-Meek, Hearing, Groteluschen, and Krampf (1999) reported that students who had experience working with people with disabilities displayed more positive attitudes than those students without such experience. Development of positive attitudes toward people with disabilities comes from ongoing and informal opportunities to interact with them (Modell, Rider & Menchetti, 1997).

Krajewski and Flaherty (2000) interviewed 144 high school students about their attitudes toward individuals with disabilities and found that frequency of contact had a significant impact on their attitudes; students who reported more frequent contact held more favorable attitudes. Because frequency of contact is important in determining student's attitudes toward individuals with disabilities, leisure services professionals could encourage this contact by offering inclusive programs.

How direct contact is structured can make the difference between an encounter being positive or negative. The direction of attitude change depends on the conditions under which contact has occurred; favorable conditions produce positive attitude shifts while unfavorable conditions produce negative attitude shifts (Tripp, French & Sherrill, 1995). Structured experiences with people with disabilities facilitate positive attitude shifts (Stewart, 1988). For example, Beck and Dennis (1996, p. 85) assessed attitudes of 186 fifth graders, some involved in an inclusive situation and others not. They concluded that results from previous studies combined with the results of this study indicate that structured, interactive programs designed to increase positive attitudes toward children with disabilities are more useful in affecting positive attitudes than programs where children are simply placed in physical proximity to one another and given limited instruction regarding interaction and communication.

To increase the likelihood of long-term behavioral change, educational experiences that include opportunities for direct exposure to persons who present positive images of people with disabilities are suggested. The direct exposure could involve interacting with people with disabilities who are guest lecturers, working on a specified task with a person with a disability, or conducting inclusive programs. Problems can result from people developing images of other people with whom they have not yet had direct contact. Hockenberry (1995) suggested that if you get close to people stereotypical images begin to break up, but they do not go away easily. When people experience repeated direct contact with other people who may be different from them, their differences become so familiar that these differences become part of people's "personal comfort zone" (Miller & Sammons, 1999, p. 7).

According to Paul (1998), an inclusive world is not really possible if people simply read and talk about other people who are different from them. Therefore, Paul concluded that the more we do things with people who are different from us, the more likely we can develop an appreciation and, hopefully, acceptance and understanding of the diversity of the human race. John Callahan, a successful cartoonist who created the cartoon series Pelswick (the first television show to feature an animated character in a wheelchair) made the following observation about making contact with people:

> If you hang around someone who's disabled, within just a few days, hours—or, in my case, minutes—you'll realize that he or she is just another person on the street. (Hauser, 2001, p. 19)

What are considerations when doing a simulation in a wheelchair?

One specific example of a simulation requires participants to pretend they have paralysis of the legs and use a wheelchair to move. The duration of the simulation can vary according to the learning situation, but a simulation brief in duration may not have the desired effect. When giving directions for a simulation, provide extensive information and guidelines regarding the preparation, implementation, and evaluation of the simulation to increase the chance that participants will approach the task in a mature and understanding fashion.

Preparation

Participants are encouraged to place themselves in challenging situations but to use sound judgment. It is recommended that participants carefully *preplan all experiences* before charging ahead. Providing sufficient time to arrive at planned destinations on time is a necessity. Often, participants will experience that even the "best laid plans" will lead them into the unexpected. Therefore, when possible, participants are encouraged to have a friend accompany them. The participant's friend should assist only when absolutely necessary. Typically, it is suggested that if a transportation system is in place specifically for people with disabilities, participants in the simulation should not use this transportation service. Participants are also discouraged from conducting their simulation with another person using a wheelchair. In any simulation, participants should *discuss personal concerns or reservations* about the experience with the person supervising the simulation.

Implementation

Throughout the experience, participants should attempt to *remain in the wheelchair as much as possible*. If, for any reason, participants must get out of the wheelchair (e.g., if the person is alone and stuck in the mud) the person should attempt to do this discreetly while others are not watching. This may mean that participants might need to wait a few moments before breaking character. If it is unavoidable to break character in front of other people (e.g., the participant is in danger) he or she should attempt to briefly explain the situation truthfully to those present. However, it is hoped that participants do not break character during the time they are using the wheelchair.

When encountering friends and family members, participants are encouraged to explain to them that the experience is an assignment and provide them with the rationale for the simulation. In some cases, it may be advisable for participants to *describe the assignment in advance* to people with whom they have close relationships. The most appropriate responses to questions about participants' condition while they are conducting the simulation are those that are direct and honest.

Evaluation

After completing the simulation, participants will not know what it is like to actually have the particular disability, due to many physical and psychological factors that exist in actual disabling conditions. However, they will *enhance awareness of disability and attitudinal and physical barriers.* In certain situations, participants may experience more problems than an individual who regularly uses a wheelchair due to lack of skill and problems with the wheelchair. In other situations, participants may experience less difficulty as they realize that they can literally walk away from the experience.

In response to employees of a hospital participating in a simulation requiring them to use a wheelchair, Scott Balko had a few of his own suggestions for the participants that illustrate the limitations of such an educational experience. He recommended that people conduct their simulation for one year. During this year, participants should get a skin ulcer that does not heal so that plastic surgery is required, experience some urinary tract problems, encounter calcium deposits, have some muscle atrophy, experience respiratory problems such as pneumonia, and encounter cardiovascular problems. In conclusion, Balko warned people participating in an educational simulation that it is no game. Balko's sentiments are a reminder that although participation in educational simulations of disabling conditions can heighten awareness, once participants have completed the simulation, they will not know what it is like to be disabled for a considerable length of time. **Figure 4.2** (p. 64) summarizes the suggestions for simulation participation.

What can be done to help process the simulation done in a wheelchair?

To enhance the effectiveness of the simulation, participants are often encouraged to record their impressions of the experience. The organization of such a report (see **Figure 4.3**, p. 65) might include the following:

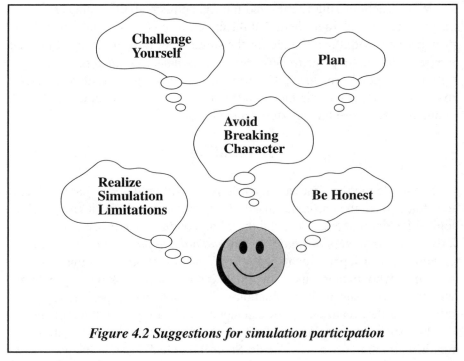

Figure 4.2 Suggestions for simulation participation

- analyze skills,
- consider environmental barriers,
- evaluate social reactions,
- describe personal reactions, and
- identify professional implications.

Analyze Skills

An analysis of the skills needed while completing the simulation can be enlightening. It is often helpful to provide specific examples of skills demonstrated while participating in the simulation and a description of some tasks that could no longer be completed independently such as cooking, eating, personal hygiene, or leisure skills.

Consider Environmental Barriers

Another consideration is environmental barriers that participants experienced. A description of various architectural barriers such as steps and heavy doors can be identified. Observation about ecological barriers such as steep hills and marshy areas can help provide insight into the experience. Many people find that it is helpful to identify any transportation barriers encountered throughout the experience. Participants' encounters with these barriers and their responses to them can be informative.

Evaluate Social Reactions

Social reactions that participants experienced appear to be critical in influencing development of positive attitudes toward people with disabilities. Identification of the verbal and nonverbal responses of people who were encountered can be very revealing. Participants are encouraged to describe specific communication behaviors and avoid making assumptions about people's intentions. Identifying specific examples of different people's reactions can help participants become aware of how they would now treat people with disabilities.

Describe Personal Reactions

When attempting to process the simulation that has influenced participants' emotions, a section of the report devoted to personal reactions can be helpful. Participants may attempt to explain their feelings before, during,

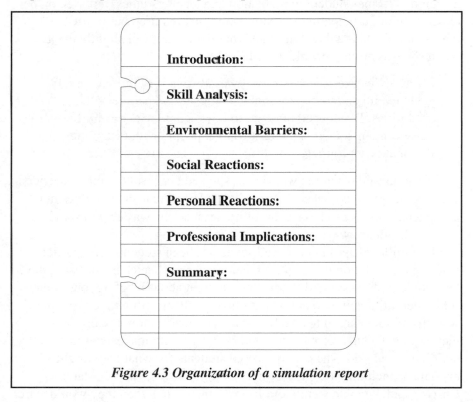

Introduction:

Skill Analysis:

Environmental Barriers:

Social Reactions:

Personal Reactions:

Professional Implications:

Summary:

Figure 4.3 Organization of a simulation report

and after the simulation. This comparison can develop insights that were not initially apparent to the participants. Trying to find the answers to such questions as: "What was your response to your abilities and disabilities?" and "How did you feel about other's reactions?" can help participants develop insights into the lives of people with disabilities.

Identify Professional Implications

Participants are encouraged to provide specific examples of how this experience will improve their ability to successfully meet the demands of their intended career responsibilities. Identification of specific actions that could be taken as a professional to provide accessible programs helps individuals develop action plans for inclusion of people with disabilities into leisure services.

What are some people's responses to doing a simulation in a wheelchair?

Yaccino, a former student in recreation and leisure studies, reported on her experience of participating in a simulation that required her to use a wheelchair for half a day. She stated that she always felt slightly uneasy when she was around people with disabilities:

> It was always very scary to me. I was always very intimidated. It's made me much more comfortable being around people with disabilities. It's opened my eyes to how people with disabilities are treated in our society. And how to treat people with disabilities in a way that is appropriate.

Yaccino said using the wheelchair showed her just how many barriers exist for people using wheelchairs. She explained that she still does not know what it is like to have a disability because she was able to stand up and put the chair away.

Eichmiller (1990) interviewed several college students who participated in a simulation that required them to use a wheelchair for half a day. One student, Chrissy, said she had not thought about it before, but in the future her attitude would not be patronizing. "People think they (people with disabilities) are in need of constant assistance. Now I realize that they're not. To have people constantly offering help makes you feel childlike," she said. The class prepared students for what they might encounter, including people staring. "Definitely, yes," people stared, Chrissy said. "People were more friendly than usual, then they would stare at my legs," she added. Although she does not think that anyone without a disability could fully understand, Deborah reported that after the simulation, she could relate much more to those with disabilities.

After completing a simulation we do *not* know what it is like to actually have the particular disability. In response to this, Linda reported that: "You can only understand to a point. I could build my upper body strength, but I couldn't get used to the staring." Nancy explained that "I sat in with a student who uses a motorized wheelchair. He thinks everybody should spend time in a wheelchair. He told me, 'You'll definitely learn from this.'" Dave admitted that: "Normally girls will look at me, but when you're in the chair, it's like you're being looked right over. They don't see you, they see the chair." Bob reported that "I think I will, in the future, approach a person with a disability differently. I won't just look at their disabilities, but at their abilities." Nancy exclaimed that, "It was definitely an eye-opening experience!" Dave added, "You don't forget an experience like that." "Even now (two weeks after the simulation), I'll go somewhere and take note if places are accessible," Deborah said. "Will this stick with me? Definitely."

Young (1990) reported that being temporarily disabled was an "eye-opening experience" for him. His strongest realization was how inaccessible the world is for people with disabilities. He observed that although many buildings have access ramps, some were angled too steeply or were in such a state of disrepair that efforts at access were hazardous. What was most surprising and disconcerting to him was the number of public facilities that had no access ramps. At times, he felt a sense of outrage at his helplessness and dependency upon the graciousness of others that he withdrew from the public. Young expressed the feeling that seeing himself as a burden to others was quite sobering. Throughout his experience, he reported that many of his friends were generous with their time and energy. Yet, Young reflected that the many years most people spend learning to be self-sufficient are difficult to ignore, and the desire for self-sufficiency can lead one to eliminate events and activities where self-sufficiency is not possible. Young's comments teach us that although it is helpful to provide assistance when required, it is even more effective to help people with disabilities access community recreation programs and create a supportive and accessible environment that allows people to participate as actively as possible without the need for assistance.

A person responded to Young's letter who has a friend (Brian) who will use a wheelchair for the remaining portion of his life. The anonymous writer reported that, fortunately Brian has refused to give up life in the mainstream—which while perhaps easier and safer would deprive him of leading as normal a life as possible and from being the exceptional role model he is. The writer stated that if people would increase their awareness of people with disabilities, all would benefit. Although awareness has improved in the last few years, communities have a long way to go to provide a workable public transportation system, rest rooms that have doors that open easily, curb cuts on both ends of sidewalks, seating that does not relegate wheelchair users to out-of-the-way areas and usable ramps. Finally, the writer suggested that it is not an issue of "them and us;" rather, we are all in this together. Those people who today consider themselves not to be disabled may acquire a disability at any time.

Thompson and Vierno (1991) reported that Don Smitley likes to refer to people who do not use wheelchairs as "shoe-bound." He relates using his wheelchair to others using shoes and said, "You would only think about shoes if they are uncomfortable, and I view the wheelchair the same way."

What else can we do?

If we are interested in developing authentic and respectful professional relationships with people who differ from us, then a step toward greater inclusion has been taken. When detecting the other person's difference it may be helpful to consider that it is natural to notice differences and it is fine to have a negative impression of a difference—at first. For example, our negative impression may be related to the fact that the disability is new to us or that we were not expecting to see a person with a disability in the current context or that the disability is disturbing to us. In any event, after detecting a difference, it is helpful to pause before acting on this first impression. Miller and Sammons (1999) suggested ways to improve how we interact with a person who happens to be different from us:

- decide what to do,
- take action by looking,
- take action by talking,
- take action by doing something, and
- debrief the encounter.

Decide What to Do

After detecting the other person's difference, the next step is to think about the difference so we can decide what to do next. Although this process can take only a few seconds, it helps us to gain control of your actions and take actions that reflect our goals and values, rather than taking action based on our sometimes uncomfortable or negative first impression of differences.

Take Action by Looking

If we can see, the first action we typically take is to look at the person. Once we see someone who looks or acts different from us, we stare, turn away, or acknowledge them. Staring involves a long, direct examination that implies an evaluation or judgment that often results in the person being stared at to feel uncomfortable. Turning away means that the person who turns away attempts to ignore the individual whom they initially saw

The other choice we have after seeing people who act or look different from us is to acknowledge them in a nonjudgmental way. Looking at a person's face is what we do in most situations, and smiling is typically a safe behavior. Consider that the difference you detect about a person is only one attribute they possess among many others. Thinking in this way may help us to positively regard a person rather than staring or turning away.

Take Action by Talking

After we see people, the next action that we typically engage in is talking to them. Often, if we are not sure how to refer to people with disabilities and discussions with them or about them can be uncomfortable for us. Sometimes we might have difficulty speaking to a person we perceive to be different because we may think that there is only one correct thing to say to the person, and, of course, there is not. Miller and Sammons (1999, pp. 92–93) offer some important examples:

> In situations that call for quick and easy accommodation, such as holding a door for a person who uses a walker or explaining the type and location of foods at a buffet for a person who is blind, there's no need to talk about the difference. You might think that it would be rude to ignore the person's disability—but you wouldn't ask questions about his other characteristics, such as personality, hair color, or shoe size when these features aren't relevant to the situation. When the disability is relevant to the situation, however, you have a lot of choices about what to say. Your options include acknowledging the difference, asking for information, and asking whether assistance is needed while waiting for a response before helping.

Take Action by Doing Something

Much of this course is designed to assist you in determining what might be the most appropriate action when encountering people with disabilities.

Generally, it is helpful if we provide assistance only after our offer of assistance has been accepted, that we accommodate differences whenever possible, and that we work to include all people into our recreation programs. The remaining chapters in the book are designed to help identify actions that reflect respect and sensitivity to people.

Debrief the Encounter

To debrief a situation, reflect on the interaction and then think about the next possible encounter with that person or to a similar situation. When debriefing it is helpful to consider what happened, how we felt about what happened, and what could happen next time.

Final Thoughts

Education of leisure services professionals about the capabilities of individuals with disabilities may improve their attitudes. To maximize the usefulness of such educational attempts, the following strategies can be employed:

- positive indirect exposure through readings, discussions, and videos,
- completion of self-awareness exercises and associated briefings,
- involvement in simulations, and
- positive direct contact with individuals with disabilities in a variety of contexts.

The strategies presented in this chapter intend to help people without disabilities reduce their discomfort around people with disabilities. A reduction in discomfort will increase the likelihood of positive attitudes being developed. As we develop more positive attitudes toward people with disabilities, leisure opportunities for individuals with disabilities will increase. When opportunities to experience leisure increase, the quality of life for individuals with disabilities often is enhanced.

By using strategies presented in this chapter, we begin to gain a sense of professional competence. It might be helpful to consider the observations of Soto and Goetz (1998) that our belief in our ability is the most important mediating variable in our professional effectiveness and consequent success of the people we serve.

Discussion Questions

1. How can you cultivate a sense of professional competence?
2. What is the value of attending presentations and engaging in discussions about people with disabilities?
3. How can you become aware of your attitudes toward people with disabilities?
4. What is the value of participating in simulations of disabling conditions?
5. What are some guidelines to follow when conducting or participating in a simulation requiring the use of a wheelchair?
6. How can you encourage people to learn from a simulation?
7. What have been some responses of people who have participated in a simulation of a disabling condition?
8. What is the value of participating in situations that provide you with an opportunity to become familiar with a person with a disability?
9. What are some techniques you could use to improve other people's attitudes about people with disabilities?
10. What is the value of reducing some people's discomfort around other people who happen to have disabilities?

Chapter 5

Improve Others' Attitudes

It is the greatest of all mistakes
to do nothing
because you can only do a little.
Do what you can.
-Sydney Smith

Orientation Activity: Examine Societal Attitudes

Directions Alone: Record your feelings about the person making each statement. What might you say if the person directed the statement to you?

Directions with Others: Find a person and discuss the implications of one statement on recreation participation. Make notes as you talk for later discussion. Once you finish discussing your responses, find another person and discuss another statement.

1. No, we cannot handle any cripples at this bowling lane. We had retarded kids here last year and it was a big pain.
2. She could not belong to the ceramics class; she's got the mind of a 6-year-old, even if she is 48 years old.
3. We're going camping this summer, and it is the first time we have had this many blind adults together in a camping trip.
4. We want the handicapped at the recreation center—that's why we have special-needs classes.
5. It is nice to have the youth group be so active in offering daytime dances for the elderly from the nursing home.
6. He can play in the volleyball league; however, if his cerebral palsy becomes a problem then he must leave.
7. Our movie theater offers discounts to handicapped persons with proper identification.

8. I saw that a girl who attends the Thursday evening social group is missing a leg, I could not look at her all night.
9. It is expensive to make our resource room accessible to the disabled; it is better if they order resources from home.
10. Sure she wants to learn sports, but our clinics are not set up for retarded people.
11. Make sure your older brother does not get wet on the bird-watching trip, you know he will not take care of himself.
12. We like to keep people busy because the idleness is hard on them. That's why we developed our diversional program.

Debriefing: People often fear what they do not know, what is different, and what makes them feel vulnerable. Negative attitudes based on fears create barriers to full participation in society for individuals with disabilities. Conversely, positive attitudes create opportunities for people that enable them to pursue active participation in their communities. Development of positive attitudes can begin with exposure to individuals that allow people to develop an understanding of and an appreciation for those that differ from them. Consider the following questions when reflecting on the activity you have recently completed:

- What are the problems associated with the aforementioned statements?
- What attitudes do you feel are being represented by these statements?
- How would you change these statements to turn them into statements reflecting positive attitudes?

Introduction

Ignorance resulting from a lack of exposure can facilitate the development of negative attitudes. A direct result of ignorance is fear, as illustrated in the following quotation by Bart, who has an observable physical disability:

> People do not know how to act towards you. They're afraid they'll say something wrong, they're afraid that they'll do something different that will make you upset, they don't know how to act with you.

Fear can be the strongest feeling people with disabilities elicit from people without disabilities (Shapiro, 1993). According to Murphy (1990), a researcher who has paraplegia, people with disabilities serve as constant, visible reminders to people without disabilities that they are vulnerable; people with disabilities represent a possibility that is feared.

Previous exposure to people with disabilities can result in development of positive attitudes toward these individuals. For example, Stewart (1988) reported that students who participated in an inclusive university weight-training course involving contact with two students with disabilities improved their attitude toward people with disabilities significantly more than participants in a university weight-training course that did not have individuals with disabilities. As another example, Kisabeth and Richardson (1985) documented significant positive changes in attitudes of students toward people with disabilities as a result of a person with a disability being included in a university racquetball class. The challenge to leisure services professionals is to determine ways to provide exposure to diversity that results in development of positive attitudes toward all of their participants.

How can we adopt inclusive beliefs that help improve our attitudes?

This section provides some ways to think about and treat people with disabilities. The ways of thinking presented in **Figure 5.1** set the stage for beneficial contact and the development of positive attitudes. They include:

- focus on similarities,
- view all people as part of humanity, and
- adopt a person-centered approach.

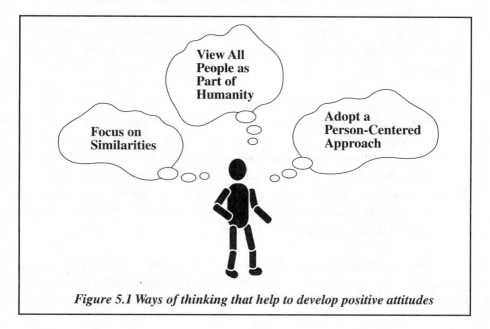

Figure 5.1 Ways of thinking that help to develop positive attitudes

Focus on Similarities

In the case of groups that are already disadvantaged, ignoring similarities adds to their challenges. If we focus only on other peoples' differences, we will develop a different impression of those differences than if we perceived them within a system that includes similarities as well (Yuker, 1988). The words of the Dalai Lama (Lama & Cutler, 1998) are relevant as he described the art of happiness:

> Wherever I meet people, I always have the feeling that I am encountering another human being, just like myself. I find it is much easier to communicate with others on that level. If we emphasize specific characteristics, like I am Tibetan or I am Buddhist, then there are differences. But those things are secondary. If we can leave the differences aside, I think we can easily communicate, exchange ideas, and share experiences. (p. 2)

Positive relationships are often established between people who believe they share common characteristics. Many factors encourage the feeling that two people belong together in some way. When a person identifies with someone because of similarity, there will be a tendency to like the other person. When a common bond between individuals is developed by focusing on similarities, people's ability to accept differences is enhanced. Differences between people can be viewed negatively by requiring conformity, or differences can be seen as exciting opportunities to learn new ways of looking at the world. Diversity is what allows people to grow and learn. Shapiro (1993, p. 4) emphasized this point when he stated that people with disabilities:

> no longer see their physical or mental limitations as a source of shame or as something to overcome in order to inspire others. Today they proclaim that it is okay, even good, to be disabled. Cook's childhood polio forced him to wear heavy corrective shoes, and he walked with difficulty. But taking pride in his disability was for Cook a celebration of the differences among people and gave him a respectful understanding that all share the same basic desires to be full participants in society.

The orientation activity presented at the beginning of this chapter was provided to encourage readers to begin considering the implications of focusing on similarities with people and identifying differences between people. Statements by two people following their rehabilitation from spinal cord injuries emphasize this point:

> I forget that I'm in a wheelchair sometimes, I totally forget that I'm any different than anybody else and it just doesn't bother me.

> I'm still the same person that I used to be . . . I just sit down instead of stand up all the time . . . can still have as much fun as I ever wanted to and ever did . . . I'm still able to do things that I used to do and want to do.

View All People as Part of Humanity

Bogdan and Taylor (1992) reported that when people are accepting of individuals with disabilities, they often describe their friends and family members as possessing characteristics of "humanness." Consequently, the disability is viewed as secondary to the person's humanness. The authors offer four primary dimensions of humanness (illustrated in **Figure 5.2**, p. 78):

- attributing thinking to the other,
- seeing individuality in the other,
- viewing the other as reciprocating, and
- defining social place for the other.

Belief in these dimensions enables people without disabilities to define people with disabilities as people "like us" despite their significant behavioral and/or physical differences (Bogdan & Taylor, 1992). The dimension of assuming that each person can think means that each individual has the capacity of free will and can make meaningful choices. The belief that each person is a unique individual suggests that each person can contribute to the community. Reciprocity implies that there is a give and take between people and that each person has the ability to make a contribution in some way. The dimension of defining a social place is based on the notion that since people are social beings each person has the right to be a part of society that includes social networks, organizations, and institutions. Bogdan and Taylor (1992) stated that:

> Within these social groups, individuals are given a particular social place. The concept of role is often used to describe a person's social place, but social place is not merely a matter of playing a social role. It is also a matter of being defined as being an integral

part of the group or social unit. There is a personal dimension to roles. Roles are particularized for each social unit and personalized by each occupant. Through fulfilling particular social roles, social factors are defined as being part of humanity. (p. 289)

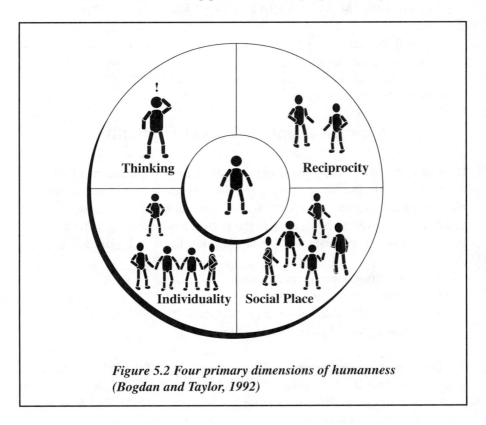

Figure 5.2 Four primary dimensions of humanness (Bogdan and Taylor, 1992)

Adopt a Person-Centered Approach

A helpful approach for facilitating access of all people to community leisure services is to adopt a person-centered approach to the delivery of services. Roberts, Becker, and Seay (1997) reviewed several person-centered models and identified the following common elements: support for inclusion is invited, connections between people are made, expectations are envisioned, problems are solved, and progress is celebrated. Hutchison and McGill (1992) described a person-centered approach as one based on the assumption that in an ever-changing world, one constant factor is our shared humanity. The authors described this approach by stating:

Our shared humanity should be what compels us to treat each other as unique human beings with unknown potential for growth and learning. A strong person-centered philosophy helps us respond to each other, first in terms of our human needs, and second in terms of our more individual requirements. (p. 75)

The person-centered approach intends to have all people feel important, have hope, and dream about developing relationships and a sense of community. A person-centered approach includes the belief that every person is unique and has the potential for growth and development. In describing a person-centered approach to community leisure services, Cipriano (1998, p. 6) concluded that, "The only course to full accessibility is programming by abilities rather than disabilities and then attending to whatever barriers may stand in the way of including any potential participant who has those abilities."

What actions can we take to change perceptions?

The next section describes some specific strategies to help people without disabilities develop more positive attitudes about people with disabilities. The strategies presented in **Figure 5.3** (p. 80) intend to promote beneficial contact and positive attitudes. We can become actively involved in facilitating acceptance of people with disabilities by all members of our community. Some strategies that can help us achieve this goal include:

- structure interactions,
- encourage extensive personal contact,
- promote joint participation,
- facilitate equal status,
- foster cooperative interdependence,
- develop effective communication,
- encourage age-appropriate behaviors,
- create naturally proportioned groups, and
- model positive interactions.

Structure Interactions

Programs structured to promote positive interactions among participants tend to promote positive attitudes. Donaldson (1980) reported that structured experiences consistently result in positive attitude changes, while unstructured contact does not. According to Wilhite, Devine, and Goldenberg (1999), leisure services providers can create a supportive inclusive environment and should take steps to ensure that the potential for appropriate contact between people with and without disabilities is realized. One way to encourage the presentation of structured interactions is to include the promotion of positive interactions among participants with and without disabilities as one of the goals of each program. Plans could be developed to stimulate positive interactions and to devise methods for responding to negative interactions.

Inclusion is clearly beneficial to all people involved; however, it does require some effort on the part of the leisure services professional. Simply placing people in the same environment does not ensure positive interactions between them. Planning ways to structure and promote meaningful interactions between participants can help professionals to increase the likelihood that the benefits of inclusion will be realized.

Encourage Extensive Personal Contact

The goal of providing extensive contact between people with and without disabilities is to increase communication and understanding. For example, Hoenk and Mobily (1987) reported that children who had extensive contact

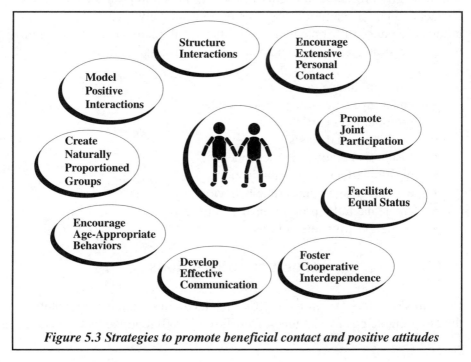

Figure 5.3 Strategies to promote beneficial contact and positive attitudes

with other children with disabilities in an inclusive play environment demonstrated more positive attitudes toward interacting with peers with a disability than those with little contact. In addition, Rowe and Stutts (1987) demonstrated that a one-semester practicum experience that provided contact with people with disabilities improved attitudes of undergraduate students.

When we use volunteers to assist people with disabilities in an inclusive leisure program, we may wish to consider the implications of the volunteers' roles. If volunteers are placed in situations where they have ample opportunities to interact with individuals with disabilities, it appears they may be in a better position to develop positive attitudes toward these individuals than if they were placed in situations where they encountered difficulty interacting with the participants. One-time interactions with people with disabilities that are brief in duration, such as special events, may not create an environment that fosters positive attitudes by volunteers toward participants with disabilities.

Promote Joint Participation

Agencies that offer inclusive leisure services have more of a chance to achieve the goal of frequent contact between people with and without disabilities than those departments that do not actively promote inclusion (Roper, 1990). Participation in inclusive recreation activities can provide opportunities for people residing in the community to experience positive interactions that dispel existing stereotypes.

Since participation in recreation activities offers us many opportunities for close personal contact, involvement in inclusive leisure services can provide an effective way to change societal attitudes toward people with disabilities. By facilitating inclusive leisure opportunities for all community members, we can contribute to the acceptance of people with disabilities.

Facilitate Equal Status

The most positive attitudes result from contact between individuals with and without disabilities on an equal status basis (Levy, Jessop, Rimmerman & Levy, 1992). Equal status refers to participants assuming roles that result in similar degrees of respect from other participants. Inclusive recreation activities that bring people together on an equal basis have the potential for positively influencing the public's perceptions of people with disabilities.

To promote equal status of participants, we must clearly communicate the contributions that each individual makes to a given activity. We can direct participants' attention to insights they gain by being exposed to diversity among participants. All participants can be encouraged to view their involvement with others as a means to facilitate leisure participation for the entire group, rather than simply helping those "less fortunate" people. We can take steps to avoid the experience reported by Wilhite and colleagues:

> Molly talked about her embarrassment when one of her teachers asked in front of the class, "Who wants to be Molly's helper?" Molly explained, "I knew a few people in there, but not well. So nobody raised their hand which embarrassed everyone." Clearly, Molly was not being given equal status with her peers. A better approach might be if a buddy system was initiated for all partici-pants and buddies were encouraged to help each other. (p. 21)

Foster Cooperative Interdependence

Johnson and Johnson (1984) reported that cooperative activities, rather than competitive ones, were effective in promoting positive interactions and good attitudes. These findings supported previous observations by Amir (1969) who reported that when common goals rank higher than individual goals, improved relationships and fostering of positive attitudes occur. Yuker (1988) also concluded that positive attitudes result from contact between individuals with and without disabilities that are friendly, cooperative, and aimed at a common goal.

For the goal of cooperative interdependence to occur, each person must be equally dependent on the other for achieving the desired goals (Levy et al., 1992). We can provide many different recreation activities, such as team building, trust development, and adventure recreation, that require cooperation and contributions by all participants. The focus of the recre-ation activities can be on the process of collaboration to meet a challenge rather than the product of winning. Examples of cooperative activities include gardening (where everyone is assigned a particular task), making a paper-mâché project (where everyone adds a layer), bowling (when the highest possible team score is desired), making a quilt (with a group), and cooking (where everyone completes at least one step).

Develop Effective Communication

Clear communication between people can reduce interaction strain. For example, simple acknowledgment of the disability by the person with the disability can reduce the other person's discomfort (Belgrave & Mills, 1981).

Cook and Makas (1979) noted that people with and without disabilities differed in their perceptions of what constitutes the most positive attitudes toward persons with disabilities. To people with disabilities, "positive attitudes" meant either removing the special category of disability entirely, or promoting attitudes that defend their civil and social rights. However, for people without disabilities, "positive attitudes" reflected a desire to be nice, helpful, and ultimately place people with disabilities in a dependent situation. Therefore, people without disabilities may actually be perceived by people with disabilities as expressing negative attitudes when the individuals without disabilities attempt to express what they consider to be positive attitudes.

Since some people without disabilities want to express attitudes that are acceptable to and respectful of people with disabilities, it becomes clear that they can benefit from learning about how their behaviors can offend people with disabilities. Therefore, it is helpful if people without disabilities are educated about disability as a civil-rights issue, and made aware that many people with disabilities reject special treatment on the basis of their disabilities and do not desire to be perceived as different, even if "different" means "better."

According to Makas (1988), in situations in which a person makes a statement or behaves in a way that demeans or insults, an individual with a disability is justified in correcting the error. However, the author warns that if the correction is accompanied by powerful negative emotions, the content of the correction is likely to be lost. Negative reactions to a person's failed attempts at positive interaction may discourage the person's good intentions and create further misunderstanding and discomfort. Communication, particularly the sharing of one another's expectations, can be valuable in reducing barriers that contribute to discomfort.

Encourage Age-Appropriate Behaviors

Evans, Hodapp, and Zigler (1995) observed that some individuals with disabilities participate in leisure activities that are typically engaged in by those who are younger than them. Demchak (1994) stated that if we encourage individuals with disabilities to participate in activities and with materials that are typically associated with younger individuals (e.g., toys), negative stereotypes about people with disabilities are perpetuated.

However, if individuals with disabilities use materials and participate in activities appropriate for their age, they might be viewed more positively. Age-appropriate activities reflect the personalities, attitudes, and interests of a particular generational group (Jackson, Dunne, Lanham, Heitkamp & Dailey, 1993).

Selection of leisure activities for people with disabilities should occur based on activities performed by peers without disabilities in a wide variety of inclusive community environments.

Calhoun and Calhoun (1993) reported that chronological age-appropriate activities might reduce the stigmatizing effects of disability on the perceptions of adults with disabilities. Participating in age-appropriate activities may lead others to view adults with disabilities as capable of taking on more complicated and advanced tasks than would otherwise be expected.

One example of promoting age-appropriate leisure participation is associated with an adolescent boy, Jason. As a child he loved to listen to any toy that emitted sounds and flashed lights. When he got older, his parents bought him a portable video game. This game was extremely reactive with sounds and lights that flashed. Jason very much enjoyed playing the video game. Now that he is older, Jason enjoys playing video games with his friends in video arcades, movie theater lobbies, and bowling alleys.

Create Naturally Proportioned Groups

The company a person keeps influences our perceptions of this person. Inclusion is almost impossible if there are many individuals with disabilities congregated in any one place. When people with the same impairments are placed together in an activity, this conveys the idea that such people "belong together" to others (Wolfensberger, 2000).

Biklen (1989, p. 237) stated that it is difficult to see the person and not the category when the individual is surrounded by others who share similar salient characteristics, such as obvious disabilities. If people who are devalued are placed in an environment in numbers that are too large for the social systems around them to relate to and assimilate, then these individuals will probably experience rejection, hostility, and efforts at segregation from the larger social system (Wolfensberger, 1995). However, if a person is seen associating with people who we view positively, then we tend to view that person in a positive manner. Therefore, Wolfensberger (2000, p. 114) advocated the idea of natural proportions by stating that people with disabilities:

are apt to acquire—or retain—positive images and role expectancies by being associated with people who are perceived as competent, vigorous, moral, distinguished, etc., and who occupy positive roles. However, in order for such positive image transfer to take place, it is generally important that only a small number of devalued persons be associated with, or juxtaposed to, a much larger number of valued ones, because it is the majority—and even predominant—identity of any social grouping that is apt to define its individual members in the eyes of observers.

The formation of *natural proportions* involves developing groups of people that resemble demographics of the society. For example, a group that contains approximately one person with a disability for every 10 people without disabilities meets the condition of natural proportions for people with disabilities. Germ and Schleien (1997) reported that approximately 70% of leisure services professionals interviewed consider natural proportions helpful in increasing the chance that inclusion would occur.

Model Positive Interactions

One way to promote positive attitudes toward people with disabilities is to model behaviors intended to make the person with a disability feel welcome. Rizzo and colleagues (1997) demonstrated that children model behaviors of adults who are in leadership positions. We can act as change agents by modeling positive behaviors and social acceptance toward including people with disabilities. This reduces resistance to inclusion by community members without disabilities and improves their attitudes (Devine & Kotowski, 1999). Devine and colleagues (1998, p. 72) provided the following example of effective modeling, specific to sports but relevant to all leisure services:

> In front of others, treat the teammate with a disability the same as everyone else. It's not, "Team, meet Johnny, our special teammate." Instead, it should be, "Team, meet Johnny. He bats left-handed and plays outfield."

Final Thoughts

Although behaviors that reflect negative attitudes can limit opportunities for people with disabilities, these negative attitudes and subsequent behaviors can be changed. We can play an important role in changing participants' attitudes so they reflect acceptance and understanding of diversity.

Structuring interactions, encouraging extensive personal contact, promoting joint participation, facilitating equal status, fostering cooperative interdependence, focusing on similarities, developing effective communication, and modeling positive interactions are ways that may help develop positive attitudes toward individuals with disabilities. Perhaps, with increased contact with people with disabilities and the awareness of a highly visible presence of people with disabilities, negative feelings toward these individuals can be eliminated.

Discussion Questions

1. What is the value of structuring interactions when people with and without disabilities are participating in recreation programs?
2. What is an example of how to structure a situation to promote positive interactions between people with and without disabilities?
3. How can you encourage extensive personal contact between participants with and without disabilities?
4. What are some methods that promote joint participation between people with and without disabilities?
5. What is the value of facilitating equal status among participants in a recreation program?
6. How might you encourage participants in your recreation programs to be of equal status?
7. How might you foster cooperative interdependence with people participating in your recreation program?
8. What are some ways you can encourage people you encounter to focus on people's similarities rather than their differences?
9. What are some strategies to increase effective communication that would help improve the attitudes of people you encounter?
10. What are some specific techniques you could utilize to improve people's attitudes toward individuals with disabilities?

Chapter 6

Use Sensitive Terminology

More people are blinded by definition than by any other cause.
-Jahoda

Orientation Activity: Change Terminology

Directions Alone: Write a substitute word or phrase for those presented
that communicates a more positive attitude toward people with disabilities.
Circle the numbers of the words or phrases most difficult to change.

Directions with Others: Divide into small groups and discuss the words or
phrases that posed the most difficulty for each participant. Allow members
of the group to explain the rationale for their choices. After a specified
time, discuss your responses with the entire group.

1.	a special kid	21.	maniac
2.	crippled	22.	crazy
3.	the retarded	23.	deaf
4.	autistic people	24.	dumb
5.	the blind	25.	deaf mute
6.	AIDS victim	26.	handicapped person
7.	the deaf	27.	normal
8.	a CP	28.	able-bodied
9.	those MDs	29.	a paraplegic
10.	wheelchair bound	30.	afflicted with autism
11.	dependent on crutches	31.	imbecile
12.	suffers from MS	32.	the amputee
13.	mental age of 3	33.	the special woman
14.	confined to a wheelchair	34.	lunatic
15.	stricken with epilepsy	35.	moron
16.	borderline retarded	36.	deformed person
17.	dummy	37.	a spina bifida child
18.	feeble-minded	38.	the schizophrenic
19.	a nervous breakdown	39.	a neurotic person
20.	a spinal-injured man	40.	psycho

Debriefing: Language and words are probably the most severe handicaps facing people with disabilities. Although breakthroughs in technology, medical treatment, and legislation are opening doors to meaningful lives for people with disabilities, language persists in developing barriers.

The use of insensitive language to describe other people often creates tension. To reduce this barrier to interaction, we can use clear and accurate communication. To improve attitudes toward people with disabilities, stop using words that convey fear, insensitivity, stereotyping, and discrimination. This chapter supplies information on terminology that encourages communication of positive attitudes toward people with disabilities. As you examine the words and phrases you substituted for the previous words, consider the following questions:

- In what situations are you not sure of how to refer to people with disabilities?
- What general rules can you offer when attempting to describe people with disabilities?
- Why is it important to focus on the words you use to describe people with disabilities?

Introduction

Young children recite the phrase "Sticks and stones may break my bones, but names will never hurt me." Agreed, words might not physically harm individuals, but the words we choose in our interactions with others can have an impact on how people feel about themselves and us. Abu-Tahir (1995) responded to criticisms about trying to use the most sensitive terminology when he stated:

> Some say, "What's the big deal? What's all the fuss about what *we* call *them*." We need to remember that how we refer to a people has everything to do with how we treat those people. The early African-Americans were labeled "slave" thereby justifying their inhumane treatment. The original Americans were called "savages," not "people." Women were called "girls." Today, labels are used to disregard people's beauty and value. (p. 2)

Gilbert, MacCauley, and Smale (1997) analyzed the content of 513 articles from *The Globe and Mail* (a prominent Canadian newspaper) from 1980 to 1990. They concluded that minimal if any change has occurred in the language used in newspaper articles to refer to people with disabilities.

The language is frequently contradictory, with 73% of the articles containing both negative and positive language. Thus, it is understandable that the public is confused about which terms to use. This chapter will help to alleviate some confusion about sensitive terminology.

Why is it helpful to use sensitive terminology?

Since people typically want to express acceptable attitudes that demonstrate respect for people with disabilities, becoming aware of behaviors that offend individuals with disabilities is important. Terminology should reflect equality of all citizens and sensitivity to the situation. An important aspect of selecting terminology is to ensure that respect toward members of the group is communicated (Luckasson & Reeve, 2001). Our behaviors toward people with disabilities can affect the quality of life, self-concept, and acceptance of those individuals. Since leisure services providers frequently interact with people with disabilities, it is critical to project a positive attitude through the use of sensitive terminology.

Byrd, Crews, and Ebener (1991, p. 41) reported that students who were briefed on rules for appropriate use of language when referring to people with disabilities performed significantly better than students who did not. They concluded, "there apparently is benefit to providing this instruction to students who are in a course where disability, disease, or exceptionality is being discussed." By advocating for sensitive terminology, people with disabilities have forced some professionals to rethink old assumptions and redefine ways to address needs identified by people with those disabilities (Ward & Meyer, 1999). According to Smith (1992, p. 1):

> Laws such as the Americans with Disabilities Act, approved in July 1990, bar discrimination of people with physical or mental disabilities in public accommodations, private employment, and government services. By passing laws, the federal government hopes to empower people with disabilities, but the battle for access may be better fought on the communication front. Educators can help the next generation of writers and the working press learn to use language that promotes the notion that people with disabilities are entitled to access. The day the ADA bill passed, *The Atlanta Journal and Constitution* announced, "Handicapped Rights Bill Awaits Final Approval" (1990, p. 11.). This usage may seem innocuous enough, but it is off the mark. The preferred usage is "people with disabilities."

What can be done to help us use words that are sensitive?

This chapter suggests ways to use sensitive terminology that communicates positive attitudes toward people with disabilities, including the following (see **Figure 6.1**):

- focus on people's similarities,
- consider the person first,
- emphasize each person's abilities,
- communicate respect for each person,
- use consistent terminology, and
- refer to people without disabilities.

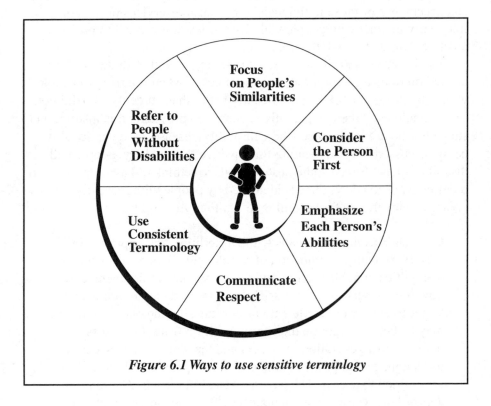

Figure 6.1 Ways to use sensitive terminlogy

Suggestions for using terminology that focuses attention on similarities shared by all people rather than differences are made. A "people first" philosophy is described with implications for terminology. Encouragement is given for us to emphasize individuals' abilities rather than their disabilities by using specific words and phrases. Recommendations for using language that communicates dignity and respect are also presented. An attempt is made to alleviate confusion with some words and promote the use of consistent terminology that represents people with disabilities in a positive manner. In addition, information is provided on preferred terminology to describe people without disabilities. The following sections encourage professionals and students to act as agents of change to help other people use the most appropriate terminology to describe individuals with disabilities.

Focus on People's Similarities

Focusing on a person's uniqueness can be a positive way to view the individual. However, an emphasis on unusual traits might become so overwhelming that the similarities shared by all people are ignored. Failure to recognize that all individuals have the same basic needs can set people apart from one another and create barriers to interpersonal relationships. Typically, it is easier to interact with a person if we initially concentrate on similarities we share with this person as opposed to differences. People's attitudes tend to be more positive when they focus on similarities (Snell, 1988).

One way that people mistakenly focus on differences rather than similarities between people is by identifying some individuals as being "special." Typically, people with disabilities express the desire to be treated with the same respect as any person. Charles Greenlaw, an official associated with the Boy Scouts, summarized the involvement of Tim Fredricks, a scout who happens to have mental retardation, in a community Boy Scout program. "The other scouts see nothing unusual about having Tim in the group, nor do they treat him as 'special.' The only way that Tim is 'special' is that he is an Eagle Scout" (Fredricks, 1987, p. 27).

When people are identified as "special" as a result of their disability, the implication may be that their disability limits all that they do. When this generalized impact of their disability is accepted, people tend to lower their expectations of individuals with disabilities. Bree Walker, a co-anchor of an evening television newscast who has a physical disability stated: "We have to reach a point where having a physical difference doesn't matter. When we do, I will feel that my time has come and I am no longer regarded as 'special'" (Dietl, 1988). Deborah McFadden stated:

> We're trying to prevent use of the word "special," because every time you have a "special" person, you make that person different. We must have the dream and the hope that our future will be inclusive of everyone. (McFadden & Burke, 1991, p. iii)

According to Wright (1988), when a person identifies with someone because of similarity, a tendency for that person to like the other person will be induced. However, the author suggested that focusing on individuals' differences could be perceived in a way that promotes prejudice. Therefore, when we use terminology to describe people with disabilities, it is helpful if we consider only using a label when absolutely necessary. For example, a supervisor may be educating her staff about the needs of Anthony being included in a program and may say, "Anthony may have some difficulty with abstract concepts; therefore, you may want to provide some demonstrations when giving verbal directions."

When writing about people with disabilities, journalists and others have been encouraged to not refer to a person's disability or other characteristics such as race unless it is critical to the story. Emphasizing the worth of all people, rather than differences between people, will encourage portrayal of people with disabilities in a positive fashion.

Consider the Person First

When relating to people who have been grouped together for whatever reason, consider these individuals as people first and then, if relevant, consider their group affiliation. According to Luckasson and Reeve (2001, p. 47), "first and foremost, we emphasize that the term given to any disability is not the essence of any individual who has the disability. Individuals are people first."

If it is relevant to use a label, emphasize the person's humanness by avoiding the tendency to make stereotypic generalizations about people who, in addition to many of the other characteristics that affect their humanness (e.g., sense of humor, reliability, honesty) happen to have a disability. To place the person first, we use the label only as a noun referring to a condition such as "a person with mental retardation" rather than a noun referring to the person such as "the retard" or an adjective such as "the mentally retarded person."

According to Helff and Glidden (1998), many professionals and parents have moved away from disability-oriented language ("the disabled") to people-first language ("people with disabilities"). Snow (1998) asked these questions and made these statements to make a point about people-first language: Are you myopic or do you wear glasses? Are you freckled or do you have freckles? Are you disabled or do you have a disability? People first language describes what a person *has*, not what a person *is* and therefore puts the person before the disability. Snow (1998, pp. 15–16) provided insight about the use of people-first language:

When we start calling things by their right names, when we recognize that people with disabilities are people first, we begin to see how people with disabilities are more like people without disabilities than they are different. My son, Benjamin, is 11 years old. He loves the Lone Ranger, ice cream, and playing on the computer. He has blond hair, blue eyes, and cerebral palsy. His disability is only one small piece of his life. When I introduce myself to people I don't tell them I'll never be a prima ballerina. Like others, I focus on my strengths, the things I do well, not on what I can't do. I don't say, "My son can't write with a pencil." I say, "My son uses a computer to do his school work." I don't say, "My son can't walk." I say, "My son uses a walker and a wheelchair."

By making reference to the person first, respect for the worth of the person is demonstrated. Coulter (1992) reported that use of disability-first language such as "the retarded" or "retarded persons" shows a lack of respect for people with disabilities. Another way to focus on the individual is to avoid labeling people into groups according to medical diagnoses or disabilities such as "the blind" or "the amputee." Focus on people first, such as "individuals with visual impairments," or "people with amputations."

In general, it is helpful to avoid using acronyms such as "CP" for cerebral palsy, "MR" for mental retardation, or "MD" for muscular dystrophy. The use of such acronyms emphasizes the condition rather than the person. In addition, use of acronyms may create confusion and make some people feel ignorant because they are unaware of the meaning of some acronyms. This breakdown in communication can limit our ability to present a positive image of people with disabilities. However, if it is relevant to identify the person's medical diagnosis, the name of the condition is lengthy, and there is high recognition of the acronym within a given society, the acronym may be appropriately used. For example, Acquired Immune Deficiency Syndrome is most frequently identified as AIDS because the acronym has a higher recognition rate. Therefore, in some limited situations, use of an acronym may be accepted.

When identifying individuals, it is useful to recognize their humanness and identify them as "people" or "program participants" rather than "patients" or "cases." The use of patients or cases implies that individuals are ill and in need of medical assistance. Many people with disabilities are not receiving medical care, are in excellent health, and therefore should not be identified as patients. Most of us, at some time, will be receiving medical care and be identified as a patient in the context of the medical environment; however, this does not imply that we should then be identified as a patient in all contexts of our lives. The condition of being a patient or a case varies according to the situation and, therefore, the use of these terms as a label for people with disabilities is often inaccurate. The word "client" may be used to describe people participating in a variety of leisure services. If client is used consistently to describe all participants, then it is more acceptable than when client is used only to describe those individuals with disabilities.

An example of people first terminology occurred on May 10, 1988, when former President Reagan signed Executive Order 12640 establishing the President's Committee on Employment of the Handicapped as the President's Committee on Employment of People with Disabilities. People working to improve the language concerning disability enthusiastically supported the name change (*Rag Time,* 1989). Chairperson Harold Russell stated that the new name demonstrated that the President's Committee was sensitive to the desires of people with disabilities. In addition, other legislation such as the Individuals with Disabilities Education Act (formerly known as the Education of the Handicapped Act) and the Americans with Disabilities Act, clearly demonstrate a focus on people first terminology.

Inclusion encourages people to focus on similarities and to accept differences. Considering this goal, Smith and Hilton (1997, p. 6) talked about people first terminology:

> At first glance it may seem a trivial matter whether a child is called "child with mental retardation" rather than "retarded child," but the change in attitude this kind of difference in language reflects may be crucial for these students. When disabilities are seen as secondary to the overall humanity of the student, attitudes may change to reflect a greater openness to the person and a greater optimism regarding the amelioration of the disability.

Emphasize Each Person's Abilities

It is important for us to emphasize individuals' abilities rather than focusing on limitations. For example, it is more accurate to say "a woman who uses a wheelchair" rather than "she is confined to a wheelchair" or "she is wheelchair-bound." The use of the phrase "he walks with crutches" is more accurate than "he is dependent on crutches." Typically, when people access forms of transportation other than walking such as an automobile, bicycle, or skateboard, they are not described as being "confined to" or "dependent on" that particular means of transportation. It is helpful to be consistent with this line of reasoning when describing people with disabilities who use alternative forms of transportation or mobility.

Many words used to describe individuals with disabilities reflect concepts of dependency and helplessness that perpetuate negative attitudes and corresponding patterns of response and expectation. At times, fundraising efforts have employed the use of counterproductive terminology intended to evoke impressions of needy, fragile people requiring special treatment. Organizations using such tactics to raise funds intended to promote independence may in fact foster a sense of dependency through the fundraising campaign. Describe people as simply having a disability rather than using words that imply pain and suffering. Phrases such as "afflicted with... suffers from…a victim of…crippled by…stricken with…" sensationalize the disability and tend to evoke sympathy toward individuals. Instead, it would be more appropriate to say "the person has…the condition is caused by…a disability resulting from…"

In a February 1988 issue of *Time* magazine entitled "Roaming the Cosmos," the lead sentence to the article describing the renowned physicist Stephen Hawking was: "Physicist Stephen Hawking is confined to a wheelchair, a virtual prisoner in his own body." This description can be contrasted with the lead sentence in the article entitled "Black Holes Figured Back in Time" reported in a June 1988 issue of *Insight* magazine: "Through the intricate equations devised over two decades, cosmologist Stephen W. Hawking has advanced intriguing visions of the universe's origin and structure." The differences between the two representations are striking.

Frequently, sympathetic views evoked by such words as "confined" or "prisoner" restrict people's independence by limiting other people's tendency to treat individuals who have disabilities with dignity and respect. For instance, at the second AIDS forum in Denver in 1983, individuals with AIDS condemned attempts to label them as "AIDS victims." People attending the conference stated that the phrase AIDS victims implied defeat and identified the phrase "persons with AIDS" as the most preferred terminology.

Communicate Respect for Each Person

The practice of classifying individuals according to mental age has been drastically reduced in recent years. It is important that we avoid using the phrase "mental age," because the label tells us nothing about the person's cognitive strengths and weaknesses (Baroff, 1986). For instance, when discussing the implications of following written directions by a woman, say "a woman who is 35-years-old and currently identifies a few words" as opposed to stating "the woman who has the mind of a 3-year-old." Use of the phrase "mental age" may result in mistakenly treating a person with a mental impairment such as Alzheimer's disease, mental retardation, or a learning disability as a child.

Using terminology that labels adults with mental impairments as children, such as "he is childlike" or "our kids" can show disrespect. Instead we can communicate dignity provided to other adults in our society by using age-appropriate terminology to describe individuals. Age-appropriate terms encourage development of programs that are appropriate for the age of the participants and do not require participants to compromise their dignity.

We can also use terminology that demonstrates respect by avoiding the use of any terms to describe people with disabilities that communicate racism or ethnocentrism. For instance, sometimes people with mental retardation who have Down syndrome are referred to as "Mongoloid." This term was used because of one of the characteristic features of persons with Down syndrome—their eyes resembled individuals of Asian descent. Therefore, if it is relevant to describe the specific form of mental retardation caused by an extra 21st chromosome, professionals are encouraged to use Down syndrome rather than Mongoloid.

Many words that have been used in the past to describe people with disabilities have communicated ideas of deviancy, helplessness, and dependency. Words such as imbecile, lunatic, moron, borderline, dummy, feeble-minded, maniac, crazy, deaf and dumb, or deaf mute are no longer acceptable because of their strong negative overtones. Instead, we can use phrases such as people with developmental disabilities, individuals with mental retardation, people with psychological disorders, individuals with communication disorders, or people with speech and hearing disorders. Through the use of these words and phrases, we will better communicate a positive attitude about people with disabilities.

Use Consistent Terminology

Impairment, disability, and handicap are three distinct words defined in different ways. Unfortunately, many people use the words interchangeably and often inaccurately.

The word *impairment* means to diminish in strength and refers to identifiable organic or functional conditions that may be permanent (such as an amputation) or temporary (such as a sprain). When an individual possesses an impairment, the focus is on the problem—a disease or injury with a specific portion of the body. For instance, a visual impairment involves a deficit with the eye, such as that caused by clouding of lenses resulting in cataracts. When cataracts are mentioned, the problem with the eye is emphasized. Another example may be that a person has a neurological impairment, such as cerebral palsy, that prevents independent leg movement. In this situation, when the phrase "neurological impairment" is used, attention is directed toward the central nervous system that was damaged. The focus of the discussion related to impairment is not on the person; rather, the discussion is directed to the actual condition.

Able is defined as having sufficient power, skill or resources to accomplish a task. When the word able is combined with the prefix *dis,* which refers to being deprived of, the definition of the word disability becomes apparent. The word *disability* describes the reduction or deprivation of a skill or power. This reduced ability is a result of an impairment. For instance, a person with cataracts has a visual impairment that may result in a reading disability even when corrective lenses are used. When the word disability is used, attention is given to the interaction of the visual impairment with the functioning ability of the individual. When discussing a person's disability, it is necessary to examine the individual and the effect that the impairment has on that person. However, according to Whyte and Ingstad (1995, p. 3):

> A preliminary common-sense definition of disability might be that it is a lack or limitation of competence. We usually think of disability in contrast to an ideal of normal capacity to perform particular activities and to play one's role in social life. Sickness also inhibits ability, but we distinguish between sickness, which is temporary (whether ended by healing or death), and disability, which is chronic.

Although, at first glance, this definition might seem harmless, Talle (1995) warned that the notion of disability is heavily charged with implications of social inferiority or stigma.

The word handicap was originally used to denote a disadvantage in sport (Hale, 1979). A *handicap* is a game in which forfeits were held in a cap (hand in cap), a content in which artificial advantage is given (or disadvantage imposed) on a contest to equalize chances of winning. Howe-Murphy and Charboneau (1987) identified the word handicap as being linked with the practice of beggars who held cap in hand to solicit charity. These definitions demonstrate that the labeling of people as handicapped represents an impression of society that these individuals are dependent on others.

The important aspect of the word handicap is that it varies from one situation to another. In effect, a handicap is an interaction between environmental conditions and the individual, rather than simply inherent in the person. For instance, a person with a visual impairment may be handicapped when going to the theater to watch a movie but may not be handicapped when listening to music on the radio. A person with a neurological impairment who uses a wheelchair may be handicapped when playing soccer but may be extremely skilled at billiards. Because a person may be handicapped in one situation and not handicapped in another, it is inaccurate to label the person as handicapped. The word handicap implies that the person is handicapped in every situation. This generalization of a condition to all life situations imposes unnecessary restrictions on the individual.

Since being handicapped is a social phenomenon influenced by our society (Lord, 1981), people with disabilities can handicap themselves by believing that they cannot do something and society can handicap people with disabilities by denying them opportunities to participate. The term "handicap" is reserved for describing obstacles that lessen a person's chance of success. These obstacles often will prevent people from doing something. Jack Kemp (1994), an attorney and an advocate for people with disabilities who was born with multiple limb anomalies stated:

> One day I came home crying that these kids had been making fun of me. They said I had wooden arms and wooden legs *and* a wooden head—which probably isn't too far off the mark! My dad said, "Well, those kids have a handicap too." He told me that I might have a disability, but other people who don't accept me have a handicap. A handicap is something external to me that interferes with my freedom to be a part of my community. A curb without a curb cut is a handicap to someone in a wheelchair. People's negative stereotypical thinking about individuals with disabilities is a handicap to our acceptance. That was the first time someone had lifted the burden of "handicapism" off of me. I got teased, but my dad put it into perspective. (p. 28)

Miller and Sammons (1999) identified four types of handicaps: social, personal, physical and those associated with resources. *Social handicaps* are associated with other people's negative attitudes toward people with disabilities. *Personal handicaps* occur when people lack adequate information about their own disability or about ways to become involved in various activities. *Physical handicaps* can include inaccessible buildings, parks, or transportation. *Resource handicaps* are when people have insufficient funds, training, and people to assist them.

To illustrate the point that these handicaps or obstacles can shape a person's quality of life as much or more than a person's specific medical, physical, or cognitive disability, Miller and Sammons (1999, p. 29) provided the following example:

> Imagine that you have arthritis (impairment) and cannot climb stairs (disability). You want to go to a concert, but the theatre has no elevator or ramp. You have a handicap because of the architectural inaccessibility of the theatre. Similarly, a person who is deaf has a handicap while watching television without closed captioning; a person who is blind has a handicap in an elevator without Braille signs; and a person who uses a wheelchair has a handicap when shopping in a store that does not have accessible parking entrances, restrooms, and aisles.

Many people have stated that they want to be identified with a disability rather than a handicap. For instance, Karol Davenport, a leisure services provider who also happens to use a wheelchair, explained that she preferred to be referred to as a "person with a disability" rather than "handicapped" (Jesiolowski, 1988). Ms. Davenport's preference was supported by a survey conducted by *The Disability Rag* ("The results are in!" 1986) that reported the preferences of the magazine's readership. Nearly three-fourths of the respondents with disabilities stated that they would prefer the phrase "a person with a disability" when referring to themselves, while only 3% preferred "handicapped person." Shapiro (1993) stated that the term "disabled" has replaced "handicapped" and is becoming the first word to emerge by consensus from people with disabilities.

Refer to People without Disabilities

The word "normal" is acceptable when referring to statistical norms and averages; however, this term is demeaning to people with disabilities when used in reference to people with no disability (National Easter Seals Society, 1981). The use of the word normal to describe people who do not possess an apparent disability implies that a disability is the one distinguishing factor that separates people into two primary categories: normal and disabled. Not only is the word normal demeaning to many people with disabilities, but also many people without disabilities resent being labeled as normal. Normal implies that people act similar to many other people in almost all aspects of their lives. This view stresses conformity and ignores individuality, creativity, and diversity.

When describing people without disabilities, it is helpful to apply the same principles described earlier in this chapter. If not having a disability is irrelevant to a particular situation then we can simply avoid labeling the individual. However, if it is important to identify the person as not having a disability we can use the phrase "people without disabilities" to refer to people who do not possess an apparent disability. Some people use the phrase "able-bodied" to describe individuals without disabilities. This phrase can cause confusion, however, because individuals with disabilities may also possess bodies that are very able such as people with mental retardation, autism, and learning disabilities.

Why does sensitive terminology change?

Language is the means by which we attempt to accurately communicate with others. Over time our words change to reflect changes in attitudes, thinking, and expression (Crouser, 1999). According to Hartman (1998), like other stigmatized groups, people with disabilities are in a continuous and evolutionary process of choosing language they prefer to be used to describe themselves and their experiences. What is identified today as being sensitive terminology may no longer be sensitive tomorrow. History has shown us that acceptable terms in the past often are no longer accept-able today. Crouser (1999) provided the following example when discuss-ing the American Association on Mental Retardation:

> We were founded to serve idiotic and feebleminded persons and eventually we moved on to serve imbeciles and morons. Decades later our constituency was described as mentally deficient and now we support people who are mentally retarded. And now we must ask ourselves, again . . . Is it time to change our terminology?

Changes in the way we think about people with disabilities result in changes in the terms we use. However, Warren (2000) suggested that changing terminology that describes people with disabilities every few decades is no solution and that ultimately we must find a way to somehow transcend the issue of terminology.

There are some words and phrases that have been considered by people with disabilities and their advocates as demonstrating a positive view toward people with disabilities. For instance, Ted Kennedy, Jr. (1986) dislikes the terms "handicapped" and "disabled," because they imply inability and are negative descriptions that promote undesirable stereo-types. Instead, Kennedy prefers "physically and mentally challenged" or "persons with a disability," to stress human beings first and limitations second. Kennedy's desire to emphasize the person first is in keeping with most people's preferred terminology. However, some people view the phrase "physically challenged" as vague and ambiguous.

Some other terminology that describes people with visual impairments, such as "partially sighted," has met controversy. Some individuals feel the phrase "partially sighted" implies an avoidance of the acceptance of having a disability, while others feel it accentuates positive aspects (sight). Rana Arnold reported that when polling members of the Sight-Loss Support Group of Central Pennsylvania views regarding the phrase "partially sighted" varied from person to person.

Another controversy relates to ways to describe people who are deaf. Some people who are deaf reject "people first" terminology and prefer being described as "Deaf people." According to Dolnick (1993, p. 38), "the upper-case D is significant. It serves as a succinct proclamation that the deaf share a culture rather than merely a medical condition." The argument of deafness as culture relates to the belief that over a half a million Americans who are deaf share a common language (American Sign Language) and as a result share a common identity. However, the view that deafness is akin to ethnicity is far from unanimously held.

One problem that arises when using phrases that have yet to receive general support from people associated with a particular group is the difficulty in receiving services such as financial aid, education, and recreation. Although phrases such as "partially sighted" and "physically challenged" seem to accentuate the positive for some people, these same phrases may create problems in acquiring services and seem to offend other individuals. *The Disability Rag* ("The results are in!" 1986) reported that only a few of their subscribers indicated a preference for the phrases "physically challenged" or "inconvenienced." In describing the perceptions of the hundreds of people with disabilities whom he interviewed, Shapiro (1993, p. 33) wrote:

> Concoctions like "the vertically challenged" are silly and scoffed at. The "differently-abled," the "handi-capable," or the "physically and mentally challenged" are almost universally dismissed as too gimmicky and too inclusive. "Physically challenged doesn't distinguish me from a woman climbing Mt. Everest, something certainly I'll never do," says Nancy Mairs, an essayist and poet with multiple sclerosis. "It blurs the distinction between our lives." Only by using direct terminology, she argues, will people think about what it means to be disabled and the accommodations she needs, such as wheelchair accessible buildings or grab bars in bathrooms. Dianne Piastro, who writes the syndicated column "Living with a Disability," complains that such terms suggest that

disability is somehow shameful and needs to be concealed in a vague generality. "It's denying our reality instead of saying that our reality, of being disabled, is okay," says Piastro.

At this time it is difficult to recommend the consistent use of such phrases. It is important, however, for us to realize that identification of the most preferred terminology to describe persons with disabilities is a continuously evolving process.

Why should I consider the perspective of the person with a disability?

If we are unsure of which words to use when we make contact with people, we can ask the person with a disability what terminology he or she prefers. Words that are currently creating controversy and have yet to receive a general consensus may be the words of choice in the future. In all situations, listen to people to determine the terms and phrases they most prefer and attempt to understand their reasons for these choices. This sentiment is reflected by Coulter (1992, p. 2):

> I believe that people have a right to call themselves whatever they want, and that others should respect their choice. We should not be surprised when these choices change over time. We have seen several such changes recently: people preferring to be called gay or lesbian instead of homosexual, or people preferring to be called African-American instead of colored or black, for example. If this choice reflects a reasonable consensus of those who may be so described, then I believe we should respect it. People with disabilities have made it perfectly clear that they want us to use people-first language, and so we should.

Similarly, although many people express a desire for the use of people first terminology, as with any labels, there is not total support for its use. For example, Hartman (1998, p. 10) described Carol Gill, who based on her research, private practice as a psychotherapist, and experiences as a woman with a disability, stated that: "I don't mind people-first language, I do mind the insistence on it. My disability is an integral component of who I am—I am incredibly proud to be a disabled woman."

Dr. Gill's statements illustrate the point that, although many suggestions are provided on sensitive language by many people with disabilities, a critical suggestion to follow is to learn what each individual desires and to respect the right of that person to name him or herself. As further illustration of this suggestion, Nancy Mairs (1992, pp. 56–57) takes the extreme position as she writes the following:

> I am a cripple. I choose this word to name me. People—crippled or not—wince at the word "cripple." Perhaps I want them to wince. I want them to see a tougher customer, one to whom the fates/gods/viruses have not been kind, but who can face the brutal truth of her existence squarely. But I don't care what you call me, so long as it isn't 'differently abled,' which strikes me as pure verbal garbage designed, by its ability to describe anyone, to describe no one. I would never refer to another person as a cripple. It is the word I use to name myself.

Similarly, it is helpful for us to remember that interpretation of the meaning of words is based on our perspective, which is strongly influenced by our culture. Words and sentences used in one culture may demonstrate respect; however, use of the same words in a different culture may be viewed as offensive. Fernald (1995, p. 99) compared language preferences of people with disabilities among English-speaking countries and stated: "some terminology that Americans assume to be sensitive and stigma-free was, in fact, offensive to British colleagues." Therefore, it is important to consider that the information presented in this chapter is one perspective of sensitive terminology and when in doubt ask individuals what they most prefer.

How can we become change agents?

Based on the premise that changing social attitudes through language has been a powerful tool for the civil rights movements, Medgyesi (1988) encouraged advocates for people with disabilities to insist upon terminology that is empowering rather than demeaning. Use of empowering terminology establishes people with disabilities as a social and economic force to be considered and respected.

Use of insensitive terminology may occur because well-intentioned people are not aware of the most accurate words or phrases to describe people. Do not assume that the person using insensitive terminology was purposefully being offensive—the person may be using them out of ignorance and does not intend to be disrespectful. After reading this chapter and gaining knowledge of the most appropriate terminology, consider the perspective of the people using the inappropriate terminology when educating them about the most desired behaviors to exhibit as they interact with or represent individuals with disabilities.

Final Thoughts

One way to communicate respect for people is to avoid using words that offend them and to use words that make them feel valued. The use of sensitive terminology can set the stage for a positive interaction that can lead to successful, meaningful, and enjoyable leisure experiences for all. Snow (1998, p. 94) made the following statement:

> While people with disabilities and advocates work to end discrimination and segregation in education, employment, and our communities at large, we must all work to end the prejudicial language that creates an invisible barrier to being included in the ordinary mainstream of life.

We can become change agents within society. Although this chapter intended to describe what many people with disabilities and professionals espouse as sensitive terminology, consider that the use of acceptable terminology is an evolving process. Therefore, it is helpful if we continuously respond to the most recent information presented, demonstrate a willingness to listen to and consider other people's perspectives, and revise our terminology to best represent people with disabilities.

Finally, in reporting on the life of Judy Clouston, a recognized poet, Crabtree (1994) presented a quote by Clouston that demonstrated how she felt about sensitive terminology:

> When the clerk shouts, "Hey, Joe, there's a crippled lady up here who needs some sour cream," I wince. When a stranger says, "My aunt is an invalid . . ." I can't hear the rest of the sentence. When I hear the phrase "confined to a wheelchair" I want to jump out of mine. They're words, but they make a difference.

Discussion Questions

1. What is the people first philosophy?
2. What are six general suggestions for using sensitive terminology?
3. Why is it important to focus on individuals' similarities?
4. Why is it best to avoid the use of the term "special?"
5. Why should acronyms be avoided? When is it appropriate to use acronyms?
6. What is the difference among the terms "patient," "client," and "participant?" Which term is preferred and why?
7. What are two ways the federal government acknowledged the importance of people first terminology?
8. Why should you avoid using terminology that sensationalizes or exploits people with disabilities?
9. What is meant by the terms "impairment," "disability," and "handicapped?"
10. What is the best way to refer to people who do not have disabilities?

Chapter 7

Support Families

It's a tough balancing act.
-Jan Walters

Orientation Activity: The Family Balancing Act

Directions Alone: Collect 10 empty cardboard boxes. Read the following list of possible problems a family might experience. All families may experience these situations; however, families that have a member who has a disability are more likely to experience these situations. As you read each situation, pick up one of the boxes. Continue reading and adding boxes until you drop a box.

Directions with Others: Divide into small groups and discuss how you felt when you were attempting to carry as many boxes as possible. Describe how you felt when one or more boxes fell. Discuss your perception of the responsibilities of family members of individuals with disabilities. Generate some ideas on how leisure services providers may be able to alleviate the stress experienced by these families.

1. Since there is no afternoon recreation program for your child to attend, you must hire someone to be with your child.
2. The person you have scheduled to watch your child is sick and you must take a day off work.
3. Since there is no summer recreation facility open to your sister, you must watch her instead of working and earning money.
4. Because of the unwillingness of the preschool to accommodate your child, you must stop working and stay home with your child.
5. One of the members of your household becomes ill and you must take care of them.
6. Your child is injured while playing out in the street.
7. A person working at the bowling alley tells you that you should not bring your brother there in the future.

8. You decline an invitation to a party because the last time you were there people did not make your family feel welcome.
9. You are unable to afford to go on a family vacation this year because of the medical expenses you incurred.
10. Your friends make fun of you because a member of your family has a disability.

Debriefing: Families must respond to many circumstances that influence their lives. Each circumstance requires the family to make an adjustment. In the orientation activity, taking on a cardboard box represented the family circumstances. As families acquire "boxes," they must readjust their strategy of working together to keep them from falling and to maintain an intact family. Through a life cycle, the family accumulates numerous boxes, which they attempt to share and carry as a group. Eventually, this simulation required the addition of so many adjustments that the boxes could no longer be carried. When some boxes fell this was a time of crisis and the family could not remain stable without outside community support and intervention. With assistance from others, however, the crisis was managed. Consider the following questions when thinking about the orientation activity:

- How did you feel while participating in the activity?
- What did you learn from this activity?
- How can leisure services providers support families who have a member who has a disability?

Introduction

Behind every person with a disability is a family. A family may be generally defined as all members of a household under a roof who have a common interest and commitment to its members (Cartledge, Kea & Ida, 2000). Each family tries to manage the needs of each member of the family, as well as their collective needs. At times, families are placed in a position of having to choose which needs will be met and which ones will not. For instance, Fink (1988) stated "Because we could not find after-school care and daily respite care, we had to place our son in a group home. We want him home now, and I cannot bring him home because there is no place for after-school care, vacation, etc."

Braddock, Hemp, and Fujiura (1987) reported that the trend within the last couple of decades of moving people out of large residential institutions (identified as the deinstitutionalization movement) has resulted in an increased number of people with disabilities residing in their communities (see **Figure 7.1**). Families have become a major source of care and support for these individuals, but attempts to provide this care create major challenges. The attitudes, values, and behaviors of family members are very important in shaping the leisure decisions of individuals.

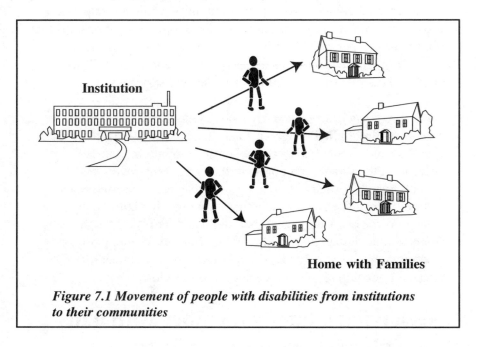

Figure 7.1 Movement of people with disabilities from institutions to their communities

What is the value of inclusive leisure services for families?

Kloeze (1999, p. 6) concluded that since leisure occurs more within the family context than any other, "the home is most people's leisure center, and the family their main leisure group." Despite the growing support for inclusion of individuals with disabilities, ample evidence exists that families and communities experience significant barriers to accomplishing successful inclusion (Turnbull & Ruef, 1997). Working with families to help foster inclusive programs is an important challenge for leisure services professionals.

Johnson, Bullock, and Ashton-Shaeffer (1997) observed that because most children with disabilities spend much of their free time at home with their families, families should be natural partners in leisure education for youth with disabilities. Many families are aware of the value of inclusive services. For example, when asked to identify the most significant benefit that followed inclusion most parents referred to acceptance by others, participation in typical educational activities with peers without disabilities, exposure to normal expectations, and membership in a typical educational group (Ryndak, Downing, Jacqueline & Morrison, 1995).

Participation in "special" programs may actually contribute to a family's sense of isolation from their community, while participation in inclusive community programs allows families to build relationships that do not focus on a person's disability or difference (Umstead, Boyd & Dunst, 1995). Umstead and colleagues (p. 36) provided the following example to illustrate the value of inclusive leisure services:

> One parent said she particularly enjoyed the friendships she made while waiting for her daughter, Lakeisha, at swimming and gymnastics classes. She told us that when she ran into these other parents at the supermarket or mall, they had many things to talk about, including their children's accomplishments and activities. Parents also talk about the benefits of giving other community members the chance to know their child and family. Other children come to understand that children with disabilities share many of their own talents and interests. Children who play and learn together develop respect for each other's abilities.

Does having a family member with a disability place stress on a family?

Children produce an element of stress for parents, and children with disabilities are no exception. Although children with disabilities contribute in positive ways to their families, they have daily care needs and associated problems that create challenges for parents.

Rowitz (1992) reported that many families with a member who has a disability perceive they do not have control over what happens to them. In addition, they often do not know how to access resources and feel intimidated by the system. Saetermoe, Wideman, and Borthwick-Duffy (1991) reported that many parents who have a child with a disability are working, have no free time, and are barely able to take care of their own responsibilities. These families often must struggle with the rising costs of many services such as respite care, transportation, and medical support. Roach, Orsmond, and Barratt (1999) reported that family members become frustrated because they feel there are very few resources provided to them to continue their efforts in taking care of their son or daughter.

According to Gill (1994), for some people, having a relative with a disability alters family roles. Children often feel a deep sense of anger and loss when a parent no longer functions in an accustomed manner as a result of a disability or caring for a family member with a disability. Struggles faced by families of people with disabilities include financial and time constraints, lack of resources, fatigue, and social isolation. Family duties and responsibilities may change from member to member as the realities of living with a person with a disability become apparent.

Hintermair (2000) concluded that any physical or mental disability is unanimously regarded as a considerable stress potential for parents. Many parents with children with disabilities face challenges regarding long-term support for their children and may become exhausted over time (Lin, 2000). Pedlar, Haworth, Hutchinson, Taylor, and Dunn (1999) interviewed families with a member who was disabled and concluded that family members committed much time and energy to trying to ensure that their relative was well cared for, was receiving appropriate support, and continued to live as a valued member of the family.

What are examples of types of support for leisure and family stress?

Mary Ulrich has been an active advocate for people with disabilities. She is a contributing member of her community and a leader in several national organizations. In addition, Mary is a wife and a parent. One of her children happens to have a severe disability. Based on her personal experiences, Mary made a significant contribution to this section of the chapter.

Community Support for Beverly

Many local communities have responded to the needs of typical families. For example, Beverly's parents accessed the services of daycare for Bev when she was younger. Currently, they piece together public and private community programs to help support their family. During the summer when school is not in session, Bev, who is now 13 years old, rides her bike to the community recreation center at 8:00 a.m. as her mother and father go to work. She begins diving lessons at 8:30 a.m., swim team practice at 9:30 a.m., and free swim with her friends until noon. She then rides her bike to a nearby park for tennis lessons from 1:00-3:00 p.m. After a short bike ride home, Bev calls her mother or father at work to provide them with an update on her status and then starts a few chores before dinner.

When examining Bev's life during the school year and in the summer, the time blocks appear similar: classes, free time, home, and chores. During the summer, Bev's family adjusts their routines to accommodate their needs. As a result of a little creative planning, the availability of financial and community resources, and Bev's growing skills and independence, Bev's family is able to maintain a balance between their needs and community support.

Community Support for Karen

Now, let us examine the balance of family needs and community supports for the family of a person who requires extensive support. Karen is 13 years old and lives in the same neighborhood as Beverly. She goes to the same school, and her mother works with Bev's mother in the same business. Karen, however, cannot go alone to the community recreation center. The swimming program for children with disabilities is only on Thursdays from 3:00-4:00 p.m. Karen is currently not able to ride her bike to the park independently and is not eligible for tennis lessons because of her disabilities. The sports leagues, Bible schools, Scout camps, and community camps either have no programs for children with disabilities, or they have programs at specific times which are suitable for personnel working with these programs but inconvenient for Karen's family. Daycare centers will not accept Karen. Although Karen's family contacts the school and many social service agencies, they are unable to locate any ongoing programs that would meet Karen's needs. Further, though many professionals are sympathetic, it is clearly the family's problem. The inability to provide community leisure services adds more stress to the family.

The family worries about Karen's future. They know she is going to learn fewer skills than most of her peers. Karen is also going to need an increased number of teaching trials to learn those few skills. She frequently will forget skills she does not practice, and then it takes her longer to relearn these skills. Karen has problems with transfer of skills from one place to another. The family is also aware that Karen enjoys a variety of recreation activities and wants to be with other people. Unfortunately, instead of engaging in opportunities for growth and enjoyment, frequently Karen finds herself alone and wasting time.

Karen's mother and father have reluctantly taken their vacation days on Mondays during the summer and count on different babysitters for the remainder of the week. They resent that they cannot plan an extended, relaxing, and fun vacation. The additional emotional stress affects their jobs and other relationships. Karen's mother also resents that the caregiving responsibility for Karen is almost totally hers.

Karen's life during the summer is dramatically different than during the school year. Karen has very little to do during her free time. She has no friends and spends a great deal of time engaging in self-stimulatory and destructive behaviors. Her behaviors reflect an attempt to communicate her desire to actively participate in enjoyable and satisfying activities. Because Karen's schedule during the summer is not physically demanding, Karen does not sleep through the night. By the end of the summer, 12 babysitters had resigned their services for Karen. During the summer, Karen had not received opportunities for practice and growth of many of the skills she had mastered during the school year. Karen also had no one in her life, except a very exhausted family, who saw her strengths, gifts, and talents. It appeared there was no one who wanted to be around Karen in the beginning of the summer, and now that Karen's skills regressed throughout most of the summer and her inappropriate behaviors increased, the likelihood of finding someone who would care about Karen seemed remote. Although Karen's family tries desperately to listen to her and made many attempts to meet her needs, in the end they realize they had failed the young woman for whom they cared so deeply.

Karen's family was under tremendous stress and felt extremely frustrated with their lack of options, community support, and their inability to support their daughter. They began to see themselves not as a "family with one member who happens to be severely disabled," but rather as a "handicapped family." Karen's family began to question their parenting skills and their ability to meet Karen's needs. They sadly joked that in their county, the only way to receive after-school, school holiday, or summer vacation programming was to place Karen in an institution. Unfortunately, if Karen's family does become dysfunctional through divorce, abuse, or other tragedies, some people in the community will conclude they failed because a member of the family had a disability, rather than attributing the failure to a lack of community resources and supports.

Community Support for Aaron

Public schools are designed to support families in educating their children. Unfortunately, many people perceive the support of public schools as all that is necessary for families with children with disabilities. However, it is important for us to keep the amount of support received from the public schools in perspective.

For example, Aaron who is 15 years old has a life expectancy of 74 years. His school has a responsibility for his education for approximately 22 years. In a 365-day calendar year, the school year is usually about 180 days, and the school day is approximately 8:00 a.m. to 4:00 p.m. (including transportation), which totals eight hours or one third of a 24-hour day. Therefore, the school has responsibility for one third of the 180 days of the 22 years, a total of 1,300 hours. Aaron's family's responsibility totals 25,700 hours, or approximately 20 times the amount of time their child is under the supervision of the public schools.

During the 8 hours of the school day, Aaron has a large support staff composed of teachers, aides, therapists, administrators, maintenance and transportation staff, cafeteria workers, and clerical personnel, but the other 16 hours he has only the support of his family. Although there have been exciting reports of inclusion facilitators, community developers, and leisure and recreation support staff, the only way that Aaron can be in any extra-curricular activity is for one of his parents to attend and assist him. Although there are some positive trends for connecting people to their communities, in Aaron's last evaluation, his circle of friends was desperately small. There are some resources to help families learn to choose their priorities, address stress, and manage their problems. Yet, many family members pray that their child dies before they do, because even with their strongest advocacy efforts they cannot meet their child's needs, especially if they choose the value system that embraces inclusion.

Whose responsibility is it to provide inclusive leisure services?

Schleien and Werder (1985) asked professionals from community education agencies and parks and recreation:"Who should be responsible for the educational and recreational programs of their students on weekends, holidays, and in the summer?" They found that 93 percent of community education agencies named the parks and recreation staff, and 78 percent of the parks and recreation staff chose the community education agencies. This inability of professionals to assume responsibilities for meeting the leisure needs of youth with disabilities is extremely disconcerting for families. Families are often forced to compromise needs of family members with disabilities to access leisure programs and services (Shapiro, 1994).

To illustrate the many frustrations parents feel toward the absence of adequate community leisure support, consider the following dream that continues to haunt Mary Ulrich:

> The dream begins in a community recreation center during a "handicapped family swim night." Her husband Tom, sons Tommy and Aaron, and Mary along with their friends are splashing

and playing in the water. The pool is an excellent facility that has new equipment and has been painted with black racing lines across the bottom. On "handicapped swim night" professionals with an "LG" (lifeguard) on their T-shirts are stationed between each black line. The LG has been told to save the lives of people drowning in his or her area that are divided by the large black lines. As the families are swimming, they notice that the pool water starts to change. Instead of calm water, now there are swift currents. The water keeps rising and whirlpools are pulling them under. Tom and Mary attempt to keep Aaron and Tommy above water. The other families are also struggling. The participants paddle and try to go to the side of the pool, but they continue to be thrown back into deeper water. They cry to the LGs on the side of the pool, but the LGs do not seem to hear them. Every time a family member sinks to the bottom of the pool, it seems they land on a black line. Finally, the families all gather in the middle of the pool and shout in one loud voice, "Help, please help, we cannot do it ourselves." The families' shouting causes the LGs to look at the family members. However, the LGs appear confused because the family members continue to land on the black lines, and the LGs cannot decide whose territory the family members are in. Each LG has specific rules and guidelines regarding whom they can save. The situation gets grave. One or two of the LGs throw life preservers into the pool or shout encouragement such as "Swim faster," "Remember the strokes I taught you," "We are doing all we can," "You parents just need an organized effort," and "It is up to you, parents, you can do it!" In time, the water begins moving more swiftly, and the families become weaker. As the situation gets desperate, the first LG turns to the second LG and says, "What do you think?" The second turns to the third LG and says, "What do you think?" This line of questioning continues from one LG to another until finally, all eyes are on the Head LG who is sitting high in a chair in the middle of the facility. As the families sink into unconsciousness, the Head LG begins shaking his head as he frantically pages through a rule book.

What can we do to help families cope with stress?

Meeting the needs of individuals with disabilities may contribute to the family's sense of competence (Roach et al., 1999). To involve families in the services we provide, we can:

- create family-centered leisure services,
- develop cross-cultural competence,
- work to avoid overprotection,
- help families relieve stress, and
- communicate with family members.

Create Family-Centered Leisure Services

Family-centered leisure services focus on realizing the visions of individuals with disabilities and their families through collaborative partnerships with the individual, family members, friends, professionals, and the community (Turnbull & Turnbull, 1996). These services typically concentrate on strengths of individuals and their families and on development and maintenance of relationships that enable them to be integral parts of their communities (Blue-Banning, Turnbull & Pereira 2000). Family-centered leisure services identify the importance of individuals and families receiving social support from key members of the community, such as leisure services providers. Services focus on helping the family experience leisure together rather than focusing on only one family member.

Social support is an important aspect of family-centered leisure services. Cobb (1976) stated that social support emphasizes personal interactions that lead a person to feel cared for, valued, and included in mutually dependent relationships. Social support influences families' ability to cope and adjust (Gill, 1994). Herman and Hazel (1991) called for greater emphasis and reliance on family-based care for people with disabilities and noted that it is important for public agencies such as leisure services departments to emphasize family-centered approaches to services (see **Figure 7.2**). Family-centered approaches to leisure services delivery require support by each professional to help families overcome barriers to leisure participation.

Research has consistently demonstrated that family time and family leisure are highly valued. In a review of family leisure and leisure services, Shaw (1992, p. 13) reported that, "family leisure is an important aspect of leisure and an important part of life for many people in our society." Shaw also noted that family-oriented activities within and outside the home are the most common forms of leisure activity. Shaw suggested that recreation programming for families represents a challenge because of the mix of ages and both sexes, and because of the variety of interests, skills, and needs that individual family members bring with them. This challenge is often intensified when a member of the family possesses a disabling condition.

Develop Cross-Cultural Competence

The presence of a culturally diverse society has implications for developing inclusive programs. Current best practices in services that include people with disabilities are family-focused with emphasis on diversity and cultural issues (Parette, Huer & Brotherson, 2001). Kalyanpur and Harry (1999) observed that increasingly professionals are working with culturally diverse individuals and families whose values and beliefs may significantly differ from those of the dominant culture. Addressing the needs of culturally diverse individuals and their families in the development of programs requires that service providers recognize and respect the cultural differences of people with disabilities (Blue-Banning et al., 2000). Since all families (even ones from the same cultural group) differ, leisure services providers should anticipate differences, value these differences, and incorporate the family's perspective into actions.

Disability is interpreted in a variety of ways by people from different cultures. Hanson, Lynch, and Wayman (1990) reported that views related to disability and causes of these conditions range from those that emphasize the role of fate to those that place responsibility on the person or the person's family. For example, people who ascribe to the more fatalistic view of disability (e.g., people from Vietnam) may see little recourse or remedy to their condition, feel they have little power to escape their fate,

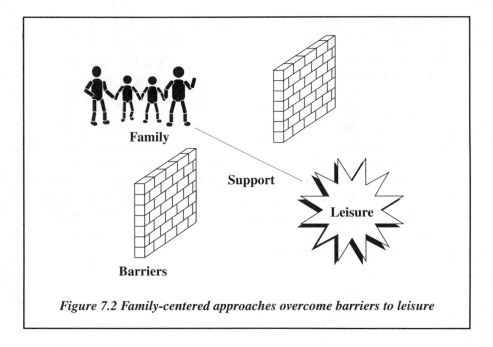

Figure 7.2 Family-centered approaches overcome barriers to leisure

and therefore, seek to achieve harmony in this life (Green, 1982). In other cultures people believe that people are responsible for their conditions and may attribute the cause of a disability to the parents who are being punished for their sins or who had taken inappropriate actions while the mother was pregnant. In some of these cultures the person with a disability can be viewed as being possessed by evil spirits or having a mind-body imbalance (Hanson et al., 1990)

In the American culture the cause of a disability may be assigned to a variety of factors, including disease, brain injury, genetic disorders, chemical imbalances, or environmental factors such as child abuse. Some disabilities are caused by many factors while for others no single factor of causation can be identified (Hanson, 1998). The views held by families concerning disability and associated causes influence the degree to which a family will participate in leisure services. For instance, some families may be uncomfortable about discussing ways to make adaptations that facilitate inclusion of a family member into a recreation program while others might be very eager to do so. As we become more effective at working cross-culturally, we will be able to tailor services to address these cultural differences.

For families of all backgrounds subtle ethnic and social class differences exist, and imposing our own ethnically influenced standards about a variety of issues including leisure services may limit our ability to provide meaningful services (Hanson et al., 1990). Reiter (1999, p. 334) concluded:

> Respect for the client means that he or she also has an opinion, a recommendation, a vision. Cultural sensitivity should lead to a dialogue based on mutual respect and open communication and assist in avoiding any power struggles.

Craig, Hull, Haggart, and Perez-Selles (2000) suggested that it is important for us to move beyond cultural awareness and work toward developing cultural competence. *Cross-cultural competence* refers to our ability to respond optimally to all participants and their families and understand the cultural contexts of participants and their families (Berrera & Kramer, 1997). Although cultural awareness and sensitivity are necessary elements of cultural competence, these approaches are not enough in and of themselves to significantly alter the practices and perceptions of many of us delivering leisure services (Hernandez et al., 1998). Lynch and Hanson (1998, p. 48) stated:

> Achieving cross-cultural competence requires that we lower defenses, take risks, and practice behaviors that may feel unfamiliar

or uncomfortable. It requires a flexible mind, an open heart and a willingness to accept alternative perspectives.

To be culturally competent we must become knowledgeable about the unique characteristics and backgrounds of participants and their families. In addition it is critical that we be committed to changing services so that our programs are sensitive to the perceptions of participants and their families. Also, being culturally competent implies that we develop skills that allow us to work effectively across a variety of cultural situations (Schacht, 1999). Hernandez and colleagues (1998) suggested that culturally competent agencies and individuals are characterized by accepting and respecting differences, continuing self-assessment regarding culture, attending to the dynamics of difference, expanding cultural knowledge and resources, and adapting service models.

Work to Avoid Overprotection

Professionals and parents of children with disabilities report that families facilitate opportunities and situations where social inclusion can occur across the life span. However, they also feel that families constrain inclusion by being overprotective and not allowing their family members who are disabled to make independent decisions (Mahon, Mactavish & Rodrigue, 1998). Therefore, Minow (1990, p. 39) raised the following question and attempted an answer:

> Shielding a minority or disabled child from community dislike may allow her to develop a sense of self-esteem but disable her from coping with that community—or from recognizing hostility when it comes her way. Experience with community hostility may injure the child's sense of self, yet such experience could also itself be the best educator and strengthen the child to deal with a world where her difference has been made to matter.

Turnbull, Blue-Banning, and Pereira (2000) reported that several parents of children with disabilities discussed overprotection as a barrier that prevented them from giving their children sufficient freedom to explore friendships. Overprotective parental practices and limited friendships restrict opportunities for adolescents with disabilities to learn social skills necessary for establishing and maintaining intimate and mutually responsive relationships (Zetlin & Morrison, 1998). Because peer relationships during adolescence serve as foundations for relationships with spouses, neighbors, and future coworkers, it is critical that the social opportunities of youth with disabilities be broadened.

Bruun (1995) studied people with disabilities and reported that his observations and comments by the individuals themselves indicated that overprotection was a problem for personal progress. Specific comments from one family (the Davis family) may help provide insight into the notion of family members being overprotective. Scott Davis describes himself in many ways, but when asked about his disability by Mary Rugg and John Weber (1995), Scott stated: "I was born too early and I have what's called cerebral palsy. That means I'm handicapped and cannot walk. I am working on learning to walk, but my wheelchair—Mad Dog—helps me get around." Scott's mother, Janet, talked about how overprotection can rob children of experiences needed to enrich their lives and she said: "You have to let them experience the perks and frustrations that a kid not in a wheelchair is going to experience. You have to step away enough and let them do that."

While overprotection can stifle a person, Janet Davis reported that inclusion nurtures friendships and in the end friendships are what count. To illustrate, she described a roller skating party with Scott's schoolmates:

> He gets out there on the rink in his wheelchair with 10–15 kids hanging on behind him in a train. He'll go as fast as he can and then stop and they all come together like an accordion. They say, "Come skate with me, Scott" and "Scott's skating!" And the only ones who are surprised to see him out there are the parents.

Help Families Relieve Stress

Leisure services professionals are in an excellent position to develop services that can be enjoyable for participants with disabilities and beneficial to their families. One benefit is the knowledge that the family member with a disability is involved in an enjoyable and safe program. In describing the "Respite and Recreation Project," Lashua, Widmer, and Munson (2000) suggested that leisure services professionals may use recreation not only to provide participants with enjoyable and meaningful experiences but also to provide parents and family members with a temporary reprieve from the demands of caring for a family member with disabilities.

Communicate with Family Members

After considering the reports by parents regarding their frustrations over not being heard when speaking with professionals, Minnes (1998) concluded that it is important to develop channels of communication among parents and professionals if service delivery for people with disabilities is to improve. An important aspect of such communication involves our willingness to listen to the desires, concerns, and dreams of family members. Marcia Rock (2000), a teacher, commented on the value of being a good listener when meeting with families:

> I conferenced extensively with parents regarding the wonderful educational programs I had created for their children. The parents nodded and smiled in agreement. In fact, they were quite appreciative. Yet they said little about their child. At the time, I was perplexed and often bewildered about their reluctance to contribute to the dialogue. In retrospect, how could they have responded any differently? I was the one monopolizing the discourse. (p. 30)

Reiter (1999) stated that communication is the key to any meeting between service providers and service recipients—including families in these communications is extremely helpful. We can connect with families if we respect, acknowledge, and learn more about their family patterns and values (Cartledge et al., 2000).

Are there benefits to having a family member who is disabled?

Victor Frankl (1984) wrote a compelling book documenting how his time as a prisoner of war transformed his life. Other survivors of major crises have identified positive changes and personal growth as a result of these experiences. Such a *transforming experience* involves a life event that causes substantial and lasting psychological change (Palus, 1993). Transformation involves letting go of a previous way of life in favor of a new and clearly better way of living.

Similarly, Scorgie and Sobsey (2000) noted that many parents of children with disabilities have asserted that though the challenges in their lives have been great at times, they have not only merely coped successfully with them, but they have experienced beneficial outcomes. For example, after surveying 80 parents of children with disabilities about their experiences, Scorgie and Sobsey reported that they are experiencing positive changes in their lives—many of which would not have occurred apart from parenting a child with a disability. Based on their research the authors stated:

> Some parents resent the assumption that living with a child who has disabilities must be a distressing and difficult experience. Although they would be the first to admit that there are times when life is exceedingly difficult, and want others to recognize how difficult parenting a child with a disability can be, they also ardently attest to ways in which they have been transformed . . . through their parenting experience. (p. 205)

Final Thoughts

If we truly embrace inclusion, and if we really want families to resist institutional care in favor of living in the community, then stronger support systems must be developed. Supportive leisure requires professionals to examine the individual desires and needs of people with disabilities and concentrate on coordination of resources and development of community support systems. As exemplified at the beginning of this chapter, through a cooperative approach to meeting individual leisure needs professionals will be in a position to assist families with some of their boxes.

One important aspect in facilitating inclusion is working with family members of individuals with disabilities. According to Hunt and Goetz (1997), family involvement is an essential component of effective inclusion. Families can be a valuable resource for leisure services professionals in determining ways to promote inclusion.

Considering the cultural background of the family members can help in determining effective ways to communicate with them. In addition, an understanding of the impact of overprotective family members can also help in determining ways to promote inclusion. By listening to the desires and dreams of families one gains considerable insight into ways to enhance their leisure. In summarizing her feelings about pursuing inclusion for her child, a mother interviewed by Turnbull and Ruef (1997, p. 225) stated:

> You're untrained and unskilled to meet the enormous needs of your child; but, boy, do you try, even when you don't sleep enough or eat your "balanced" meals. You live with the fears, frustrations, and lots of sacrifices, but you just never give up. For this is your child, and the love and commitment will see you through. Parents need support and encouragement.

After interviewing 40 mothers (half had a child with a severe disability), Lehman and Baker (1995) concluded that all the mothers expressed the same hope—that their children would achieve independence from their family. Consider the statement of Jeff and Cindy Strully (1989, p. 61) about their daughter, Shawntell:

> There are a number of skills in which Shawntell needs to show improvement—toilet training, eating properly, verbal communication, and walking stability. However, despite our active efforts to help her in these areas, whether Shawntell achieves such skills during her lifetime is not what concerns us most as parents. It is that there will be no one in our daughter's life who will want to be with her . . . that people will not spend the time to get to know Shawntell; that she will be isolated, lonely, and without friends.

The following statement illustrates the value of participating in community recreation with one's family. Wanda made this response when discussing how she felt when going to an amusement park with her family. The trip to the amusement park occurred soon after Wanda returned to her community following completion of a treatment program conducted at a rehabilitation center.

> I just had so much fun; I loved it. I was out with my family and I had aunts and uncles and cousins there with my parents and brothers and sister, and it was really fun . . . we just had a great time and didn't care about anything and it was just terrific.

Discussion Questions

1. What is the value of inclusive leisure services for families?
2. How does having a member of a family with a disability place stress on a family?
3. What are five suggestions for community support that could help Karen and her family?
4. Why is it important for community education agencies and parks and recreation staff to work together to meet the leisure needs of individuals with disabilities and their families?
5. What can be done to help families alleviate their stress?
6. What is family-centered approach to leisure services?
7. What are cultural considerations when involving families in leisure services?
8. What can be done about overprotection of individuals with disabilities?
9. What are the benefits to having a family member who has a disability?
10. How does the concept of transformation relate to families with a member who has a disability?

Chapter 8

Be Aware of
Barriers to Leisure

*I have learned that success is to be measured not so much
by the position that one has reached in life, as by the obstacles
which one has overcome by trying to succeed.*
-Booker T. Washington

Orientation Activity: Whose problem is it?

Directions Alone: Read the following scenario and write a brief paragraph describing its relevance to understanding people with disabilities.

Directions with Others: Divide into small groups and have each person describe his or her interpretation. When everyone has presented his or her ideas, determine how many different interpretations there were. Discuss your response with the entire group.

> I thought my wife was losing her hearing, so one day I decided to test it. I quietly walked in the front door and stood 30 feet behind her. "Suzanne," I said, "can you hear me?" There was no response so I moved 20 feet behind her. "Suzanne," I repeated, "can you hear me?" Still no reply. I advanced to 10 feet and asked, "Now can you hear me?" "Yes dear," Suzanne answered, "for the *third* time, yes!"

Debriefing: Many of us have observed that problems confront a number of people when they try to experience leisure. Some rarely initiate contact with others, some do not follow rules and misbehave, some withdraw from participation, and others indicate a lack of interest in available leisure services. If we view these problems as originating from the person as a result of their disability or other characteristics, little can be done to facilitate inclusive leisure services. If problems experienced by people are viewed from the perspective that professionals, family members, and community members contribute to these problems, then leisure services professionals can assist these individuals in many ways. For example, some people may rarely attempt to communicate because others control communication exchanges by not allowing an individual who may take a bit longer to communicate enough time. Other people may withdraw from participation as a result of repeated failures within a program. Without intervention these people may begin to feel helpless.

This chapter will highlight some of the barriers encountered by people with disabilities and the role leisure services professionals may play in overcoming them. As you consider the orientation activity ask yourself the following questions:

- What are some problems people with disabilities encounter when participating in community recreation programs?
- How might recreation professionals contribute to these problems?
- What can be done to overcome these problems?

Introduction

When asked to describe the leading barrier they experience, people with disabilities consistently report that negative attitudes are the most devastating. These negative attitudes (described in Chapter 1) do not occur in isolation. The following barriers are presented in this chapter:

- reactance,
- learned helplessness,
- controlling environments,
- unresponsive and negative environments,
- direct competition, and
- boredom and anxiety.

Why do people want things they are unable to get?

Brehm (1977) stated that the experience of freedom involves a set of behaviors that requires physical and psychological skills. To experience *freedom* individuals must have the knowledge and understanding that they are able to make a choice. Behaviors that are free include only those acts that are realistically possible for the individual. Given a set of free behaviors, *reactance* will occur when any of these behaviors is eliminated or threat-

ened. The relationship between freedom and reactance is illustrated in
Figure 8.1.

Reactance increases the desirability of the eliminated or threatened
behavior—the behavior becomes more attractive to the individual. For
instance, if a child is to select one recreation activity from several attractive
alternatives (e.g., hiking, dancing, or reading), elimination of one activity
(e.g., hiking) will result in that activity becoming even more desirable (see
Figure 8.2, p. 130).

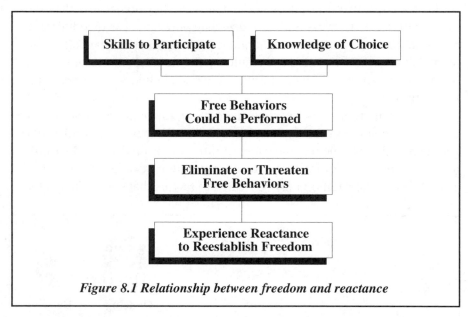

Figure 8.1 Relationship between freedom and reactance

A person who experiences reactance will be motivated to remove the
threat to the free behavior or regain the lost free behavior. When reactance
occurs, the person tends to engage in the threatened free behavior, engage
in behaviors that imply continued engagement in free behaviors, and encourage
other people of similar abilities and status to engage in threatened or eliminated
behaviors.

David, a boy playing a basketball game, is told by a leisure services
professional to stop yelling obscenities. The individual may continue or
even increase the use of obscenities, reduce the use of obscenities but
increase physical aggression, or encourage other players to use obscenities.

How do some people learn to be helpless?

When people expect to influence a certain outcome, but find their control
and freedom jeopardized, initially they exert more effort to establish control

(reactance). However, the perception of *helplessness* occurs if people become convinced that further attempts will not produce a desired outcome.

Seligman (1975) described helplessness as a psychological state that frequently results when events are uncontrollable (i.e., independent of a person's voluntary actions). Reinforcement or punishment can modify voluntary actions. Certain consequences of voluntary behavior will increase or decrease the chance of the behavior occurring. As individuals are exposed to uncontrollable events, they begin to learn that responding is futile. They feel that it just does not matter what they do because they will fail and therefore they experience *learned helplessness*. Learned helplessness undermines a person's motivation to respond, reduces the ability to learn that responding works, and results in emotional disturbance such as depression or anxiety. The occurrence of learned helplessness is presented in **Figure 8.3**.

People find it difficult to assess their ability to control a situation when they first encounter events that are troublesome for them to control. Often, people initially assume that the cause of difficulty is unstable and specific to the situation. Therefore, they increase their attempts to exert control. They feel that their failure may be related to factors that could change the

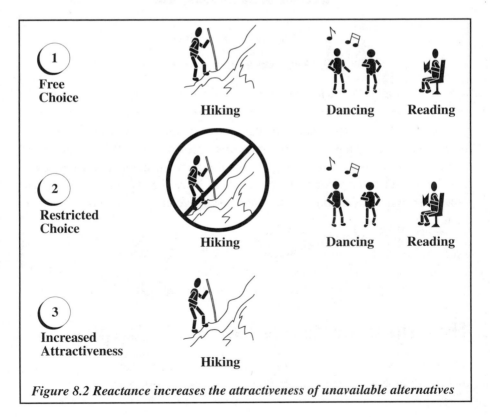

1
Free Choice

Hiking   Dancing   Reading

2
Restricted Choice

Hiking   Dancing   Reading

3
Increased Attractiveness

Hiking

Figure 8.2 Reactance increases the attractiveness of unavailable alternatives

next time they try, such as the difficulty of the recreation activity, the people associated with the activity, their luck, or the amount of effort and concentration they expend. However, if they are still unable to gain control after repeated attempts to do so, they may begin to assume the outcome is uncontrollable and will experience helplessness.

A person will eventually give up the desire for freedom when reestablishment of freedom proves impossible. The length of time required for

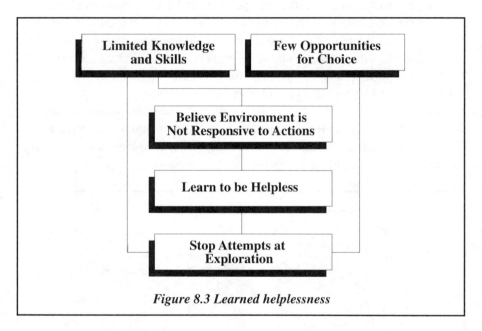

Figure 8.3 Learned helplessness

individuals to stop believing that they have freedom to engage in the eliminated or threatened free behavior depends in part on the certainty of elimination. The more apparent the inability to experience the free behavior becomes, the more quickly the person will give up that freedom.

Garber and Seligman (1980) recognized that once people perceive the absence of a relationship between their actions and the desired consequence, they attribute their helplessness to a cause. Two types of learned helplessness—personal and universal—are presented in **Figure 8.4** (p. 132). When people expect outcomes to be dependent on others' actions and not their own, *personal helplessness* is experienced. This personal helplessness results from failures that erode self-determination.

As an example of personal helplessness, Laura may be on her first ski trip with a group of peers. She may see other people receiving instruction in snow skiing and think that it is fine for those people to learn to ski. However, Laura believes that she could never learn to do it.

Some people may expect outcomes not to be dependent on their own actions or other people's actions. This is identified as *universal helplessness*, and produces feelings of hopelessness.

As an example of universal helplessness, Matthew may decide not to attend a program on volunteerism. He does not attend the program because he thinks that nobody really wants anyone else's help. Also, Matthew believes that even if other people try to help, it would not do any good.

In each situation the outcome expectancies are not absolute; rather, they are on a continuum ranging from total dependence on one's responses to very limited control of a situation. People do not necessarily adopt the perception of helplessness or mastery in every situation. Our challenge is to try to move participants in our programs away from perceptions of helplessness toward a more mastery-oriented orientation.

Learned helplessness may be revealed in the way the person thinks (cognition), feels (emotion) and shows interest in an activity (motivation). These consequences of helplessness are important considerations as we try to promote meaningful leisure participation for people.

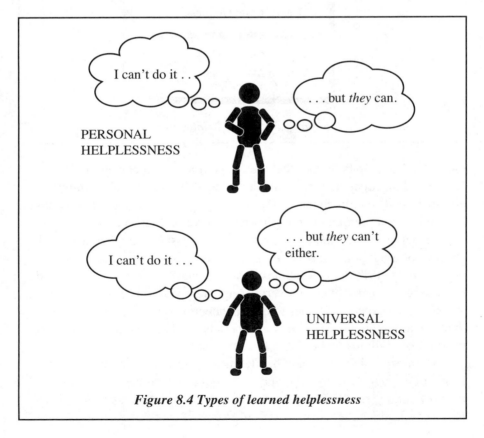

Figure 8.4 Types of learned helplessness

Cognitions

People who learn to be helpless will experience difficulty understanding that their responses produce outcomes. Consequently, they will have problems learning to take control of their lives.

Talie, who is attending a dance class, may feel that no matter how hard he tries he will never learn to dance. As a result of this belief, he finds it difficult to concentrate and learn what is presented.

Emotions

People who expect outcomes to be independent of their responses will tend to become depressed. As individuals attribute their negative outcomes to internal, stable, and global factors, and their positive outcomes to external, unstable, specific behaviors, their self-esteem decreases.

Each time Rudy experiences failure in outdoor adventure recreation activities he attributes his failures to his ability—which is internal, stable, and global, and he attributes his successes to luck—which is external, unstable, and specific. Therefore, Rudy's self-esteem may be lowered and he may become unhappy.

Motivation

People who expect their responding to be futile will reduce their initiation of voluntary actions. Some people have less knowledge and fewer skills than their same-age peers. Consequently, they are given fewer opportunities to make choices and demonstrate self-initiated leisure participation. Repeated futile experiences result in the perception that one is helpless. With the perception of helplessness comes an elimination of attempts to explore the environment. As exploration decreases, opportunities to experience enjoyment also decline.

Cleo feels that no matter how hard she tries to learn judo she will never learn it. Because of Cleo's beliefs she will not be motivated to go to judo class.

People respond to failure in different ways at different times. The manner in which people react to failure depends on their perspective. Their responses may be categorized as a mastery orientation or a helplessness orientation (see **Figure 8.5**, p. 134).

Mastery Orientation

For some people failure can result in increased effort, intensified concentration, increased persistence, heightened sophistication of problem-solving strategies, and enhanced performance. When people respond in this way, they are identified as having a *mastery orientation*. If they assume a mastery orientation they perceive their mistakes are rectifiable. In addition, they view their failure as a result of a lack of effort and therefore look forward to the future. People with a mastery orientation emphasize the positive aspects of their failures and/or engage in active problem solving.

Helplessness Orientation

Others may respond to failure with curtailed effort, reduced concentration, decreased persistence, a deterioration of problem-solving strategies, and a disruption in performance. These responses are indications that a person has learned to be helpless. If people come to expect that they cannot control outcomes, they might perceive that their mistakes are inevitable and view their failure as a result of a lack of ability. Individuals who have a *helplessness orientation* tend to dwell on the present and focus on negative aspects of a situation. Therefore, they stop attempts at solving the problem associated with failure.

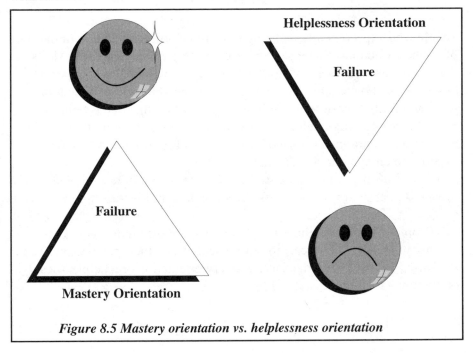

Figure 8.5 Mastery orientation vs. helplessness orientation

What happens when people experience controlling environments?

A controlling environment does not respond to people's initiatives; however, it does demand behaviors from individuals. When an environment directs and controls people, they often become motivated by external rewards (i.e., they experience external motivation). The presence of certain rewards and deadlines that pressure people toward specific outcomes tends to undermine intrinsic motivation, promote compliance or defiance, and inhibit enjoyment. Deci and Ryan (1985, p. 57) noted:

> Research has substantiated that extrinsic rewards and controls can affect people's experience of self-determination. In such cases, the events will induce a shift in the perceived locus of causality from internal to external, a decrement in intrinsic motivation for the target behavior, less persistence at the activity in the absence of external contingencies, and less interest in and enjoyment of the activity.

Studies by Lepper and Greene (1978) and others have demonstrated the effects of a controlling environment. Typically in these studies children are engaging in some activity, such as drawing, and then experimenters offer to pay the children for the products they produce. Productivity increases while rewards are offered; the children draw more. However, when rewards are withdrawn, children show less interest in the activity than they did before rewards were offered and less than children who were not offered rewards. Referred to as the *overjustification effect*, such studies show that intrinsic motivation can be undermined by extrinsic rewards. The relationship between motivation and overjustification is illustrated in **Figure 8.6** (p. 136). Certain extrinsic rewards such as money, prizes, and food, tend to decrease intrinsic motivation.

Deci (1971) had two groups of students work on a set of puzzles. Half the students were rewarded with a dollar for each puzzle they solved, and the others received no reward. All students were then observed in a subsequent free-choice period, and results indicated that the students receiving rewards spent significantly less free-choice time with the puzzles than did the students who were not rewarded.

Orlick and Mosher (1978) first provided children with a free-choice period. Next the children played in either a reward condition (where they received a task-contingent trophy) or a no-reward condition. Four days later, they returned for a post-test free-choice period. The children who had participated to obtain the trophy displayed a decrease in free-choice time spent on the task, as compared to the students who did not receive any rewards. These results suggest that extrinsic incentives can undermine intrinsic motivation for interesting recreation activities.

In another example, Mahteka, a baseball coach, may emphasize to her players the need to win the championship trophy. The enjoyment associated with participation in a baseball league may be reduced for many of her players.

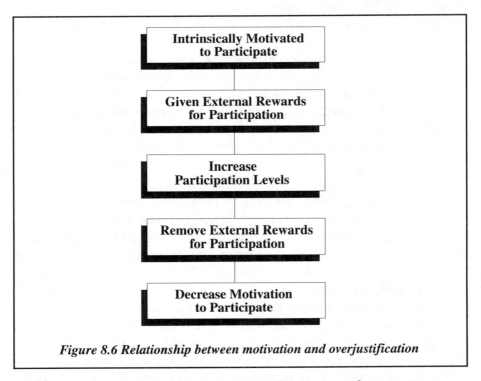

Figure 8.6 Relationship between motivation and overjustification

What happens when people experience unresponsive and negative environments?

Some individuals experience environments that do not respond to their initiatives. As a result of these *unresponsive environments* outcomes are perceived to be unrelated to their behaviors. In this type of an environment, the relationship between an action and associated consequences is not clear and cannot be mastered by the individual.

Environments that contain *negative feedback* not contingent on a person's behaviors also tend to reduce motivation. When we provide general, nonspecific praise or criticism to participants as they attempt to learn a new leisure skill we will inhibit rather than stimulate learning. Participants will have difficulty determining the effectiveness of their actions when we fail to provide them with informational feedback.

When Paulo, the instructor in a painting program, only tells participants that they need to work harder even after they have made considerable progress, they may become frustrated. At the same time, if participants complete their projects and Paulo never seems to have time to provide useful feedback, they may lose their desire for the activity.

What happens when we emphasize direct competition?

Competition can make many recreation activities fun and exciting. In activities such as swimming laps or shooting baskets, people can compete against themselves, striving to surpass some internal standard they have set. This *indirect competition* provides purpose and direction and is the basis for satisfaction when the standards are met.

Direct competition, which involves pitting oneself against another, can also be fun, exciting, and challenging, and can encourage intrinsic motivation. Doing well in a competitive situation provides clear competence feedback and could enhance a person's intrinsic motivation. However, focusing on winning rather than on doing well at an activity is problematic. The focus on winning can impair performance and lead to aggression. Therefore, direct competition can impair performance and result in aggression (Deutsch, 1969).

Deci, Betley, Kahle, Abrams, and Porac (1981) had two groups of students work on puzzles, with each student working in the presence of another person. Students in one group were instructed to solve each puzzle faster than the other person, while students in the other group were told to solve the puzzles as quickly as they could. When given a chance for free choice afterwards, the direct, face-to-face competition led to a decrease in intrinsic motivation. In a similar example, Vallerand, Gauvin, and Halliwell (1986) reported that competition undermined the intrinsic motivation of children. The children worked with a motor task, and those who competed at it spent less subsequent free-choice time working with the activity than those who had not competed.

Many people tend to experience competition as controlling and feel like they have to win. When they do win, although they feel satisfied, participants are less intrinsically motivated for the activity itself. They will be motivated to continue competing and will still want to win; however, the activity itself will no longer be inherently rewarding (Deci & Olsen, 1989). Weinberg and Ragan (1979) demonstrated that participants who had won a competition were more eager to compete again than those who had not, but less eager to engage in the activity in the absence of the competition.

How does people's arousal level influence their participation?

Although recreation activities can offer people opportunities to control their lives, increase their personal development, experiment with roles, and take part in self-appraisal, recreation activities are not necessarily positive, nor do they necessarily produce positive results.

Boredom and anxiety may occur because of an incompatible match between skill level and challenge. As seen in **Figure 8.7**, too little challenge coupled with a high skill level is likely to produce *boredom*. Conversely, too much challenge and too little skill may produce *anxiety*. Activities that require performance at their maximal level or require them to "stretch" and expand their skills to some degree tend to motivate people. People tend to gravitate to recreation activities that provide them with challenges that require some effort and concentration while permitting some degree of success.

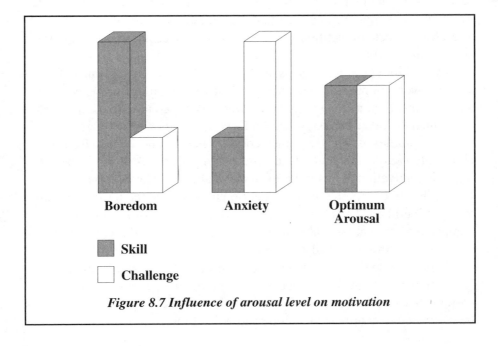

Boredom   **Anxiety**   **Optimum Arousal**

■ **Skill**

□ **Challenge**

Figure 8.7 Influence of arousal level on motivation

As an example of how arousal level influences participation, people were given the choice to play ring toss. They were first instructed to throw several rings to a post placed near their feet where they consistently achieved ringers, one a few feet away where they had about a 50% success rate, and one several yards away where they rarely, if ever, achieved a ringer. After being given the chance to try each post, participants were asked to throw rings toward the post of their choosing. Most participants chose the post a few feet away because it required them to concentrate and afforded them the opportunity for success. They reported that throwing rings at the post at their feet was boring and throwing at the post far away was frustrating.

Although from time-to-time all of us become bored in various situations, when people consistently experience boredom during their free time they can encounter a variety of related problems. For example, after a review of the literature, Lee, Mittelstaedt, and Askins (1999), concluded that boredom in general (and boredom in free time in particular) can lead to problems such as drug abuse, delinquency, vandalism, hostility, stress, and depression. For example, after analyzing results from questionnaires, interviews and activity diaries of 82 adolescents, Caldwell, Darling, Payne, and Dowdy (1999) concluded that intrinsic motivation and self-determination, as hallmarks of leisure, are counter to boredom and are associated with high levels of involvement in an activity. To reduce feelings of boredom, Caldwell and colleagues encouraged leisure services professionals to facilitate adolescent choice of activities, mitigate adult control and structure, and reduce feelings of obligatory participation.

On the other hand, if challenges are too high, an individual becomes frustrated, then worried, and eventually anxious (Czikszentmihalyi, 1997). Martens, Vealey, and Burton (1990) referred to anxiety as negative expectations about personal success in an activity. These negative expectations occur when people believe their skills are insufficient to be successful in a situation. Furthermore, when people experience repeated failure when engaged in various activities, their fears may increase and result in anxiety.

Final Thoughts

There are several explanations of human behavior that provide insight into the problems people with disabilities experience relative to their leisure participation. An understanding of barriers helps to clarify difficulties experienced by some individuals in becoming self-determined. Sensitivity to barriers experienced by people with disabilities such as reactance, learned helplessness, overjustification, boredom, and anxiety should help professionals to design leisure services that alleviate these barriers rather than contribute to their development.

Discussion Questions

1. What is the leading barrier to participation as reported by people with disabilities?
2. How can reactance influence leisure behavior?
3. What causes people to perceive helplessness?
4. What is learned helplessness?
5. What are two types of learned helplessness?
6. What are the three consequences of helplessness?
7. What are the two different reactions people experience to the interaction of failure and helplessness?
8. How does the overjustification effect undermine intrinsic motivation?
9. What are two types of competition and how do these influence motivation?
10. What is the relationship between skill, challenge, boredom, and anxiety?

Section B

Facilitate Participation

Chapter 9

Respond to the Americans with Disabilities Act

Ignorance of the law excuses no man.
-John Selden

Orientation Activity: Describe the ADA

Directions Alone: Write a brief paragraph describing the Americans with Disabilities Act (ADA). Write as if you are explaining the ADA to someone who is not aware of this legislation.

Directions with Others: Move about the room and share your description with someone. Have that person tell you what he or she learned from your description, recording any key points. Listen to that person's description. Tell the person what you learned from the description, making notes on important ideas you learned. Repeat this exercise with other people until you are given a signal to stop. Come together as a group and discuss what you have learned.

Debriefing: As a civil-rights legislative act for people with disabilities, the ADA guarantees the rights of full inclusion into the mainstream of American life. While there have been some improvements toward inclusion during the last decade, segregation and discrimination of individuals with disabilities continues to be a pervasive social problem. The opportunities created by the ADA should transform the quality of life for all people (Wehman, 1993, p. xxi). Reflecting on the orientation activity consider the following questions:

- What are some implications of the ADA?
- Why is it necessary to have the ADA?
- Who is influenced by the ADA?

Introduction

The Americans with Disabilities Act (ADA, Public Law 101-336) is a civil-rights law intended to eliminate discrimination against people with disabilities by the guarantee of equal opportunities, full community participation, enhanced independent living, heightened self-sufficiency, and access to every critical area of American life.

According to the ADA, public facilities—leisure agencies, restaurants, hotels, theaters, retail stores, museums, libraries, and parks—cannot discriminate on the basis of disability. Private clubs and religious organizations are exempt. To respond to the ADA we must make reasonable changes in policies, practices, and procedures so that discrimination and segregation do not occur. It is hoped that the ADA will encourage and empower people with disabilities to explore preferences and pursue choices, including leisure. Lana Shaw (Spirit of ADA, 2000, p. 6) stated:

> [The ADA] has definitely had a big impact on my life. With the passage of this act, I gained a sense of self-respect and equality that I had not felt in a long time. Doors have been opened and I have opportunities that so many others take for granted. No longer do people look at someone with a disability and shake their head in pity because now we are given a chance to be productive and influential citizens.

Although the ADA has resulted in greater awareness of disabilities and the barriers that prevent many people from participating fully in American society, statistical evidence for real improvements in their lives, such as greater levels of social inclusion, has been slow to materialize. According to Kaye (1998, p. 1):

> While there are indications that many barriers in the built environment have been removed, improving accessibility of public buildings and some transportation systems, many problem areas remain. And low levels of participation in social, cultural and commercial activities do not seem to have increased measurably since the ADA became law. People with disabilities continue to live in relative social isolation.

Who is covered by the ADA?

As described in Chapter 1, the ADA applies to people with any type of *disability*—a physical or mental impairment that substantially limits one or more major life activities. Although the ADA does not specifically say whether the law covers "correctable" disabilities, in 1999 the Supreme Court ruled on Murphy v. UPS and decided these types of disabilities (e.g., diabetes) are not covered (Clemetson, 1999).

Although the ADA covers mental impairments, many people are confused on how to make accommodations for these individuals. As a result, the Equal Opportunity Commission in 1997 issued guidelines to help agencies determine how to make accommodations—especially those associated with employment—for people with mental illness. In reporting on the accommodation of people with mental illness in the workplace, Gleick (1997) stated that one goal of the ADA is to remove the stigma of talking about mental illness and coping with it. Unlike sometimes costly alterations such as installing ramps or lowering drinking fountains, accommodating people with mental illnesses often requires little more than an attitude adjustment.

What are the major titles of the ADA?

The ADA contains five major titles, illustrated in **Table 9.1** (p. 146). Title I prohibits employers from discriminating against "otherwise qualified individuals with a disability" in any employment action. Title II, Subtitle A prohibits the more than 85,000 state and local government agencies from discriminating against people with disabilities in the provision of services and opportunities. Title II, Subtitle B prohibits providers of public transportation from discriminating against people with disabilities. Title III prohibits private entities that offer public accommodations, goods, facilities and services—restaurants, theaters, hotels, zoos, and museums—from discriminating against people with disabilities. Title IV requires the availability of communication systems for individuals with hearing impairments. Title V covers a variety of miscellaneous issues, including regulation and enforcement. Specific agencies enforce the different titles (see **Table 9.2**, p. 147).

Who must comply with the ADA?

The ADA addresses many issues that facilitate realization of the rights of each person. To be sure they are in compliance with the ADA, leisure

Title I	Employment Practice
Title II, Subtitle A	Government Services
Title II, Subtitle B	Public Transportation
Title III	Public Accommodations by Public Agencies
Title IV	Communication Systems
Title V	Miscellaneous

Table 9.1 Major titles of the Americans with Disabilities Act

services providers should consider the major groups targeted by the ADA, including:

- employers,
- transit systems,
- private agencies,
- government agencies, and
- telecommunications.

Employers

Employers may not discriminate against an individual with a disability in hiring, promotion, or other employment activity if the person is otherwise qualified for the job. Employers can ask about one's ability to perform a job, but cannot inquire if someone has a disability or subject a person to tests that tend to screen out people with disabilities.

Employers must provide reasonable accommodations to individuals with disabilities. This includes job restructuring and modification of equipment. Employers do not need to provide accommodations that impose an "undue hardship" on business operations. Employers of fewer than 15 people are exempt from Title I, unless the employer is a state or local government.

Transit Systems

Public transit buses ordered after Aug. 26, 1990 must be accessible to individuals with disabilities. Transit authorities must provide comparable transportation services to people with disabilities who cannot use fixed-route bus services, unless an undue burden would result.

Private Agencies

Private entities that offer goods, services and facilities to the public may not discriminate against people with disabilities. Auxiliary aids and services must be provided to individuals with disabilities, unless an undue burden would result.

Physical barriers in existing facilities must be removed if removal is readily achievable, inexpensive, and easy to do. If not, alternative methods of providing the services must be offered, if they are readily achievable. All new construction and alteration of facilities must be accessible.

Government Agencies

State and local governments may not discriminate against qualified individuals with disabilities. All government facilities, services, and the information they communicate must be accessible.

ADA Regulations	Enforcing Agency
Employment	Equal Opportunity Employment Commission (EEOC)
Buildings, facilities, rail passenger cars, and vehicles; Recreation facilities and outdoor developed areas	Architectural and Transportation Barriers Compliance Board (Access Board)
Transit	Department of Transportation
Telecommunications	Federal Communications Commission
Public accommodations State and local public services	Department of Justice

Table 9.2 Who enforces the ADA?

Telecommunications

Companies offering telephone service to the general public must offer telephone relay services to individuals who use text telephones, teletype-writers (TTYs), or similar devices.

Although the ADA requirements vary according to the type of agency such as state funded or private and size of the agency, many procedures outlined by the ADA would be beneficial for any leisure agency to follow. The guidelines presented in **Figure 9.1** are procedures that have been gleaned from the ADA and would assist agencies in providing inclusive community based programs.

How can we plan for inclusion?

Planning is a critical aspect of the delivery of leisure services. During the planning phase, compliance with the ADA is considered. To encourage this consideration, the following suggestions are provided:

- conduct a self-analysis,
- provide notice of compliance,
- determine essential eligibility,
- complete a transition plan,
- ensure coordination,
- adopt a procedure for handling complaints,
- consider employment concerns, and
- develop inclusive services.

Conduct a Self-Analysis

To determine deficits in delivery systems and barriers to participation that result in discrimination against people with disabilities, we can initiate a self-analysis. Professionals must examine all leisure programs to determine how to accommodate a person with a disability who meets essential eligibility requirements for participation. Any architectural, transportation, communication, or service barriers should be identified.

Leisure services providers must solicit input from interested people with disabilities or advocacy organizations. Ongoing self-analysis should be available for public review, contain a list of the interested persons consulted, and provide descriptions of areas examined, problems identified, and modifications made.

Figure 9.1 Respond to the Americans with Disabilities Act: Plan for inclusion, make appropriate purchases, advertise to everyone, and facilitate accessibility

Provide Notice of Compliance

The intent of the agency to comply with the ADA and how this intent will be achieved should be provided. For example, some agencies may report that compliance to the ADA will occur by making reasonable accommodations such as changing rules, policies, and procedures; removing architectural, transportation, and communication barriers ; and providing auxiliary aids and services. Notice of compliance is reported in all agency materials. For example, business cards and letterhead should include the agency TTY phone number. (Information on TTYs and other technology is presented in Chapter 19.)

Determine Essential Eligibility

Leisure services providers examine a set of factors to determine who participates in which service. These essential eligibility factors often include whether the person registers before the capacity is exhausted, whether required fees are paid, and whether the individual agrees to and adheres to rules of conduct, with a reasonable accommodation made by the agency. For example, Trina may not participate in a program because when she tried to enroll the available slots had been filled.

Complete a Transition Plan

A transition plan for the removal of barriers and other structural modifications should be developed. The transition plan must include an identification of the alterations required to achieve accessibility, the cost of the alterations, and a timeframe for when the alterations will be completed.

Ensure Coordination

Designate at least one employee to coordinate agency efforts to comply with the ADA and promote inclusion. This employee must have authority to make decisions regarding compliance, ensure cooperation of staff, and investigate alleged complaints against the agency. The name, office address, and office telephone number of this employee must be made available to the public.

It is also helpful if at least one member of a leisure services delivery agency has received specific training associated with including people with disabilities (such as a therapeutic recreation specialist); however, many agencies do not have such a person. Galambos and colleagues (1994) suggested that if departments do not have staff with a therapeutic recreation background, steps can be taken to prepare the agency to include people with disabilities into existing services. Enlist the support of people with disabilities and local agencies to teach staff about the ADA and how to include people with disabilities into existing services.

Adopt a Procedure for Handling Complaints

Develop a procedure for responding to complaints of noncompliance against the agency. The procedure should be similar to procedures established for employee grievances. It must allow for prompt attention to allegations of noncompliance.

Consider Employment Concerns

Consider alternate ways to address employee needs. For example, supplemental unpaid leave may be a viable option for qualified people with disabilities who, because of their disability, may require additional time away from work. Individuals associated with a person with a disability, such as a family member, may also require additional unpaid leave.

Develop Inclusive Services

The ADA has been a catalyst for promoting the inclusion of people with disabilities in community life (Devine, 1999). Although many people and agencies have embraced the spirit of the ADA, the ADA requires inclusion by public agencies. If compliance with the mandates stipulated in the law does not occur, a process is established to enforce adherence to the law.

A ruling by the U. S. Supreme Court in the case of Olmstead v. L. C. provided clarification of the ADA interpretation of placement of individuals into segregated programs without a choice of participating in those that are more inclusive (Perez, 2000). The Olmstead case involved two Georgia women who lived in state-run institutions whose disabilities included mental retardation and mental illness. Professionals had determined that they could be appropriately served in a community setting, and the plaintiffs asserted that continued institutionalization was a violation of their right under the ADA to live in the most integrated setting appropriate. The court concluded that:

> Unjustified isolation . . . is properly regarded as discrimination based on disability . . . institutional placement of persons who can handle and benefit from community settings perpetuates unwarranted assumptions that persons so isolated are incapable or unworthy of participating in community life. (Perez, 2000, pp. 1, 11)

How can we make appropriate purchases?

There are many things to consider when making purchases. This section examines ADA requirements related to the following:

- vehicles,
- furniture and equipment, and
- capital purchases.

Vehicles

Ensure that requests for bids to buy or lease vehicles for transporting participants specify that the vehicles are readily accessible to and usable by people with disabilities. This requirement should be followed regardless of whether any individual with a disability is known to require the use of such a vehicle. In addition, all donated or leased vehicles used for the transportation of participants need to be readily accessible to, and usable by, individuals with disabilities.

Furniture and Equipment

When leisure professionals purchase furniture and recreation equipment, a portion of the product must be accessible. The Architectural and Transportation Barriers Compliance Board issued the Americans with Disabilities Act Guidelines (ADAG) for Building and Facilities designated as Play Areas. These guidelines provide detailed information concerning the purchasing of equipment and construction of play areas. (These regulations are described in Chapter 10.)

Capital Purchases

Include consideration of access and use by people with disabilities for capital purchases. A *capital purchase* refers to equipment such as a computer, swing set, or boat that becomes a major acquisition. Typically, capital purchases require a procurement request, unlike less expensive items sometimes purchased with petty cash. An agency should demonstrate that people with disabilities could access capital purchases or that a plan is in place for making the purchase accessible to all. Capital improvement plans must include removal of architectural and communication barriers.

How can we advertise to everyone?

A critical aspect of promoting inclusion and responding to the ADA is ensuring that people with disabilities are aware of our programs. Therefore, the following suggestions are provided when considering advertising leisure services:

- include a compliance statement,
- provide alternative formats, and
- make advertisements accessible.

Include a Compliance Statement

Agencies should include a statement in all brochures and publications about compliance plans for the ADA. For example, state that the agency does not discriminate on the basis of an individual's disability, and the agency does make reasonable accommodations (e.g., changing rules, removing barriers, providing auxiliary aids and services) to enable a person with a physical or mental disability to participate.

It is also helpful to include a statement inviting people to communicate their needs. For example, a brochure may include the following statement: "To assist staff in planning programs, please call in advance of programs if you or a family member requires an accommodation."

Provide Alternative Formats

We can develop brochures in alternative formats such as large print, braille, and cassette tapes for use by individuals with sight or cognitive impairments. The creation of a brochure on cassette as part of the program planning and brochure planning processes is easy, and may have other uses, too. For example, when presenting a description of services to a group of children, a brief spoken rewording can be more effective than a written one. (Information on using technology to develop alternative formats is presented in Chapter 19.)

Make Advertisements Accessible

Leisure services providers must ensure that brochure display areas are accessible to and usable by individuals with disabilities. Features of such displays include a shelf positioned at the correct height for an individual using a wheelchair, or making staff available to distribute brochures that may be out of reach of an individual in a wheelchair. A Braille message regarding the type of brochures available and how these may be obtained should be made available.

After surveying over 300 directors and staff affiliated with therapeutic adventure programs in the United States, Herbert (2000) reported that while directors followed hiring and promoting policies consistent with the ADA, promotional materials describing programs were not available in alternate formats such as large print, Braille, or audiotape. Bruno (1997, pp. 58–59) concluded:

> In recent years, more and more companies are showing people with disabilities in their print and TV ads, and the image of a person in a wheelchair has become a kind of shorthand: It suggests a corporate policy of inclusion in regard to both employees and customers . . . But for this message to actually be credible, the model in the ad must have a genuine disability and use the product she's selling.

How can we facilitate accessibility?

Recreation and leisure services professionals must provide opportunities for people with disabilities to register for programs. People with disabilities can be a wonderful source of support, and soliciting their input can provide valuable information. The contributions people with disabilities can make toward helping to develop inclusive services can be very useful because of their perspective of the situation. This section considers the following methods of facilitation:

- modify registration,
- make meetings accessible, and
- obtain input.

Modify Registration

Professionals must be prepared to change registration procedures to accommodate an individual with a disability who, because of that disability, cannot perform registration in the manner required by procedures. Alternative registration procedures may include, but are not limited to, mail-in registration, phone registration, or personal registration by appointment.

As a precaution, personnel may request that a person provide proof of disability (e.g., documentation from a physician or educational clinic) in exchange for the opportunity to register in an alternative manner. However, personnel shall permit the individual accommodation in the registration process, pending submission of proof. If satisfactory proof is not provided within a reasonable time, or if proof is insufficient, the registration may be canceled.

According to the ADA, agency brochures must have a statement acknowledging the departmental policy of adherence to the ADA and must invite people with disabilities to register for any program they choose. Devine, McGovern, and Hermann (1998, p. 72) provided the following suggestions associated with a sport program registration and planning:

> Each registration form must ask if potential participants need an accommodation to enjoy or participate in a program. When a registrant does require a special accommodation, you, your staff, or team volunteers must contact this individual before the session begins. Discuss the types of activities, the level of social interaction, and prerequisite skills, and ask if the registrant will require assistance to play the sport. Allow yourself plenty of time to secure staff, plan program changes, develop behavior plans, purchase or make adaptive equipment, and make other changes to allow successful inclusion.

Make Meetings Accessible

Ensure that any public committee or advisory group meetings are conducted in an accessible fashion. Notices for such meetings could include the following: "If you plan to attend the meeting and will require an accommodation because of a disability, contact our office at least one working day in advance of the scheduled meeting." Be ready on short notice to seek an interpreter or provide other accommodations necessary for participation by an individual with a mobility, sight or hearing impairment, even if the notice requirement is not met. We should plan all meetings to be held in rooms without architectural barriers.

Obtain Input

It is critical to ensure that nominees for advisory boards, citizen panels, or other groups involved in guiding the agency include people with disabilities. Invitations to participate should be posted in large print or Braille or available in alternative formats.

With the passing of the ADA in July of 1990, people with disabilities have been more visible in society as a result of requirements associated with nondiscrimination. Because these individuals have now been recognized as an important market sector, especially to the travel and tourism industry, Peniston (1996, p. 29) concluded that:

> Since the passage of ADA, the lodging industry has greatly improved services to people with disabilities, but this industry can continue to make strides by including the opinions of travelers with disabilities as important data to determining the future trends of hotel customer satisfaction.

How can we determine essential eligibility requirements?

The ADA requires that people who meet essential eligibility requirements, or could meet them with reasonable accommodations, be given the opportunity to participate in leisure programs regardless of age, sex, mental or physical ability, race, or religious beliefs. An individual meets essential eligibility requirements for participation in most leisure programs if the following conditions are present (see **Figure 9.2**):

- capacity,
- fee,
- rules of conduct,
- safety,
- skill,
- age, and
- residence.

Capacity

The person must register for the leisure program before other registrants have filled the program to capacity. The capacity of a program is based on factors such as the size of the facility, the number of staff available, and the amount of resources available.

For example, if a program has a capacity of 50, and Sylvia is the 51st individual desiring registration, she may be denied the opportunity to register. This may occur whether or not the individual has a disability.

Fee

The person must pay the appropriate registration fee for the leisure program. However, individuals may not be charged a higher fee to offset the costs of accommodations.

For example, if a fee of $20 is required for a one-hour golf lesson, and Andrew is registered for the lesson, he must pay the fee or have the fee paid by another, such as his parent, sibling, guardian, or sponsor.

Rules of Conduct

The person must agree to abide by any reasonable rules of conduct for participation in that leisure program. If an individual violates reasonable rules of conduct, the agency may suspend or modify that individual's involvement after reasonable accommodation has been made.

For example, in a swimming lesson, the individual must not dive from the deck into the shallow end of the pool. In a sports program, the individual must not strike other participants. In a public outing to a theater, the

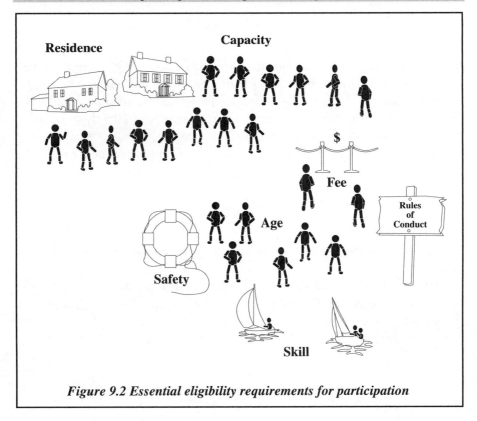

Figure 9.2 Essential eligibility requirements for participation

individual must not speak so loudly during a performance or presentation as to disturb the enjoyment or listening of others in the audience. These examples are applicable to all participants, whether a disability is present or not.

Safety

Safety concerns may be a factor when a direct threat of imminent physical harm exists. This threat must be real, and not perceived. Employees must be cautioned against allowing their perceptions of an individual's disability to result in an inaccurate belief that the threat of harm is imminent.

For example, if Lydia has harmed other participants and could not be reasonably accommodated, employees may elect to refuse her admission to a general swimming program. However, the opportunity to swim must still be offered through such methods as individual lessons. In addition, based on this one experience some employees may assume that all people with mental health disorders pose a direct threat of imminent physical harm. This belief is based on a misconception and results in discriminatory treatment of people with mental health disorders who are not aggressive.

Relative Skill

Relative skill may be a factor in a few programs, such as highly competitive sports programs. This is applicable whether or not the person has a disability.

For example, Ira could not register to participate in an annual musical performance for the public without basic competencies. Therefore, staff could refuse to allow Ira to perform in a concert, but should consider providing other music options, such as joining a choir or enrolling in music lessons.

Age

The age of participants may also be a factor in an analysis of essential eligibility.

For example, it is inappropriate for Terrance, a 15-year-old, to be registered in a program for children ages 3 to 5. Regardless of whether he has a cognitive impairment, it will likely be inappropriate to place Terrance with younger children.

Residence

If agencies exclude nonresidents from certain programs for legitimate reasons such as limited capacity, then nonresidents with disabilities may be excluded.

For example, where fees charged for nonresidents are higher than those for residents, that standard may be applied to people with disabilities. However, whenever possible, services should be available to residents as well as nonresidents. No person living outside the geographic boundaries may be excluded solely because of disability.

How can we make reasonable accommodations?

The ADA includes reference to a number of specific accommodations to enable people to participate. Application will vary, depending upon the type of activity (e.g., sports, crafts, social, educational) the location of the program, whether it is an individual or group activity, whether it is competitive, recreational, or instructional, the age of the participants, and other factors. Generally, accommodations are not expensive and can occur by removing barriers, changing procedures, and providing assistance.

Based on a survey of over 200 recreation agencies throughout the United States, Devine (1999) reported that the most common accommodations provided to participants with disabilities included pool lifts, relocating of classes to accessible facilities, adapted sport and recreation equipment, sign language interpreters, formal inclusion plans, participant skill assessments, and braille, large print, or cassette tape information.

An example of how the ADA helped a person to receive a reasonable accommodation occurred in golf. Casey Martin is a professional golfer who has Klippel-Trenaunay-Weber Syndrome, a congenital degenerative circulatory disorder manifested in a malformation of his right leg that causes him severe pain and atrophy in his lower leg. He is unable to walk for extended periods of time and at risk of fracture or hemorrhaging when he does. When the PGA denied Martin's request to use a golf cart in a tournament, Martin sued under Title III of the ADA. He won because the court concluded "the provision of the golf cart to Martin was a reasonable accommodation to his disability, and that use of the cart did not fundamentally alter the nature of the PGA and Nike Tour tournaments" (Kozlowski, 2000). The PGA appealed, but on May 29, 2001, the Supreme Court confirmed that Martin has a legal right to use a golf cart during tournament play.

How can barriers be removed so that accommodations are made?

A variety of barriers can impede inclusion. In addition to the major barrier of negative attitudes, we can systematically address removal of the following barriers:

- architectural barriers,
- transportation barriers, and
- communication barriers.

Remove Architectural Barriers

Architectural barriers that exclude people with physical impairments from entering a facility must be removed. Such barriers result in unlawful discrimination. If we provide services on several floors, accommodations must be made to allow people with mobility impairments to access services on the upper floors. An immediate solution facilitating access would be to install an elevator. Although this is an excellent solution, other alternatives are possible, such as moving services to an accessible portion of the building.

Many leisure services providers own and operate historical facilities. Removing architectural barriers from a historical structure could compromise the integrity of the building.

To avoid damaging the historical significance of a facility and still accommodate people with disabilities curators could develop a model to scale of upper floors and display this model on ground level. Also, a videotape presentation of the upper floors could be developed. Photographic and other displays of the upper floors would also help to accommodate people unable to access the top floor. A cassette tape or narrator to describe the upper floors is an additional option.

Remove Transportation Barriers

Not being able to participate in a program because of a transportation barrier may result in the exclusion of a person with a disability. When a program is made available to the public, and a person cannot get to the program because of a disability, these barriers must be removed when transportation is provided as a part of a program.

Remove Communication Barriers

If a person with a disability cannot understand communication media used because of a hearing, sight, or cognitive impairment, the communication poses a barrier to participation.

For example, to register for a leisure program, Leon must complete a registration form. This requires the ability to see and understand the words on the registration form. For Leon, who has a cognitive impairment, the written form is a communication barrier that can be removed by providing an employee to read the form to him. This accommodation could also help a person with a visual impairment.

Other actions that could be taken for people with visual impairments include providing cassette tapes that explain registration procedures or registration forms with Braille instructions.

As another example, when providing food services, servers can prepare themselves for customers with visual and cognitive impairments by being ready to read the menu to customers and developing alternative menus, such as Braille or larger type.

What can be changed so that accommodations are made?

A variety of agency procedures can be changed to help include people with disabilities into leisure services. The following areas are addressed in this section:

- modify services,
- reassign programs, and
- adapt equipment.

Modify Services

Modify rules, policies, or practices that result in the exclusion of or discrimination against an individual with a disability to enable a person with a disability to meet essential eligibility requirements to participate in the program.

For example, a rule prohibiting the use of personal flotation devices in swimming pools may exclude Cybil, who has a physical impairment and requires additional support. The rule could be modified to permit certain types of flotation devices to accommodate Cybil. In another example, a policy requiring a driver's license instead of an identification card to fish would be discriminatory to individuals who are old enough to have a driver's license but do not currently have one due to impairments. As a final example, an agency that forbids all animals from entering particular areas of their facility such as dressing rooms and swimming pool areas discriminates. This rule must be revised to accommodate animals that provide mobility assistance to people with various visual and motor impairments.

Reassign Programs

Reassign programs from an inaccessible site to a site free of architectural barriers. We can consider bringing the leisure program to the participant at his or her home. In certain instances, home visits may be a less costly accommodation than transportation to and from a site where a transportation barrier exists. Home visits can be made when a person with a disability cannot attend a program and the inability to attend is clearly a result of the disability and not a choice made by the registrant.

Adapt Equipment

When equipment is integral to the leisure program, such as camping equipment or sports equipment, adaptive devices may be used to help a person with a disability. Such devices may alter the degree of strength or dexterity required to manipulate the equipment (such as a bowling ramp) or assist an individual in holding equipment (such as a brace or Velcro straps).

What can be provided so that accommodations are made?

Providing assistance is one of the most important ways to promote inclusion and respond to the ADA. If we provide some very simple help to a person, it can make the difference between them being actively involved in leisure or being isolated and bored. Although the ADA is designed to promote the independence of people with disabilities, everyone is dependent on others each day. By providing assistance we promote interdependence. The following ways to provide assistance are presented in this section:

- provide aids,
- supply personnel, and
- conduct in-service training.

Provide Aids

We must provide auxiliary aids and devices that will enhance participation and communication. If a person with a hearing or sight impairment has registered, for a leisure program, aid must be provided to enable the person with a sensory impairment to have an equal opportunity to enjoy the program.

For example, in a youth sport skills program, oral instructions and demonstrations will be used to instruct participants in skill acquisition. For Milton, who has a hearing impairment, the oral instructions will be difficult to interpret, even if heparticipant has some lip-reading ability. An appropriate accommodation may be the provision of an interpreter for Milton during the leisure program. Another accommodation may be the instruction of an employee in elementary sign language, with an emphasis on terms used in the sport, and the eventual assignment of that employee to the sport skills program in which the individual with a hearing impairment has registered. However, care must be taken to ensure that the interpreting skill of the employee is adequate to the task.

Supply Personnel

Provide additional staff as needed. This may be appropriate when a participant has a lower cognitive ability than other registrants and requires more staff time to make the opportunity for leisure participation equivalent to individuals without disabilities.

For example, a staff member or volunteer at an amusement park could be available to assist children with disabilities to participate or to help children without disabilities whose parents may encounter difficulty due to restricted mobility.

Conduct In-Service Training

Conduct in-service training for agency personnel and volunteers. Training may include information such as programming strategies, adaptive techniques, principles of the ADA, use of sensitive language, or awareness of attitudinal barriers.

For example, an appropriate training for personnel and volunteers of a nature center would be to receive information on assisting people with disabilities with participation on interpretive tours. Agency personnel and volunteers using adaptive equipment receive appropriate training prior to use.

What is considered an undue burden?

At times, making accommodations to include people with disabilities can result in an undue burden to various agencies. The ADA recognizes this possibility and provides directions for such instances. Undue burdens can occur in the following areas:

- economic,
- administrative, and
- programmatic.

Economic Burden

The Justice Department has not upheld the denial of an accommodation solely because of an economic burden. Because agencies vary greatly in size and cost of accommodations, they must determine the cost of the accommodation in comparison to the operating budget, availability of tax funds, number of employees affected, potential number of beneficiaries, nature and location of the program, and other factors.

To address the topic of economic impact of the ADA, Shaw (1994) reported on statistics collected by the Job Accommodations Network, a federally funded consulting service that provides free information to employers and people with disabilities. Shaw stated that 15% of recommended accommodations needed to respond to the ADA cost nothing, 52% cost less than $500, and only 22% would cost more than $1,000.

Administrative Burden

An administrative burden is typically associated with an agency having the necessary personnel to accommodate people. If there is a severe shortage of qualified personnel needed for a specific accommodation, an undue administrative burden may result.

For example, if there were no certified interpreters in the area the agency would be permitted to employ a noncertified interpreter who lived in the area.

Programmatic Burden

The third consideration includes an accommodation that results in a fundamental alteration of the nature of the program. This accommodation opposes the concept of "most integrated setting," but if the individual cannot leave his or her home because of a disability, home visits may be appropriate.

For example, a home visit for Peg, a woman with a severe health impairment, where an employee brings the activity to her home could result in a fundamental alteration. If the program for which the individual registered were a team sport program, it would not be reasonable to bring the entire team and the opposing team to an individual's home. However, with a crafts program, instructional music program, or art program, a home visit would be an effective accommodation.

How can we meet the spirit of the ADA?

The ADA helps set the stage for inclusion. However, even if agencies are in compliance with the ADA, people with disabilities still might not be included in various programs. Baylor (1996, p. 14) explained how the ADA mandates accommodation rather than inclusion:

> ADA was designed to "accommodate" rather than to include. That is, it makes an assumption that if we accommodate people with disabilities, inclusion will automatically result. Unfortunately, it does not. I can be accommodated by a ramp, but I will be included if someone invites me in their door . . . Changing architectural design is one thing; changing peoples' hearts is another.

We must go beyond responding to the letter of the law and respond to the spirit of the law. We must take whatever actions necessary to help people become included in community leisure programs. Jill Smolowe (1995, p. 54) spoke to this point:

> While the specific aim of the landmark legislation was to provide America's 49 million physically and mentally disabled people with access to public areas and workplaces, the larger spirit of the law was to puncture the stifling isolation of the disabled and draw them into the mainstream of civic life.

After interviewing 55 people with disabilities, Bedini (2000) found that having a disability could compromise leisure. She encouraged leisure services providers to ensure that their language, signage, titles, advertisements, and staff are appropriate and respectful of all participants. Sometimes it is the little things that people do that can help encourage others to feel comfortable with being in a situation. For example, Smolowe (1995, p. 54) wrote:

> It is often the small gesture that can make an inhospitable world seem welcoming. After a sunglasses vendor in Palatine, Illinois, advertised her sign-language skills, people with hearing impairments flocked to her stand to discuss frame shapes and lens tints. At the Chicago Botanic Garden, shelves and pulley systems enable wheelchair users to inspect a special exhibit. In the rest rooms there, a cheap innovation safeguards the disabled from the nasty scalding their legs routinely endure in public places: the hot-water pipes beneath the sinks are wrapped in insulation.

Embracing the spirit of the ADA and developing inclusive leisure services allows us to contribute to the entire community. We must not only respond to recent federal legislation such as the Americans with Disabilities Act, but also respond to the people with disabilities who are demanding leisure services (Beland, 1993).

When thinking about the ADA, Oliver (1996) encouraged professionals to adopt a philosophy that focuses on personal identity. With this philosophy, difference is not merely tolerated and accepted but it is positively valued and celebrated. According to Oliver it is not simply a matter of providing a legal framework that results in inclusion, but rather that the framework creates a sense of moral obligation to ensure its enforcement. In discussing how people avoid personal responsibility, Barry (1997, pp. 72, 75) talked about the relationship between laws and morality:

> Laws are intended to institutionalize the highest moral ideals of a people. Were we always true to those ideals, we'd need no laws — we'd be self-regulating. That we have legal limits in almost every area of our lives is public proof of the countless individual failures to honor some ideal or other, which law piled upon law can do little to alter. If we were more caring and considerate, more respectful and fair-minded, more understanding and empathetic, we'd have fewer laws because we'd need laws less.

Final Thoughts

The ADA intends to improve the quality of life for people with disabilities by involving them in all aspects of life, including leisure services provided in their communities. According to McGovern (1992), leisure services professionals deal with quality of life issues on a daily basis and have the opportunity to make compliance with the ADA a visible and positive statement for the entire leisure industry and for people with disabilities.

Although progress has occurred in support of the inclusion of people with disabilities, more is needed. John McGovern (1996, p. 34) offered the following examples of ADA compliance associated with leisure services:

- A woman with multiple sclerosis should be able to get in and out of a newly constructed swimming pool to enjoy swimming, even if it means installing a lift at the pool.
- A young boy who has autism should have the same opportunity as his brothers and sisters without disabilities to enjoy a summer camp program, even if it means an extra staff member or a behavior plan.
- An adolescent girl who is deaf should be able to understand the strategy discussed by her hockey league coach—thanks to a sign language interpreter provided by the league—and enjoy the camaraderie of sports.
- A boy using a wheelchair should be able to get across a playground surface and enjoy the new and exciting playground equipment.

Weinum and Mitchell (1997) presented a model to encourage leisure service professionals to support and include every participant in programs and services, regardless of ability by getting ready, being willing, and being able. To *get ready*, prepare staff to accept inclusion as a process that begins with a customer service attitude. Ask participants or family members for more information to increase the chance of success. Recruit staff members who are willing to learn or may already have the skills needed to work with a diverse consumer group. Know whom to contact for training on management strategies, crisis prevention, and disability awareness. To *be willing*, know the why and how of inclusion and know that everyone benefits from inclusion. Implement inclusive strategies. To *be able*, go the extra mile to include any individual. Identify success stories as reported by participants and family members. Note the growth in numbers of people with disabilities attending programs.

Leisure service providers who embrace the spirit of the ADA are in a good position to develop inclusive leisure services. The hope is that we move beyond simply accommodating people to openly including them in our programs. John Hockenberry's (1994, p. 33) comments emphasize these sentiments:

Our struggle for inclusion in this society is a test of whether American society truly wants diversity and freedom for all . . . It is in this world that we celebrate our victories with legal symbols like the Americans with Disabilities Act . . . Real inclusion is not measured in laws and lawsuits, but instead by what the community builds together in order to bring everyone together. Inclusion is a subway everyone can use, a building everyone can enter. There is no single definition of inclusion, but you'll know it when you see it.

Discussion Questions

1. What is the purpose of the ADA?
2. What leisure services agencies must comply with the ADA?
3. What are the different titles associated with the ADA and what major topics do each of them cover?
4. What should be considered when making purchases that are consistent with the intent of the ADA?
5. How can advertisements of leisure services respond to the ADA?
6. How can registration for leisure services be facilitated for people with disabilities?
7. What are essential eligibility requirements for the provision of leisure services?
8. What are some examples of reasonable accommodations for people with disabilities in leisure programs?
9. What is meant by the existence of undue burden?
10. How can we meet the spirit of the ADA?

Chapter 10

Employ Principles of Universal Design

All the world's a stage, and all men and women are merely players:
They have their exits and their entrances.
-William Shakespeare

Orientation Activity: Test Design Awareness

Directions Alone: Read each statement below and decide if they are true or false. Once you have finished, read the debriefing to check your answers.

Directions with Others: Move about the room and find another person to share one aspect related to accessibility that you have learned. Continue this process until a signal to end the activity has been given.

1. Ramps are easier for everyone to use than stairs.
2. Most guide dogs stop at intersection curb cuts.
3. Universally designed buildings should have heat-sensitive elevator controls (touch the number and it lights up).
4. Most people with visual impairments can understand direction signs in Braille.
5. Even short-nap carpets can cause barriers for wheelchairs.
6. Public bathroom signs marked "Ladies" and "Gentlemen" may pose barriers to some people with mental retardation.
7. If a door is wide and has no threshold, it is accessible to wheelchairs.
8. A person with epilepsy should have many bathroom grab bars.
9. Many older adults and people with disabilities should have a telephone in their bathrooms.
10. Some people experience heat stroke in their shower or bathtub.
11. Rooms for people with limited mobility should be furnished with soft, overstuffed furniture.
12. Round doorknobs are generally the most difficult kind to use.

13. A dark sign with light lettering is generally easier to read than a light sign with dark lettering.

Debriefing: This Design Awareness Test has been adapted from an exercise developed by Interface, Human Factors Design Consultants in Raleigh, North Carolina. Answers to the statements follow.

1. False: Some people prefer stairs and can use them more easily than ramps.
2. False: Dogs are trained to stop at curbs; they may lead their masters into traffic if a curb ramp is in their direct line of travel.
3. False: They are nearly impossible for people who are blind to use; they may be especially deadly if used for wheelchair evacuation during a fire. Raised buttons must be placed on elevators to be accessible to persons with visual difficulties. They must be placed at a height that is accessible to people of small stature, and to those using wheeled assistive devices.
4. False: At least 90% of persons who are blind cannot read Braille.
5. True: Some short-nap carpets have a tendency to pull wheelchairs to one side as they roll.
6. True: Some people are taught to distinguish between restroom facilities by the length of the word on the door; short word means MEN, long word means WOMEN.
7. False: Doors can have many barriers: door handles may be difficult; doors may close too fast and too hard; doors may be too heavy to push open.
8. False: Grab bars may be a dangerous obstruction during a fall. Cushioning the fall would be more effective.
9. True: The bathroom is the most dangerous room in your house and phones are often used to call for help.
10. True: The heat from bath or shower water can cause heat stroke, especially in elderly persons. Lowering the hot water thermostat may prevent this.
11. False: Soft furniture does not support the spine adequately; it may be nearly impossible for some people to get up.
12. True: Lever handles require much less hand and wrist action.
13. True: That is why most interstate freeway signs are dark green or blue with white letters.

Introduction

During an average day, most people give little thought to how they get around in their environment. Mobility concerns arise, however, when people are confronted with personal limitations (e.g., broken bones, sprains, pregnancy) or experience external hindrances (e.g., carrying heavy packages, using a baby stroller). At some point in our lives, most of us will experience a temporary or permanent limitation. When this occurs, the issue of accessibility or usability suddenly becomes important. McGill and Holden (1995, p. 11) wrote about a man's struggles with access:

> In the midst of his struggles, the simplest things became issues. He says, "My house, for example, had the wrong doorknobs." One day, he saw the doorknobs as symbols of independence. "If I just had the right kind of doorknobs, I could open more doors for myself—both literally and figuratively. I could take more responsibility for myself.

What is meant by universal design?

Universal design refers to attempts to make all products and environments accessible to all people (Moon, Hart, Komissar & Freidlander, 1995). In describing the design of his home by he and his wife, William Rush (1999, p. 1) taught readers about universal design:

> Universal design is making products and environments to be useable by all people, to the greatest extent possible, without the need for adaptation or specialized design. The idea of universal design is to simplify life for everyone by making products, communications, and the built environment more usable by as many people as possible at little or no extra cost. We could see that universal design benefits people of all ages and abilities.

Often, universal design can benefit many individuals other than those who have a disability. For example, Minkoff (1997, p. 22) described the use of a surf chair on the beach of Ocean City New Jersey:

> Initially, it was thought that the chairs would provide assistance for individuals with disabilities; in most cases that is true. However, the chairs have proven to benefit a variety of individuals who have

difficulty maneuvering through the city's soft, wide beaches . . .
senior citizens, pregnant women and people recovering from
surgery are just some of the beach goers who have taken advantage
of the program.

Webster's defines *access* as "freedom or ability to obtain or make use
of" or "ability to enter, approach, communicate with, or pass to and from."
Access also has social connotations and involves total experiences. Positive
or negative feelings and attitudes influence these experiences.

Accessibility or usability of a facility is the degree to which a person
with limitations can get to, enter, and use a building or surrounding area.
The term barrier implies that there is an obstruction that impedes an individual's
progress. A single stair can allow an individual to move from one level to
another level with ease. However, that same stair can deny a person using a
wheelchair or a parent with a child's stroller the right to enter that facility.

Although the term *accessible* suggests that something is made usable
through some adaptation, the term universal design moves beyond the idea
of being accessible. It creates a broadly inclusive environment that blends a
variety of design concepts, including accessibility, into a range of meaningful options for all people (Rogers, 2000).

What types of access barriers exist?

When many people think of access they often think of physical access—
installing a ramp or renovating bathrooms for wheelchair users. But access
does not end there. Consider the situation presented by Laird (1992):

> What about the person who is deaf or has a hearing impairment?
> They can enter a building, but once they are inside, the information
> being transmitted when a leader is giving directions, a play is
> performed, or information discussed at a meeting is inaccessible to
> them because a sign language interpreter or an assistive listening
> device has not been provided for the occasion. What about the
> person who is blind or has a visual impairment? Once again the
> person can enter the building, but if it is a meeting in which
> information is being distributed on paper and must be read, then
> the meeting is inaccessible to this individual. Why? Because the
> information has not been produced in an alternate format such as
> Braille, large print, or on a cassette tape. What about the person
> who has mental retardation? This person may require the assis-
> tance of a support person to participate in community activities.

People who have disabilities face architectural barriers and attitudinal barriers every day. Although much of this chapter will focus on physical access, barriers that prevent people with disabilities from participating in activities on a daily basis can be eliminated if attitudes are improved. Laird (1992) suggested that if people could change their attitude from one where implementing changes to structures or producing or providing information in alternate formats is considered to be "special treatment" to one where making these changes benefits the whole community, other barriers will begin to fall. Our willingness to actively make our communities accessible can be the driving force for the removal of barriers to access.

Architectural barriers consist of structures constructed by humans that present an obstacle for people who have a mobility, visual, or sensory disability. Architectural barriers not only inhibit people with disabilities, but also affect the elderly, parents with carriages, and people with temporary disabilities.

Devine and colleagues (1998) reported results of a survey of park and recreation agencies across the United States. They identified environmental and structural areas that presented obstacles to leisure participation for people with disabilities. Of the agencies surveyed 75% had either not retrofitted existing sites or had made renovations for access but felt more were needed. They identified problems such as baseball dugouts with narrow openings, tennis courts with lips or steps or a difficult-to-manipulate latch at the gate, outdoor racquetball courts with narrow and short entrances, or the lack of Braille signage at facilities.

Attitudinal barriers tend to be the most difficult to identify and overcome. As discussed in Chapter 1, an attitude is a way of thinking or feeling. Thinking or feeling negatively about a disability or a person who has a disability creates an attitudinal barrier. Attitudinal barriers often arise from fear, lack of knowledge about a disability or lack of communication. To rectify this problem, people must start looking at the individual's ability, not the disability, and focusing on potential, not limitations.

What are principles of universal design?

Universal design is equitable, results in something useful, and is marketable to any group. Flexibility is important — the design should accommodate a wide range of individual preferences and abilities. Universal design implies that the design is simple (easy to understand) and informative (it communicates information needed to operate). Another aspect of universal design is tolerance — it minimizes adverse consequences of accidental or unintended actions. The design is not strenuous and used comfortably with minimum fatigue. Universal design makes things available to people, with allowances made for approach, reach, and manipulation independent of size, posture, or mobility. (These principles have been adapted from the Trace Center, 1995.)

Cangemi, Williams, and Gaskell (1992) suggested that leisure service professionals should consider adopting several strategies that can greatly improve the process of removing barriers to accessibility. As indicated in **Figure 10.1**, these include:

- incorporate barrier-free design into the planning process,
- acquire knowledge of the laws and accessibility standards,
- include people with disabilities as planning team members,
- include an accessibility specialist on your planning team,
- exceed standards whenever possible,
- extend accessibility beyond the parking lot,
- incorporate accessibility into outdoor environments,
- plan for a continuous path of travel,
- consider aesthetics and environmental values when planning, and
- ensure materials comply with governmental standards.

Which access guidelines should we follow?

Changes in both federal and state laws have indicated an increased societal commitment to the rights of people with disabilities. These laws led to the development of standards and creation of agencies charged with implementing the legislative mandate for access. We must review federal, state, and local requirements, adhere to the most rigorous and specific standard, evaluate regulations for all items, and implement the regulation that provides the greatest amount of accessibility.

The American Transportation Bureau Compliance Board issued a comprehensive set of federal standards entitled *Minimum Guidelines and Requirements for Accessible Design*. These standards, and those contained in the Uniform Federal Accessibility Standards and the Americans with Disabilities Act Accessibility Guidelines, serve as the major sources of accessibility criteria for recreation facility planners (Cangemi et al., 1992). Agencies must follow the Uniform Federal Accessibility Standards to assure compliance with federal accessibility legislation and comply with state and local building codes, where applicable. Development of the Uniform Federal Accessibility Standards reflects the legislative mandate for equal access for persons with disabilities to public accommodations, facilities, and programs.

What access guidelines have been established by the ADA?

Title II and Title III of the Americans with Disabilities Act (ADA) require, among other things, that newly constructed and altered state and local government facilities, places of public accommodation, and commercial facilities be readily accessible for individuals with disabilities. Recreation

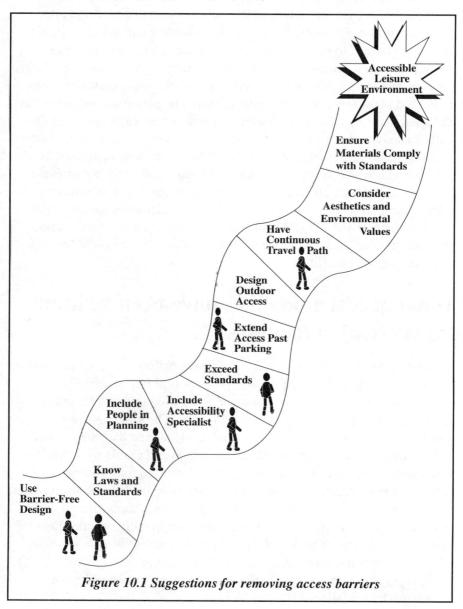

Figure 10.1 Suggestions for removing access barriers

facilities, including play areas, are among the types of facilities covered by the ADA.

The Americans with Disabilities Act Accessibility Guidelines (ADAAG) provide information on the purpose of the guidelines, general considerations, and specific instructions and definitions. In addition, ADAAG contains specific recommendations for providing accessible elements and technical requirements associated with a variety of areas that are relevant to leisure services. Guidelines are provided for construction associated with exterior facilities, new buildings, additions to and alterations of buildings, historic preservation of buildings. In addition, guidelines are provided to permit entrance to a building, such as provision of accessible routes, ground and floor surfaces, parking and passenger loading zones, ramps, protruding objects, curb cuts, stairs, doors, elevators, windows, and platform or wheelchair lifts. There are guidelines for restrooms and related areas that include drinking fountains and water coolers, toilet stalls, urinals, sinks, mirrors, bathtubs, shower rooms, handrails grab bars, dressing and fitting rooms. Safety considerations are also addressed by guidelines such as detectable warnings and alarms. There are also guidelines associated with other areas such as telephones, fixed or built-in seating and tables. The description of accessible elements and spaces is followed by detailed ADAAG guidelines for restaurants and cafeterias, medical care facilities, businesses, libraries, accessible transient lodging, and transportation facilities.

What access guidelines have been written for recreation facilities?

In October 2000 the Architectural and Transportation Barriers Compliance Board (Access Board) issued the ADAAG for Building and Facilities designated as *play areas*. These guidelines are used in the event that a complaint is filed against a particular play area. The guidelines were developed to ensure that newly constructed and altered play areas meet ADA requirements and are readily accessible to and usable by individuals with disabilities. Play areas designed and constructed for children age 2 and over are addressed in the guidelines. (There is insufficient information to develop guidelines for children under age 2.) The Access Board will provide technical assistance materials to help small entities understand the play area guidelines. The Access Board also has accessibility specialists who can answer questions about the guidelines. Many companies that sell playground equipment adhere to the guidelines and can be used as a resource. The guidelines include provisions for:

- ground-level play components,
- elevated play components,
- accessible routes,
- transfer systems,
- ground surfaces, and
- soft-contained play structures.

Ground-Level Play Components

A ground-level play component is a play component approached and exited at the ground level. Examples include spring rockers, swings, sand-digging toys, and stand alone slides. The intent of this provision is to ensure that these components, which can be accessed by children with disabilities, are integrated with other ground-level play components.

Grouping all ground-level play components that can be accessed by children with disabilities in one part of the play area would not be considered integrated. Where certain types of ground-level play components are separated for safe use, the integrated provision can still be met. For example, if one part of the play area has activity panels and another part has swings, as long as an accessible route connects to both parts of the play area and at least one activity panel and at least one swing is located on the accessible route, the ground-level play components would be integrated.

Elevated Play Components

An elevated play component is approached above grade and is part of a composite play structure consisting of two or more play components attached or functionally linked to create an integrated unit providing more than one play activity. Generally, there must be access provided by ramp or transfer system to at least one fourth to one half of the elevated components of a play area. To clarify this revised definition, Hendy (2001, p. 114) identified the following example:

> A horizontal ladder that is free standing with no platform access is considered a ground-level play component. The same horizontal ladder attached to a platform as part of a composite play structure is then considered an elevated play component, and not a ground-level component, even though it can be reached and used from the ground.

Accessible Routes

This guideline stipulates that there be at least one accessible route within the boundary of the play areas as well as one connecting the play areas to parking, drinking fountains, rest rooms, and other elements. Accessible routes provide children who use wheelchairs and other mobility devices the opportunity to access play components. Accessible routes should coincide with the general circulation path used within the play area.

Where possible, designers and operators are encouraged to provide wider ground-level accessible routes within the play areas or consider designing the entire ground surface to be accessible. If transitions at the boundary of play areas accessible routes and site accessible routes exceed 1/2 inch, such as where a rubber surface is installed on top of asphalt to reduce effects of impact, then a sloped surface must be installed with a maximum slope of 1:12. This means that for every inch that a ramp rises above the ground there are 12 inches of ramp length. This prevents the development of ramps and transitions that are too steep for people who use wheelchairs.

A maximum slope of 1:16 is required for ground level ramps; however, a lesser slope will enhance access for those children with limited strength. Ramps are preferred over transfer systems since not all children who use wheelchairs or other mobility devices may be able to use or may want to use transfer systems. Where a stand-alone slide is provided, an accessible route must connect the base of the stairs and the exit point on the slide. Where a sandbox is provided, an accessible route must connect to the border of the sandbox. Accessibility to the sandbox would be enhanced by providing a transfer system into the sand or by providing a raised sand table with knee clearance.

Transfer Systems

Transfer systems are ways to access play structures that generally include a transfer platform and a series of transfer steps. Children who use wheelchairs or other mobility devices transfer from their wheelchair or mobility device onto the transfer platform and lift themselves up or down the transfer steps and scoot along the decks of platforms to access elevated play components. Some children, however, may be unable to use a transfer system or choose not to leave their wheelchair or other mobility device.

The distance between the transfer system and the elevated play component should be kept to a minimum, since moving between the transfer platform and a series or transfer steps requires extensive exertion. Transfer supports are required on transfer platforms and transfer steps. Transfer supports allow people an opportunity to use their upper body to make a transfer, and include items such as a rope loop, a loop type handle, a slot in the edge of a flat structure, and the use of poles or bars.

Ground Surfaces

Ground surfaces must be accessible as determined by measuring the amount of work required to propel a wheelchair straight ahead and to turn across the surface. The force is measured using a force wheel on a rehabilitation wheelchair as the measuring device. It is required to be less than that required to propel the wheelchair up a ramp with a 1:14 slope. Ground surfaces must be inspected and maintained regularly and frequently to ensure the continued compliance.

Generally, for a play component to be accessible it must be located over an accessible surface, such as rubber tile, poured-in-place rubber, or engineered wood fiber (Owens, 2001). Companies that produce accessible playground surfacing should provide verification that their product adheres to accessibility and impact-absorption guidelines. When using a combination of surface materials, careful design is necessary to provide gradual transition between surfaces.

Soft-Contained Play Structures

A soft-contained play structure is composed of one or more components where people enter a fully enclosed play environment that uses pliable materials such a plastic, netting, or fabric. If four or more entry points are used, at least two must be located at accessible routes.

What are some benefits of the ADAAG for play areas?

In the opinion of the Access Board, the civil rights benefits of the guidelines ensure that children with disabilities, and parents and other adults with disabilities who supervise children on play areas, have an equal opportunity to use and enjoy play areas. Parents of children with disabilities will benefit from lower travel costs to transport their children to accessible play areas. Businesses that provide play areas as part of their facilities may benefit from increased profits as families with individuals with disabilities are more likely to patronize their establishments. Children with disabilities benefit from increased opportunities to play and to have social interactions with other children. Children without disabilities may also benefit from this diversity. Hendy (2001, p. 109), made the following observation:

> One of the most frequently asked questions during the National Playground Safety Institute's training is "Do I have to make all my playgrounds accessible?" It is time as a society that we realize that by making our playgrounds and recreation areas accessible to persons with disabilities, we are making them enjoyable for people of all ages and abilities.

What is the potential impact of universal design?

The letter written by a friend from Springfield was printed in *Parks and Recreation Magazine* in an article written by Oestreicher (1990). The letter helps to illustrate the importance of accessible recreation environments and the need for access.

In another example, a woman went to a basketball game with her husband who uses a wheelchair. She accompanied her husband to the wheelchair section and was told by the attendant that she could not remain there — the area was reserved for people in wheelchairs. This situation is repeated all too frequently at coliseums, sports arenas, and stadiums.

Implementing principles of universal design means more than just providing an entrance ramp and a section with seats removed to accommodate wheelchairs. Often these sections are situated in areas with the poorest view of the event. This practice also segregates people, separating them from their friends or families and setting them apart from the other spectators. Seating sections should be arranged so as to provide people a choice of seating locations and ticket prices. Portable chairs should be used in these sections to allow people with and without disabilities to enjoy the event together.

What does the International Symbol of Access mean?

The International Symbol of Access (see **Figure 10.2**, p. 184) represents the hope of independence and mobility to people with disabilities. Wherever it is displayed, people can be assured that obstacles will not prohibit them from participation (Alderson, 1985).

Dear Playground Director:

I was told about the playground you want to build for kids like me and regular kids, and that you were looking for ideas from handicapped kids. We really need a place to play, and maybe, if I tell you about my normal day in the summer, you will understand.

I lie in bed an hour to an hour-and-a-half, after I wake up, while Mom makes breakfast. I can help Mom make breakfast. I just don't do it as fast as Mom, and with two brothers and sisters, I "get in the way."

After breakfast, I roll out to the sun porch, while Mom cleans the house, or does the laundry. I could help with the cleaning, but Mom can do it faster, and . . . I "get in the way."

Most days, I go outside in the backyard and play by myself, or with our dog. We have a basketball hoop on the garage, and I'm pretty good, especially my hook shot. I know I could play with my brothers and their friends, but I slow down the game, so most days I sit in the backyard reading or playing with the dog. It seems to me, we are both put out here so we won't be in the way. The only difference is the dog can run off and play with his friends when he wants . . . I can't . . . Deep down inside I know I can do just about anything anyone else can do, just a little different, just a little slower. It just seems I don't get a chance very often . . . or at all.

For a week every summer I go to camp for special kids. It's fun, but it's only for a week a year, and even when I enjoy playing and winning against another handicapped kid, it would be much better to play and win against a regular kid.

So Mr., I'm sorry I don't know how to spell your name . . . it's too long, but if you build a playground where I can go anytime and can play with regular kids, and not be in anyone's way, I'll play in it and I'll buy you a "Big Mac" with cheese and a Coke.

I won't sign my name, because it might hurt my family a little, and they do love me, very much . . . so do your best please.

Yours truly,

A friend from Springfield

Use of signs to convey information to visitors and participants is an important consideration in the provision of access. The International Symbol of Access is often used in parking lots to indicate reserved stalls and in buildings to indicate accessible bathrooms. It can also be used in conjunction with directional symbols or a written message such as "Ask for Information Here," which tells the visitor that there are other services available. Such services may include interpretive cassettes, the availability of a wheelchair for loan, and accessible transportation services.

The Symbol is used in informational materials such as maps, program announcements and information, and registration brochures, to indicate accessibility. Care should be taken in the use of these symbols. For instance,

Figure 10.2 International Symbol of Access

a building that has an accessible entrance should not have the access symbol displayed unless the facilities and services inside the building are also accessible. The 1975 Assembly of Rehabilitation International meeting presented the following policies to govern the use of the International Symbol of Access:

- the Symbol shall always be used in the design and proportions approved by the Assembly, reproduction of which shall be disseminated with this resolution;
- the colors used shall always be in sharp contrast and, unless there are compelling reasons to use other colors, the Symbol and its background shall be reproduced in either black and white or dark blue and white;
- no change in or addition to the design shall be permitted; and
- the Symbol shall be used only to mark or show the way to facilities that are accessible to persons whose mobility is restricted by disability.

To preserve the meaning of the Symbol of Access, to maintain the dignity of individuals for whom the Symbol was designed, and to avoid confusion to the general public, the Symbol of Access is to be displayed properly at all times. Any organization is permitted to display the Symbol in published material relevant to services for people with disabilities. The

Symbol must be clearly identified as the International Symbol of Access, and it must always face to the right, unless it is meant to be a directional signal, such as identifying that an accessible restroom can be found down a particular hallway.

The Symbol of Access was not intended to identify a person who is disabled, and it should not be used in that manner. The Symbol is intended to mark facilities that use universal design and are usable by people with disabilities. The Symbol of Access tells people that they can enter a building or facility without fear of being blocked by architectural barriers. To use the Symbol of Access for reasons other than to denote an accessible building or facility for use by persons with disabilities is prohibited.

How can different leisure contexts be universally designed?

There a many different contexts in which leisure services are provided. Examples of the application of principles of universal design to the following contexts is presented in this section:

- playgrounds
- outdoor recreation,
- rest rooms and locker rooms, and
- special events.

Playgrounds

Handy (1999) stressed that designers, purchasers, and providers of playground equipment and play areas have a responsibility to provide safe, challenging play environments that do more than simply comply with safety standards. Handy emphasized that when selecting playground equipment and components to be placed on a play structure, there are many questions to ask, including "How will accessibility be provided for persons with mobility impairments?" She provided the following suggestions regarding access:

> When designing a structure for the preschool age group, an appropriate means of access is critically important. A wheelchair-accessible ramp with a slope of 1:12 is the least challenging form of access. A ramp should not be the only means of accessing a play structure, as the distance required to move from one point to

another via a ramp is not practical for all users. A ramp that is not intended for wheelchair access, with a slope that does not exceed 1:8, is the next level of challenge . . . Most transfer platforms enable a wheelchair child to transfer from the chair to the platform to access the equipment, then back to the chair. These transfer platforms are very easy to access and are considered a minor challenge. When a child with limited mobility exits a slide, it is important to provide a way back to the wheelchair or walker. The location of access components is an important issue for all users. (pp. 87, 90)

Outdoor Recreation

The Association for Experiential Education has established standards with the intent of transcending disability rather than compensating for the lack of ability (Rogers, 2000). This approach is solution oriented and ability focused and emphasizes socially meaningful roles.

To illustrate the point that people with disabilities can participate safely in outdoor recreation programs (e.g., ropes challenge courses) and that the programs can be designed to be inclusive (i.e., accessible to community members of all ability levels), Curulla and Strong (2000, p. 49) provided the following example of Martha, a 35-year-old social worker:

[She] found herself very nervous. Having seen a video of what was in store—climbing 30 feet up a Douglas fir tree and then sliding across a system of cables and ropes on a small platform called "the Stagecoach"—she didn't think it would be possible for her since she used a wheelchair. Her fears were genuine, but unfounded. By the end of the day, she had not only climbed the tree herself, she had assisted others in climbing, traversing, and succeeding in their challenge course efforts. At the group debriefing following completion of the course she proudly expressed the empowering sense of accomplishment she felt after completing a full day of emotional, social, and physical challenges. With the group's support, she felt she had broken through some of her own personal barriers. She was sure that reflecting on what she had accomplished that day would boost her confidence in the future when she or others doubted her capabilities.

Rogers (2000) provided several illustrations of the application of the principles of universal design to challenge courses. One specific example Rogers (p. 85) identified was related to horizontal components:

Incorporate parallel components that anyone can use. A traverse element may have a log and a cable that run next to each other and participants choose how they want to negotiate it, or there may be very large climbing holds that constitute a route up a climbing wall with small one next to them. This approach allows for exciting two-person team experiences on a variety of elements.

Rest Rooms and Locker Rooms

Important features of any recreation and park facility are the restrooms and locker rooms. An example of how universal design can solve many problems is by including family locker rooms. Ahrweiler (2000, p. 12) stated that family locker rooms are self-contained rooms, about 60 square feet, with a toilet, shower, and changing area that can be used by an entire family. Family locker rooms provide privacy and safety for children accompanied by a parent of the opposite sex. People with disabilities desire them, especially those accompanied by a caregiver or family member of the opposite sex.

Ahrweiler (2000, p. 14) provided the following statements about universal design, quoting frequently from William Tracey, a manufacturer of plumbing fixtures:

> Hand controls, which use sensors to turn water on and off, gained prominence in locker and restroom facilities for the benefit of disabled users but are now popular with a broad spectrum of users and facilities operators as well. "Hands-free controls are valuable for the maintenance and sanitation end," Tracey says. "Able users appreciate the fact that they don't have to handle the controls, and the facility managers find they keep restrooms cleaner." ADA requirements have led to greater interest in universal design, where facilities are designed to accommodate all users, disabled or not. "As facilities began switching over to ADA-compliant designs, more and more people realized that instead of installing one or two special areas just for disabled users, it makes sense to create fixtures that can be used by everyone—handicapped or not," Tracey says.

Special Events

When planning conferences, workshops, and special events we must recognize the need to plan ahead for attendance of people with disabilities. McCarty (1991) recommended including people with disabilities when planning services and events. The questions presented in **Table 10.1** can be used as a general guide when surveying a potential meeting site for accessibility.

When visiting the potential location of a special event, we can make certain doorways are wide enough to accommodate wheelchairs, check for handrails and raised toilet seats in the bathrooms, and look for ramps, parking spaces, and fire alarms with audio and visual notification systems. When considering travel arrangements questions such as the following can be asked:

- Is there a lift-equipped van for transportation from the airport to the conference?
- What are local taxi service policies about transporting passengers with disabilities?
- Will these services transport people who use wheelchairs?
- Will these services assist the passenger who is disabled?

Final Thoughts

Universal design is a critical step to inclusion. People must be able to get to a desired recreation activity, interact with the equipment, and interact with other participants if they are to engage in community leisure pursuits. By being creative and persistent, we can expand the leisure options for people by applying principles of universal design. A brief story by 11-year-old Lucas Parker (1998, p. 250) illustrates this point:

> One day, when I was five, I went to a local park with my mom. While I was playing in the sandbox, I noticed a boy about my age in a wheelchair. Since I was only five, I couldn't understand why he couldn't just get in the sandbox and play with me. He told me he couldn't. I talked to him for a while longer, then I took my large bucket, scooped up as much sand as I could and dumped it into his lap. Then I grabbed some toys and put them in his lap, too. My mom rushed over and said, "Lucas, why did you do that?" I looked at her and replied, "He couldn't play in the sandbox with me, so I brought the sand to him. Now we can play in the sand together."

Lucas can teach us a valuable lesson about bringing the leisure experience to people. Some professionals argue, however, that they rarely (if ever) observe people with disabilities in their community accessing their facilities. Therefore, they conclude that even if they made their facilities

Parking
- Are parking spaces available for individuals with physical disabilities?
- Are parking spaces near the building entrance?
- Are parking spaces easily accessible to the front entrance by a level or ramped path at least 4 feet wide and free of obstructions?

Route
- Is the surface of the parking lot smooth and firm but not slippery?
- Are walks leading to the facility level or nearly so?
- Are there curb cuts at crossways?

Entrance
- Is at least one primary entrance usable to individuals who use wheelchairs?
- Do all doorways have a clear opening of at least 32 inches?
- Are doors operated by a single effort?
- Is the door light enough for the person with a disability to open it?
- Are sharp inclines or abrupt changes in level avoided at thresholds?

Ramps
- Are ramps provided where there are stairs?
- Do ramps conform to standard of no more than 1:12 slope?
- Do ramps have non-slip surfaces with a 32-inch handrail on at least one side?

Elevators
- Are guest elevators accessible and usable by people with physical disabilities?
- Are all elevator controls 48 inches or less from the floor?
- Are tactile identifications located beside elevator operating buttons?

Bathrooms
- Do all bathroom doors provide a minimum of 32 inches of clear opening?
- Is the bathroom floor the same level as the floor outside of the bathroom?
- Does the bathroom contain a floor clearance area of at least 5 feet by 5 feet to permit a person in a wheelchair sufficient turning space?
- Is there at least one bathroom stall usable by a person who uses a wheelchair?
- Are sinks, mirrors, and dispensers usable by people in wheelchairs?
- Are there handrails in the toilet and shower area?
- Is there sufficient turning space and maneuvering in the bath for a wheelchair?
- Are hanging rods for clothing located within 48 inches of the floor?

Telephones
- Are there conveniently located public phones 48 inches or less from the floor?
- Do public telephones have volume control devices?
- Are TTYs available?

Miscellaneous
- Are water fountains available and have a clearance of 28 inches?
- Are tables convertible to wheelchair use with floor clearance of 28 inches?
- Is the meeting space accessible and usable by persons with disabilities?
- Are all common areas accessible to all people?
- Is help available for those who might need assistance?
- What is the general attitude of personnel towards persons with disabilities?

Table 10.1 Guidelines for surveying a potential meeting site

and programs accessible, people with disabilities would not attend. The information presented in this chapter encourages us to apply principles of universal design and thereby create opportunities for people with disabilities to engage in community leisure pursuits.

Discussion Questions

1. What is the meaning of universal design?
2. What types of access barriers exist?
3. What are some principles of universal design?
4. What access guidelines have been established by the ADA?
5. What access guidelines have been written specifically for recreation facilities?
6. What is the potential impact of universal design?
7. What is the meaning of the International Symbol of Access?
8. How can playgrounds be universally designed?
9. How can outdoor recreation programs be universally designed?
10. What are some considerations for universal design when planning special events?

Chapter 11

Facilitate Self-Determination

*Few human concerns are more universally
central than that of self-determination.*
-Edward Deci

Orientation Activity: The Choice Is Theirs

Directions Alone: Choose any recreation program that you might offer as a leisure services professional. While thinking of this recreation activity, record answers for each of the following questions. Be sure to include specific examples.

Directions with Others: One person will be assigned as recorder and will write the responses on a chalkboard or easel that all participants can see. Address each question and report the different methods identified. Attempt to produce as comprehensive a list as possible.

- How might we encourage participants to choose activities within a given recreation program?
- How might we determine what a participant has chosen if he or she does not speak?
- How might we encourage participants to make choices once we begin conducting a recreation activity?
- If participants do not have the skills to respond to a survey or interview questions concerning their enjoyment associated with a program, how might we determine if they are enjoying an activity?

Debriefing: Self-determination is a highly valued personal characteristic in our society (Abery, 1994). If we identify self-determination and choice as important elements of leisure and enjoyment, then it appears logical to encourage participants in leisure programs to make as many choices as possible and to take responsibility for their participation.

Providing opportunities for individuals with disabilities to cultivate self-determination can be challenging and often requires systematic planning (Wehmeyer, 1994). The goal of enhancing self-determination has merit, since it appears that people's perceptions of freedom and their ability to determine their own participation patterns is more important than the specific recreation activity which they choose. The aforementioned questions encourage leisure services professionals to provide opportunities for choices whenever possible within programs.

The fact that some participants may have fewer skills, respond in different ways, or exhibit behaviors not demonstrated by most does not preclude them from valuing their freedom and from experiencing enjoyment. Leisure service professionals are in an excellent position to facilitate self-determination for all individuals. Their support will help individuals experience leisure as much as possible. Consider the following questions related to the orientation activity:

- What is the value of encouraging participants to make choices and increase their sense of self-determination?
- What is the primary responsibility of leisure services providers to people with disabilities?
- Why is it important to provide opportunities for people with disabilities to empower themselves?

Introduction

On December 25th 1971, Dr. Jesse Jackson encouraged the crowd he addressed to join him in his famous proclamation: "I am somebody." With this phrase people announced that they viewed themselves as valued people who have much to share and contribute—a sense of self-determination (Pomeranz, 1997). People learn that they are somebody by experiencing positive interactions with others that nurture and support their sense of inherent value as a human being and their sense of self-determination.

Self-determination is necessary for the optimal experience of enjoyment. Self-determination makes effort and the investment of attention worthwhile for a person. These factors bring about enjoyable involvement. This experience serves to develop competence, thereby reinforcing self-determination. To better understand the impact of self-determination on leisure participation, the psychology of enjoyment will be explored.

This chapter encourages leisure services providers to consider the impact of the way in which they deliver their services to people with disabilities. Leisure services are primarily designed to set the stage for people to enjoy themselves. At times, we become so concerned with "keeping people busy" that we lose sight of the more important goal of our services: facilitating enjoyment.

What is self-determination?

Self-determination involves people having control over their lives in areas they value. Self-determined people exert control over what happens to them, when and where it occurs, and with whom it takes place (Stancliffe, Abery & Smith, 2000). Generally, people who perceive themselves as capable and self-determining are able to effectively deal with the challenges of day-to-day life and may avoid undesirable outcomes such as depression, distress, substance abuse, and physical illness. Deci (1980) asserted that self-determination involves the flexibility and ability to choose options and to adjust to situations with only one available option.

Wehmeyer (1998) proposed four essential characteristics of self-determination required for the individual to act autonomously. The person acts on his or her own preferences without external pressure. In addition, the person must regulate his or her behaviors by considering skills and the task, then formulating, implementing, and evaluating a plan. The person must also initiate and respond in an empowered manner (i.e., believe in his or her capacity to influence outcomes). Finally, acting autonomously requires that the individual realize the impact of his or her actions that provides an accurate understanding of his or her strengths and limitations.

After analyzing almost 200 studies involving close to 1,400 participants with disabilities, Hughes and colleagues (1997) discovered an increasing trend to involve people with disabilities as active participants by targeting outcomes related to self-determination, autonomy, and choice. In an analysis of information on the quality of life and self-determination of 50 adults with cognitive disabilities, Wehmeyer and Schwartz (1998) concluded that self-determination contributes to a more positive quality of life. Therefore, by considering another person's choices, preferences, and aspirations we can promote a sense of self-determination and communicate a sense of respect (Hughes & Agran, 1998).

Although acting autonomously is an important characteristic of self-determination, people are not completely autonomous. Few would choose to meet all their daily living demands independently, without assistance and support from others. Given this need for *interdependence*, Pumpian (1996) asserted that being autonomous includes being interdependent with families and others with whom we interact. Brown, Gothelf, Guess and Lehr (1998) encouraged professionals to acknowledge this interdependence and focus on supporting people with disabilities to become more autonomous within the context of interdependence.

How is intrinsic motivation related to self-determination?

Intrinsic motivation energizes behavior and increases autonomy. Performance of the behavior does not require external rewards or control. The experiences of interest, enjoyment, and excitement provide reinforcement for such behaviors. These are the experiences most often associated with leisure and recreation.

Intrinsically motivated people will seek challenges commensurate with their competencies—they will avoid situations that are too easy or too difficult. The balancing act between competencies and challenges associated with intrinsic motivation is depicted in **Figure 11.1**. Individuals who are intrinsically motivated are more likely to learn, adapt, and grow in competencies that characterize development.

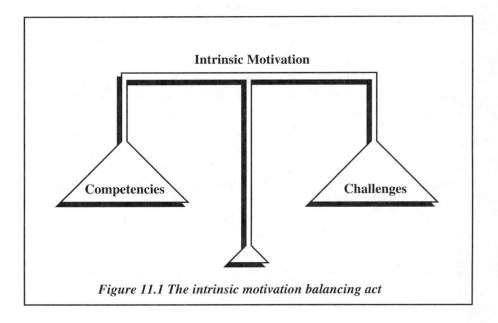

Figure 11.1 The intrinsic motivation balancing act

What causes people to enjoy something?

Leisure services professionals can bring about the experience of enjoyment. Whatever additional benefits enjoyment may bring, it is in and of itself the reason for the provision of services designed to include people with disabilities. Leisure professionals seek to identify the factors that interfere prohibit enjoyment, as well as those that facilitate enjoyment. The nature of enjoyment, however, has not always been made clear.

The work of Csikszentmihalyi (1997) and his associates on optimal experience offers a useful starting point for this examination. These investigators have studied, with various methods including interviews and surveys, the qualities of subjective experience. By examining the experiences of dancers, rock climbers, writers, basketball players, artists, surgeons, and others who love their work, these investigations have isolated characteristics of enjoyment, or what they refer to as *optimal experience*.

The studies show that the experience of enjoyment is distinguishable from pleasure. *Pleasure* is the result of satisfying basic biological drives such as hunger, thirst, sex, and stimulation. *Enjoyment* is the experience derived from investing one's attention in intrinsically motivating action patterns. The activity is often so compelling that one becomes deeply absorbed in it and loses consciousness of self and awareness of time. The word used to describe this subjective quality of the optimal experience is *flow*. The sense of movement that this word implies is created by the merging of action and awareness around the challenges provided by an activity and the feedback that defines a person's capability to meet those challenges.

While many activities can create an optimal experience, the activity must become more challenging (in keeping with expanding skills) to maintain the experience. Unlike pleasure, enjoyment is consistent with concentration, effort, and a sense of control and competence. Enjoyment is often used colloquially as the equivalent of "fun," or simple positive affect, but it is being used here to reflect a considerable degree of psychological involvement as well.

The research of Csikszentmihalyi and others shows that concentration, effort, and a sense of control and competence are all critical aspects of the experience of enjoyment. Thus, these factors must be understood and managed by leisure professionals if enjoyment is to be facilitated. See **Figure 11.2** (p. 198) for a depiction of the conditions of enjoyment.

While there are other agendas for leisure professionals, teaching people to generate optimal experiences and establishing environments conducive to flow is especially important. Creating conditions that help concentration, effort, and a sense of control and competence, while promoting freedom of choice and the expression of preference is the engineering of enjoyment. To do that, leisure services providers must understand self-determination and the factors that interfere with it.

How does the environment stimulate self-determination?

Self-determination occurs when people take control of their freedom. The environment can encourage self-determination by being responsive and informational or it can discourage self-determination through controlling and capricious responses to behaviors. A responsive and informational environment reacts to a person's initiatives, provides information about the person's competence, and encourages further action. It fosters intrinsic motivation and internal causality, resulting in self-determined behavior.

Events involving choice and positive feedback provide information to the person, thereby enhancing self-determination. For example, Maughan and Ellis (1991) demonstrated that the administration of praise and persuasion for accomplishments associated with a video game enhanced perceptions of adolescents. By creating environments that are option-rich, responsive, and informative, we can increase the likelihood of participants becoming self-determined.

How can self-determination in leisure be facilitated?

Because self-determination involves a lifelong interplay between the individual and his or her environment, a supportive, responsive context is

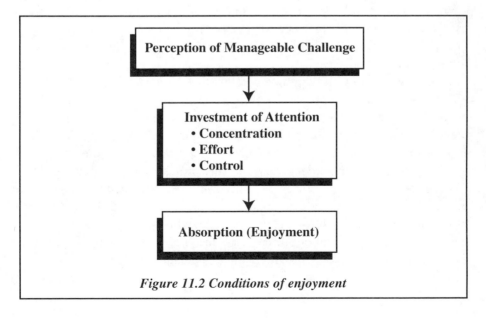

Figure 11.2 Conditions of enjoyment

important when encouraging people to become self-determined. Optimum environments offer individuals the opportunity to express and further develop self-determination. To promote self-determination we must begin to shift from services directed by professionals to services directed by participants (Wehmeyer, Palmer, Agran, Mithaug & Martin, 2000).

Many strategies can facilitate self-determination. **Figure 11.3** previews the seven strategies identified in this chapter. An environment that facilitates self-determination can be established by encouraging participants to:

- provide opportunities for choice,
- promote communication,
- respond to preferences,
- foster active participation,
- encourage empowerment,
- increase competence, and
- advocate goal setting.

Provide Opportunities for Choice

One characteristic common to most discussions of self-determination is choice; however, some families and professionals make choices for people

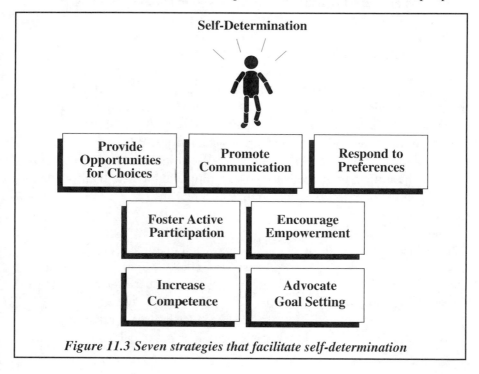

Figure 11.3 Seven strategies that facilitate self-determination

with disabilities rather than allowing participants to decide for themselves. Opportunities to express interests and preferences have been prevented by people who incorrectly assume that people with disabilities are incapable of making informed choices (Heller, Miller, Hsieh & Sterns, 2000).

When people are given choices they improve their engagement, interest, and enthusiasm in activities (Moes, 1998), increase their participation level, and reduce their challenging behaviors (Sigafoos, 1998). To encourage self-determination, we can support initiation of activities by providing participants with opportunities to express preferences, allowing them to make choices regarding their leisure participation, and permitting them to experience outcomes based on their choices. We can encourage participants to make choices within activities if we present multiple and diverse options, such as what materials to use, with whom to participate, and when to stop an activity. Choice opportunities can also be facilitated during the course of an activity by simply following the person's lead and interests (Bambara, Cole & Koger 1998).

Freedom of choice is vital to the pursuit of enjoyable, satisfying, and meaningful experience. Personal autonomy for people with disabilities is an essential aspect of independent functioning and self-reliance. Heyne, Schleien, and McEvoy (1993, p. 46) emphasized this point:

> When people with disabilities are allowed to choose activities, they are more eager to learn the skills necessary to participate, they more readily generalize those skills to other settings, and they are more likely to continue to participate in those activities.

Opportunities for choice associated with leisure participation must be taught to individuals with disabilities. The ultimate goal of any leisure program is to facilitate self-initiated, independent use of free time with chronologically age-appropriate recreation activities. When we provide opportunities for individuals to make self-determined and responsible choices that reflect their needs to grow, explore, and realize their potential, this enhances their ability to experience leisure.

For example, Anne's favorite recreation activity is doing artwork. When she attends her art class she is encouraged to select the paper she will use; she chooses between different colors, sizes, and textures. In addition, she decides to use watercolors today rather than chalk or markers. After she has her materials, Anne is invited to position her easel where she prefers and begins her chosen project while carefully selecting her color scheme.

It is important to maintain a delicate balance between providing opportunities for choice and encouraging development of culturally normative age-appropriate leisure behaviors for people with disabilities. Sometimes people choose to exhibit behaviors that society has identified as being offensive or detrimental. These people are often redirected to participate in socially acceptable activities of their choosing that do not bring psychological or physical discomfort to themselves or other people. Leisure instruction related to helping individuals determine the appropriateness of behaviors is often useful. All people must learn that humans are rarely completely free to do anything they wish. To experience leisure on an ongoing basis, people must learn to assert their rights as well as respect other people they encounter. The appropriateness of behaviors may vary according to the following:

- location (e.g., bedroom versus public swimming pool),
- frequency (e.g., asking once versus asking several times in a brief duration),
- timing (e.g., laughing when someone is crying), and
- relationship of people present (e.g., brother versus teacher).

Encouraging individuals with disabilities to make choices and take charge of their lives is an important aspect of leisure services delivery. The earlier opportunities for choices are presented to people, the more likely they will acquire behaviors associated with self-determination. An important action in trying to support people with disabilities to become more self-determined is to invite them to try new experiences while at the same time continuously offering chances to make choices.

Promote Communication

Effective communication facilitates involvement with others. However, for a variety of reasons, some people may take considerable time to formulate a communication turn. At times, professionals responding to these individuals do not provide them with adequate time to respond. This unwillingness to wait for people to take their turn results in the professional taking control of the conversation and often the entire situation. Since the ability to choose to initiate involvement is critical to the leisure experience, people should be encouraged to initiate interactions and share conversations.

Construction of a supportive environment that is responsive to the communicative attempts of these people is important. A supportive environment can be created when we approach the person, attend to the person, and wait at least 10 seconds for that person to initiate interaction. This will encourage leisure involvement and, more importantly, demonstrate respect for that person.

When providing leisure services it may be helpful to take a *nondirective approach,* which strongly considers the individual's preferences and choices. Nondirective instructional strategies can help us avoid instilling a sense of dependency within our participants. Since a perception of freedom to choose to participate in meaningful, enjoyable, and satisfying experiences is fundamental to the leisure experience, independent leisure participation is achieved more readily when reliance on *directive approaches*, which promote professional control and limit choice for participants, is avoided.

Since much daily communication is not verbally prompted, encouraging people with disabilities to initiate communication is an important goal. As people engage in reciprocal exchanges stimulated by their ability to initiate interaction, this enhances their ability to communicate preferences, make meaningful choices, and experience leisure. Simply providing people with limited communication skills with an alternative form of communication is not sufficient—specific attention to responding to conversational attempts is needed. We should be as responsive as possible to the communicative attempts made by people with limited communication skills.

If the person does make a communicative initiative, speaking partners can reinforce these attempts such as by providing people with objects they have requested, returning greetings to people, and extending and expanding their comments. However, if the person does not initiate interaction, professionals are encouraged to ask open-ended questions beginning with "what" and "how" as opposed to those questions that force people into a yes/no response.

Respond to Preferences

de Villiers (1987) explained that *preference* refers to a desire for an option following a comparison of that option against a continuum of other options. *Choice* refers to the act of selecting one option, ideally a preferred one, from among others simultaneously available (Newton et al., 1991). The distinction between choice and preference is subtle but important. For example, arbitrarily dispensing an option that is preferred by someone robs that person of the right and pleasure of making the choice (Newton, Horner & Lund, 1991). Likewise, helping someone to choose among less-preferred options only substitutes for the kind of choice-making most people value.

When attempting to provide opportunities for expressing preferences and making choices, we should determine the person's preferences and create supporting opportunities for the person to choose among preferred options. Each day presents many opportunities for participants to express preferences and make choices about their activities. These choices include not only what to do, but also where, with, and with whom to perform the activity. To respond to the needs of people with disabilities, we can assess participants' preferences and develop strategies for determining the most preferred activities.

Foster Active Participation

Individuals with disabilities are often excluded from recreation activities due to their assumed inability to perform independently. However, an individual who is deemed unable to engage in an activity independently should not be denied the opportunity for partial participation.

All individuals should be provided the opportunity to participate in natural environments rather than in artificial settings. Partial participation involves the use of adaptations and provides assistance needed to facilitate leisure participation, thereby affirming the right of persons with disabilities to participate in environments and activities without regard to degree of assistance required (Baumgart et al., 1982). Through partial participation, individuals with disabilities may experience the exhilaration and satisfaction associated with the challenge inherent in a particular recreation activity.

Adaptations to enhance participation or to make partial participation possible include providing personal assistance; adapting activities by changing materials, modifying skill sequences, altering rules, and using adaptive devices and alternative communications systems; and changing physical and social environments to promote friendships.

As an example of partial participation, Michael, who uses a walker, and his colleagues at work decided to enter a softball league sponsored by the community recreation and parks department. At the beginning of the season, a few rules were adjusted to facilitate his participation in league play. Instead of the ball being pitched to him, he hit the ball off a tee and after he made contact a teammate (Nichole) ran the bases. When his teammate scored a run, the team congratulated both Michael and Nichole.

The principle of partial participation ensures that even those people who might never be able to acquire a large enough complement of skills to completely participate in recreation activities could still learn enough to partially participate. Ferguson and Baumgart (1991) identified three problems that have arisen when professionals have attempted to promote partial participation. First, some professionals have narrowly defined participation as simply presence. When passive participation is the dominant form of participation, the practice becomes problematic. Recreation professionals should attempt to encourage active participation by all participants, including people with disabilities. Second, sometimes professionals fail to consider the person's preferences, long-term learning needs, family priorities, reactions of peers, and other socially validated, community-referenced guidelines. It is important to gain this information from the participants and their families. Third, we may interpret "doing things independently" as doing them alone, which can result in too narrow a prescription for performance. The supportive presence of another person offers leisure services providers and participants the opportunity to enhance an individual's participation by having the other person perform those parts of the activity that are burdensome, time-consuming, or image-damaging for the person.

Encourage Empowerment

Service providers do not always allow people with disabilities and their families the right to make their own major life decisions. Cognitive, physical, communicative, or sensory impairments may make it difficult for an individual to express his or her preferences and be accurately understood by another person.

West and Parent (1992) stated that for many individuals with disabilities, the opportunities for learning and practicing decision making and self-direction are limited or circumvented. The reasons that these individuals experience such powerlessness and lack of self-direction have less to do with their limitations and impairments than with attitudes and practices of caregivers, service providers, funding agencies, and social institutions.

Every person, regardless of the severity of his or her disabilities, has the right and ability to communicate with others, express everyday preferences, and exercise at least some control over his or her daily life. Each individual, therefore, should be given the choice, training, technology, respect, and encouragement to do so (Williams, 1991, p. 543).

Empowerment may be defined as the transfer of power and control over the values, decisions, choices, and directions of human services from external entities (e.g., government funding agencies, service providers) to consumers of services. This results in increased motivation to participate and succeed and greater dignity for the consumer (West & Parent, 1992). Leisure services providers need to create environments in which people with disabilities and their family members are given information to make rational choices as well as opportunities to exercise their choices. "One important component of self-determination, personal control, typically refers to direct exercise of civil and individual rights through personal choices with the goal of exerting control over one's daily life and future plans" (Stancliffe, Abery, Springborg & Elkin, 2000).

Learning to make good choices requires experience with the process of decision making, choosing among viable alternatives, and dealing with the consequences of decisions. When independent choice making is not feasible or safe, choice making can be adapted or supported, and individuals may partially participate in decision-making processes. Hanline and Fox (1993) observed that most professionals agree that the development of autonomy, the importance of choice-making, opportunities for self-initiation, and environmental manipulation all facilitate learning, enjoyment, and empowerment.

Making timely and correct decisions leads to a sense of personal effectiveness and interest that subsequently promotes investment of attention and enjoyment. People who do not possess the decision-making skills needed for activity involvement are more likely to acquire these skills if they participate in recreation activities and are given considerable autonomy in doing so. Participants can be encouraged to evaluate their decisions, determine the effectiveness of their decisions, and decide whether they would act in a similar fashion in a similar circumstance. Encouraging people to locate facilities, learn about participation requirements, and obtain answers to questions can stimulate decisions about leisure involvement.

After studying 54 young adults with intellectual disabilities, Jenkinson (1999) noted that those people who had experiences leading to learned helplessness may require a lengthy period of supported practice in making decisions to gain greater confidence and feelings of control. In addition, Jenkinson encouraged practitioners to present manageable decisions that do not present people an abundance of information from which they must make a decision. Leisure services providers who want to encourage all participants to become self-determined would do well to give participants as many opportunities as possible to practice making manageable decisions.

Increase Competence

Perceived competence refers to a person's evaluation of his or her competence compared to others of the same age and gender. Perceived competence is an important feature of leisure because it results in feelings of personal control. Psychological comfort is perceived when people compare performance to standards adopted internally and feel satisfied with their performance. This comfort is important because it allows for the possibility that people may use a criterion other than social comparison to judge their competence.

People with disabilities who have more free time activities to choose from are in a better situation to experience leisure than those who do not. Participation in activities in which people perceive themselves as competent throughout their lives is important for leisure services professionals to consider when planning their services. Therefore, expanding a person's leisure repertoire—those activities an individual does for fun—would increase feelings of competence. Mobily, Lemke, and Gisin (1991) reported that the development of a leisure repertoire is a collection of activities capable of producing perceptions of competence and psychological comfort. What people do often for their leisure they will do well, and what people do well in their leisure they will do often. West and Parent (1992, p. 75) provided a note of caution when expanding people's leisure repertoires:

> More activity does not necessarily mean a better quality of life. Some individuals may actually choose to engage in a few repetitive, but highly enjoyable, activities per week. The issue is ensuring that meaningful opportunities for choice are actually provided.

Advocate Goal Setting

Ward (1988) referred to self-determination as the attitudes and abilities that lead individuals to define goals and to take the initiative to achieve those goals. Activities with clear goals are more likely to lead to participant enjoyment (Csikszentmihalyi, 1990). In many activities the goals are implicit, and therefore goal setting is not important. For example, when completing a painting, the main concern is to develop the skills which, when used, result in recognizing a finished product.

One role of service providers is to encourage participants to set goals when they are not apparent and work toward achieving them—usually problem-solving in the process—within an environment which fosters interdependence. According to Deci (1995, p. 152) "goals need to be individualized—they need to be suited specifically to the person who will work toward them—and they need to be set so as to represent an optimal challenge."

Final Thoughts

In summary, self-determination is necessary for the optimal experience of enjoyment. It makes effort and the investment of attention worthwhile for a person. As seen in **Figure 11.4**, this experience of enjoyment serves in turn to develop competence, thereby reinforcing self-determination. All people need to have opportunities to take charge of their own lives. Their experiences can be organized by principles that promote self-determination.

Wehmeyer and Bolding (1999) examined 273 people with intellectual disabilities and found that those who lived or worked in the community were more self-determined, had higher autonomy, had more choices, and

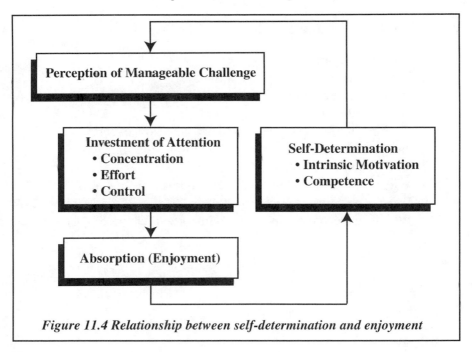

Figure 11.4 Relationship between self-determination and enjoyment

were more satisfied than were peers of similar ages and IQs who were living or working in segregated environments. Therefore, the authors surmised that if people are supported to make choices, participate in decisions, set goals and experience control in their lives they will become more self-determined. Conversely, as people become more self-determined, they will be more likely to assume greater control, make more choices, improve their ability to set goals, make better decisions, enhance their problem solving, and have greater belief in their capacity to influence their lives.

Discussion Questions

1. What is self-determination?
2. Why is self-determination important?
3. What is enjoyment?
4. What is an optimal experience?
5. How can we create conditions to promote flow experiences?
6. How can the environment encourage self-determination?
7. Why is choice important?
8. What is the difference between a preference and a choice?
9. What is perceived competence?
10. Why is perceived competence an important feature of leisure?

Chapter 12

Develop Leisure Education Programs

Education is what survives when what
has been learnt has been forgotten.
-B. F. Skinner

Orientation Activity: Go Beyond Recreation Activity Skills

Directions Alone: Select a recreation activity and answer the following questions to assist you in developing a comprehensive leisure education program.

Directions with Others: Find other people who chose the same recreation activity as you. If no one else identified your activity, find another person who has identified an activity similar to yours. Once groups have been formed, share your ideas about leisure education with the other person(s) in your discussion group. After a specified time, discuss what you have learned with the entire group.

- How can we encourage participants' awareness of preferences related to the activity?
- How can we develop a sense of appreciation of the value of the recreation activity?
- How might we encourage development of self-determination with this activity?
- How could we encourage decision making within the context of this recreation activity?
- How might we teach people about resources associated with this recreation activity?
- What social skills could we encourage so that participants may be successful in this activity?

Debriefing: Limited leisure awareness, knowledge, and skills become major barriers for many individuals in making successful transitions into active community living. To overcome these barriers it can be helpful to provide systematic and comprehensive leisure education. Attempt to answer the following questions related to the orientation activity:

- What is the value in addressing the questions listed in the orientation activity?
- What are the implications of offering a leisure education program?
- How might we incorporate leisure education into our current or future position as a leisure services provider?

Introduction

Leisure describes a person's perception that he or she is free to choose to participate in meaningful, enjoyable, and satisfying experiences. As individuals get in touch with the positive feelings—control, competence, relaxation, and excitement—associated with the leisure experience, they will be intrinsically motivated to participate. That is, they will participate in leisure simply to be involved in the experience, not for some tangible outcome or external reward.

This chapter describes the content of a leisure education program that develops opportunities for all people to experience leisure. Leisure education programs designed with the goal of facilitating the leisure experience are needed. This chapter provides a rationale for leisure education for all people, including people with disabilities. The structure and content of a leisure education model are presented to assist professionals in providing comprehensive leisure instruction. The model for leisure education presented in this chapter focuses on facilitating inclusive community leisure experiences for people with disabilities.

This chapter provides the structure and content of a leisure education curriculum for persons with disabilities attempting to successfully transition into adulthood. In addition, the chapter contains leisure participation evaluative procedures that can be used as indicators of successful community adjustment. The model emerged in response to the clear need for leisure education for people with disabilities and is based on previous suggestions identified in articles and texts reported throughout this chapter.

What is leisure education and why is it important?

The term *leisure education* refers to the use of comprehensive models focusing on the educational process to enhance a person's leisure lifestyle. Leisure education provides a vehicle for developing an awareness of recreation activities and resources and for acquiring skills needed for participation throughout the life span. The need for incorporating leisure education into leisure services for persons with disabilities is strong.

Some people with disabilities lack adequate knowledge and skills needed to participate in activities that allow them to experience leisure. Based on the knowledge that specific factors (e.g., self-concept, social skills, and inclusion in community life) can be enhanced through recreation participation and awareness, Bedini, Bullock, and Driscoll (1993) reported that the application of a leisure education program that teaches these skills can prepare individuals with disabilities for life in their communities.

What content could be included in a leisure education program?

Leisure education provides individuals the opportunity to enhance the quality of their lives in leisure; understand opportunities, potentials, and challenges in leisure; understand the impact of leisure on the quality of their lives; and gain knowledge, skills and appreciation enabling broad leisure skills. Therefore, as illustrated in **Figure 12.1** (p. 212), an effective leisure education program could include, but not be limited to, seven major domains:

- awareness of self in leisure,
- appreciation of leisure,
- self-determination in leisure,
- decision-making skills,
- knowledge and utilization of resources,
- social interaction skills, and
- recreation activity skills.

Awareness of Self in Leisure

An important aspect of developing a meaningful leisure lifestyle is to engage in self-examination (Hoge, Dattilo, Schneider & Bemisderfer, 1997).

"Basic to all learning, growth, and positive behavioral change is awareness; therefore an important ingredient of leisure education programs is in assisting participants to explore, discover, and develop knowledge about themselves in a leisure context" (Barry, 1997, p. 6). "Self-examination and self-knowledge must be accurate and comprehensive if one is to make effective life choices autonomously." (Sands & Doll, 1996, p. 61).

To facilitate recreation participation people must possess knowledge of their preferences. When people become aware of what they prefer they are more likely to select and do the things that they enjoy. For example, small groups could go for a brief walk outside and be instructed to identify objects or activities they enjoy. Participants could collect objects or the leader could record the communicated preferences. Upon returning, each group could share the findings. Another learning activity might involve the use of equipment used with various recreation activities such as baseball bat, ice skates, or a skateboard. Participants would be asked to choose equipment associated with their favorite activities. Opportunities for participation in those activities, characteristics of the activities, and previous experience with these activities could be explored.

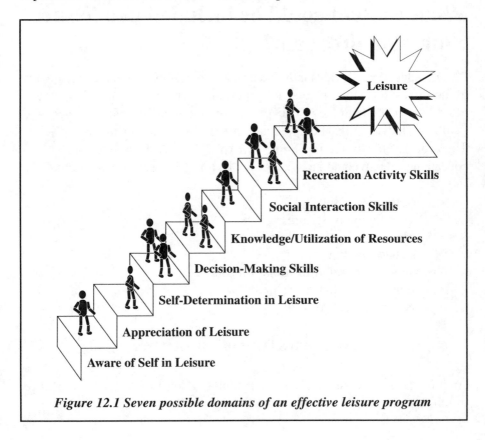

Leisure

Recreation Activity Skills

Social Interaction Skills

Knowledge/Utilization of Resources

Decision-Making Skills

Self-Determination in Leisure

Appreciation of Leisure

Aware of Self in Leisure

Figure 12.1 Seven possible domains of an effective leisure program

Examination of personal attitudes toward leisure may provide individuals with information about their own barriers to leisure participation. One way to have individuals examine their attitudes is to place them in a forced-choice situation.

For example, a room can be divided in half with one half of the room representing one way of approaching leisure participation and the other half of the room representing a different approach such as exciting vs. relaxing, outside vs. inside, alone vs. with others. Participants must go to one side of the room or the other as the leader places large poster-board pictures associated with these concepts on each side of the room. When they arrive at their chosen destination they are asked to talk about the reasons for their selection.

For some people, considering leisure patterns and desires can be valuable. Reflecting on past leisure pursuits may permit people with disabilities to gain insight into skills they possess. Analyzing individuals' current leisure involvement will assist them in identifying activities they enjoy as well as determining barriers they would like to overcome. We can also encourage participants to look beyond their past and present leisure participation patterns and to consider areas for future discovery to enhance motivation for leisure participation.

For example, to help individuals focus on what makes them happy now and what could make them happy in the future, a learning activity could be conducted requiring participants to identify as many enjoyable recreation activities as possible. They could identify these activities by pointing to them in a book, verbalizing them, or drawing them. After they have completed this task, materials associated with one activity chosen by each person could be gathered. Participants can be encouraged to observe or join each individual participating in a chosen activity. Following demonstrations, participants' desire to learn any of the activities presented could be assessed. Exploration of what activities they have yet to master but are motivated to learn about is often helpful.

Appreciation of Leisure

To gain an awareness of leisure, it is useful to develop an appreciation of the concepts of leisure and leisure lifestyle. When people understand these concepts, their ability to participate in satisfying and enjoyable recreation activities will be enhanced.

For example, one way to help individuals gain an understanding of the difference between work and leisure may be achieved by dividing participants into two groups. One group is given paints and brushes and required to paint a specific object on a large piece of paper such as a car. The other group can be provided with the same materials and permitted to paint anything they like. After 10 minutes, have the groups switch tasks. Questions and statements can be made about the differences between the activities and the role freedom plays in leisure participation. By focusing on leisure appreciation, participants can begin to develop sensitivity for the uniqueness of leisure.

Because many people with disabilities have been overprotected, their ability to take personal responsibility for leisure involvement may be reduced. People with disabilities are capable and responsible for their own leisure, and they can change and improve their present leisure status. For example, to encourage a sense of responsibility within individuals, leisure education sessions can be divided into two parts. One portion of the session could involve instruction to teach individuals how to participate in specific recreation activities such as table games. The following portion would permit them to engage in socially acceptable activities of their choosing. During this time they would be in control and responsible for their participation. The amount of time individuals are placed in this situation would vary according to their skills.

Self-Determination in Leisure

Self-determination occurs when people take control of their freedom. According to Wehmeyer (1996), self-determination involves acting as the primary causal agent in one's life—making decisions free from external influence or interference. Self-determination, which includes the perception of freedom to make choices and the ability to initiate chosen leisure activities, is an important consideration in facilitating leisure. Wall and Dattilo (1995) suggested that by creating option-rich, responsive, and informative environments, both participants and professionals would increase the likelihood of becoming self-determined.

After reviewing the literature on leisure education, Bambara and Ager (1992) reported that professionals are advocating a broad-based agenda for leisure education—one that emphasizes choice and the facilitation of self-directed activity along with direct skill instruction. Unfortunately, choice and self-determination have been rarely addressed when facilitating leisure for people with disabilities.

Development of a sense of self-determination facilitates the ability of individuals to make choices and sets the stage for acquisition of more complex decision-making strategies. According to Luken (1993), for leisure education to be effective it must encourage participants to go beyond mere leisure awareness and instill the ability and confidence to take personal action and choose to participate independently in meaningful experiences. (See Chapter 11 for ways to promote self-determination.)

Decision-Making Skills

Some individuals have difficulty making decisions related to many aspects of their lives. Based on observations that persons with disabilities frequently fail to adjust to community living as a result of inappropriate use of free time, Hayes (1977) recommended instruction in decision making and encouraged selection of recreation activities by people with disabilities. Making a decision related to leisure participation is facilitated by individuals' awareness of themselves relative to leisure, appreciation of leisure, and their sense of self-determination in leisure involvement.

One way to teach people decision-making skills is to involve them in a cooperative small group activity. For example, divide participants attending a leisure education session related to camping into small groups. Give each group one backpack and have them enter a storage area containing camping equipment, food, clothing, and other supplies. Ask members to prepare for an overnight hike to a particular location. Participants must select items they will take; however, they can only take what can fit in the backpack. Each group must keep a list of the items they include and identify why they chose the selected items.

Knowledge and Utilization of Resources

Difficulty in making appropriate leisure decisions may result from people's lack of knowledge about leisure resources. Ashton-Shaeffer and Kleiber (1990) reported that a major reason some people with disabilities experience problems adjusting to life in their communities is their lack of awareness of recreation resources. Knowledge of leisure resources and the ability to use these resources appear to be important factors in establishing an independent leisure lifestyle. It can be helpful to teach individuals not only how to participate in an activity but also how to answer questions about leisure options, including:

- Where can one participate?
- With whom can one participate?
- How much does participation cost?
- What type of transportation is available?
- Where could one learn more about a recreation activity?
- What equipment is required?

For example, one way to help people learn about the equipment needed for participation is to have them participate in a matching game that will stimulate their memory and concentration, and provide information on recreation activities and equipment. Two sets of cards, one with names and pictures of activities and one with names and pictures of equipment are placed facedown on a table. The number of cards varies according to participants' skills. The object of the game is to match an activity with the equipment used in the activity by turning over the related cards. A discussion regarding the equipment needed could then occur after each match is made, accompanied by exposure to the actual equipment and activity whenever possible.

In addition to the need for people with disabilities to acquire knowledge of community leisure resources, they must be able to utilize these resources. To encourage use of leisure resources, it is helpful to inform families and friends about the leisure resources available within their community.

Joswiak (1979) developed a leisure education program for people with disabilities emphasizing development of an awareness of leisure resources within the home and community. Anderson and Allen (1985) conducted an investigation incorporating Joswiak's leisure education program with 40 people with disabilities. Upon completion of their study, the investigators concluded that participation in the leisure education program emphasizing knowledge of leisure resources appeared to enhance frequency of activity involvement.

Social Interaction Skills

A lack of social skills prevents many people from developing a satisfying life. Although people with disabilities experience different problems that prevent them from developing a satisfying leisure lifestyle, this remains a prevalent problem (Stumbo, 1995). An absence of social skills is particularly noticeable during leisure participation and frequently leads to isolation and an inability to function (Chadsey-Rusch, 1992). Lord (1997, p. 35) reported:

> The lack of social competencies is in fact the greatest barrier to full inclusion for individuals with disabilities. This is due in a large degree to associated communication deficits, as well as, the lack of social training and opportunities.

After conducting 18 focus groups with people with disabilities, family members, and caregivers, Mahon, Mactavish, and Bockstael (2000) reported that family members and service providers suggested the degree to which the individual with an intellectual disability mastered social skills had " . . . a tremendous impact on the extent to which an individual is socially integrated and the nature of the social integration" (p. 34).

Because peer relationships during childhood and adolescence are critical, social skill instruction for individuals with disabilities is important (Zetlin & Morrison, 1998). Therefore, development of social skills used in leisure situations appears to be important for people with disabilities because acquisition of these skills promotes inclusion. Successful inclusion of participants into leisure services may occur by teaching people how to make verbal statements, maintain eye contact, maintain appropriate physical proximity, make appropriate physical contact, share equipment and materials, cooperate and develop friendships.

For instance, people with disabilities can be instructed to participate in an activity to help them practice how to introduce themselves to a group. In turn, participants will communicate to the group their first name, and for 30 seconds share with the group positive information about themselves such as accomplishments, desirable personal traits, or friendships. Participants will be instructed to communicate only positive information during this time. Leisure education learning activities such as this are designed to encourage social inclusion.

Recreation Activity Skills

Since choice is critical to leisure participation and choice involves options and alternatives, then people must possess a repertoire of recreation activity skills and related interests. We can encourage participants to select and develop recreation skills having the most potential for enjoyment and satisfaction. Therefore, the recreation activity skills that an individual is taught should be based on the individual's needs, interests, motivations, preferences, and aspirations as well as the availability of the activity within their community and available resources such as money, equipment, or clothing needed to participate.

Recreation activity skill development can provide physical and emotional support assisting participants, family members, friends, and community professionals to overcome fears of the unknown and failure. Reduction of fears associated with leisure participation should reduce hesitancy of people to become active participants in community life as well as develop support systems comprised of family members, friends, and professionals. Determination of which recreation activity skills a person is taught should result from participants' preferences, their ability to engage in the recreation activity in the near and distant future.

What processes could be used to deliver a leisure education program?

Leisure education contains three components designed to facilitate meaningful leisure participation for people with disabilities (see **Figure 12.2**). One component involves development and implementation of a leisure education course. This component of the model is supplemented with community support through leisure coaching and family and friend support for leisure participation. Systematic follow-up on community leisure participation facilitates generalization and maintenance of leisure skills and knowledge. This section addresses the following processes:

- leisure education course,
- community support through leisure coaching, and
- family and friend support for leisure participation.

Leisure Education Course

A leisure education program can include a structured course that teaches participants skills that can assist them in actively participating in meaningful and enjoyable experiences. A detailed curriculum for leisure education is identified in *Leisure Education Program Planning: A Systematic Approach* (Dattilo, 1999).

Goals written as general participant outcome statements guide course development. The course goals can be divided into a number of behavioral objectives with corresponding performance measures. A performance measure is a statement of the exact behavior that will be taken as evidence

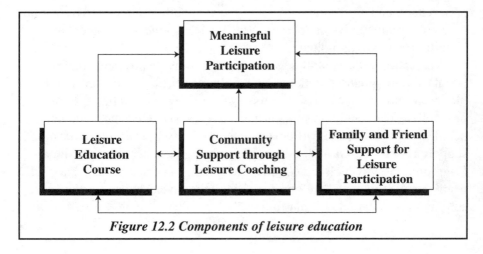

Figure 12.2 Components of leisure education

that the intent of the objective has been achieved. The majority of information contained in the course describes content and process required to conduct the program. Each program's content specifies what is to be done in the program to achieve the intent of the objectives.

Community Support through Leisure Coaching

A leisure education course can be supplemented with systematic community-based leisure instruction and support by a leisure coach. The primary purpose of a leisure coach is to help participants with disabilities become actively involved in existing community leisure services. Initially, leisure coaches can meet with professionals delivering recreation programs to provide collaborative, consultation and support for integration of people with disabilities. As indicated in **Figure 12.3** (p. 220), leisure coaches are available to respond to questions and concerns of the community recreation professional, to act as advocates for both recreation professionals and the people with disabilities, and to provide assistance to participants as needed while they participate in inclusive community recreation activities. A leisure coach can help identify existing community recreation activities that are compatible with interests and skills of the individual with disabilities. In addition, a leisure coach can determine requirements of an activity, assess the skills of the participant, and identify if specific accommodations are required.

Leisure coaching can occur in conjunction with a formal leisure education course permitting skill enhancement and alleviation of identified barriers to leisure participation. To facilitate participant independence and autonomy, as well as create a more cost-effective system, the presence of the leisure coach is phased out systematically as the person with a disability gains skills and confidence.

In summary, the leisure coach acts as a support person. The leisure coach gives support to recreation professionals conducting programs that include people with disabilities while providing support directly to participants to help them participate in community recreation programs of their choosing.

Family and Friend Support for Leisure Participation

Parent, guardian, sibling, and friend participation in the process of leisure education can be stimulated by providing workshops designed to increase their ability to promote independent leisure functioning for the person with disabilities. The workshops can highlight information communicated in the leisure education course, focusing on identifying leisure resources available in the community.

Family and friend participation can be encouraged through regular meetings that inform them of accomplishments and problems experienced

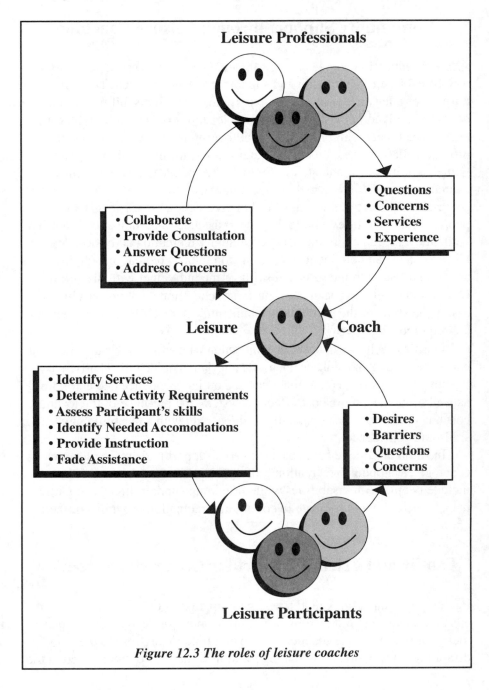

Leisure Professionals

• Questions
• Concerns
• Services
• Experience

• Collaborate
• Provide Consultation
• Answer Questions
• Address Concerns

Leisure   **Coach**

• Identify Services
• Determine Activity Requirements
• Assess Participant's skills
• Identify Needed Accomodations
• Provide Instruction
• Fade Assistance

• Desires
• Barriers
• Questions
• Concerns

Leisure Participants

Figure 12.3 The roles of leisure coaches

by the person at community recreation agencies. Strategies encouraging continuation of participants' successful efforts and methods for reducing barriers to community leisure involvement can be addressed.

What are some examples of leisure education programs?

The programs described in this section are just a few examples of how leisure service providers have begun to develop leisure education services for people experiencing a variety of challenges. Great value exists in community leisure service providers offering programs that go beyond diversional recreation activities and incorporate efforts to systematically provide leisure education. The programs described here include:

- promote health,
- decrease stress associated with caring for an older adult,
- increase satisfaction of adults,
- contribute to adolescent development,
- enhance the lives of children and youth, and
- decrease free time boredom.

Promote Health

Payne, Orsega-Smith, Spangler, and Godbey (1999) encouraged local parks and recreation agencies to offer community-based leisure education programs that focus on health promotion. Such programs allow community members to bridge the gap between clinical rehabilitation and public recreation and park services. Besides being affordable, accessible, and attractive, local park and recreation agencies offer a variety of programs and facilities that make them ideal for offering health promotion programs. To illustrate the possibility of using leisure education to promote good health, Payne and colleagues (p. 74) provided the following example:

> For an older person who is recovering from a health problem, initial involvement in community recreation and park services may be limited to physical activity programs. However, to ensure long-term adoption of enjoyable physical activity, recreation and park staff could conduct individualized or small-group leisure education counseling sessions. In these sessions, staff could help older people identify and encourage involvement in other self-chosen, meaningful, enjoyable, and beneficial sponsored recreational activities.

Decrease Stress Associated with Caring for an Older Adult

With the increasing number of older adults in our society, especially those residing in their communities, many people will experience caring for an older adult at home. As more adults are in need of long-term assistance, the people providing their care experience stress (Perlin Mullan, Semple & Skaff, 1990). Hagan, Green, and Starling (1998) proposed a leisure education program designed to decrease stress associated with caring for an elderly adult. The leisure education program proposed by Hagan and colleagues included personal time management, information about leisure activities, information about leisure support resources, ways to develop leisure appreciation, and ways to develop awareness of self in leisure.

Increase Satisfaction of Adults

Mahon and Martens (1996) demonstrated that adults with cognitive limitations enhanced their leisure satisfaction and increased their community adjustment as a result of participating in a leisure education program that included leisure awareness, personal futures planning, and action planning. Using a modified version of the leisure education program, Mahon and Goatcher (1999) observed that after involvement in a program that helped participants plan for later life, adults with mental retardation increased their leisure and life satisfaction significantly more than their peers who did not participate in such a program.

Contribute to Adolescent Development

Since leisure provides opportunities for individuals to experiment with self-expression and various roles, it is an important context for adolescent development (Larson, 1994). However, Caldwell and Smith (1998) warned that this same leisure context is where many unhealthy behaviors occur, such as cigarette smoking, alcohol and other drug use, and early promiscuous sexual intercourse. Therefore, there is value in developing leisure education programs for adolescents that teach them about leisure opportunities in their communities so that an alternative to high-risk behaviors, such as promiscuous sexual behaviors that may lead to HIV infection, can be avoided. Risisky, Caldwell, and Fors (1997) suggested that a leisure education program for adolescents emphasize leisure skills building, decision making, and enhancing self-esteem.

Enhance the Lives of Children and Youth

A primary goal of leisure education in the schools should be the development of free time and leisure-related skills that enhance the quality of daily life for children and youth (Heyne & Schleien, 1997). Provision of leisure education in the school setting can create optimal environments for achieving students' goals related to inclusion. Specifically it can encourage refinement of social skills, promote social interactions, and develop friendships between classmates with and without disabilities. Since recreation and play are important aspects of the socialization and education of children, leisure education can play a vital role in the growth, maturation, and quality of life of young people.

Decrease Free Time Boredom

Lee, Mittlstaedt, and Askins (1999) encouraged leisure service providers to design leisure education programs for people experiencing free time boredom, focusing on enhancing participants' awareness of self in leisure. Such programs could encourage individuals to explore, discover, and develop knowledge about themselves in a leisure context. Within the context of such educational programs, practitioners may find it helpful to assist participants to explore new alternative values, goals, and leisure activities. According to Lee and colleagues, participation in meaningful leisure education programs can help people experiencing free time boredom make important, positive changes to their lives.

Final Thoughts

A primary purpose of leisure services is to meet the leisure needs of participants. Our ability to meet the needs of people with disabilities is impaired without effective service delivery systems. This chapter identified the need and rationale for including leisure education in inclusive leisure services. Information provided support for people with disabilities having difficulty experiencing meaningful leisure. The suggestions for leisure education intend to encourage participants to develop characteristics that facilitate successful inclusion in community life.

Discussion Questions

1. What is leisure education?
2. What is meant by awareness of self in leisure?
3. How could people attending a leisure education program develop an appreciation of leisure?
4. Why is self-determination an important component of a comprehensive leisure education program?
5. What are some components of the decision-making process?
6. What are some questions relative to leisure resources that are important for people to be able to answer?
7. What are some examples of important social interaction skills when participating in inclusive leisure services?
8. What are some guidelines to follow when teaching recreation activity skills?
9. What are some actions that could be taken to develop a course on leisure education?
10. What are the primary responsibilities of a leisure coach?
11. How could family and friends be included in leisure education?
12. What are some examples of leisure education programs?

Chapter 13

Promote Social Interactions and Friendships

A candle loses none of its light by lighting another candle.
-Taylor

Orientation Activity: Connecting People

Directions Alone: Choose an agency with which you are familiar or imagine an ideal job. List at least five different ways you could encourage participants to get to know one another and promote the development of friendships between participants with and without disabilities.

Directions with Others: Move about the room with your list, find a person, and introduce yourself. Discuss one idea you had about encouraging friendship and have the person identify one different idea. Record the person's name and her or his idea on your list. Once you have discussed the information move to another person. Continue this process until you have shared all the items on your list. See how many different ideas you can list by talking to as many people as possible.

Debriefing: If given the choice, most people want to participate in inclusive recreation activities. Often the degree to which people enjoy an activity is based on their social interactions with other participants. Continued participation is often linked to the relationships they have developed with their peers involved in the same activity. Consider the following questions when thinking about connecting people:

- How might we prepare a situation to help people interact?
- How can we encourage social interactions between participants?
- How might we help to develop friendships among participants?

Introduction

Development of relationships—the core of inclusion—involves providing support to help people who have been devalued establish relationships with valued members of their community. For people to have access to valued social roles, they need to grow and learn with their peers. Dolnick (1993, p. 43) reported:

> Historically, advocates for every disabled group have directed their fiercest fire at policies that exclude their group. No matter the good intentions, no matter the logistical hurdles, they have insisted, separate is not equal. Thus buildings, buses, classes, must be accessible to all; special accommodations for the disabled are not a satisfactory substitute. All this has become part of conventional wisdom. Today, under the general heading of "mainstreaming," it is enshrined in law and unchallenged as a premise of enlightened thought.

With a growing preference of people with disabilities and their families for inclusive leisure programs and legislation supporting and mandating services for people with disabilities in inclusive community environments, leisure services professionals must be prepared to provide services to people with disabilities in inclusive settings. Unfortunately, despite research showing benefits of people developing relationships through inclusion, implementation has been slow and has sometimes been met with resistance.

This chapter includes two major areas. The first addresses information about benefits of inclusive leisure services that primarily relate to the provision of opportunities for social interaction and development of friendships. A variety of groups of people can benefit from inclusive leisure services, including people with and without disabilities and leisure services providers. The second covers ways to foster social interactions and ultimately encourage development of friendships. Prior to the activity we can prepare people and situations so that positive interactions between all participants are encouraged. In addition, we can take various actions while an activity is occurring to promote positive contacts between participants.

What are benefits of inclusion for people with disabilities?

Some people assume that only people with disabilities experience the benefits of inclusion; however, people without disabilities can experience benefits of inclusive leisure participation. Inclusive leisure participation prepares people with disabilities for life in a diverse society, and prepares society to accept individual diversity. While there are many benefits of inclusion, greater social acceptance by peers and social inclusion into the community may be the most important (Favazza, Phillipsen & Kumar, 2000).

By including all people in community programs, people with disabilities prepare for life in their community, practitioners improve their professional skills, and, according to Karagiannis and colleagues (1996), society makes the conscious decision to operate according to the social value of equality for all people. Some of the benefits of inclusion are that participants:

- cultivate friendships,
- acquire social skills,
- engage in social interactions,
- develop life-long skills,
- enhance their image,
- observe role models, and
- improve academic performance.

Cultivate Friendships

People with disabilities can develop friendships with other participants when they participate in inclusive community leisure programs. Sable (1992) reported that youth with and without disabilities were able to develop spontaneous friendships that emerged out of shared interests as a result of an inclusive leisure experience.

For example, Dwayne and Marcia reported that as a result of developing friendships during participation in a community recreation program, their daughter Sasha was invited to birthday parties, received telephone calls from friends, and had friends come over to her house to play.

When parents are asked about what they want for their children, often they indicate that they want their child to have friends. For example, in a report to the U.S. President (U. S. Department of Health and Human Services, 1994) Linda Charlton talked about her dreams for her 2-year-old daughter, Katie, who has Down syndrome (a condition that frequently leads to mental retardation):

Our goals for Katie include wanting her to feel loved, to give her a sense of high self-esteem so that she can experience life with confidence. She is a very social child and while I think she has a great capacity to make friends, I wonder how other children will accept her. (p. 2)

Hultsman (1993) reported that activities that permit interaction with a person's peers provide opportunities for shared interests, a sense of accomplishment and belonging, and personal identity and mastery over the environment. Inclusive leisure services help to reduce barriers and create a forum for emerging relationships.

Acquire Social Skills

People with disabilities are more likely to develop social skills needed to develop relationships when participating in inclusive leisure opportunities. For example, Cole and Meyer (1991) reported that children with severe disabilities in inclusive environments improve their social competence, whereas those in segregated settings did not.

Since having friends is important to the quality of every person's life, people with disabilities learn best when learning what their friends are learning. Kliewer (1999) reported that inclusive environments give people a chance to learn to get along with others, interact, seek and lend assistance, understand when assistance is needed, make sense of changing contexts, ask questions, communicate with others, and behave appropriately.

Engage in Social Interactions

After observing play groups that contained children with and without disabilities and groups that contained only children with disabilities, Guralnick and Groom (1988) concluded that inclusive play groups facilitated peer interaction, whereas segregated play groups constrained peer interaction and promoted adult-child interaction. In addition, Dreimanus and colleagues (1992) reported that children with severe disabilities interacted more often with other children when they were in inclusive environments, and that preschoolers with disabilities exhibited more socially advanced skills in inclusive settings. Schleien, Ray, Soderman-Olson, and McMahon (1987) also observed that social behaviors and interactions of children with disabilities increased during an inclusive art education program.

Develop Life-Long Skills

The presence of appropriate inclusive options promotes development of life-long functional recreation skills. People with disabilities can learn appropriate interdependent behaviors such as asking for assistance as needed by experiencing challenges that are part of inclusive community life. Enjoyment associated with leisure participation can reward different levels of ability, if professionals encourage valuing each individual's contribution.

Enhance Their Image

Storey, Stern, and Parker (1991) examined the attitudes of college students towards a woman with disabilities participating in either Special Olympics or in typical recreation activities within an inclusive setting. The research-ers reported that in the Special Olympics presentation, the woman was regarded as younger and more in need of segregated treatment settings than in the typical activities presentation. This investigation lends support to the belief that the image of a person with disabilities is higher with inclusive participation as opposed to segregated participation.

Observe Role Models

Inclusive recreation environments provide role models that promote age-appropriate participation for people with disabilities. For example, Stainback and Stainback (1987) reported that participants without disabilities pro-vided models of age-appropriate dress, language, gestures, and social behavior for their peers with disabilities. Inclusive play opportunities stimulate and motivate children with disabilities, offering them opportuni-ties to imitate and model play behaviors of their peers without disabilities (McGill, 1984).

Improve Academic Performance

Individuals with disabilities who are involved in inclusive programs do better academically and socially than comparable individuals in segregated environments (Baker, Wang & Walberg, 1995). After conducting longitu-dinal observations of the performance of students with disabilities in public schools, Rankin and colleagues (1994) concluded that all children who were in inclusive classrooms were doing better than they did in previous years when they were in self-contained classrooms. Parents reported that for their children with disabilities inclusion has resulted in removing barriers to learning, using increased vocabulary, employing coping strategies during difficult situations, being less dependent on parents, being more interactive with peers, and reducing inappropriate behaviors (Ryndak et al., 1995).

In summary, people with disabilities accrue many benefits from participating in inclusive leisure services. The most prominent benefits associated with inclusion relate to participants' abilities to engage in social interactions with their peers and develop meaningful friendships.

What are benefits of inclusion for people without disabilities?

When discussing benefits of inclusion, people often focus on the benefits experienced by people with disabilities. Although benefits to individuals with disabilities are numerous, benefits to people without disabilities are also plentiful. Learning to live, work, and play with people who are different is a critical part of a person's development (Passentino & Cranfield, 1994). In inclusive communities:

> people are enriched by having the opportunity to learn from one another, grow to care for one another, and gain the attitudes, skills, and values necessary for our communities to support the inclusion of all citizens. (Vandercook et al., 1989, p. 19)

People without disabilities acquire many benefits from participating in inclusive programs. Through regular social contacts with individuals with disabilities people without disabilities:

- improve attitudes,
- increase understanding,
- develop acceptance,
- experience personal growth,
- increase understanding, and
- improve social development.

Improve Attitudes

People who are not disabled often positively alter their attitudes about individuals with disabilities as a result of joint participation in selected activities. For example, Schleien and colleagues (1987) reported that after participation in an inclusive art education program, the attitudes of children without disabilities toward their peers with disabilities changed positively. Carefully planned inclusive programs result in positive developmental and attitudinal outcomes for young children without disabilities (McLean & Hanline, 1990).

Increase Understanding

Enjoyment of recreation and education opportunities that reward different levels of ability can occur when people value each individual's contribution. According to Schleien and Green (1992), exposure to inclusive leisure services results in a greater understanding and acceptance of individuals with varying backgrounds and ability levels, creating the potential for integration to have a positive impact on the social development of all individuals.

When involved in inclusive programs, people without disabilities become more accepting of differences and begin to appreciate the capacities of persons with disabilities (Ray & Meidl, 1991). The following quote from the Georgia Advocacy Office (1992) illustrates the benefits people without disabilities receive when participating in inclusive programs:

> Our world includes a vast array of people who, we believe, are more alike than different. We have watched education become more and more exclusive in the definition of which students "belong" in the regular classroom. We believe that what children learn from each other about difference and acceptance is equally as important as the technical education that they receive. We all need to learn how to live and work together (p. 4). Students develop more fully when they welcome people with different gifts and abilities into their lives and when all students feel secure that they will receive individualized help when they need it (p. 9).

Develop Acceptance

By encouraging and facilitating inclusive leisure opportunities for all community members, leisure services professionals can contribute to the acceptance of people with disabilities by people without disabilities. Leisure services professionals can take an active role in reducing social stigmas associated with persons with disabilities by emphasizing similarities rather than differences. Brown and colleagues (1989) concluded that long-term interactions between people with severe disabilities and people without disabilities facilitate development of skills, attitudes and values that will prepare both groups to be sharing, participating, and contributing members of complex communities.

Galambos and colleagues (1994) stated that as a result of participation in inclusive leisure services people without disabilities learn new ways to solve problems and adapt to difference, develop more positive attitudes toward people with disabilities, and increase acceptance of people in general. Similarly, after surveying 1413 high school students from two high schools (one inclusive and one segregated), Fisher, Pupian, and Sax (1998) found that youth educated in an inclusive setting expected and recommended the inclusion of youth with disabilities. However, if youth attended a school that provided limited inclusion, they expected and recommended segregation. Fisher and colleagues argued that, as a group, youth who had the inclusive experience are better prepared for their adult life since they will likely encounter people with disabilities in the community and in their jobs.

Experience Personal Growth

As a result of participation in inclusive leisure opportunities, many people report that they experience personal growth and increased social sensitivity, including improved capacity for compassion, kindness, and respect for others. Others report that they develop skills and attitudes needed to live harmoniously in communities that include people with and without disabilities.

Improve Social Development

Kliewer (1998) noted that researchers have consistently found improved social development—such as feelings of self-worth, communication and interaction abilities, leadership skills, and tolerance of diversity—for children without disabilities involved in inclusive environments. After a review of the research literature, Kliewer concluded that children without disabilities included in classrooms with children with mild to severe disabilities achieved at levels equal to or above their peers in classes that do not include children with disabilities.

Helmstetter and colleagues (1994) asked 166 high school students without disabilities to indicate their agreement or disagreement with a variety of outcome statements related to inclusion. The adolescents reported that inclusive experiences:

- increased responsiveness to the needs of others,
- encouraged valued relationships with people with disabilities,
- increased tolerance of other people,
- developed personal values,
- increased appreciation of human diversity, and
- promoted positive changes in personal status with peers.

In summary, benefits of an inclusive leisure opportunity extend beyond leisure services providers and the participants with disabilities. All people benefit from inclusion.

What are benefits of inclusion for leisure services providers?

Leisure services providers also experience benefits associated with having diverse individuals access our services together. Inclusive services can encourage us to:

- increase our acceptance, and
- improve our financial situation.

Increase Our Acceptance

As leisure services agencies embrace the concept of inclusion and respond to the needs of a diverse participant group, they comply with the ADA. According to Galambos and colleagues (1994), by providing inclusive services, leisure services providers are exposed to and educated about individual needs, and subsequently they increase their acceptance of people in general.

Improve Our Financial Situation

While there are many benefits to inclusion from educational, social, and psychological perspectives, benefits of inclusion are also realized from an economic standpoint. After examining the instructional costs of inclusive schooling for one school district, Salisbury and Chambers (1994) concluded that providing inclusive services was substantially less expensive than contracting for segregated services. Referring to the economic benefit of inclusion, Tiersten (1994, p. 4) made the following statement:

Ultimately, inclusion could help, rather than harm, the bottom line. In ignoring people with disabilities, organizations are missing a superb business opportunity. "Americans with disabilities are an emerging market," according to Steven Hacker, president of the Dallas-based International Association for Exposition Management.

How can we prepare people to promote social interactions and friendships?

Although the ADA and other civil rights legislation mandate agencies to accommodate individuals of varying abilities both architecturally and programmatically, often these agencies only remove architectural barriers. Unfortunately, physical access and physical proximity between people with and without disabilities does not in and of itself ensure positive results.

Without programmatic access, participants without disabilities continue to view their peers with disabilities and inclusion efforts negatively (Schleien, 1993). Many programmatic strategies can be used to encourage the inclusion of people with disabilities into community leisure programs. This section highlights the following strategies to prepare people to help encourage social interaction and develop friendships:

- be aware of isolation,
- learn about benefits of friendships,
- teach leisure services providers,
- assess participants interest, and
- include people in planning and decision making.

Be Aware of Isolation

People with disabilities are most often isolated from their peers without disabilities if interactions are left to chance (Hutchison, 1990). Hanline (1993) reported that children without disabilities tend to communicate with other children without disabilities more often than they communicate with peers with disabilities. They choose other children without disabilities as playmates and friends more often than they choose children with disabilities and prefer to sit next to peers without disabilities in group activities. Children without disabilities do not interact with their peers with disabilities unless they are supported and encouraged to do so (Favazza et al., 2000).

Typically, people who have limited social networks usually spend their free time alone, with family, with friends of family, or in structured group activities with other people with disabilities (Hutchison & McGill, 1992). Therefore, it is important that we encourage interactions at a very young age and help people without disabilities understand and respond to the unique behaviors of peers with disabilities so that they may develop meaningful friendships.

Learn about Benefits of Friendships

The impact of leisure participation on social support is likely to be significant for those who have limited friends or few social contacts. Friendships serve many important functions for children, including teaching social skills, encouraging separation from parents, developing a sense of autonomy, enhancing self-esteem, instilling a sense of belonging to a community, achieving feelings of intimacy, being assured of being valued and loved, and enriching quality of life.

Larson, Zuzanek, and Mannell (1985) concluded that regular social contact through leisure activities helps overcome a considerable deficit in perceived social support for people who are isolated. By engaging in leisure pursuits conducive to social interaction, Coleman and Iso-Ahola (1993) suggested that people are more likely to make friends and develop closer friendships.

Teach Leisure Services Providers

Another way to prepare people for inclusion is to provide training for all leisure services personnel. Possible topics for training include presentations on the rationale for inclusive leisure that address the benefits of inclusive leisure services for people with and without disabilities, information about the Americans with Disabilities Act and how it supports inclusion, and information on the value of social interactions, friendships, and inclusion.

Roles and responsibilities of people who contribute to inclusive services, such as parents, participants, advocacy groups, schools, and leisure services professionals, can be identified through staff training situations. It can be helpful to describe specific strategies for promoting social interactions between participants, ways to develop meaningful friendships, and how to design services that foster inclusion, such as encouraging accepting attitudes, implementing program methods to attract and support individuals, evaluating and soliciting feedback, and developing networks and resources.

Assess Participant Interests

It can be helpful to administer surveys and questionnaires to obtain input from potential participants about their interests and desires. To discover people's needs and interests one should not rely solely on surveys but observe participants' expressions and ways of communicating as they participate. Participants can be provided with repeated opportunities to choose between two or more activities to establish a preference profile.

Once preferences are identified, we can encourage people to act on their interests and provide opportunities to learn and to practice leisure skills in various settings. Dreimanus and colleagues (1992) reported that grouping children by mutual interests helped increase acceptance of children with disabilities by their peers and promoted social connections.

Include People in Planning and Decision Making

Some professionals have found value in involving participants and families when designing modifications that promote social interaction and participation in inclusive programs. The act of soliciting feedback can facilitate inclusion and identify ways to promote social interactions. An invitation to people with disabilities and their family members to assist in staff development can be an effective way to promote social interactions and develop a context for development of friendships. The designation of a staff person to be a facilitator of inclusive experiences and to promote positive social interactions may also be useful. Another approach involves including statements in promotional literature on policies of inclusion giving potential participants someone to contact.

How can we prepare the situation to foster social interactions and friendships?

Positive interaction between people with and without disabilities can be increased by limiting space, selecting materials and activities that promote social interaction, and rotating and limiting materials (Favazza et al., 2000). To address the issue of how to prepare the situation so that it will foster social interactions and the development of friendships, this section is divided into the following areas:

- design cooperative activities,
- divide participants into small groups,

- provide a small area for participation, and
- choose interactive materials and equipment.

Design Cooperative Activities

Activities that require cooperation can facilitate inclusion. A cooperative learning structure can create interdependence between people because completion of a task by a group requires that everyone contribute in some way. Each person should encourage all other participants to achieve realistic group goals (Ivory & McCollum, 1999).

Participation in joint activities may result in peer acceptance and interaction between children with and without disabilities. For example, Green and DeCoux (1994) reported that modified rules of a basketball league promoted the inclusion of a child using a wheelchair. Rynders and Schleien (1991) recommended that to facilitate cooperative interactions we should provide prompts for positive interactions when these behaviors are not occurring, reinforce positive interactions as they occur, and redirect behaviors if participants get off task.

Divide Participants into Small Groups

After reviewing the literature, Chandler, Fowler, and Lubeck (1992) reported that peer interaction typically occurs more often in small groups that contain two or three people. As the number of people becomes smaller, the opportunity for expression is typically enhanced, and thereby creates situations conducive to social interaction.

Provide a Small Area for Participation

A small area in which activities are enjoyed stimulates interaction and integration. Small areas result in more peer interaction than large play areas (Brown, Fox & Brady, 1987). Peer interaction occurred more often when children with disabilities were within 1 or 2 feet of each other than when they were 10 feet apart (Speigel-McGill, Bambara, Shores & Fox, 1984).

Choose Interactive Materials and Equipment

Limited numbers and varieties of materials tend to promote sharing and positive peer interaction (Skellenger, McEvoy, McConnell & Odom, 1991). Specific types of toys such as cars, games, gross motor equipment, and sociodramatic materials promote peer interaction, whereas other toys such as clay, books, and puzzles inhibit social interaction (Chandler et al., 1992).

Ivory and McCollum (1999) identified that clay, LEGO toys, books, paints, paintbrushes, paper, scissors, crayons, markers, and puzzles tend to isolate children, while blocks, dress-up clothes, dolls, dollhouse, house-keeping materials, puppets, and vehicles tend to promote social interaction. When they compared the behaviors of young children involved in an inclusive playgroup they noted that cooperative play occurred significantly more often with the social toys as compared to the isolating toys.

How can we manage an activity so that social interactions and friendships are encouraged?

Leisure services providers can take various actions to encourage people to interact with one another while engaged in leisure pursuits. These interactions can act as the foundation for development of friendships. Some of the strategies include:

- teach social skills,
- encourage age-appropriate behaviors,
- provide social support,
- promote development of peer companions, and
- foster friendships

Teach Social Skills

Placing children in the same physical environment without any assistance does not necessarily lead to social interaction or social acceptance between children with and without disabilities. Programs that teach children with disabilities social skills or how to initiate and respond to peers' social contacts can promote positive peer interactions. Systematic efforts to allow children to interact frequently with a small, stable group of peers is likely to lead to some increase in interaction between children with and without disabilities (Antia & Kreimeyer, 1992).

Encourage Age-Appropriate Behaviors

Treat participants with disabilities the same as others their age by expecting them to be as independent as possible, encouraging others to interact with them, supporting and assisting only when necessary, and encouraging accomplishments. Compare a participant's abilities to what is expected of all participants, and if there are aspects of the activity that a person cannot perform independently, problem solve to determine what types of supports are needed. Emphasize using age-appropriate materials and methods, accommodating for individual patterns of development, learning through interacting with peers, teaching within natural environments, and using meaningful routines when providing services that include people with disabilities (Hanline & Fox, 1993).

Provide Social Support

To facilitate friendships it is important for us to provide needed social supports. Supports can range from incorporating volunteers to providing helpful reminders to assisting people with equipment to providing help during some aspects of participation. Regardless of the level of support, it is helpful if participants learn and to become independent and interdependent in recreation activities.

Although independence is discussed frequently as a goal for all people, another important goal associated with development and maintenance of friends is interdependence. *Interdependence* implies a reciprocal relationship where we depend on another person as she or he helps us and, in turn, that person depends on us as we help him or her.

Promote Development of Peer Companions

Peer companions promote positive social interactions between people with and without disabilities. All people should be encouraged to view the relationship between two peers as being relatively equal. Goldstein, Kaczmarek, Pennington, and Schafer (1992) reported that peers can be taught to encourage social interaction between children with and without disabilities in inclusive settings, and it is helpful to teach peers with and without disabilities to interact with each other.

Foster Friendships

Leisure is an excellent social context for the development of friendships and for the expression of social identities (Kleiber & Rickards, 1985). Friendships developed and fostered through leisure participation and perceived availability of social support generated by leisure engagement help people cope with stress as well as maintain or improve health (Coleman & Iso-Ahola, 1993).

According to Coleman and Iso-Ahola (1993) friendships may be facilitated by situations characterized by perceived freedom and intrinsic motivation (e.g., leisure). As an example, Rook (1987) suggested that choosing to be with a companion in free time communicates to the companion the existence of a close relationship. In another example, Larson, Mannell, and Zuzanek (1986) reported that the ability of friends to generate positive feelings is partly associated with a greater rate of active leisure activities with them.

Inclusive leisure participation can play an important role in facilitating the development of friendships. The leisure context can encourage friendships because it gives people something to do together, a reason for spending time together, and a way to get to know one another through shared experiences.

What are examples of inclusive leisure programs that promote social interaction and friendships?

There are numerous examples of leisure programs that encourage interaction between people with and without disabilities and the subsequent development of friendships, including:

- fitness and leisure for everyone,
- bankshot,
- every buddy,
- shared interest at home, and
- acting together.

Fitness and Leisure for Everyone

People with and without disabilities were encouraged to participate in inclusive recreation activities during a special event entitled "Recreation and Fitness for Everyone" (Weirs, 1988). This event lasted for three hours and featured activities led by university athletes, people with disabilities, and members of Hand in Hand, a nonprofit organization designed to promote community awareness and integration for individuals with mental, physical, social, and emotional disabilities. Activities included aerobics led by a woman with a hearing impairment; wheelchair games; soccer, coordinated by a man with mental retardation in conjunction with a player from the university team; beep ball, a baseball game featuring a noise-making ball that permits people with low vision to participate; and a sing-a-long performed by people with and without hearing impairments. In addition, an information table was provided where people registered to volunteer for future Hand in Hand events and obtained information about inclusion and diversity.

Bankshot

Miller (1991) reported on "Bankshot," a modified version of basketball that allows participants with and without disabilities to compete with one another. The nonexclusionary basketball contest was developed so that entire families can play. Although the configuration of the ball and rim is not modified, the rim has been lowered to eight feet from the floor, different backboards have been designed, and running and jumping is not permitted.

The format for Bankshot is similar to miniature golf, with 18 stations plus a tiebreaker in an area approximately half the size of a tennis court. The stations have uniquely shaped backboards that require different types of shots. At each hoop, the shooter takes aim from three different circles on the ground. A complete circuit usually takes approximately 45 minutes. Distance and difficulty of the shots determine points. Bonus points are gained by hitting from all three circles at any given station. Bankshot is being played at miniature golf courses and parks in over 60 cities across the United States and in Israel.

Every Buddy

Ledman, Thompson and Hill (1992) reported on a cost-effective program—the Every Buddy Program—developed to provide supervised after-school services to children with multiple disabilities. Participants were included in the YMCA programs by adding trained staff to three of the YMCA's after-school program sites. These personnel provided individualized support needed by children with disabilities to participate in the program alongside their peers. Parents strongly agreed that the environment was safe, children were eager to attend the program and were participating in activities, and the needs of families and children were being met. They enjoyed telling others that their children were attending the program.

The YMCA staff felt that children with and without disabilities benefited from the effort and that there had been no negative response to the program from the parents of children without disabilities. To the contrary,

the parents of the children with disabilities reported that they were frequently approached by the other parents who expressed not only acceptance of the children with disabilities but also gratitude that their children
had the opportunity to be with people with disabilities.

Shared Interests at Home

Montgomery (1992) reported that when a child meets another child who is
different, they are naturally curious and may ask uncomfortable questions.
The child without the disability may not have the experience to handle the
situation, and the child with the disability may not have had much experience meeting new people.

A parent reported that the quickest way to help young visitors connect
with her son was to suggest that he show them his room. Once there, his
model horses collection, rather than his disability, usually became the
center of attention. As interests are shared, or skills identified, acceptance
and integration is enhanced. A child with a disability who knows sign
language can teach some simple signs to new friends or a child who is
competent with the computer or card games might invite guests to play.

Acting Together

Miller, Rynders, and Schleien (1993) reported on the results of a project
entitled "Acting Together," a drama class incorporating theater games and
improvisational acting experiences for children. According to the authors,
"Acting Together" demonstrated the value of creative drama as an approach to promote inclusion. Since drama is essentially a social art, it does
not exist in the absence of an audience or in the absence of a society of
players (actors). This quality may make it a particularly useful medium
when participants have very limited repertoires of social skills.

Final Thoughts

At the center of feeling included in one's community is the ability to
experience leisure with friends. Mahon and colleagues (2000, p. 28) quoted
Martin, a man with an intellectual disability, as saying:

> I know what integration means! It means coffee with friends,
> walks to the mall with friends, getting together with people who
> like to do stuff you like, having a good time and being included.

There are many social benefits that are realized when inclusive leisure services are provided. As an example, Linda Preston made the following statement about her 12-year-old son (U. S. Department of Health and Human Services, 1994):

> We went to a forest preserve one weekend and a group of young people had an impromptu concert with bongos, drums, and other instruments. We went over to listen. One of them gave Elisha some maracas. And for the next hour, Elisha was just one of the band, making music, dancing and keeping the beat. They didn't see his disabilities. They just saw the music in him. (p. 36)

Discussion Questions

1. What are some benefits of inclusion for people with disabilities?
2. What are some benefits of inclusion for people without disabilities?
3. What are some benefits of inclusion for leisure services providers?
4. How can cooperatively structured leisure activities be designed to promote social interactions?
5. What are the benefits associated with developing friendships?
6. Why is it important to foster age-appropriate behaviors to stimulate social interactions?
7. How does the size of a group influence social interactions?
8. What kinds of play and recreation materials promote social interactions?
9. What is the value of including people in the leisure services planning process?
10. What are some examples of successful inclusive efforts?

Chapter 14

Make Reasonable Adaptations

The more things change, the more they are the same.
-Alphonse Karr

Orientation Activity: Be Flexible and Change

Directions Alone: Record the name of a recreation activity that requires materials or equipment for participation. Keeping this recreation activity in mind, answer the following questions to encourage you to make adaptations to your programs.

Directions with Others: Attempt to find other people who chose the same recreation activity as you. Share your ideas about making adaptations with the other person(s) in your group. After a specified time, discuss what you have learned with the entire group.

- What materials or equipment could be changed to promote inclusion of people with disabilities?
- What aspects of the activity could be changed to promote inclusion of people with disabilities?
- What about the environment could be changed to promote inclusion of people with disabilities?
- What could be changed about the way we teach to promote inclusion of people with disabilities?

Debriefing: When attempting to adapt existing recreation programs to meet the needs of current participants, many facets of a given program can be considered. As you reflect on the orientation activity, respond to the following questions:

- What is the value of making adaptations for people with disabilities that provide them with the opportunity to participate in community recreation programs with their families and friends?

- What can you do in your current or future position to encourage personnel to make adaptations that facilitate participation by people with disabilities?
- What can you do to maintain the enjoyment of all participants when making adaptations for one person or only a few people?

Introduction

Making adaptations to materials, activities, the environment, participants, and instructional strategies can make the difference between a person being excluded from participation or being included. It is clear that adaptations can have a positive impact on individuals' leisure participation. There are many examples of how simple and creative adaptations have resulted in successful leisure participation.

Leisure services providers must possess the knowledge and skills needed to make adaptations and be prepared to make accommodations based on the individual's abilities and limitations (LeConey, Devine, Bunker & Montgomery, 2000). Adaptations are a vital component in effective inclusion efforts. Appropriate activities draw on individual's strengths and allow participants to learn from each other (Hunt & Goetz, 1997). Making adaptations to skills, rules, and equipment makes it possible for us to meet the needs of individuals with disabilities participating in inclusive settings. People should not be separated from their peers and friends because the program requires adaptation and modifications; rather, these adaptations must be made so that inclusion can be achieved.

After surveying 484 community leisure services agencies, Schleien, Germ, and McAvoy (1996) reported that both rural and urban agencies cited adaptations of program materials and environments and partial participation strategies as the techniques most frequently implemented to serve participants with disabilities. Similarly, Devine and colleagues (1998) reported results of a survey of park and recreation professionals and found that difficulty with program modifications was the fourth most common problem encountered when implementing inclusion in recreation. When interviewed about inclusion practices, elementary physical education instructors reported that they frequently modified their instructional plans, the equipment they used, and opportunities for practice (LaMaster et al., 1998).

This chapter, devoted to adaptations, encourages us to modify our programs as necessary. When needed, these adaptations should permit us to meet the varying needs and abilities of the people receiving leisure services. The suggestions for adaptations are not intended to be complete. They are, however, intended to communicate some options to make accommodations that can facilitate active leisure participation for people with disabilities.

How can we emphasize the person first when making adaptations?

Realizing that participants are people first can create an important starting point for including all people into the services we provide. To encourage focus on the person first, leisure services professionals can:

- individualize adaptations,
- focus on abilities, and
- match challenge and skills.

Individualize Adaptations

A key to adapting recreation programs is to consider the individual needs of each participant. Because many people possess differing levels of skills, and experience a variety of consequences as a result of different disabling conditions, it is important for us to individualize adaptations. Each participant has different life experiences, different support systems, different health considerations, and different resources.

Focus on Abilities

A person-first philosophy also requires us to focus on participants' *abilities* rather than on their *disabilities*. Too often assessments conducted identify what participants cannot do. Next, adaptations are designed to accommodate this limitation. Perhaps a more useful procedure may be to initially focus on the skills and abilities of participants and then make adaptations building upon these skills. When people's abilities become the focus of attention, we are more likely to allow participants to be as independent as possible; therefore, we will tend to avoid stifling these people by making unnecessary adaptations that fail to capitalize on their skills.

Match Challenge and Skills

Each recreation program contains learning experiences that possess a certain degree of challenge. Prior to conducting a recreation program, we can systematically assess the skills and interests of the people for whom the program is designed. Then when conducting programs we will be in a position to better achieve the delicate balance between the challenge of specific activities and skills of the participants.

If an imbalance exists between the degree of challenge of a program and the participants' skills, barriers to leisure participation may be created. As discussed in previous chapters, if a specific activity is too easy for participants, boredom often results. However, if an activity is too difficult, frustration can occur. One way to reduce these barriers is through adaptation. Adaptations can permit modifications of the challenge associated with participation to meet the abilities of the participants. Once adaptations are made, these adaptations must continually be adjusted to meet the changing skills of the participants. A summary of the suggestions to help place emphasis on the person is presented in **Figure 14.1**.

How can we encourage participant autonomy?

Since an important aspect of leisure involves freedom to make choices, it is important that people perceive that they are autonomous. The following suggestions are provided to facilitate this sense of control and choice:

- facilitate independence,
- determine necessity of adaptations, and
- view adaptations as transitional.

Facilitate Independence

Modifications should decrease the necessity of participants to rely on others for assistance and provide people with disabilities with increased opportunities to actively participate in leisure as independently as possible.

Determine Necessity of Adaptations

Because many people with disabilities experience barriers to leisure participation, sometimes we may be quick to change a recreation program. Changes may be readily made to a given program because leisure services professionals may be skilled at making modifications. However, sometimes these changes are made with the knowledge of the general characteristics of a group rather than with explicit information about the specific participants. Although this may be practical in some situations, it may also create a problem.

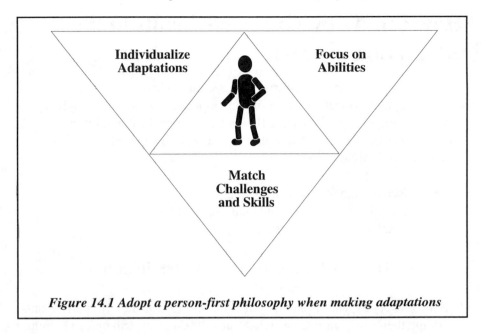

Figure 14.1 Adopt a person-first philosophy when making adaptations

Some aspects of recreation programs may be changed when they need not be. Therefore we must examine each adaptation and determine its necessity.

View Adaptations as Transitional

Adaptations can permit active participation for people with a wide range of knowledge and skills. The very nature of leisure services implies that individuals will learn and change. As people learn and change, their skills and knowledge fluctuate. Therefore, if an adaptation was made at one time, it may no longer be appropriate because the individual has now acquired the ability to participate without any adaptations. At that point, the adaptations may impair rather than encourage leisure participation.

Some people participating in recreation programs may possess degenerative or progressive conditions that require continual modifications. A previous slight adaptation to a particular activity may later be insufficient to provide the person with the opportunity to participate. We must be willing to adopt the view that any adaptations made may need to be altered in the future. A summary of suggestions to help encourage participant autonomy is presented in **Figure 14.2** (p. 250).

How can we involve participants in the adaptation process?

It is important for leisure services professionals to involve people with disabilities in all aspects of program development. These individuals can provide an important perspective that helps to improve the delivery of inclusive leisure services. The following suggestions stimulate ways to include these individuals in the adaptation process:

- discuss adaptations with participants,
- determine feasibility of adaptations, and
- ensure safety of adaptation.

Discuss Adaptations with Participants

In almost every aspect of planning, it is helpful to consult with participants regarding their opinions and desires (Smith, 1993). A critical task in helping people become motivated to participate is to encourage them to offer input into the chosen program. Active involvement in shaping a recreation program can provide individuals with a sense of investment that may increase their motivation to initiate and maintain participation.

Discussions with participants may provide valuable information about ways to adapt the activity and instill feelings of control and commitment by

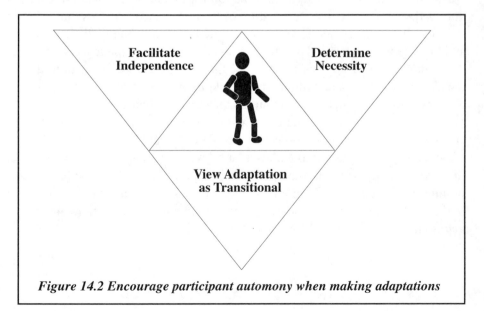

Figure 14.2 Encourage participant autonomy when making adaptations

participants. When participants do not currently possess the skills to effectively communicate their feelings and ideas toward an adaptation, then observations can be used to obtain input from these individuals.

Determine Feasibility of Adaptations

Involving participants in the process of adapting recreation programs can provide us with a means to determine the feasibility and usability of the adaptation. If participants feel that the adaptation detracts from the program, their motivation may be reduced. Therefore, asking participants their opinions and encouraging them to make suggestions can enhance our ability to make feasible adaptations. Discussion with people prior to and during adaptations can help encourage active leisure participation following adaptations.

Ensure Safety of Adaptations

The most critical element for us to remember when making changes to any recreation program is safety. Commercially available equipment, materials, and games typically have been tested and retested to determine their safety for potential participants. Anytime an adaptation is made, the previous research conducted by the manufacturers is compromised and associated safety claims change. Therefore, we must examine and evaluate any program we adapt and consider the safety of participants.

One strategy to help evaluate the safety of an adaptation is to actively seek participants' input regarding ways to ensure and increase the safety associated with a given aspect of a recreation program. A summary of ways to involve participants in the adaptation process is presented in **Figure 14.3** (p. 252).

How can we evaluate adaptations?

Competent professionals must continuously evaluate effects of their services. The evaluation process allows us to be aware of our actions, to improve our services, and to respond to the needs of the people we serve. To encourage evaluation of the adaptations made to materials, equipment, activities, people, and environments, the following suggestions are provided:

- conduct continuous observations,
- make necessary adjustments, and
- retain aspects of the original task.

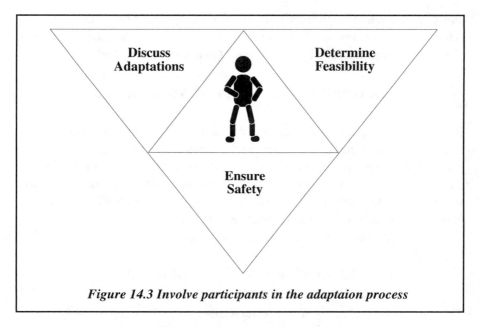

Figure 14.3 Involve participants in the adaptaion process

Conduct Continuous Observations

When adaptations are made to specific aspects of a recreation program, continuous observation of individuals participating in the program is suggested. Observations of individual participation can allow us to determine if the adaptations are achieving their intended goals. These observations provide us with a way to examine unanticipated difficulties participants may be experiencing relative to the adaptations. Continuous observations put us in a position to be able to understand the effectiveness of the adaptations.

Make Necessary Adjustments

Observations provide us with the opportunity to discover problems with adaptations. When problems are identified, we must then be willing to respond to any difficulties associated with adaptations. This willingness to change an adaptation must stem from the belief that even if a great deal of time and energy is put into a given task, it may need to be altered to permit active leisure participation for persons with disabilities. A slight adjustment to an aspect of a recreation program may make the difference between active and meaningful participation and failure.

Retain Aspects of the Original Task

Each time an adaptation is made, that aspect of the program becomes less like the original task. Therefore, adaptations can limit the ability of individuals to participate in different programs that do not contain such adaptations. Keep features of the program as close to the original program as possible to encourage participants to generalize their ability to participate in the activities in other environments and situations.

Lee, Dattilo, Kleiber, and Caldwell (1996) and Mobily, Mobily, Lessard, and Berkenpas (2000) described the desire of individuals who have acquired a disability to establish continuity with experiences that existed before their illness or accident occurred. People often strive to achieve positive experiences associated with leisure participation similar to those that they had encountered before their disability. The sense of continuity can be fostered by keeping the activity as similar to the original activity as possible yet providing an accommodation that promotes meaningful leisure participation for individuals. A summary of considerations for evaluating adaptation is presented in **Figure 14.4** (p. 256).

What aspects of leisure services can be adapted?

The following information encourages leisure services providers to consider a variety of aspects of leisure services when attempting to make adaptations that facilitate participation. Identification of possible adaptations of leisure services are divided into five major areas:

- materials,
- activities,
- environment,
- participants, and
- instructional strategies.

These five (not necessarily mutually exclusive) areas intend to organize suggestions for adaptations. The materials used during a recreation program can be adapted to meet the needs of the participants. The specific requirements associated with the learning activities may be changed. The environment provides another adaptation alternative for us to facilitate active involvement for participants. Efforts toward adaptation can be focused on the participants themselves to increase the likelihood of their success.

Finally, it can be helpful to turn our focus of adaptations inward and examine possible ways to modify instructional strategies to teach people with disabilities about leisure.

The descriptions related to these five areas are not intended to be all-inclusive, but to help develop plans for adaptations for recreation programs. Examples given in many of the following situations are made with recreation activities to provide instances that enable visualization of the suggested adaptation.

How can materials be adapted to promote inclusion?

Many aspects of materials used in recreation programs can be adapted. Some examples of possible methods for adapting materials are presented below relative to the following areas:

- size,
- speed,
- weight,
- stabilization,
- durability, and
- safety.

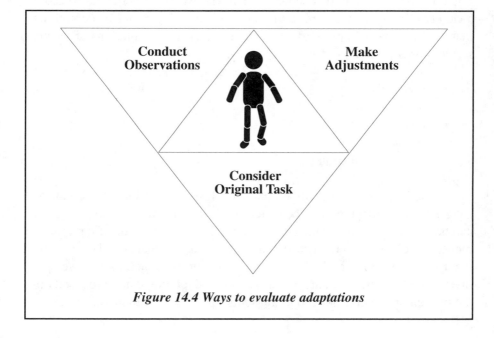

Figure 14.4 Ways to evaluate adaptations

Size

The size of materials can be adjusted for participants by making objects such as puzzle pieces larger for those having difficulty grasping small objects. Tape can be wrapped around handles to increase their size and permit manipulation. Conversely, other people may have difficulty grasping larger objects such as felt-tip markers so smaller ones could be used.

The size of objects to be inserted into an opening can be reduced (e.g., basketball) while the opening can be enlarged (e.g., basketball hoop). Large, colorful cards can assist individuals with visual problems in playing board/card games. If individuals are participating in racquet sports, the racquets can be shortened for more control or lengthened to allow participants to cover more ground.

Speed

Some individuals with disabilities may experience problems associated with gross motor coordination. A coordination problem can be quickly observed as individuals respond to moving objects. One way to increase the success of persons responding to objects is to change the speed of the moving object. Air can be removed from a ball so when struck it will move at a slower speed. Wedges can be placed under any angled surface to change the incline to decrease or increase the speed of a ball. For example, wedges can be used to slow down the ball (e.g., pinball) or speed up the ball (e.g., bowling).

Weight

The weight of objects can be adjusted to meet the strength of the participants. Wooden and metal materials can be exchanged for those that are made from plastic or rubber. For instance, plastic balls, sponge balls and balloons can be substituted for heavier balls in some situations, while lighter plastic or Nerf bats can be used in lieu of heavier metal or wooden bats.

Stabilization

Sometimes people who have unsteady movements may be prevented from using some expensive technology because they are likely to break the equipment. Suction cups and clamps can be used to stabilize the material such as a tape recorder or compact disc player. In this way, the person can use the material without fear of accidentally damaging it.

People participating in craft projects who possess grasping skills with only one portion of their bodies can be assisted by securing the project to a board or table such as taping paper to a desk for drawing or painting.

Durability

Materials for recreation programs should be made durable so that the material will last as long as possible. Duct tape is often helpful in reinforcing many different pieces of equipment. Game boards and playing cards should be laminated to increase the ability of the objects to withstand regular use. Velcro can also be used to secure objects that need to be removed at different times.

Safety

When making any adaptations to objects, continuously evaluate each adaptation in reference to safety. If objects change in any way they should be examined closely. Use only nontoxic substances and remove any sharp edges. Possibilities of ingestion of objects and suffocation should be considered and prevented. In all cases, problems should be anticipated and steps taken toward prevention of any injuries.

How can activities be adapted to promote inclusion?

Many traditional recreation activities can be adapted to facilitate more active participation by individuals with disabilities. Some examples of possible methods for adapting activities are presented below relative to the following areas:

- physical aspects,
- cognitive requirements, and
- social conditions.

Physical Aspects

Individuals participating in leisure pursuits vary a great deal relative to physical strength, speed, endurance, energy level, gross motor coordination, hand-eye coordination, flexibility, agility, and many other physical skills. To adapt a physical requirement of a program, several adjustments can be made. The typical number of people associated with a game can be changed. For instance, the number of people participating in volleyball can be changed from 6 to 10 people for persons with limited speed and agility. People with limited endurance and strength may benefit from making the requirements to complete an activity less strenuous by reducing either the number of points needed or the length of time a game lasts. For example, needing to score 8 points to win a table tennis game rather than 21 or changing the length of time to complete a recreation activity from 30 to 15 minutes. While learning some activities, the physical movements can be changed by requiring participants to walk instead of run, such as in basketball. For those individuals who have impaired mobility, changing the required body position from standing to sitting may provide opportunities for participation such as throwing Frisbee. Some people receiving recreation services may possess limited physical endurance; therefore, we may wish to provide more opportunities to rest during a particular event, such as hiking.

Cognitive Requirements

People with disabilities may encounter problems associated with cognitive requirements as a result of many disabling conditions. For example, people may have impaired cognitive functioning because of a trauma (e.g., head injury), a neurological disorder (e.g., cerebrovascular accident), a developmental disability (e.g., mental retardation), a learning disability (e.g., dyslexia), a mental health problem (e.g., depression), or a side effect (e.g., from medications taken for physical illness). To accommodate these individuals' reduced cognitive functioning, the rules associated with different games can be changed. For instance, if short-term memory appears to be a problem for persons with head injuries, the number of cards used in a card game can be reduced. For example, rather than using all cards in a deck in a game of concentration, only the face cards can be used.

People who do not yet possess counting skills may be able to play a game by substituting matching of colors, instead of requiring the recognition of numbers or words to move game pieces. If the requirements for scoring during an activity are too difficult for participants, changes can be made such as having people with cognitive limitations initially keep track only of the number of bowling pins they knock down, rather than using scoring procedures associated with calculating spares and strikes.

Some individuals with learning difficulties may require some minimal assistance with reading cards used for a table game. We may wish to change the game from requiring individuals to play alone to participation with partners. Often, teams of participants can be developed that allow the individual team members to complement each other's skills and abilities.

Social Conditions

As discussed in previous chapters, many people may experience barriers to their leisure involvement. Frequently, these barriers are related to problems encountered in a social context. Some individuals may be intimidated by activities requiring larger groups. A reluctance to participate in larger groups may be a result of previous experiences associated with failure and perhaps ridicule.

To assist people in gaining the confidence needed to participate in large group activities, we may initially choose to reduce the number of people required to participate in an activity and begin instruction and practice of an activity in small groups, or if resources are available on a one-to-one basis. For instance, social skills instruction related to learning how to make friends may be conducted initially with a few individuals. As participants acquire the social skills, the context could be expanded to include more participants.

The pressure involved in some activities involving direct competition against another team may be extremely threatening for some people with disabilities. A person's failure to perform may result in the entire team losing to an opponent. This failure can decrease confidence and self-esteem and contribute to a reduced motivation to participate. One approach to adapting an activity could be changing the activity so cooperation is emphasized and direct competition against another team is eliminated. To accomplish this cooperative atmosphere, we may decide to eliminate the opposing team. The opposing team would be replaced by a series of established goals to be achieved by the team. In lieu of the traditional game of basketball, one team could participate by establishing goals related to making a basket. For example, beginning at the opposite end of the court requiring all five team members to dribble the ball as it is brought down the court while trying to make a basket in the least amount of time.

How can the environment be adapted to promote inclusion?

The environment can play an important role in the ability of individuals to actively pursue leisure involvement. We may be in a position to adapt the environment in which leisure participation is intended to occur or to make recommendations for changing the environment. Because we are often attempting to provide leisure services in a variety of contexts, possible adaptations to the environment are suggested that relate to:

- sensory factors, and
- participation area.

Sensory Factors

Participation can be enhanced for some individuals by simply manipulating the sounds occurring within the environment during participation. For instance, when playing a recreation game, some people who are easily distracted may have difficulty concentrating when the game is being played in a multipurpose room with other people talking to one another as they engage in other activities. Moving the recreation game to a small, quiet room where only people participating are present may facilitate more active participation for some individuals.

Some people using hearing aids can experience difficulty when participating in a gymnasium because of the echoing effect that can occur. Placement of drapes and sound absorbing tiles near the ceiling may muffle some distracting sounds and provide persons with hearing impairments the opportunity to attend to directions more easily.

Providing an environment that permits people to see as much as possible is important when attempting to teach people. Therefore, examine the context of an activity to determine if adequate lighting is available. Simply adding a lamp may enhance completion of craft projects.

Some people's vision may be substantially impaired as a result of glare. Therefore, it is helpful if we consider the angle of the lights and realize the possibility that some lights may be too bright and inhibit, rather than enhance, participation.

Participation Area

The area in which an activity is played can be adapted to facilitate more active participation. This can allow participants with limited speed to successfully participate. For instance, rather than using an entire baseball field to play kick ball, participants can be required to keep the ball in play within the infield. In softball, participants can be required to hit to one side of the pitcher's mound allowing more individuals to cover a small area.

Boundaries designating the end of the playing areas can also be changed to make people more aware of these designations. Wider chalk marks can be used on soccer fields to allow people to see more clearly when they are approaching an area designated as out-of-bounds. Ropes can be placed along a walking trail to permit individuals with visual impairments to follow the trail and maintain their awareness of boundaries.

The surface area can also be changed to permit some people to more easily access activities. A person who uses a wheelchair may be able to join a hiking expedition when some firm foundation has been applied to a trail. Changes in textures on the ground and adjacent walls of playgrounds can indicate to children with visual impairments that they are moving toward different equipment.

The facility where the activity is conducted may be also changed. For instance, we may place ramps in a swimming pool to permit access for people with limited mobility. In addition, the water in the swimming pool could be lowered to only two or three feet to initially accommodate those people with significant fears associated with water.

How can participants be adapted to promote inclusion?

When considering adaptations, the changes associated with materials, activities, and the environment often come to mind. If, however, adaptations are viewed as changes that are made to facilitate active leisure participation, then another category for making adaptations may be considered. The participants themselves may actually be altered to encourage active participation in those experiences that bring them joy and satisfaction.

This section provides suggestions on how to make some of these adaptations to the participants. Modifications can dramatically influence participants' level of participation. These modifications include:

- position the person,
- provide physical aids that support,
- recommend evaluations for sensory aids,
- provide opportunities for increased mobility,
- be open to alternative ways to communicate, and
- teach skills.

Position the Person

The optimal condition in which individuals learn and actively participate is the *ready state*. That is, participants should be sitting or standing as erect as possible, comfortable, able to reach materials and objects associated with an activity, and facing in the direction of the activity. Pillows, foam wedges, and support belts can be used to help individuals prepare for activity involvement.

If individuals who have limited muscle control wish to read or look at a book or magazine, they can lie on their stomach on the ground. A triangle wedge can be placed under their chest with the larger side close to their neck and the smaller side near their stomach. The book can be placed on the floor and can be controlled with their hands.

A person using a wheelchair can be securely fastened into the chair and provided access to toys by placing them directly on a lap tray attached to the chair. For swimming, life jackets can be used to support individuals as they learn to swim. If people using wheelchairs wish to actively contribute to the development of a mural that is being painted, they can be positioned sideways to the wall or easel to allow them to reach the mural.

Provide Physical Aids that Support

Providing physical aids that support the individual can enhance many people's participation in recreation activities. For instance, people may encounter difficulty grasping a fishing pole because of severe weakness associated with their wrists. A brace may be used to help support the wrist when holding the fishing pole.

Some participants involved in a nature walk may have a limited range of motion. This reduced range of motion would typically limit their ability to bend at the waist and collect samples of leaves, bark and other items used for debriefing sessions following the walk. Providing them with a scooping device attached to an extended handle would permit them to participate more actively in the walk and accompanying discussion. In addition, people who have limited grasping capabilities can paint, if a paintbrush is strapped to their hand by using Velcro.

Recommend Evaluations for Sensory Aids

If we notice that participants appear to have difficulty seeing demonstrations or responding to other visual cues used to facilitate participation, they should check to determine when the person was last seen for an eye examination. If there has not been a recent eye exam, the practitioner should recommend one. The eye exam may result in the prescription of corrective lenses or contacts, which would then promote more active participation.

In addition, some participants may not respond quickly to verbal instructions. At times, they may seem confused or inattentive. These characteristics may be indicative of a hearing loss. Records should be checked to determine the most recent audiology examination. Again, if a recent evaluation has not been performed, it would be important for us to make a recommendation for the person to have a hearing examination completed. The examination may result in people using some form of hearing aid to enhance their ability to hear and thus reduce barriers to leisure participation.

Provide Opportunities for Increased Mobility

Some individuals participating in leisure services may have reduced mobility. For instance, mobility may be limited because of a degenerative disease, such as multiple sclerosis; a traumatic accident resulting in injury to the central nervous system, such as a spinal cord injury; or from an orthopedic disorder resulting in reduced range of motion, such as arthritis. In response to this reduced mobility, people may find assistance by using a variety of aids such as wheelchairs, crutches, walkers, or braces.

Although their primary means of ambulation may be effective in the majority of situations across their life experiences, they may be able to participate more actively in some recreation activities with a different variation of the mobility aid. For children who use wheelchairs and are participating in activities in a gymnasium, a scooter board can inject fun and increased speed into the activity. For instance, when playing kickball, children could use scooter boards to move about. This adaptation could be made in conjunction with an activity modification by establishing the rule that participants use their hands to hit the ball and then move to the bases quickly on the scooter boards.

Personal wheelchairs may be the most appropriate for daily experiences. There are, however, many commercially available sport wheelchairs designed specifically for the requirements associated with particular types of sports. For instance, there are chairs designed for activities that require a great deal of rapid turning. These types of chairs may be used when participating in activities such as tennis, basketball, and racquetball. Other people may be interested in participating in races on or off the track. These individuals frequently use chairs designed for speed and movement in a forward direction. It is helpful if we examine the participation patterns of people experiencing reduced mobility and consider variations to their typical mode of transportation that could enhance leisure involvement.

Be Open to Alternative Ways to Communicate

Some individuals cannot meet their communication needs through standard forms of spoken communication. Therefore, we must be willing to modify the required response mode for a particular activity. These individuals may require augmentative and alternative communication (AAC) systems to fulfill their needs.

AAC systems include unaided systems (e.g., gestures, sign language, and finger spelling), nonelectronic aided systems (e.g., communication boards and books containing symbols, words, or pictures), and computer-based assistive technology (e.g., speech synthesis and word printouts). AAC systems vary considerably according to message storage and retrieval systems, communication speed, and communication-aid output capabilities.

There is a large range of competencies and abilities across individuals using AAC systems resulting in an extremely heterogeneous population of AAC users. It is useful if leisure services professionals are open to these alternative forms of communication and be willing to change the required mode of communication for a specific activity to permit active participation by persons using communication systems other than speech. (Further information about AAC systems is provided in Chapter 19.)

Teach Skills

As stated previously in this chapter, if an imbalance exists between the degree of challenge of a program and the participants' skills, barriers to leisure participation may be created. The majority of this chapter has focused on adaptations that can permit modification of the challenge associated with a recreation program to meet the abilities of the participants. However, we have another option when trying to help individuals meet the requirements of an activity. Recreation is designed to teach people skills and knowledge that facilitate their ability to meet the challenges encountered when attempting to experience leisure. For instance, if people do not possess the skills to access public transportation to go to a fitness club, instruction related to use of public transportation will increase the ability of individuals to meet the challenges associated with enhancing their physical fitness.

How can instructional strategies be adapted to promote inclusion?

The four areas for making adaptations previously mentioned have required us to focus attention away from providers and onto materials, activities, environment, and participants. The fifth area encourages us to consider the way we deliver services and provide instruction.

If people receiving leisure services are not developing leisure skills and knowledge at a rate consistent with their potential, there may be ways to modify the instructional strategies we employ to allow individuals with disabilities to more effectively and efficiently meet their needs. The next section will address the following considerations related to instructional strategies:

- establish objectives,
- develop instructional steps,
- offer opportunities for practice,
- include instructional prompts,
- provide reinforcement, and
- consider personnel.

Establish Objectives

Some participants in leisure programs may encounter difficulty achieving established objectives. We may continue to focus on the inability of individuals to achieve their objectives and thus create further difficulty. It is important to be willing to reassess the objectives and change them to meet the needs of participants. This is not to say that objectives not be challenging. In fact, they should be monitored closely for the possibility of having objectives that are too easily completed by participants. While overly rigorous objectives can create frustration for both participants and practitioners, development of objectives demanding too little of individuals can create an environment conducive to boredom and apathy.

Develop Instructional Steps

A useful tool in providing leisure services for people with disabilities is task analysis. Task analysis involves segmenting a task into components that can be taught separately. The instructional components can then be sequenced together to allow individuals to complete an identified task. The procedure of task analysis is used when attempting to teach a multifaceted task that may appear complex for participants.

Although task analysis requires identification of components that, when accomplished in sequence, permit completion of the task, the number of components identified for any given task may vary considerably. For instance, in one situation the act of swinging a table tennis paddle to hit the ball may be divided into four steps, while in another circumstance the task may be divided into 10 components.

The skills of individual participants should determine the level of specificity associated with a task analysis. Therefore, if people experience problems learning a skill we can examine the components being taught. We can then determine if further delineation is needed for those individuals who are not progressing on a particular component, or if some components should be collapsed to accommodate people who feel they are not being sufficiently challenged.

Offer Opportunities for Practice

To educate people with disabilities about leisure, we develop content and then attempt to present this content in a systematic fashion. Sometimes people enrolled in recreation programs fail to progress at the rate we expect. One reason people may not acquire skills and knowledge associated with a particular aspect of recreation is that they may not have received sufficient opportunity to practice the information presented in the program. Another way to adapt the instructional strategy is to change the amount of practice associated with a particular objective.

Repetition through practice can allow individuals to integrate the newly acquired knowledge and skill into their existing leisure repertoire. Continuous practice of previously learned skills can increase the chance that individuals will maintain the skills over time. When planning practice sessions, it is important to be creative and make these opportunities as interesting and fun as possible. Frequently, people do not understand a concept the initial time they are presented with the idea. Practice provides experiences that permit repetition of concepts and ideas that enable people to retain that information more easily.

Include Instructional Prompts

As we provide instruction, we may observe that participants do not respond to our directions. Therefore, we may wish to consider the use of prompts to assist participants. Prompts can provide auditory cues for individuals, typically through verbal instructions. There are, however, other forms of prompts that can be used.

Environmental prompts can encourage participant involvement by simply manipulating the context in which an activity is provided. For instance, one way to encourage use of recreation table games in a recreation lounge may be for the practitioner to place the games on tables in the room or open the closets where they are stored so that participants entering the area will see the games.

Visual cues may be provided to stimulate participation. Modeling appropriate behaviors and providing systematic demonstrations may allow participants to more clearly see the desired leisure behavior. In addition, hand-over-hand physical guidance may permit individuals to feel the specific movements associated with participation and thus increase their ability to correctly perform the skill. Because people may respond differently to various prompts, examine the procedures and be willing to modify the way participants are prompted to learn and apply new leisure skills.

Provide Reinforcement

We often provide individuals with a reinforcer—an object or event that encourages the acquisition of leisure skills and knowledge. The object or event, however, may not be perceived by the participant to be a reinforcer. Selection of an object or event to serve as a positive reinforcer must be person specific—something that will effectively influence that individual's behavior. Therefore, we must monitor the participants' responses to a consequence to determine if it is truly a powerful enough reinforcer to influence behavior. If over time behaviors do not increase in response to administration of a specific item or activity, we must be willing to make adaptations. Testing various items and activities until reinforcers are identified may provide us with a systematic procedure for identification of reinforcers.

Consider Personnel

Interaction between participants and practitioners is highly complex. Some participants may respond to some leisure providers more energetically than to others. Failure of some program participants to progress at an anticipated rate may be influenced by who delivers the services. Closely monitor interactions with participants as well as other personnel delivering recreation services. In-service training can be provided to improve skills. In addition, adapting schedules to accommodate both staff and participant needs may also encourage more effective implementation of recreation programs.

What are examples of adaptations that facilitate leisure participation?

Growth in the development of adaptive equipment has met the desires of individuals with mobility impairments to experience the excitement associated with many outdoor adventure activities. Smith (1995) observed that acts to which the word "extreme" can be attached—such as skiing, hang gliding, motorcycling, kayaking, skydiving and mountaineering—have generated development of extensive medical adaptive devices and rehabilitation equipment.

Kaminker (1995) described a variety of adaptations that have been made to allow individuals with quadriplegia to participate in physically active recreation activities:

- Buddy system for scuba diving. Julia Dorsett, East Coast Director of the Handicapped Scuba Association, explained, "Under water, we're all the same."
- Chin-activated joystick to fly a plane. "You have to have arm muscles, but you don't have to have hands." says Ray Temchus, President of Freedom's Wings International.
- Sip-and-puff-activated switch for sailing. Sam Sullivan, an engineer with the Disabled Sailing Association, stated, "The exciting thing about sailing is that people of all abilities can compete against each other with no special categories or allowances."
- Adapted saddle and reins for horseback riding. "Hand use is not necessary, a horse can be trained to respond to wrist-controlled reins," says Evelyn Refosco, co-chair of the American Handicapped Riding Association's Adult Riding Committee.

There are many examples of adaptations that have facilitated participation. One example is associated with Dennis Walters and his approach to golf as reported by Perry (1995, p. 65):

Golf hasn't been the same since Dennis Walters mounted a barstool on a golf cart so he could return to the links following an accident that left him paralyzed from the waist down. Proving that a disability doesn't necessarily translate into a big handicap, Walters has received the prestigious Ben Hogan Award for the Golf Writers of America in honor of his remarkable comeback . . . Walters shows people with disabilities they can enjoy the challenge and satisfaction a good round of golf brings. He demonstrates how to adjust swings to correct any problem—from slices to hooks. But his lessons also have a broader application that extends far beyond the links: Obstacles can be surmounted with a little ingenuity and a lot of hard work.

Final Thoughts

Although there are many commercially available materials that have been developed to facilitate participation in recreation activities by people with disabilities, a critical ingredient in promoting inclusion is to identify barriers. Once these barriers are identified, then we must take on the challenge of making the necessary adaptations to promote inclusion. These efforts occur not in isolation, but with assistance from people with disabilities, families, colleagues, advocates, and experts. When we believe that all people deserve to be included in any program and we are willing to do what it takes to make it happen, inclusion becomes a reality.

This chapter focused on ways to make adaptations. These adaptations should permit us to meet the varying needs and abilities of the people attending recreation programs. The suggestions communicated some options available to facilitate active leisure participation for people with disabilities. General considerations provided guidelines to follow when making any adaptation intended to promote leisure involvement. The chapter also provided suggestions on adaptations related to materials, activities, environment, participants, and instructional strategies.

Discussion Questions

1. What are ways to emphasize the person first?
2. How can participants' autonomy be encouraged?
3. How can participants be involved in the adaptation process?
4. What are ways to evaluate adaptations?
5. What are possible methods for adapting materials used in recreation programs?
6. How can activities be adapted to facilitate recreation participation by people with disabilities?
7. How does the environment play an important role in the ability of individuals with disabilities to participate in recreation activities?
8. How can the environment be adapted to facilitate inclusion of individuals with disabilities?
9. What are ways of altering the participants to facilitate participation?
10. What are ways instructional strategies can be adapted to promote inclusion?

Chapter 15

Advocate for Services

*On an occasion of this kind it becomes more than a
moral duty to speak one's mind. It becomes a pleasure.*
-Oscar Wilde

Orientation Activity: Be an Advocate

Directions Alone: Identify 10 of the following advocacy actions that you
would like to adopt as personal goals. Prioritize these 10 actions, assigning
the number 1 to the most important and the number 10 to the least important.

Directions with Others: Move about the room and find another person
who chose one of the same activities as you. Introduce yourself, find out
the person's name, and discuss why you each chose the item. Once you
have finished, find another person and continue the process.

1. Invite people with disabilities to attend programs.
2. Ask adults with disabilities to serve as leaders.
3. Organize a Diversity Awareness Day.
4. Survey architectural barriers and share results.
5. Write news releases about barriers facing people with disabilities.
6. Educate people about recreation and support services available to
   all people.
7. Talk with people with disabilities to learn more about them and
   their disability.
8. Discuss the problems architectural and attitudinal barriers create.
9. Volunteer to record materials for people with visual impairments.
10. Develop public service announcements for radio and television.
11. Contact organizations for ideas about their work with citizens who
    have disabilities.
12. Write letters to local newspaper editors urging removal of barriers
    from facilities.
13. Plan exhibits to create awareness and dispel myths about people
    with disabilities.

14. Ask people with disabilities to appear in advertisements for leisure services.
15. Learn about building codes and laws concerning access.
16. View a film on problems that people with disabilities face.
17. Conduct an evaluation or complete research on people with disabilities and share the results.
18. Teach awareness activities to community groups.
19. Keep the media informed of successes obtained by people with disabilities.
20. Campaign for the display of the Access Symbol where appropriate.
21. Learn requirements for using the Access Symbol and check buildings for compliance.
22. Conduct a poster contest related to the removal of barriers.
23. Volunteer at an agency that serves people with disabilities.
24. Develop services to assist families that have a member who has a disability.
25. Form an advocacy committee to work on removal of barriers.
26. Meet with a legislator and learn about policies and laws.
27. Write to television stations complimenting them on positive portrayals of people with disabilities.
28. Encourage community groups to sponsor sign language courses.
29. Invite a person with an auditory impairment and an interpreter to talk to your agency.
30. Sponsor an idea exchange among people and agencies on ways to promote inclusion.
31. Discuss ways to involve people in community activities and remove barriers.
32. Read children's stories and discuss how people with disabilities are portrayed.
33. Identify different forms of transportation for people with disabilities.
34. Learn about technology that assists people with disabilities.
35. Select a recreation activity, choose a disability, and identify helpful accommodations.
36. Interview people with disabilities at work in the community.
37. Speak about recreation opportunities to parents of children with disabilities.

Debriefing: Most attempts at advocacy, by and on behalf of people with disabilities, have been to urge opportunities for all people to participate as fully as possible in community life, and to end discrimination based on disabilities. The demands for community inclusion and civil rights have been widely recognized as just (e.g., The Americans with Disabilities Act).

Advocates are needed not because people with disabilities are inherently weak and incapable, but because they are members of a group that has been oppressed. People with disabilities should receive community services because they have a right to them. The services are provided because people with disabilities are citizens. If disabilities interfere with citizens' rights, then society must make the changes that will enable them to enjoy those rights—regardless of costs. Ultimately, people with disabilities should be their own advocates. The advocate lets people manage their own affairs. As you reflect on the orientation activity consider the following questions:

- What is an advocate?
- How can you begin to advocate for people with disabilities?
- Why is advocacy necessary?

Introduction

At times, people with disabilities are socially isolated and disconnected and therefore have difficulty getting their voices heard by the community. They are devalued in our society and are often cut off from social roles that bring power, status, influence, and opportunities. According to Gill (1994), people without disabilities often find it difficult to accept people with disabilities as equal members of society.

Some people with disabilities do not have the skills to communicate their wishes effectively and may need a spokesperson. Many people with disabilities need services and supports to facilitate participation in society. Unfortunately, the systems to provide these are often complex, segregated, and controlling. Advocacy is an important means to facilitate inclusion of people with disabilities because it is concerned with securing rights, encouraging full participation, promoting access, and empowering people.

What is meant by advocacy?

To *advocate* means to recommend, to be in favor of, or to plead for. An advocate pleads the cause of another or gives support to a particular cause. The word "advocate" is derived from the Latin *avocare,* "to summon." The advocate is called upon to provide assistance. An advocate seeks to correct situations in which discrimination, disempowerment, or disconfirmation occurred, and to remove barriers. (Kaufman-Broida & Wenzel, 1994).

Advocacy is required when ordinary actions have been unsuccessful in ensuring that a person's rights are being met. To illustrate this point, Hutchison and McGill (1992) developed a list of characteristics that distinguish between advocacy and other everyday activities, stating that advocacy:

- involves in-depth feelings and commitment to a cause,
- calls for doing more than what is done routinely,
- involves risk (advocates' actions are open to criticism), and
- must be structured to be free from conflict of interest.

As stated in the previous chapter, a *barrier* is any obstacle or obstruction (natural or man-made) that impedes progress but is not necessarily impassable. An *architectural barrier* is any feature of the man-made physical environment that impedes or restricts the mobility of people to the full use of a facility. An *attitudinal barrier* is a way of thinking about or perceiving a disability in a restrictive, condescending or negative manner.

To *empower* someone is to give power or authority to that person. All people have the right to live life to the fullest and experience leisure, but many people with a disability face barriers that prevent them from doing so. These barriers may be in the form of limited access to facilities, transportation, information, programs or job opportunities. Whatever the reason for the barrier, advocacy—the process of speaking up and working for changes in policies, opportunities, and attitudes—can help.

Who is responsible for advocating for people with disabilities?

A major role of professionals who provide public services is to advocate on behalf of people with disabilities in a variety of community forums (Beckwith & Matthews, 1995). According to Peniston (1998, p. 84), "Advocacy is a vehicle for change, whether the change is on a singular level affecting one person or on a multiple level affecting an entire country; change generates progress." In addressing the importance of advocating for people with disabilities, Bieler (2000, p. 18) provided the following analogy:

In Brazil, we tell a story of a hummingbird that, during a very big fire in the forest, was seen coming back and forth, carrying water in his beak and dropping it over the fire. The other animals, most of them bigger and stronger than the hummingbird, were all running away as fast as they could, thinking only to save their own skins. While running, a lion watching the hummingbird asked him if he had not yet realized that he would not extinguish the fire with such drops of water, but instead, he would get himself killed. Without stopping to rest, the tired hummingbird told the lion, "I'm just doing my part."

After conducting in-depth interviews with 17 families of children and adults with disabilities, Turnbull and Ruef (1997, p. 223) concluded that families have been the catalyst in most situations when any positive action has occurred related to attaining inclusion. Most families express exhaustion and frustration in always needing to be the initiators.

Heyne and Schleien (1997) encouraged leisure services professionals to work together with parents of children with disabilities to help facilitate inclusive leisure participation. In their article they spoke about our responsibility for advocacy:

> Many recreation professionals who work with children with disabilities recognize that parents are often our strongest allies in promoting inclusive services. Yet, the responsibility for advocating for and facilitating inclusion must shift from parents to recreation providers who are competently equipped to offer inclusive services. As the American with Disabilities Act (ADA) of 1990 mandates, the readiness and willingness to provide inclusion must be adopted by recreation providers to the extent that, even before a parent or a person with a disability approaches a recreation facility, the door to inclusion is open. (p. 77)

Kaufman-Broida and Wenzel (1994, p. 73) encouraged leisure services providers to view advocacy as a responsibility associated with their jobs. We must see ourselves and be seen by others as advocates as well as services providers because advocacy is a force for change rooted in our values and beliefs.

How can we become advocates?

Since advocacy is an important component of professional behavior it may be helpful to consider ways to advocate for people who have been oppressed in various ways. The following areas are ways to become an effective advocate: prepare a strategy for advocacy, follow guidelines to become an active advocate, and evaluate attempts at advocacy.

How can we prepare a strategy for advocacy?

Establishing advocacy goals, becoming informed about people with disabilities, and listening to people with disabilities are all helpful ways to prepare for advocacy. **Figure 15.1** identifies the following techniques:

- establish advocacy goals,
- become informed, and
- listen to people's perspectives.

Establish Advocacy Goals

Formulate goals specific to advocacy and develop an effective strategy to meet those goals. Next, prioritize goals that have been established. Be persistent, and realize change may take time. Many advocacy efforts can take years to achieve desired results.

Become Informed

As we become informed about the rights and desires of people with dis-abilities we are taking an important step toward advocacy. Credibility is lost when we are unable to answer pertinent questions. Failing to be aware of significant events relating to the issue being pursued can be equally problematic. However, an honest response that a topic has not been studied

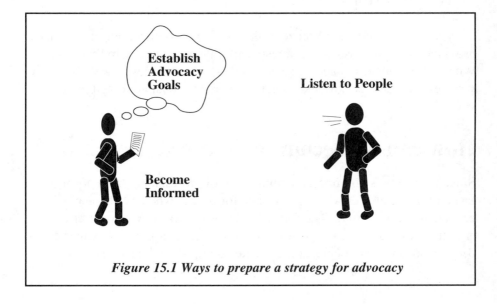

Figure 15.1 Ways to prepare a strategy for advocacy

and that the answer is not known can be disarming—and helpful. There is not a need to become an expert, just the desire to be resourceful and know where to find information.

Listen to People's Perspectives

It is critical that advocates listen to other people's perspectives about inclusion, disability, and providing a supportive environment for people with disabilities. Resistance to including people with disabilities into services may be an indication of negative feelings or fears. It can be helpful if we respond by listening to concerns, opinions, and fears of others to keep communication open.

How can we be active advocates?

Presenting information that is clear, tactful, and contains humor may be useful when advocating for people with disabilities. In addition, we may try to make suggestions to help people improve their approach to interacting with people with disabilities. The following techniques are illustrated in **Figure 15.2** (p. 278):

- present information,
- be clear,
- be tactful,
- use humor appropriately, and
- suggest alternatives.

Present Information

Present information about the rights and desires of people with disabilities to other people. An informal discussion emphasizing how inclusion can benefit all people is often a good beginning. We can provide examples of successful attempts at inclusion that have been achieved within an agency or program.

Be Clear

Based on basic principles of communication, it must be clear whose interests we are representing. We can talk with people with disabilities to verify if they agree with our perspective of certain issues. Advocates should define and present the issue in a comfortable way.

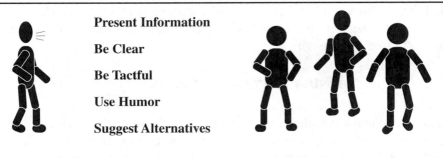

Present Information

Be Clear

Be Tactful

Use Humor

Suggest Alternatives

Figure 15.2 Suggested techniques of active advocates

Be Tactful

When serving as an advocate, avoid being unnecessarily confrontational. Remain consistent and present facts accurately. Demonstrate appreciation to people and organizations that are helpful and willing to listen, show concern for problems, and show enthusiasm for solutions.

When addressing people we can demonstrate that we will provide assistance if we are aware of the problems and understand methods for remediation. We can offer to show others how to comply with the ideals of inclusion and the spirit of the ADA.

Use Humor Appropriately

Advocates and individuals with disabilities who have gained acceptance often are able to use playfulness and humor effectively. If done appropriately humor can dissipate tension and lead to common understanding. If we are playful we can often put people at ease and create an environment where they may be receptive to change. However, many of us struggle with using humor in a respectful manner and encounter people who may be using humor in a disrespectful way.

Suggest Alternatives

Sometimes direct information or responding to feelings is not enough to break through rationalizations. We can suggest alternatives to people after initial dialogue and negotiations. Alternatives to time and financial constraints are often appreciated.

How can we evaluate attempts at advocacy?

Leisure services providers often take pride in their ability to effectively evaluate their services. Evaluation of advocacy efforts that include analyzing the content presented, examining the presentation style, and identifying successful advocacy attempts may be useful. The following techniques are presented in **Figure 15.3**:

- analyze informational content,
- examine the process, and
- identify successful advocacy attempts.

Analyze Informational Content

It is helpful for advocates to closely examine the content of the information we present. We can consider if people understand what we attempt to convey. In addition, it is useful if we determine if other, more helpful information may be available.

Examine the Process

Examine the way in which the information was presented. Considering the limitations as well as the strengths of the different advocacy approaches can be useful. We can consider the effectiveness of the approach and if it reached the intended audience.

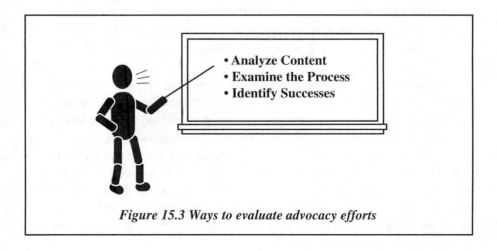

Figure 15.3 Ways to evaluate advocacy efforts

Identify Successful Advocacy Attempts

We can celebrate our successful attempts at advocacy. It is important for us to reward ourselves and others associated with these efforts. We can use our successes as examples in future advocacy efforts.

How can humor relate to advocacy?

Sapon-Shevin and Smith (1999) wrote that as advocates for people with disabilities we are committed to ending oppression of people with disabilities and to educating the public about disability issues. In addition, the authors stated that they believe humor can be helpful and that it is important to be able to laugh and not take disability too seriously; humor is an important part of the educational and advocacy work that they do. Shapon-Shevin and Smith provided several questions to ask when trying to decide how we might feel about specific jokes related to people with disabilities:

- In the presence of a person with this disability, would you feel comfortable sharing this joke? Hearing this joke?
- Does this joke make you feel like you have something in common with a person with a disability? Closer to people with a disability? More understanding of this disability? More relaxed with people with disabilities?
- Does this joke make you feel "they" are irrevocably different? More distant from "them?" That "they" are somehow less than human? Does this joke provide or reinforce incorrect information about the disability or make you tense or awkward in the presence of a person with this disability?
- Is this joke laughing *at* people with disabilities or *with* them? Is the joke exploitative? Who benefits from humor of this type?

The above questions can be applied to just about any interaction we might have with other people. Although raising these questions can help us decide how comfortable we are about specific jokes, the question still remains: "What do we do when we are uncomfortable with a joke?"

In any advocacy situation carefully consider the context of the situation. Thinking about where the conversation is occurring, our relationship with the person talking, and people present all play a role in how we might handle a situation. For example, if in a group situation a student uses terminology that some people with disabilities find insensitive, wait and speak with the person individually.

Once the context of the situation is assessed, Sapon-Shevin and Smith (1999) offered several strategies that might be helpful in determining what to do when we consider certain humor to be inappropriate, including:

- Ask the joke teller a question such as "I have heard that term used several times lately and I have been wondering why people use it; what do you think?"
- Say something like "Did you know that . . .?" Sharing accurate information presented in this course may be helpful if we work from the position that the joke teller is ignorant rather than malicious (even if we think differently).
- Simply do not laugh or smile.
- If you are then asked why you did not laugh, an explanation such as the following might be helpful, "I thought you were a caring person, but did you know that what you said offended me and would probably offend some other people?"

Direct methods of interaction might create a negative experience and result in the person becoming defensive. Again, it is critical to keep in mind the context to determine when to use a particular advocacy strategy and realize that many people are simply not aware of what is and is not sensitive behavior.

How can we encourage self-advocacy?

Advocacy has traditionally meant speaking on behalf of others. In recent years the term *self-advocacy* has been coined to refer to individuals and groups who have traditionally been powerless and largely voiceless speaking up on their own behalf to try to change their social status and situation. The self-advocacy movement among people with disabilities has been influential in improving opportunities and is an important part of the civil rights movement of people with disabilities (Cone, 2001).

Advocates and advocacy groups that act on behalf of others risk becoming paternalistic—defining what is in the best interest of the individuals or groups and working for that without really stopping to ask the people what they want. To avoid this the actions of advocates must reflect the expressed wishes of the individuals or groups they are representing, not upon what others believe is best for them.

Initiate advocacy efforts with an honest and open approach and to be willing to negotiate and to compromise when necessary. If we are serious about empowering people who have been powerless, however, we need to recognize that a certain amount of confrontation, and a certain adversarial relationship will always be part of advocacy.

Empowering people inevitably means taking some power away from one person, or group, to give it to another. Neither individuals nor organizations typically relinquish power willingly. Some advocates will need to be adversarial, others cooperative. These two approaches complement each other and are necessary for the social change that people with disabilities seek.

Many people with disabilities have formed self-advocacy groups. Self-advocacy groups began among people with disabilities who thought that together they could help each other become more independent, learn to speak for themselves, and gain a measure of self-respect and confidence that they had not had in the past. Self-advocacy groups do many things. They organize socials, learn social skills, learn about rights and responsibilities, acquire the skills needed for running meetings, and more. Regardless of what they do, the important thing is that the activities grow out of the needs of consumers, and they promote independence and the ability to speak and act on their own behalf.

The underlying assumption in self-advocacy is that dependence encourages dependence, and independence encourages independence. Thus, self-advocacy groups seek to provide peer support that can help break established patterns of dependency. People with disabilities become self-advocates because they want to become more independent. Parents, friends, and organizations often encourage self-advocacy because they recognize that as people with disabilities learn to make decisions and accept greater responsibility for their lives, everyone—people with disabilities and those without disabilities—benefits.

What are some examples of advocacy efforts?

There are many examples of ways to advocate. The list provided in the orientation activity of this chapter is just a sample of the many actions we can take to advocate for people. The following are ways that some people and companies have begun to advocate for people with disabilities, including:

- making toys, and
- reading the newspaper and writing letters.

Making Toys

Mattel formed a not-for-profit corporation called "For Challenged Kids" to produce and market toys specially designed for children with disabilities.

All profits from the sale of these toys will be dispersed among organizations that work with children with disabilities.

The first "For Challenged Kids" product line, "Hal's Pals," consisted of five, 19-inch soft-sculptured dolls, each with a different disability. Hal, who is one of the best skiers in Colorado, is a ski instructor with one leg. Bobby is an athletic little boy who uses a wheelchair for mobility. Suzie is an adventurous girl who is sight impaired and uses her cane and guide dog to explore her neighborhood. Laura is a ballerina who wears hearing aids. Kathy is a little girl wearing a party dress, a big smile, and leg braces. Mattel believes "Hal's Pals" are really mainstream toys and not just for children with disabilities. Each doll portrays its disability in a familiar, comfortable way, focusing on ability and strengths. The dolls have been identified as useful educational tools, providing insight and improved understanding into what it is like to have a disability.

Reading the Newspaper and Writing Letters

In an editorial in a college newspaper, a person wrote:

Have you seen what they're doing to Atherton Hall? They're destroying it. They are going to build up the front courtyard and level it off so that wheelchairs will be able to get to it easier. I'm not against the idea that buildings should be accessible to the handicapped, but Atherton is not the building to do it to. Every floor except the second has some levels that are connected by stairs. This means that the only places that a wheelchair could get to once it was inside the building was the lobby, the TV room, the second floor, and the parts of the others that the elevator is level with (and that elevator only goes to the ground, first, and second floors).

Another problem is the bathrooms. Every bathroom in the building has a step at the doorway that you have to step over to get in. Also, there are no handicapped toilets, showers or sinks. There is going to have to be a lot of work done just to make the University and a couple of senators or representatives who want to make this building accessible happy. Again, I'm not against the idea in general, but it is not a feasible option in the case of Atherton. Besides the monetary and time expenditures, there is the problem of a major inconvenience to the inhabitants of the dorm (e.g., noise, privacy, physical inconveniences of closing the front entrance when they rebuild parts of the interior) and even more importantly is the historical nature of Atherton Hall. It is one of the older and most beautiful dorms on campus. Its beautiful main entrance has greeted many dignitaries and honored guests of the hall and this "remodeling" will destroy the original landscaping and architecture of this building. After considering limitations of this project and the inconveniences and the problems it will cause, I have to conclude that the work currently being done to Atherton Hall is inappropriate, unnecessary, and should be halted before any further destruction takes place.

The following is a response to the previous editorial entitled "All or None" that was prepared by three students majoring in Recreation and Leisure Studies.

We would hardly refer to a building that is being altered for better accessibility as a building that is being, as you stated, "destroyed." You seem to only be concerned about the minor inconveniences that the inhabitants of the dorm will experience during the construction period. You complain of the "physical inconvenience of closing the front entrance" to the building. Did you ever stop to consider the constant inconvenience people who use wheelchairs face daily because they can not get into a building that has only stairs as a means of entrance? Typically, it would only take a couple of months of "inconvenience" to make a building accessible, yet it would provide a lifetime of accessibility to people who use wheelchairs. You refer to the "many dignitaries and honored guests" that this hall has greeted. Speaking of dignitaries, do you realize that one of our presidents, Franklin D. Roosevelt, used a wheelchair? In addition, you also stated that you are "not against the idea that buildings should be accessible to the handicapped, but Atherton is not the building to do it to." Isn't this a bit contradictory? If you are going to support a cause, you must support the entire cause—it is not right to exclude a portion just because it may cramp your lifestyle for a brief time. This reminds us of those people who used to say, "I'm not against blacks riding buses, but not my bus." If your description of how making Atherton Hall accessible is accurate, it is possible that the University is not going about it in the most efficient manner. However, this does not suggest that Atherton Hall is not a feasible building to make accessible. We suggest that rather than focusing your efforts on condemning accessibility to Atherton Hall by people using wheelchairs, that you focus your efforts on examining the plan for accessibility. In the past few years considerable strides have been made which have provided individuals with disabilities access to buildings. These breakthroughs have enabled integration into the mainstream of society a reality instead of only a dream.

Final Thoughts

Developing an understanding of actions relevant to advocacy can help encourage us to become advocates. As we learn more about ways to promote self-advocacy and are exposed to different examples of how to be an advocate we can become more empowered to advocate for inclusive leisure services. Once we gain knowledge about a topic relevant to our professional duties we then have the responsibility to share this information with others who may be naïve about the information we have acquired. We have the social obligation to act in a responsible way and be an advocate. Dunn (2001, p. 7) commented on the importance of taking action when we see injustice occurring:

To speak out might not do any good, but to remain quiet sure does a lot of bad. When no one challenges wrong, then wrong doers gain strength and confidence. They can go beyond speaking harmful words to committing harmful actions . . . speaking out against injustice opens a person to isolation and ridicule. Been there, done that. But, I'd rather be attacked proudly for standing up for what's right than to be ashamed of myself for not speaking at all. So, I'd like to encourage you to stop standing in silence as you witness discrimination, intolerance, and erosion of programs designed to level the playing field.

A fundamental aspect of being an advocate is to perceive a sense of responsibility for the way the world is. As we take more responsibility for our actions, we become more likely to be an advocate for people who are in need of our support (Barry, 1997).

Discussion Questions

1. What is meant by the term *advocacy*?
2. How does advocacy relate to barriers experienced by people with disabilities?
3. How does empowerment relate to advocacy?
4. What methods can you use to help prepare yourself to be an effective advocate?
5. When presenting information to other people on behalf of people with disabilities, what should you consider?
6. What are some ideas to consider when evaluating your ability to be an advocate?
7. What is the value in encouraging people with disabilities to be their own advocates when possible?
8. What is one action you could take today to advocate for people with disabilities?
9. Why is advocating for the rights of people with disabilities your responsibility?
10. Who benefits from advocacy efforts?

Section C

Consider Individual Characteristics

Chapter 16

People, Inclusion, and Physical Limitations

Photo by Lynda Greer

Jon Franks

Jon Franks is a chiropractor who owns a fitness center in Venice, CA. He sustained a spinal cord injury in a motorcycle accident in 1985. Jon is a triathelete who has raced all over the United States, China, and the Virgin Islands.

Jon's Story

It was November, 1985. I was on my way to a UCLA basketball practice (I was working with the team) when the engine on my motorcycle seized up on me, doing a curve at about 40 mph and I slammed into a utility pole. As a chiropractor I do know about the spine, so I knew right away what the score was.

Basketball and fitness have been part of my life since I can remember, so well-meaning people suggested that I go for wheelchair basketball. No way would I settle for less with a sport I excelled in on my feet. So in the hospital I set my mind on the triathalon. I've always been a competitor and the accident didn't kill that spirit. The triathalon is a grueling event . . . just what I wanted. Two months after the accident I was training 15 to 20 hours a week. I'm most competitive in the swimming and running events, weaker in the cycling division. For swimming I wear a wet suit and webbed gloves to give me power, and I do the backstroke . . . breathing's easier. For the run I use a lightweight chair and I use a hand-powered bike designed and built by my friend, Bruce Eikelberger. We're working to develop a better bike.

I love the challenge of racing. But it isn't just for me that I do this. I intend to change the image most adults have of people in chairs. And I'm doing it in an effort to raise bucks as well as consciousness. Attitude-wise I want to teach people that being in a chair isn't the most disabling thing; it's the attitude of others. Sometimes it's very difficult for athletes to participate in certain events. I've had my share of rejection because I'm in a chair and a pain in the butt to work around. This segregating athletic events along able-bodied/disabled lines has to stop. And I'm also racing to get sponsors to help raise money for research and technical advances. I believe I'll be out of this chair someday and that kids . . . anyone with a spinal cord injury . . . deserve the chance of complete recovery.

But as long as I'm in this chair I'm going to prove to others that people in chairs are really no different from them. A lot of people don't feel comfortable with wheelchairs . . . and that's got to change. Believe me, it will be better for everybody.

*Latent abilities are like clay. It can be mud on shoes, brick in a
building or a statue that will inspire all who see it. The clay
is the same. The result is dependent on how it is used.*

-James A. Lincoln

Orientation Activity: Zhenya, Kostas, and Susan—What to do?

Directions Alone: Read each of the following situations and answer the questions posed.

- Zhenya, an accountant in your hometown, would like to participate in a tennis program offered by the private country club of which she is a member. As the director of recreation for this country club, what might you do to facilitate participation by Zhenya, who has paraplegia, in the tennis program?

- Kostas, a college student, has expressed a desire to participate in a hiking expedition planned for a weekend adventure with a local community outing club. As a member of this club, what suggestions might you make to assist Kostas, who has spina bifida, to successfully participate in the program?

- You are the assistant coach of your child's softball team. Susan, a 12-year-old, would like to play on the team. Susan has muscular dystrophy and is still able to walk. What are some things you may wish to consider when coaching Susan and what is some information you may wish to discuss with Susan, the coach, and perhaps her parents?

Directions with Others: Move about the room with your answers and share your strategies for including Zhenya, Kostas, and Susan with another person. Record any strategies that he or she identified that you did not. After a specified time, discuss what you have learned with the entire group.

Debriefing: To include Zhenya in the tennis program we can ensure that the parking lot and the path to the tennis courts are accessible to people using wheelchairs. Also, we can advertise that the tennis program is available to every member in the club. Modification to the rules as established by the National Foundation of Wheelchair Tennis will help to assure success for Zhenya. For example, players who use wheelchairs are allowed two bounces of the ball. Ensure that she is able to participate with her friends. If she is a new member, arrange matches with peers of similar ages. We can also identify other resources she could take advantage of to improve her skills. If Zhenya has limited strength and endurance, the use of a ball retrieving basket or a person to pick up the loose balls may be helpful.

To facilitate Kostas's participation in the hiking expedition, we could first talk with Kostas about his skill and experience as a hiker. Also, we can obtain the difficulty level of the trail and match the skill level required to Kostas's skills. We may want to hike the trail in advance conducting an environmental inventory to identify obstacles that will need to be negotiated. It may be helpful if we determine what the weight of his pack should be based on Kostas's endurance, strength and agility. As with any camping expedition, a communication device that can signal distress to others may be useful. We also will want to determine strategies to accommodate people on the expedition who move at slower speeds. It can be useful to schedule breaks to allow participants who are moving more slowly than others to catch up and rest. In addition, we can identify meeting points along the trail to encourage people on the expedition to come together. If Kostas is unsteady on his feet, he may wish to use a hiking stick or cane or he may feel comfortable being paired with someone who can assist him as needed.

To encourage Susan's inclusion on the softball team, we can visit with Susan and her family to discuss her strengths as well as concerns for participation. Also, we can have her share any adaptations she has already made when playing softball. If Susan has difficulty running, we may suggest she hit and have another player run the bases for her. If she has difficulty moving, perhaps she may prefer to play the position of catcher, pitcher, or first baseman. She may be paired with someone playing other positions that could catch the ball, throw it to her, and then allow her to make the play. Rotating the entire lineup to avoid fatigue may be useful if endurance is a problem. For instance, players only play for two consecutive innings and then are rested for one inning.

Consider the following questions as you think about the orientation activity:

- How can you promote participation of individuals with physical limitations in your recreation program?
- Why is it important for recreation providers to talk to new participants when they begin a program?
- What are some considerations for the inclusion of participants who may have limited strength, balance, or endurance?

Introduction

People acquire physical disabilities in many different ways. Consider the perspectives of people with disabilities when attempting to assist them in participating in meaningful leisure pursuits. This chapter presents some information to address these issues. To set the tone for this chapter and to identify the possibilities for people with disabilities, consider the words of Gloria Brawn (1995, p. 13):

> I am a quadriplegic from a car/moose accident seven years ago. Since my accident I have been up in a helicopter twice. I also have been on the back of a Harley Davidson and had a wonderful time. I've gone snow sliding with my granddaughters here in Maine. I go swimming in our pool and fishing in our boat in the summer. I have been camping and on a trip to Nashville. Did everything I wanted to do down there. I want to go skydiving this summer. I feel the days of keeping the disabled in the closet are gone.

Meet Joan, Who Has Many Interests

People describe Joan as a lifelong activist, committed to a wide range of issues and interests, such as the peace movement and international affairs. Recently, she has become an activist for the rights of people with disabilities. "When you don't have something wrong, it's not part of your life," she said. "It didn't hit home until it hit me."

Joan's range of interests is obvious in even a quick visit to her apartment. Huge flower boxes made of railroad ties, overflowing with her flowers, flanks the wheelchair ramp to the door. The most prominent object in the living room is a loom—she says she made 10 sweaters one year as Christmas gifts. Delicate Japanese rice-paper cutouts, gifts from a friend, decorate the walls. And of course, there are the books and records. Joan has no intention of slowing down.

> I have to keep going—there's a lot left to do. There's so much— the homeless, the hungry . . . civil and social rights. We are not facing the needs of the poor, the homeless, the children . . . These are the problems we need to face as a country, a state, and as a county right down here in the local level. I hate this flag-waving, this superficial patriotism. It's just blinders to cover the real problems.

Joan has multiple sclerosis. The symptoms became noticeable during her freshman year in college, approximately 20 years ago. In addition to other physical traumas, the multiple sclerosis has weakened her legs so that she has used a wheelchair for the past 13 years. Joan said she has learned from her disability.

> My aims and goals in life changed a great deal because of my illness. Things that were so important weren't important after all. You learn to smell the flowers, look at the trees. I'm really pretty normal—that's all part of our advocacy, to get people to see that persons with disabilities are just like anyone else.

What are characteristics of multiple sclerosis?

Multiple sclerosis is a progressive disease affecting the central nervous system, which includes the brain and spinal column. *Multiple* means many or varying and *sclerosis* means scarring or hardening.

Although there is no known cause of or cure for multiple sclerosis, some patterns exist. It affects more women than men and Caucasians more than other ethnic groups. It typically occurs anytime from adolescence until the early 50s, with the average age of the onset approximately age 30.

Multiple sclerosis involves spontaneously appearing lesions at the nerve endings of the central nervous system and the disappearance of the protective nerve coverings. As the lesions heal, the sclerosis (scarring) occurs. The scars prevent neurological impulses from traveling to and from the brain. The result of these damaged transmissions include numbness and tingling of hands or feet, weakness of lower extremities, loss of voluntary movements of muscles, loss of vision in one or both eyes, and facial numbness. Most individuals with multiple sclerosis will also develop cognitive problems and affective disorders which result in personality changes, memory loss, and decreased planning and organizational abilities (Sanford & Petajan, 1990). The location and severity of the sclerosis will determine the degree of disability.

For most individuals, multiple sclerosis follows a course of exacerbations and remissions. A new outbreak of lesions, an *exacerbation*, is characterized by increasing severity of the symptoms. When lesions heal, relief of some symptoms may result. These episodes are known as periods of remission. At times, exacerbation is characterized by decreased motor ability and remissions by increased motor proficiency. Periods of exacerbations and remissions are unpredictable and depression is a common emotional response by individuals with this disease (Sanford & Petajan, 1990).

As the disease progresses, the individual may need to rely upon a cane or wheelchair for mobility.

What are considerations for inclusion of people with multiple sclerosis?

Be Prepared for Fluctuations in Behaviors

Since the skills of people with multiple sclerosis vary from time to time because of exacerbations and remissions, being prepared to deal with fluctuations in performance may enhance a person's success. Some people may require the use of a wheelchair during times of exacerbations and then later be able to walk with assistance during a period of remission.

Some participants may interpret fluctuation in performance as a lack of effort or commitment to an activity. Being aware of this variation in abilities can allow us to make accommodations for the person and facilitate positive interactions between participants.

Provide Support

Fluctuation and reduction in participation skills, as well as the cognitive and affective changes, can be frustrating for a person with multiple sclerosis. Providing support for this person and demonstrating sensitivity to the experience can help us increase the likelihood of successful leisure participation.

Meet Chuck, Who Enjoys Lifting Weights

Fabbri (1991) reported that as a youth playing tackle football games between neighborhoods, Chuck awkwardly pursued running backs and took on blockers. He wore a pair of steel leg braces at his defensive line position. "The offensive linemen looked at me kind of funny and played me namby-pamby. But after the first couple of plays, they realized I could play and started taking clean shots at me." Chuck progressed from neighborhood noseguard to world champion weightlifter. He won the gold medal at the 1988 Paralympics in Seoul, Korea, and has won four world titles.

> I wanted to be a wrestler. When I was a sophomore in high school, I asked the wrestling coach if I could try out for the team. He told me that I couldn't come out because of the handicap, but he asked me if I wanted to be the damn equipment manager.

Another coach suggested he try the weight room instead. In six months, Chuck was bench-pressing 260 pounds. That year, he finished second in the national championships and two years later he was the national champion. His national bench-pressing record in the 165-pound division was 485 pounds and his world record was 462 pounds. Chuck fits his training schedule around a full-time job as a stockroom manager.

Some people may view Chuck's participation and excellence in athletics as unique because he is paralyzed from the waist down by spina bifida. He can walk with the aid of braces and crutches and has been able to make many adaptations to recreation activities of interest allowing him to continue active participation.

What are characteristics of spina bifida?

Spina bifida means cleft spine and is a congenital disability of the spinal column that occurs early in prenatal development, as the central nervous system forms. The defect, usually located in the lumbar area, occurs when the covering of the spinal cord is displaced and forms a sac-like protrusion. The protrusion then causes improper formation of the vertebrae and results in externally exposing the abnormal protrusion. The effects of this congenital disability range from no noticeable effects to paraplegia.

Although there are different forms of spinal bifida the most severe form of spina bifida is called mylomeningocele. With *mylomeningocele*, a portion of the spinal cord itself protrudes through the back, sometimes exposing tissue and nerves. Most children born with this form of spina bifida also have *hydrocephalus*, which occurs because spinal fluid is not absorbed properly and this fluid builds up in a person's head. A surgical shunting procedure can control hydrocephalus by draining the fluid into portions of the body that can dispose of the fluid. Without this procedure the pressure can cause an enlargement of a person's head, seizures, blindness, and brain damage.

Effects of mylomeningocele may include muscle weakness or paralysis below the affected area of the spine, accompanied by loss of sensation and loss of bowel and bladder control. Children with this type of spina bifida often need mobility assistance in the form of crutches, braces, or wheelchairs. Furthermore, children with both spina bifida and hydrocephalus may have difficulty attending to tasks, expressing thoughts, and understanding language. This can result in learning problems; however, early intervention can help to reduce the severity.

What are considerations for inclusion of people with spina bifida?

Consider Decreased Sensation

People with spina bifida often have reduced sensation in their legs and may not be able to differentiate between temperatures. Care should be taken in activities to prevent burns from hot water or other sources of heat. In addition, with the loss of pain sensation, people with spina bifida may not feel the friction of their braces, resulting in *decubitus ulcers* (pressure sores).

Communicate with Participants to Determine Their Preferences

Keeping open lines of communication with individuals who have spina bifida will help alleviate possible problems. Speak with participants who have spina bifida to determine their interests and preferences. Avoid being overprotective of participants and do not make assumptions about their interests. For example, Zoerink (1988) found that many of the young people with spina bifida in his study preferred active and group-oriented leisure experiences and sports activities. Together with the participant we can explore ways to facilitate optimal participation with attention to safety and health.

Meet Marty, the "Family Man"

His friends consider Marty a "family man." His wife, children, and grand-children are the most important aspects of his life. He takes great pleasure in spending time with them and talking about their accomplishments. In addition to his family, he has two major leisure pursuits.

Since his retirement, Marty volunteers at a local hospital, assisting nurses with office management tasks. Although the nurses appreciate his contributions to office operations and his strong work ethic, they value even more his friendship and sense of humor. They characterize him as a person who is playful and fun to be around while he accomplishes a great deal of work.

Walking is another one of Marty's passions. He rises early in the morning to complete a vigorous 30-minute walk. Marty views walking as an activity he enjoys and something that offers him a sense of accomplishment, including significant health benefits. Since developing osteoarthritis,

Marty awakens in the morning stiff and in pain. However, after his morning stroll, the pain subsides and he is able to go about his day with increased range of motion and vigor.

What are characteristics of arthritis?

According to the Arthritis Foundation, arthritis occurs among one in seven people (including children and adults) and one in three families. It affects three times as many women as men, and with over 100 different forms it is the most common crippling disease in the United States. While many people will not experience serious physical problems, many people have arthritis that requires medical treatment. A common denominator for more than 100 different forms of arthritis is pain and stiffness in or around the joints of the body (Reyes, 1995). Inflammation of joint tissues or breakdown of joint cartilage (spongy tissue at tips of bones that acts as a shock absorber) often causes arthritis.

The word *arthritis* is derived from the Greek word *arthros*, which means joint, and the suffix *itis*, which is translated to mean inflammation. Understanding the derivatives of this word help us define arthritis as a group of conditions that involve an inflammation of the joints. Most types of arthritis are characterized by inflammation of the joints, tissue, and bones, which results in stiffness, swelling, redness, and pain. Two of the more recognized types of arthritis are osteoarthritis and rheumatoid arthritis.

The most common form of arthritis—osteoarthritis—affects more than 20 million Americans (Lemonick, 1998). *Osteoarthritis* is a degenerative joint disease, rarely found in people younger than 45, caused by the erosion of cartilage. This degenerative disease creates stiffness, swelling, and pain. As the cartilage erodes, bones begin to rub against one another, resulting in pain, stiffness, and joint deformity. Fortunately, osteoarthritis usually responds to medication and exercise.

Rheumatoid arthritis is one of the more profound forms of arthritis, typically resulting in severe inflammation that attacks primarily the joints. It can also affect the skin, blood vessels, muscles, spleen, heart, and even the eyes. Individuals may report feeling "sick all over," with fatigue, poor appetite, fevers, weight loss, enlarged lymph glands, and excessive sweating or cold tingling hands and feet. It is a progressive type of arthritis characterized by unpredictable fluctuations in the degree of pain and stiffness. Lemonick (1998) reported that rheumatoid arthritis can occur at any age and is experienced by over 2 million Americans.

What are considerations for inclusion of people with arthritis?

Talk with Participants

Since some people with arthritis may be in considerable pain, maintain open communication with them when participating in activities. Open lines of communication will increase the likelihood they will feel comfortable discussing with you their mobility limitations in certain situations. In addition, it is often useful to consider the existing weather conditions, because they can affect the extent of stiffness and pain associated with the joints. Typical treatment for many people with arthritis is rest, exercise and the use of nonsteroid anti-inflammatory drugs such as aspirin.

Consider Using Exercise

Research supports the belief that most people with arthritis who follow a sensible exercise program may ease pain and avoid disability (Boling, 1995). Walking, swimming, stretching, and even aerobics can help reduce joint and pain stiffness, build stronger muscles and bones, and improve overall health. Aquatic programs such as water walking, swimming, and water aerobics are frequently recommended forms of exercise for people with arthritis. The Arthritis Foundation offers extensive recommendations for activities and exercise programs tailored for people with differing forms and severity of arthritis.

When people experience pain during periods of exercise, encourage them to take a brief rest. If affected joints are hot and inflamed the activity may be too strenuous. Recommend that they discontinue the exercise at that time. The goal for an exercise program is typically mobility rather than strength. Moving the joints through their full range of motion at least twice daily can help in continued free movement.

Make Adaptations

There are many benefits of making adaptations to recreation activities so that individuals with arthritis may continue to participate. Some adaptations require minor adjustments, such as adding a Velcro strap to a lap pillow to help a person hold a book. Cardholders can be improvised as simply as sticking cards upright in Silly Putty or Play-Doh or standing them in a shallow box filled with sand. Buildings meeting the requirements of the ADA in regard to faucet handles, door openers, and ramps enable people with arthritis to move about with dignity and independence.

Meet Stacy and Jimmy, Who Are Quite in Love

Sleek, aerodynamic racing wheelchairs spin around the practice track, pushed by athletes intent on bettering a previous time. As he finishes his last lap, Jimmy rolls to a stop, panting, and gratefully accepts ice water from his coach. "Pretty good time," she says, consulting her stopwatch. The coach is Jimmy's wife, Stacy. The two met at a track meet several years ago when Stacy was a student intern. They hit it off immediately. In one year, they were married. "My parents thought I was crazy," she admits. "They had that old-fashioned way of thinking that people in wheelchairs can't do a lot of things. They said, 'You love scuba diving, dancing, sports—think of all the things you'll miss!'"

As they got to know Jimmy, Stacy's parents' fears dissolved. And from the many interests the couple shares, it appears that neither of them misses out on anything. "We're both very athletic, and training for wheelchair sports competitions keeps us pretty busy. Often when he's training for a race, I'll ride my bike alongside for exercise," says Stacy. The two introduced each other to new interests that they now share. Due to Stacy's love of scuba diving, Jimmy got his certification and the two go diving in the Florida Keys almost every year. Jimmy sparked Stacy's interest in deer hunting, and now they hunt together. Jimmy hunts from an all-terrain vehicle that he drives to the spot he chooses after he drops Stacy off at her chosen location.

Things weren't always picture-perfect for Jimmy. "I was 23 when I was paralyzed in a car accident. After that, I went into seclusion for about a year. I didn't want to see my old friends because I didn't want them to feel sorry for me. I had been dating several girls, but I dropped them, too. I had no interest in seeing anyone. I thought, "What would a girl see in me, in a chair?" After he finally started getting out of the house and being active, his confidence returned. "You eventually realize you're the same person you were before. And as you meet people and find that they still find you attractive, your self-esteem comes back. You have to keep believing in yourself in order to be a likable person. No one's interested in being with someone who's having a pity party for himself! When I was injured, it was kind of like I ended one life and started another one. Of course, I'd love to walk again. But honestly, if the choice came down to giving up Stacy and wheelchair sports and going back to my life the way it was before, I'd choose to stay in a chair."

What are characteristics of spinal cord injuries?

The spinal cord, contained within the vertebra, transports impulses to and from the brain. Impairment of the transporting of impulses occurs as a result of the extent and location of an injury to the spinal column. Impairment experienced from a spinal cord injury is permanent because the spinal cord is not able to regenerate.

The degree of disability associated with a spinal cord injury is classified according to the level of the injury to the spinal column, as well as the severity of the injury. Spinal injuries are classified as *complete* (no sensation or movement) or *incomplete* (some sensation and motor function).

Paraplegia describes injuries to the sacral, lumbar, or thoracic areas. The sacral and lumbar regions of the spine are the areas below the waist. Injury to this area may cause some paralysis, which can result in needing leg braces for mobility and some loss of sensation in the lower extremities. People with injuries in the thoracic area (between the waist and shoulders) can typically live independently in a wheelchair accessible environment.

Injuries to the cervical area or neck are the most serious and result in *quadriplegia*, which causes the greatest amount of disability. With an injury to the lowest portion of the cervical area, some individuals can live alone, independently, with alterations to their homes. With an injury at the highest portion of the cervical area, individuals can control some neck muscles. They can typically control their wheelchairs with the assistance of a chin control or a sip-and-puff apparatus. They are able to control their environments or work a computer with a mouth stick, but need human assistance for daily care needs.

Traumatic spinal cord injuries occur in a split second, but necessitate a life-long adjustment to almost all domains of life, including leisure (Lee, Mittelstaedt & Askins, 1999). In-depth interviews were conducted with 14 adults with spinal cord injuries who had returned to their communities. Not surprisingly, these people reported how the loss of their physical ability was a constraint to returning to their community (Dattilo, Caldwell, Lee & Kleiber, 1998). Two of the respondents made the following statements:

> I like to hunt a lot . . . before I could hold a rifle like this, but now when I hold it I fall forward because I don't have the balance. I haven't been hunting yet . . .
> I tried playing racquetball for the first time two weeks ago, after two or three games I was exhausted where normally I could go five or six games, so it's definitely more tiresome for me now.

Although the respondents identified their physical limitations as a constraint to leisure, they reported a strong desire to participate in community-based recreation activities. The social networks and relationships with members of the community were critical. Use strategies that promote inclusive leisure services and use leisure education to help people with physical disabilities become involved in community life.

As an example of the role leisure can play in someone's sense of identity consider the words of Curtis Lovejoy, who was injured in a car accident when he was 29 years old. Curtis described what he says to people who have recently experienced a severe physical trauma (Grizzle, 1994, p. 5):

> I tell patients I visit that the sky's the limit, and that they all have the same opportunities I have. When they can't see the light at the end of the tunnel, I tell them to take a look at me. I broke my neck and went from 175 pounds to 85 pounds. Now I can scuba dive, water ski, and I've taken up swimming competitively.

What are considerations for inclusion of people with spinal cord injuries?

Adapt Activities as Needed

People with spinal cord injuries have reduced mobility and motor strength. Therefore, some recreation activities that have extensive physical demands may need to be adapted. If an adaptation is required, work with the person to determine the most effective adaptation.

Consider Physical Needs of Participants

Individuals with impaired sensation will need to shift their weight when sitting to avoid developing pressure sores; therefore, inserting breaks into extended activities may be helpful. Many people must attend to bathroom needs on a strict schedule so it is important to have accessible restrooms near areas where programs are provided. Because individuals with spinal cord injuries are unable to regulate their body temperatures below the level of injury, it is helpful for us to be sensitive and provide appropriate means for cooling and warming, such as water spray bottles or blankets.

Consider Participants' Motivation and Promote Their Inclusion

When they are first injured, some people with spinal cord injuries think their lives are over. Some think they will never be athletic again, they will never be able to work again, or they will never fall in love again. Hopefully, during the rehabilitation process, these myths are stripped away one by one. They discover that there are many recreation activities available to them, there are many jobs they are qualified for, and relationships can be as meaningful as they ever were.

Avoid Setting Limits on What People Can Do

An important contribution that we can make to the lives of people with spinal cord injuries is to not set limits on them because of their reduced mobility. Whenever people think an individual with a spinal cord injury cannot participate in a given recreation activity, such as mountain climbing or hang gliding, people who have spinal cord injuries prove them wrong and successfully participate in these activities. We must work to make our programs available to all people and work with individuals to find ways to foster their ability to experience leisure.

Sadowsky (1997) reported on a four-day adventure skills workshop that focused on introducing people with physical disabilities to water sports and outdoor recreation activities. Of the many people with physical disabilities who participated in the workshop, Tommy Baug, a 28-year-old avid outdoorsman and farmer who sustained a spinal cord injury three years prior to the workshop, made the following observation:

> I had never even been on a jet ski until after I was injured. Now I own two, which I use regularly. I feel like the only thing I can't do is stand up and walk. I had a lot more free time after I was injured. [Sports and outdoor activities] have given me something to do instead of sitting around all the time. The most important thing you learn is that there are things you can do and ways you can enjoy life with a spinal cord injury, or whatever disabling injury you have. There's so much that you can still do.

Meet Jim, the Big-League Pitcher

Hersch (1991) wrote about the moment for which Jim had long strived. At that time, Jim was a 23-year-old left-hander who had started the baseball season by losing four games for the California Angels. His critics complained that he had no control, no off-speed pitch to confuse hitters, and no minor-league seasoning to draw on. The words missing were the ones Jim was most accustomed to hearing, the ones that said he could not succeed because he had no right hand. "It was all about pitching—this guy stinks. I thought, there it is. Finally, I've arrived."

After untold fastballs in Little League, three successful years at the university, stardom at the Olympics, award-acceptance speeches, and three seasons in the majors, Jim was at last being seen as he had always seen himself—as a pitcher. He was no longer the feature attraction of a media circus or the living embodiment of a made-for-TV movie—he was one fifth of the Angel rotation. True, he is visible proof that what appears to some a limitation need not be. But he is equally notable for the commercial ventures he turns down and for the time he takes with the children with physical disabilities who flock to him. Interestingly enough, immediately following his disastrous start, he went on to win 14 games, losing only 4, and becoming one of the best pitchers in the American League.

Since he was 5, Jim has practiced switching his glove from his left hand to his right arm and back again, a maneuver that is now fluid and routine. He can do it in that instant before the bat meets the ball. Jim is living his dream, and he appreciates it. He is also living the dream of many others who aspire to overcome their disabilities, and he appreciates that, too. He still answers more than 300 pieces of mail a week, sometimes giving personal responses to writers who need encouragement or reassurance. In each city he goes to, Jim chats easily with youngsters who come to the park just to see him.

What are characteristics of amputations or congenital absences?

The absence of a portion of a limb is an *orthopedic impairment* that can occur in two possible ways. A person who is born with a portion of one or more of their limbs missing is identified as having a *congenital absence*. If, however, a person is born with all their limbs but experiences a trauma or infection that results in the need to remove a portion of a limb, then the person is identified as having an *amputation*. Sometimes individuals will wear a prosthesis. *Prostheses* are customized to the person and, with growing children, need to be changed periodically.

What are considerations for inclusion of people with amputations or congenital absences?

Help Care for Prostheses

In the case of amputation, changes in the residual limb may require adjustment of the prosthesis. Since prostheses are very expensive, care should be taken not to damage them by exposing them to extreme heat, cold, dampness, or wetness. Typically prostheses are removed before entering a swimming pool area and may be covered when participating in recreation activities requiring active physical contact. Individuals with missing lower limbs or an amputation may choose to use a wheelchair for mobility and for sport and recreation participation.

Promote Active Participation

Nissen and Newman (1992) reported that the inability to participate in recreational activities was the most restricted aspect of a person's reintegration to their community following an amputation. There is a specific need for many individuals having a loss of some or all of their lower limbs to increase mobility skills for walking on uneven ground during such activities as hunting and fishing. People with amputations and those born without a portion of a limb should be supported to receive the benefits of actively participating in recreation activities of their choosing.

Meet Darren, Who Loves to Travel

Darren, who has childhood muscular dystrophy, attributes much of his success to his parents' support. His motorized wheelchair allows him to be active within his community and facilitates his involvement in travel and tourism.

I use an electric wheelchair and my father looks after most of my daily physical needs. Movement is fairly restricted and I must rely on others to hand me things. This does not stop me going out or doing many things. It does mean, however, that activities must be planned in advance. I have gone out with a number of girls, but I have not had a long-term relationship. Nonetheless, I have lots of friends, I have traveled overseas a number of times, I frequently go out socially and I work part time. I really believe that you must live your life, do your best and experience as much as you can. (Gething, 1992)

What are characteristics of muscular dystrophy?

Muscular dystrophy is a general designation for a group of chronic, hereditary diseases characterized by the progressive degeneration and weakness of voluntary muscles. It is not typically painful. *Childhood muscular dystrophy* (Duchenne), the most common type of muscular dystrophy, displays the most rapid progression and has a poor prognosis. The condition involves general weakening and loss of voluntary muscle control. It occurs only in males and typically onset occurs prior to age six. The pelvic musculature is affected first, resulting in some loss of independence by age 10.

What are considerations for inclusion of people with muscular dystrophy?

Consider the Condition's Progressive Nature

Since common characteristics of muscular dystrophy include slowness and fatigue, make adaptations to activities requiring physical participation and incorporate rest periods into prolonged activity. Because muscular dystrophy is progressive and not static, observe participants frequently and make adaptations as skills deteriorate.

Provide Social Support

Provide social support to help people with muscular dystrophy adjust to a reduction in skill levels. Attempts to make accommodations that permit continued participation with peers is critical to avoid the possibility of social isolation in response to reductions in physical skills. Development of skills associated with recreation activities that require limited vigorous physical exertion may provide additional avenues for individuals to experience leisure.

Meet Roberta, Who Enjoys Her New Image

Roberta was an active girl involved in many activities, including her high school cheerleading team. At the age of 16, a drunk driver hit the car Roberta was driving and she sustained a spinal cord injury that resulted in paraplegia. After months of intensive rehabilitation, she could walk again with the aid of crutches and long leg braces. Roberta soon discovered however, that walking took considerable time and effort, and despite her early insistence about walking, she began to use a wheelchair for mobility.

Roberta's insurance company covered the cost of her wheelchair: a 40-pound, stainless steel chair with padded armrests. In 1974, this chair was state-of-the-art. By 1991, Roberta's wheelchair was badly worn: the armrests were torn and the broken vinyl covering scratched her arms. One footrest now dragged on the ground, impeding her mobility. Although Roberta had a good job at a hospital, she could not afford a new wheelchair. She was embarrassed to go out socially in her worn-out chair, which hindered her leisure lifestyle. Her only outlet now was a new performing arts group that included people with disabilities. This was her opportunity to be able to dance and act in a supportive environment. Dancing and acting were activities she had wanted to participate in since her accident, but had found acceptance in other groups difficult.

Through Roberta's participation in the performing arts group, she learned about a small grant that would buy her a new wheelchair. Roberta applied, and six months later she finally got a new wheelchair. She was ecstatic! She picked a bright red chair built for speed and agility. The new wheelchair weighed only 18 pounds, allowing her to transfer it into the car with much less effort than her old chair. Roberta loved her new-found freedom. She took up tennis, and even went out socially with her friends from work. She claimed:

> Not only am I able to participate in recreational activities that were almost impossible with my old chair, I feel like I look better. I used to be embarrassed to leave my house, now I feel like a new person. This is better than a new car.

What are considerations associated with wheelchair technology?

The modern wheelchair has changed considerably from the "wicker chair on wheels" used earlier in this century. Today wheelchairs can be customized to meet individual needs and lifestyles. In addition, wheelchairs can be equipped with seating systems to accommodate individuals with specific positioning needs. Some wheelchairs are designed to be used for specific sports, such as those built for road racing, tennis, or fishing.

Individuals with paraplegia and lower-extremity amputations and disabilities most frequently use lightweight wheelchairs. With aluminum, titanium, or composite frames, lightweight chairs are available with rigid frames and pop-off wheels (average weight 20 pounds) or folding frames with fixed wheels (average weight 26 pounds). Other optional features include swing-away or removable armrests; flip-up, swing-away, or rigid footrests; push handles; and mag wheels. The presence or absence of these features helps individuals tailor the chair to their work and leisure lifestyle.

Highly specialized sports chairs for use by athletes, both amateur and professional, came into popular use in the 1980s. Many racing wheelchairs feature aerodynamic, tri-wheel designs for greater stability, cornering, and speed. Court chairs are used for sports such as tennis and basketball, and some feature one central front caster to facilitate sharp turns and forward stability.

The American National Standards Institute and the Rehabilitation Engineers Society of North America, an interdisciplinary organization that promotes assistive technology for people with disabilities, have developed standards for wheelchairs. The standards address seating such as dimensions, upholstery, and optional cushions; structure such as weight, frame material, and casters; performance such as minimum turn around width, camber; and safety such as flammability, and tip angles. These standards are voluntary and are designed to help consumers make more educated selections and purchases. For additional information see the chapter on assistive technology.

What are characteristics of people using a wheelchair?

Many people choose to use a wheelchair for a variety of reasons. Some people can walk with aids and use a wheelchair because they can conserve energy and move about quickly. However, other people require the use of the wheelchair to move about freely. Consider Jenny, who stated,

> I feel distinctly affectionate toward my wheelchair. I did a lot of falling down and hurting myself and wasted a lot of energy using canes and crutches. When I see a visual image of myself in my wheelchair, I see a handsome, accomplished woman instead of the "fearful-of-falling-down" woman I was when I was struggling to remain standing. Would I be happier if I could suddenly walk and not need the chair anymore? Only if I could keep the attitude toward it that I have gained up until this time as a result of being a wheelchair user. Only if I didn't lose the spiritual growth I have experienced working as a person with a disability. Without this continued growth I could not be happy.

One concern common among individuals with obvious disabilities is the fear of being viewed as "an easy target" by individuals looking for someone to victimize. Retzinger (1990) quoted Larry, who realizes that defending oneself on the street is more necessary today than ever before.

> You hear about muggings every day. People with visual impairments knocked down and robbed while they lie helpless on the ground. Purses snatched from people in wheelchairs as they go about their daily errands. Many people using wheelchairs would go out more if they had some form of self-defense knowledge. To go out by yourself, you must develop confidence that, if confronted with a situation, you can defend yourself. I've always had a strong desire to help other people who use wheelchairs feel that they're not vulnerable or easy targets for muggers. Through wheelchair karate, this has become a reality.

Jerry, a fourth-degree black belt in karate who runs a karate school, suggested to Larry that a wheelchair did not have to prevent him from protecting himself. Together the two developed a wheelchair karate system. After extensive discussion and training, the two discovered that some techniques would work on the street and others would be important in developing speed and accuracy. Wheelchair karate techniques use various movements involving wheelchair maneuvers, enabling people to defend themselves against possible assailants.

What are considerations for inclusion of people who use wheelchairs?

Speak Directly

Speak directly to the person in the wheelchair and not to someone nearby as if the person in the wheelchair did not exist. If the conversation lasts more than a few minutes, consider sitting down, squatting, or kneeling to get on the same level as the person. It is fine to use expressions like "running along" when speaking; the person likely expresses things the same way. Avoid discouraging children from asking questions about the wheelchair, because communication helps overcome negative attitudes. It may help to describe physical obstacles that could impede travel when giving directions to an individual who uses a wheelchair.

Consider the Wheelchair as an Extension of the Person

Avoid classifying people who use wheelchairs as sick because, as stated earlier, wheelchairs are used for a variety of reasons. Do not assume that using a wheelchair is a tragedy; it is a means of freedom that allows independent movement. When a person "transfers" out of the wheelchair to a chair, car, swimming pool, or bed, do not move their wheelchair out of reaching distance.

Provide Inclusive Services for Children

Children can begin to use a wheelchair for independence as early as 3 or 4 years of age. One wheelchair manufacturer even has a club for children, featuring T-shirts, a newsletter, and summer camping opportunities. Children's wheelchairs come in child-pleasing colors ranging from cotton candy pink to neon green, and in manual and power models. (See Chapter 19 for information on power chairs.)

Final Thoughts

The following passage is adapted from the verse entitled "Other People" by an anonymous author.

I don't think anybody's ugly. I think that something ugly always has something beautiful in it. I don't judge a person by ugliness and prettiness in their faces, in their figure. I don't judge a person like that. I judge a person by talent, by their personality, how they think about other people. A beautiful person smiles. I appreciate people that try to help me. But sometimes they want to help too much. Mostly, I can do everything for myself. Going downstairs, for instance. Some people try to carry me all the way. But I can do that mostly by myself unless it's too high. People that know me and are around me often, they know what I can do and can't do for myself. But people that I'm just getting to know, they want to treat me different so I try to tell them. I try to explain what they could do for me, what I appreciate. For example, if I'm getting to know somebody and the ice cream truck comes, they go "I'll buy it for you." I try to explain, "That's okay, I could do that." The way I was raised was to do things for myself. My mother is a very strict woman. I got polio when I was four-and-a-half. She always taught me to do all I could for myself and not to depend on everyone else. It makes me feel useless when people think I can't do nothing myself. I don't like them to treat me nice, or any special way. I like them to treat me like any other kid running around—just like a regular kid.

It is helpful to consider the perspectives of people with disabilities when attempting to include them into community leisure programs. Burstein (1999, p. 9) as she wrote about her initial feelings related to having multiple sclerosis and using a motorized wheelchair:

Entering the room became a command performance, starring my motorized wheelchair. "Hi, I'm The Wheelchair and this is Ellen with me." I could not tolerate the look and feel of my wheelchair and I was devastated by the loss of height. I had two choices: give up and fade into self-imposed oblivion or move on. I chose the latter. A wheelchair would not be a metaphor for my life. Rather, it would be a tool to enable me to enjoy life and participate in it.

Discussion Questions

1. What are characteristics of multiple sclerosis?
2. What are considerations for inclusion of people with multiple sclerosis?
3. What are characteristics of spina bifida?
4. What are considerations for inclusion of people with spina bifida?
5. What are characteristics of arthritis?
6. What are considerations for inclusion of people with arthritis?
7. What are characteristics of spinal cord injury?
8. What are considerations for inclusion of people with spinal cord injury?
9. What are characteristics of amputations or congenital absences?
10. What are considerations for inclusion of people with amputations or congenital absences?
11. What are characteristics of muscular dystrophy?
12. What are considerations for inclusion of people with muscular dystrophy?
13. What are characteristics of people who use wheelchairs?
14. What are considerations for inclusion of people who use wheelchairs?

Photo by Lynda Greer

Kate Gainer

Kate Gainer, pictured with her husband Willie Smith and their son
Michael, was born with cerebral palsy. Kate is an active advocate for
people with disabilities, serving as a volunteer member of various commis-
sions and advocate organizations. She also works for the Atlanta Center for
Independent Living.

Kate's Story

I guess I was one of the pioneer children in special education in Atlanta. In 1953, when I was 4, the first special education class for black children opened up. It was funded by Easter Seals and 16 of us were selected by doctors at a clinic in Atlanta. When my mother learned of the program she pushed hard to see that I got in; she wanted her baby to go to school. When I went to the elementary program, the teacher from pre-school went with us. Mrs. Muscia White was the only black teacher in the city with a background in special ed. More important than her background, though, was her belief that her "babies" deserved the best. She exposed us to a lot of things other kids didn't get . . . all kinds of field trips . . . to a farm . . . the symphony. After all this time she still keeps up with her "babies." This was a very important time in my life; it was during this period that Kate was formed.

In the sixth and seventh grades I was mainstreamed on a partial basis. It was great! Those kids treated me like one of the gang. These same kids were my classmates at Booker T. Washington H. S., the first black high school built in Atlanta. So I had a support system already. The only real problems I had were architectural barriers.

By the time I got to college those barriers weren't a problem. I wanted to go into marketing. I've always had strong writing skills and wanted to use them in the area of marketing. One of my professors told me that he didn't think I'd make it in marketing because the business world wasn't ready for a severely disabled person who made strange involuntary movements and talked with what I call the "C. P. dialect." And he was right. For every interview I had I got a ridiculous reason I couldn't have the job. None of them had anything to do with my professional ability. I was shocked and angry. Up until college I believed that if a person is smart enough and works hard enough, disability doesn't make any difference.

So I decided I was going to save the world . . . at least for kids with disabilities that would come along later. The first thing I did was serve on the accommodations committee for Federal Section 504 funding qualifications. Since then I have served on a lot of committees, councils, etc. to secure a better life for people with disabilities. The most frustrating thing is that it should be so simple. The basic level of accessibility to life . . . jobs, transportation, housing . . . should be there for all of us without such a struggle. But that's not the way it is. And until that's the way it is, Kate Gainer will be out there, WORKING!

Chapter 17

People, Inclusion, and Cognitive Limitations

Photo by Lynda Greer

Peter Thornburgh

Peter Thornburgh lives in Harrisburg, Pennsylvania, and works in nearby Mechanicsburg at the Center for Industrial Training. Peter sustained a brain injury when he was in an accident at the age of 4 months. This picture was taken in Washington, DC, at the home of his parents, Dick and Ginny Thornburgh.

Peter's Story

I'm 31 years old. I live in Harrisburg in a house with Brian, Todd and Ron, Michael and Tim. Four people come in to help. They don't live there. They help plan, remind people about things . . . just help out. Everyone who lives in the house works.

I work in Mechanicsburg at C.I.T. (Center for Industrial Training). I like my work . . . I pack boxes, sweep, help people. I have good friends at work. I take four buses to work . . . two over and two back. I like taking buses. I know how to take buses in Pittsburgh, Harrisburg, and Washington I take Greyhound buses, too. I like to fly.

My church is the Linglestown Church of God. I go every Sunday. The church van picks me up. At church I sit with Carol Grauel. Her husband is Jim. He sings in the choir. They are my church family. I love going to church. I love God. He is in Heaven, so is Jesus. And my first Mom. Mom (Ginny Thornburgh) is my second Mom.

I want to live somewhere else . . . with more room, not so many people. I want more friends my age. I want to do more things . . . shopping at malls and stores, baseball games . . . the Phillies . . . I like the Pirates, too . . . hockey games and the Hershey Bears.

I know how to get up by myself. I know when to pack my lunch. I know how to take a bus. I do a lot for myself. Sometimes I do need staff. Sometimes I don't need staff at all.

Recognizing our common humanity opened all of us to further learning.
-K. E. Eble

Orientation Activity: Bill and Shantel— What to do?

Directions Alone: Read the following situations and write a paragraph describing your reactions.

1. William, a 38-year-old man interested in joining a competitive softball league, has a wonderful sense of humor and Down syndrome. The recreation supervisor, Ron Turner, says, "Billy, come into my office. Be a good boy and we will see what it is you want." William is hurt and angry. He does not like being called "Billy"or being considered a "good boy." He thinks of himself as a man. He works, lives in an apartment, and has a girlfriend. He doesn't enjoy being treated or talked to like a child. He wishes Mr. Turner would treat him just like any other adult. William cannot understand why he is called "Billy," while Mr. Turner addresses every other man "Mister."

2. Shantel, a 21-year-old woman who enjoys bowling went one night after work with a few women from her office. Afterwards, a bowler told Shantel that she would be better off joining the bowling league sponsored by the local Association for Persons with Mental Illness, because all her "friends" would be there. Shantel was very hurt. She just wanted to bowl and meet new people. The bowler's remark made her feel different—like she didn't belong.

Directions with Others: Move about the room with your paragraph and share your reactions with another person. After a specified time, discuss what you have learned with the entire group.

Debriefing: For years people believed that individuals who experienced some disruption in their cognitive process including mental retardation, cerebral palsy, epilepsy, traumatic brain injury, and mental health problems should be "with their own kind." This belief created many of the problems we are now trying to remedy, including institutionalization, segregated services, and lack of communication. One way for us to begin to construct ways to promote inclusion is for us to consider the words of James Brady: "What's the difference between a stumbling block and a stepping stone? It's all in the way you approach it."

As leisure services providers it is our task to include people in programs even though they may not think, learn, act, or respond to situations in typical ways. One way for us to begin is by getting to know people with cognitive impairments, learn a little about their conditions, and be prepared to include them in our programs. As you reflect on the learning activity consider the following questions:

- How should you talk to recreation participants who have cognitive impairments?
- Why is it important to treat all recreation participants in a similar manner?
- How can you facilitate inclusion of individuals with cognitive impairments into recreation programs?

Introduction

The brain is the master organ of the body. It controls *autonomic functions* such as heart rate, body temperature, and respiration. These functions are automatic and do not require any conscious thought. The brain also controls *voluntary functions*, those actions that require us to think before acting, such as speaking and walking. Damage to the brain can affect either autonomic or voluntary functions or both, depending on the location and severity of the injury.

This chapter contains a description of various people and impairments caused by damage to the brain. Damage to the brain can occur at any point in the life span—before birth, during childhood and adolescence, or at any time during adulthood—and can be caused by:

- toxic agents such as alcohol, carbon monoxide, or lead,
- brain tumors,
- infection such as AIDS, encephalitis, meningitis, or rubella,
- diseases such as hypertension or sickle-cell anemia, and
- trauma such as brain surgery, concussion, and skull fracture.

Meet Nancy, Who Is a Strong Advocate

When Nancy received her high school equivalency diploma, it was like getting a key and an eraser. The diploma was a key to further education and a career in a helping profession and it helped erase the label that has dogged her for most of her 34 years: retarded. As a child, she was diagnosed as mentally retarded. That colored the image her teachers, classmates, and even her parents had of her. Teachers' low expectations for her became evident to her when in high school she was still reading from the same textbook she had in fifth grade.

Working in a series of nursing homes, Nancy realized that older adults were also victims of labeling and she decided to pursue a career in geriatrics. She entered an Adult Basic Education program, and passed the battery of tests for her General Educational Development (GED) diploma. "I loved it," she said, adding that having the GED helped dispel negative stereotypes that have stood in her way. "I feel I was definitely improperly labeled. I know I'm slow, but I don't feel I am retarded."

Nancy plans to pursue an education in human services and obtain a job helping others overcome their labels. As a vocal advocate for people with disabilities, she has had practice doing that. Nancy is a leader of a chapter of People First, an organization promoting the rights of people with disabilities. "We want people to see us as people first and not our disability," she said. "Label jars, not people" is the message on her People First T-shirt.

Nancy has testified before her state legislature on bills related to people with disabilities, and traveled to various states to help organize People First chapters. Through People First, she has worked to eliminate outdated language in state laws that refer to "idiots," "morons" and "imbeciles"— labels that she considers archaic and harmful. The lobbying has been an educational experience for both speakers and listeners, she said. "It shows that people with a disability can speak for themselves, and it also teaches us that we can do it."

What are characteristics of mental retardation?

Smith (1997) and others have reported there has been a change in the conception of mental retardation. It is viewed not as an absolute trait expressed solely by the person, but as an expression of the impact of the interaction between the person and the environment. The change in the way mental retardation is conceptualized requires that services be provided in inclusive environments that contain necessary supports based on the capabilities of the person with the purpose of empowering the individual to function within our society.

The term *mental retardation* is a social invention resulting from many factors, including the human tendency to label people based on perceived differences and development of standardized intelligence tests (Warren, 2000). According to Warren, the term mental retardation has been attacked as promoting stigma and negative stereotyping in our society, many people with disabilities hate it and consider it demeaning, and other point out that it lacks sufficient specificity for meaningful professional applications. As a result, people with disabilities, family members, and professionals have asked that we find a more contemporary, less pejorative term to describe this group of individuals (Crouser, 1999).

The American Association on Mental Retardation (AAMR, 1992) reported that the current conception of mental retardation focuses attention on the capabilities of the person related to limited intelligence and adaptive skills, their environment, and the presence or absence of the supports needed to live a meaningful life. Mental retardation:

- is characterized by significantly subaverage general intellectual functioning,
- results in, or is associated with, concurrent impairments in at least two adaptive skill areas, and
- is manifested before the age of 18 (during the developmental period).

Significantly subaverage intellectual functioning occurs when a person's score on standardized measures of intelligence is below the score of the average person taking the test to such a degree (two standard deviations) that society has determined this person requires assistance beyond what is typically provided by the family and community. The average intelligence quotient is a score of approximately 100. A score below approximately 70–75 on one or more individually administered general intelligence tests results in a determination of significantly subaverage intellectual functioning (Hatton, 1998). Large individual differences exist in performance on these standardized tests, and the meanings associated with tests results differ across societies and vary with any given society at different times. Clements (1998) stated that since all individuals require support from other people throughout their lives regardless of disability, identification of a disability such as mental retardation is relative.

Although IQ and intelligence are frequently used interchangeably, these concepts are not synonymous. The *IQ score* is only an estimate of an individual's rate of intellectual development as compared with the average rate for same-age peers. A person's lack of performance on a particular standardized measure of IQ can be the result of many factors other than actual intelligence. Some people may not have been exposed to the items presented on the test due to cultural and environmental differences, or perhaps people may have difficulty communicating their response due to physical or neurological impairments. Other people may be experiencing pain and sickness. The attitudes of the examiner and examinee can also influence test scores. These situations may reduce a person's performance on an intelligence test, and perhaps bring the scores into question.

Adaptive skills are a collection of competencies that allows for individuals' strengths, as well as areas for improvement, to be defined. By recognizing strengths and areas for improvement we can avoid focusing on deficits and emphasize individual competencies and the need for support.

The specific adaptive skill areas identified by the AAMR include:

- communication,
- self-care,
- home living,
- social skills,
- use of community resources,
- self-direction, health and safety,
- functional academics, leisure, and
- work.

For the purpose of this book, the adaptive skill area of leisure is highlighted. The AAMR described the adaptive skill area of leisure as:

> the development of a variety of leisure and recreational interests (self-entertainment and interactional) that reflect personal preferences and choices. Skills include choosing and self-initiating interests, using and enjoying home and community leisure and recreational activities alone and with others, playing socially with others, taking turns, terminating or refusing leisure or recreational activities, extending one's duration of participation, and expanding one's repertoire of interests, awareness, and skills. Related skills include behaving appropriately in the leisure and recreation setting, communicating choices and needs, participating in social interaction, applying functional academics, and exhibiting mobility skills. (p. 41)

According to the AAMR, mental retardation begins in childhood when limitations in intelligence coexist with related limitations in adaptive skills. The *developmental period* refers to the time after conception when growth and change occur at a rapid rate. This rate of development typically begins to slow as the person enters adulthood. Mental retardation is one particular type of developmental disability. A *developmental disability* refers to a severe, chronic disability that is attributable to a mental or physical impairment, is manifested before age 18, is likely to continue indefinitely, and results in substantial functional limitations. AAMR's definition of mental retardation contains the following underlying assumptions:

- mental retardation is not a general phenomenon,
- intelligence, as defined by tests, has limited use,
- no behavior clearly defines potential,
- adaptive behavior can be assumed,
- development is lifelong,
- educate people and avoid testing them, and
- mental retardation is most meaningfully conceptualized as a phenomenon existing within the society and can only be observed through the depressed performance of some of the individuals in that society.

Therefore, although the phrase mental retardation is used throughout this section, the label alone means very little. The profile of cognitive, adaptive, educational, and recreational ability, as well as the health status associated with each person, is critical for appropriate planning and implementation of effective services.

Mental retardation refers to a level of functioning that requires support from society. Therefore, the person with mental retardation is classified by the extent of support required for the person to learn, and not by limitations as to what the person can learn. The height of a person's level of functioning is determined by the amount of resources society is willing to allocate, and not by significant limitations in biological potential. The intensity levels of support have been defined and described by the AAMR as:

- intermittent supports provided as needed,
- limited supports that are not extensive, but consistent across time rather than intermittent,
- extensive supports not limited in time and provided on a regular basis in some environments (e.g., home), and
- pervasive supports that are constant, intense, and have the potential to sustain life.

The classification of mental retardation in terms of supports needed focuses our attention on expecting people to grow, believing in their potential, focusing on their personal choice, giving them opportunity and autonomy; and recognizing the need for people to be both in and of their community. This view of mental retardation results in all people being given the supports necessary to enhance their independence, interdependence, productivity, and community engagement.

What are considerations for inclusion of people with mental retardation?

Focus on the Uniqueness of Each Person and Avoid Generalizations

When relating to people who have been grouped together (for whatever reason) consider these individuals as people first and then—if relevant— consider their group affiliation. It is much easier to interact with a person if we initially concentrate on the similarities we share as opposed to our differences. Therefore, as much as possible, attempt to avoid the tendency to make generalizations about people—who in addition to many of the other characteristics that effect their humanness such as a sense of humor, reliability, or honesty—happen to be identified as having mental retardation.

Concentrate on Abilities and Potential Rather than IQ Scores

Sometimes people focus on results of individuals' scores on standardized measures of IQ and adaptive behavior scales and determine that the person with mental retardation has significant problems as well as limited potential for growth and development. If this conclusion has been drawn, with the focus of the problem on the individual with mental retardation, our work has ended. However, if we view people with mental retardation—no matter how severe the disability—as having potential for growth and development, then we can continuously attempt to determine the most effective and efficient procedures and assist these individuals in achieving their maximum potential.

Provide Age-Appropriate Communication and Services

Sometimes people mistakenly treat a person with mental retardation as a child. This occurs when an adult who happens to have mental retardation is compared to a child because he or she performs some skills such as reading at a level similar to some children. Because the adult with mental retardation has many more years of experience at living and has developed a variety of skills, the comparison to a child is misleading. We must work to avoid viewing adults with mental retardation as children and instead give them the respect provided to other adults in our society. This view of people with mental retardation encourages us to develop age-appropriate recreation programs that do not require people with mental retardation to compromise their dignity.

Promote Inclusion and Avoid Segregation

Unfortunately, many people with mental retardation have been required to participate in recreation activities with only other people with mental retardation. The only viable recreation activities have been those identified as "special." As a result, some people may be reluctant to access community recreation opportunities. Although some individuals with mental retardation might be reluctant to join community recreation programs, there are many examples of success associated with different activities.

For example, Lamplia (1998, p. 3) described how Jamie Barth, who has Down syndrome, was only seven years old when she began to attend the community karate school: "Today, Jamie holds a black belt in karate. Yes, people with mental retardation can earn black belts, not just gold medals for running faster than other people with Down syndrome." Lamplia also described a man with Down syndrome who is now attending her karate school. Lamplia (1998, p. 3) stated that the man has expressed to her that when he participates: "He feels equal, not special, when he does push-ups, sit-ups and martial arts drills with doctors, engineers, lawyers, business owners, schoolteachers, and college students."

Some people worry that people with mental retardation might have difficulty with participation in athletics with people without disabilities because athletics focus on competition against other people and there is a strong chance of failure. It may be helpful to consider that there are many community activities that emphasize competition against a standard or oneself rather than against other people such as aerobics, weightlifting, dance, martial arts, rock climbing, and hiking. The words of David Smith (2000, p. 71–72) might help put into perspective the value of including people with mental retardation into leisure services:

> Mental retardation can be a valuable human attribute. People with mental retardation can be powerful in the humanizing influence that they have on others. I am glad I have known people with mental retardation for most of my life . . . The power of those who have often been considered to be powerless may be important to our health as human beings and as cultural groups. A person with a disability may temper hateful and prejudicial attitudes. A person with mental retardation may soften a heart that has become hardened.

A person with multiple and severe disabilities may have much to teach us about love.

Meet Amanda, Who Enjoys Music

Amanda is a 15-year-old high-school student. Amanda does well in quiet areas with small numbers of students present, but has difficulty in public areas of the school (such as hallways or the cafeteria) because she does not like loud noises or anyone touching her. When not at school, she can usually be found in her bedroom. Amanda enjoys listening to music and, although she has many cassette tapes, Amanda listens to two songs, which she plays repeatedly. She has a book collection displayed in precise order. Amanda is a proficient swimmer; however, when the pool is crowded, she is too distracted to swim. Recently she indicated that she would like to learn to ride a horse. Because of her problems with communication and other behaviors, Amanda has been diagnosed as having an autistic disorder.

What are characteristics of autistic disorders?

An *autistic disorder*, also known as *autism*, is a complex developmental disability that is diagnosed through observation of an array of specific communication, social, and behavioral impairments. Although the cause of this disorder is unknown, according to the American Psychological Association, the following behaviors characteristic of autism usually appear during the first three years of life and are more common among males:

- lack of awareness of others,
- lack of social play,
- inability to establish friendships with peers,
- inability to communicate verbally or nonverbally,
- lack of imaginative activity,
- inability to initiate or sustain conversation,
- stereotyped and repetitive body movements, and
- the need to follow routines precisely.

One of the defining characteristics of autism is extreme difficulty with social interactions. Many individuals may actively avoid social contact, adhere to rigid schedules, and inappropriately focus on objects or topics (Baker, Koegel & Koegel, 1998).

The character Raymond in the movie *Rain Man* depicts an individual with an autistic disorder. Raymond was able to perform many self-care skills. He seemed to take pride in his room and the orderliness he maintained. Raymond had difficulty making eye contact, had poor social skills, could repeat a joke but did not understand the humor, and became upset when his routines were interrupted. He had unusual body posturing and would rock forward and back repeatedly when anxious. Raymond also exhibited characteristics of a savant—an extraordinary talent in one precise area, such as music, art, mathematics, or amassing facts on a particular subject. It is important to note that few people with autistic disorder actually have savant characteristics.

What are considerations for inclusion of people with autism?

Be Consistent and Open to Alternative Forms of Communication

Consistency with equipment placement and routine is often helpful to develop a positive and relaxed atmosphere. People with an autistic disorder often use alternative communication techniques, such as electronic communication boards, picture boards, and sign language. Regardless of the method of communication or level of response, speak to the participant with age-appropriate language.

Meet Christopher, Who Finds Freedom in the Written Word

Christopher has an acute mind that has found its liberation in writing, according to Sherrid (1988). Christopher was unable to make a meaningful mark on paper until age 11, when the drug Lioresal helped his muscle spasms. He approached words much as another child might approach an overturned truck of candy, says one critic. Just four years later, he published a book of poetry, *Dam-Burst of Dreams,* which won him comparisons with such literary giants as James Joyce and the 17th-century poet John Donne. Christopher, who has cerebral palsy, taps out letters on a typewriter with the help of a "unicorn" stick strapped to his forehead. His chin is supported by his mother who stands behind her son in his wheelchair for hours at a stretch in a study in their middle-class Dublin home.

His autobiography, *Under the Eye of the Clock,* won Britain's most prestigious literary award and was on the London bestseller list. The autobiography chronicles his (ultimately successful) struggle to attend high school. While heaping praise upon his family, teachers, and friends, Christopher writes unflinchingly of society's pity and intolerance.

Christopher plans to write a novel, but even some of his supporters are skeptical that his personal experience is wide enough to sustain fiction. His mother doesn't entertain any doubts. Nodding to a visiting journalist, she asks, "What do you think he is doing with all the people he meets?" Regardless of what the future brings, his work already may have changed attitudes toward people with disabilities. Says his teacher, Brendan: "Christopher experiences life so intensely, no one who reads his book could pity him."

What are characteristics of cerebral palsy?

Cerebral palsy is characterized by the inability to control muscular and postural movement. It is caused by damage to the motor portions of the brain. The condition is not degenerative (i.e., it will not get worse). There are many causes of cerebral palsy, including prenatal infection, anoxia (a lack of adequate oxygen) before or during birth, fetal cerebral hemorrhage, and metabolic disturbance.

People with cerebral palsy are classified by the muscular condition and degree of bodily involvement they display. People who have *spasticity* display increased muscle-tone stiffness (hypertonia) and immediate contraction when stretching affected muscles. People with *athetosis* have difficulty controlling movement associated with affected muscles, resulting in "worm-like" movements. Individuals with *ataxia* have a more subtle form of cerebral palsy that results in balance problems. *Rigidity* is a term used to describe an individual who appears very stiff and the person's neck, back, or limbs may be hyperextended. Individuals who exhibit frequent or constant involuntary shaking of body parts, especially the hands and arms, have a form of cerebral palsy identified as *tremors*. Individuals with more than one type are said to have *mixed cerebral palsy*.

Individuals with cerebral palsy are also classified according to the extremities that are affected. If only one limb is affected, individuals are said to have *monoplegia*. If the person's legs are impaired, the person is said to have *paraplegia*. If one side of the person's body is affected, the person is said to have *hemiplegia*. When all four extremities are impaired as a result of cerebral palsy, the person has *quadriplegia*.

What are considerations for inclusion of people with cerebral palsy?

Work with Participants

Work with the individual to determine what accommodations they have already devised. When teaching activities, try to avoid excessively loud sounds and sudden, unexpected motions that may increase uncontrollable movements and trigger the startle reflex. Consider that some individuals may have balance difficulties and be prone to falling.

Accommodate Mobility Limitations

Make necessary adaptations based on some people's limited mobility. Since gross motor coordination can often be a problem, accommodations can be made when introducing physically active activities. Fine-motor activities using hand-eye coordination or delicate finger movements can be very difficult for some people; therefore, efforts to enhance hand-eye coordination can be useful. When encouraging the grasping of an object, the use of sponges may help individuals with spastic cerebral palsy. The creation of a firm, hard surface for people with athetosis can also be beneficial.

Meet Jennifer, Who Likes to Climb

Jennifer had her first seizure just before her 13th birthday. Because of initial difficulty in regulating her medications for her epilepsy, she had memory problems that resulted in poor grades. Fortunately, Jennifer's school was understanding and explored options for assisting her to be a successful student. She graduated from prep school with honor grades and left home to attend college and live in a dorm. In the spring, Jennifer went rock climbing with skilled mountaineers.

> I never thought the best solution was to live a limited life. I'd rather do things and take risks than do nothing at all. Going to college far from home wasn't something I felt afraid of. I felt very capable of taking care of myself. (Lovell & Lovell, 1993, p. 6)

Jennifer is careful to explain to those around her that she has epilepsy and forewarn them what to do in case she has a seizure.

> What to do and what not to do is something I explain to everyone I know. I try to explain what seizures look like, why I have them, what may set them off, what I'm like afterward. (I usually forget things.) Although I've felt frustrated and occasionally angry, I've never felt embarrassed by it. I have epilepsy, but epilepsy doesn't have me. (Lovell & Lovell, 1993, p. 6)

What are characteristics of epilepsy?

Epilepsy is a common neurological disorder that occurs when there is a sudden brief change in how the brain works. When brain cells are not working properly, a person's consciousness, movement, or actions may be altered for a short time. Epilepsy is therefore called a seizure disorder.

Not all seizures are classified as epilepsy. For example, many young children have convulsions from fevers. These convulsions are one type of seizure. Other types of seizures not classified as epilepsy include those caused by an imbalance of body fluids or chemicals, or by alcohol or drug withdrawal. A single seizure does not mean a person has epilepsy. Epilepsy is classified according to three specific features:

- generalized or partial seizures,
- whether the seizures are the primary or secondary disorder, and
- the age of onset of recurrent seizures.

Generalized seizures involve cells from both hemispheres of the brain, whereas *partial seizures* result when only one hemisphere of the brain is involved. One type of generalized seizure consists of a convulsion with a complete loss of consciousness, called a *grand mal seizure*. A *petit mal seizure*, another generalized seizure, is characterized by brief periods of fixation, called *absences*, in which the individual appears to be staring into space and does not respond to external stimuli.

An example of a partial seizure is the *jacksonian*, in which convulsions begin in one part of a limb, such as a foot or hand, and quickly spread throughout that entire side of the body. Other partial seizures may cause periods of automatic behavior, such as rubbing movements with one hand, wandering, or periods of altered consciousness.

What are considerations for inclusion of people with epilepsy?

Consider the Nature of Epilepsy

Frequent occurrence of seizures by a person with epilepsy is very rare. The majority of individuals with epilepsy manage their seizures with medication; therefore, there is very little adjustment to leisure services delivery. Individuals with petit mal seizures can miss part of a sentence that may lead to confusion if instructions were provided at the time of the seizure; therefore, repetition of instructions can be helpful.

Be Prepared to Treat a Person Having a Grand Mal Seizure

Probably the most important consideration is to be prepared to follow basic first aid if a person has a grand mal seizure. Treatment during a seizure is the same regardless of the cause of the seizure, and should focus on preventing injury. When a person has a seizure, keep calm—there is nothing you can do to stop a seizure. Do not try to restrain the person, but clear the area so the person doesn't injure himself or herself. Do not interfere with movements, unless it is to cradle the head to prevent injury; Do not force anything between teeth or into mouth, but if the person is choking, turn the head to the side. Treat the incident in a calm, matter-of-fact manner and do not crowd around the individual. Allow the person to rest after the seizure.

An important consideration for first aid for grand mal seizures is if the person experiences the seizure in the water. O'Dell (2001, p. 86) made the following suggestions:

> First aid steps would include keeping her head above the water (if this is not possible, she would have to be removed from the water during the seizure); removing her from the water as soon as possible after the seizure; turning her on her left side to facilitate drainage of secretions; keeping her airway open; and observing her closely until she has returned to her baseline level of consciousness.

Meet Tara, Who Helps Other People Have Fun

Tara's favorite activity is spending time on cruise ships headed for warm sandy beaches. She loves traveling with friends to remote, isolated islands.

Although she enjoys her work as a supervisor of a community recreation and parks department, she is constantly planning, saving for, or going on a cruise.

Tara has always enjoyed traveling. She enjoys meeting new people and seeing new lands. After she received a traumatic brain injury as a result of a car accident when she was in college, she was determined to reacquire skills needed to continue to travel. She used thoughts of beaches and foreign sites to motivate her during rehabilitation. Although she requires adaptations in many activities, she is able to continue to travel. Tara reports that when hospitality staff members are open to making accommodations for her, she almost always has a great vacation.

What are characteristics of traumatic brain injury?

A *traumatic brain injury* is a physical insult to the brain that may cause problems with physical, emotional, and social functioning. These changes influence not only the present status but also the future status of a person. A traumatic brain injury frequently means that the person may never quite be the same again. The 1999 National Institute of Health (NIH) Consensus Development Panel on Rehabilitation of Persons with Traumatic Brain Injury (p. 974) provided the following details:

> Traumatic brain injury (TBI), broadly defined as brain injury due to externally inflicted trauma, may result in significant impairment of an individual's physical, cognitive, and psychosocial function-ing. The number of people surviving a TBI with impairment has increased significantly in recent years, which is attributed to faster, more effective emergency care, quicker and safer transportation to specialized treatment facilities, and advanced acute medical management. Although TBI may result in physical impairment, the more problematic consequences involve the individual's cognition, emotional functioning, and behavior, which can affect interper-sonal relationships . . . Community-based, nonmedical services should be components of the extended care and rehabilitation available to persons with TBI.

A variety of community leisure programs can be a part of the nonmedi-cal services identified by NIH Panel to help facilitate the continued recov-ery process of individuals with traumatic brain injury who are living in their communities. James Brady spoke about brain injuries:

> Each year, two million Americans sustain brain injuries, all of whom must deal in some degree with the lasting effects of this disability. Whether it be chronic headaches, sleeplessness, memory loss, paralysis or any myriad of symptoms, we all continue on the journey, persevere and gain the experience required to travel a brand new road, to a changed life. (Brady, 1995, p. 4)

It may be helpful to consider the words of James Brady when trying to gain insight into the implications of having experienced a traumatic brain injury. The most common cause of of such an injury is from a motor-vehicle accident. Males are typically affected twice as often as females. Other common causes include falls and child neglect or abuse. Common cognitive processes influenced by traumatic brain injury are attention, memory, general intellectual performance, language, and perceptual abilities.

Closed head injury is one type of traumatic brain injury that is often caused by the brain being whipped back and forth in a quick motion. This pull-and-tug places extreme stress on the brain stem—the part that connects the larger part of the brain with the spinal cord and the remaining portion of the body. A large number of functions are packed tightly into the brain stem, such as controls of consciousness, breathing, heartbeat, eye movements, pupil reactions, swallowing, and facial movements. In addition, all sensations going to the brain, as well as signals from the brain to the muscles, must pass through the brain stem. *Anoxia* (loss of oxygen to the brain) is another form of closed head injury. Anoxia may occur following cardiac arrest, stroke or accident (e.g., drowning or choking).

Open head injury, a second type of traumatic brain injury, is a visible assault that results from an accident, gunshot wound, fall, or other trauma, such as brain surgery to remove a clot or tumor. As with closed head injuries, symptoms can vary greatly and depend on the extent and location of the brain injury. Physical disabilities, impaired learning ability, and personality changes are common. Physical impairments can include disruption in speech, vision, hearing, and other sensory impairments; headaches; lack of coordination; spasticity of muscles; paralysis of one or both sides; and seizure disorders.

The most common area affected by a traumatic brain injury is *memory*, especially memory for new information. Other symptoms include difficulty with maintaining attention, problem solving, organizational skills, recognition of priorities, planning, and acting to achieve a goal. All types of head trauma may damage that part of the brain crucial to memory. Both short-term (recall of recent information) and long-term (recall of past information) memory may be impaired. *Amnesia* is a common type of memory loss, where the person can only remember bits and pieces of events that occurred in the past. Amnesia does not affect one's ability to learn new information.

Seizures, another typical result of traumatic brain injury, may also affect memory and can occur immediately after the injury or may not develop until months or even years later. At times, the memory loss may persist because a tiny seizure, called a *partial complex seizure*, will originate from the injured area and continue for an indefinite period afterward. This brain damage is often not diagnosed, however, because the identifying seizure is sometimes hard to recognize. There is only a short staring spell or period of unusual behavior, and only a momentary lapse of concentration occurs. If recognized, however, the condition is often readily treatable with prescription drugs.

A person's emotions can also be influenced by a traumatic brain injury. Some individuals with traumatic brain injury experience severe behavior disorders that disrupt their daily life. Disorders may include mood swings, denial, self-centeredness, anxiety, depression, lowered self-esteem, sexual dysfunction, restlessness, lack of motivation, inability to self-monitor, difficulty with emotional control, inability to cope, agitation, excessive laughing or crying, and difficulty in making choices. These behavior disorders can be treated with behavior management programs and medication.

Any or all of the symptoms of traumatic brain injury may occur in different degrees, and there may be other symptoms not mentioned. Intellectual ability may cease to improve after a period of time, but memory, social, and behavioral functions may improve over long periods of time. For many people, ongoing involvement in activities can decrease the severity of these symptoms.

What are considerations for inclusion of people with traumatic brain injuries?

Help Participants with Planning

Individuals who have had a traumatic brain injury often have impaired planning ability and may need individualized reminders about leisure options. Calendars, notes, and telephone calls may help to increase their attendance and participation in leisure services. Individuals who have experienced a traumatic brain injury may have difficulty working toward long-term goals. To maintain continued interest in a program, we can provide opportunities that include gratifying experiences. Preparation for participation is just as important as the activity itself. Plan activities that encourage social interaction, cooperation, challenge, and success for everyone. Measuring self-improvement in a skill is more meaningful to the person's self-concept than is competition against others, especially with people who are less skilled. Ensure full participation to promote interaction in an increasingly mature manner. Individuals may have a slower learning rate, but can still accomplish a great deal.

Use Concrete Leadership Strategies

Abstractions or generalizations often present difficulty for a person who has experienced a traumatic brain injury. It may help to introduce novel activities by relating them to a familiar activity. It is also helpful to conduct a task analysis by dividing an activity into its components, teaching small steps, and allowing for additional practice time. To gain the person's attention, saying the person's name before giving key directions may be helpful. Consistently model, demonstrate, and provide manual assistance using physical guidance, visual cues, and verbal directions when conducting activities. One-step or two-step directions are more appropriate than a series of commands; however, avoid using more guidance, direction, or cues than necessary to encourage the person to take more responsibility.

If having a short attention span is a problem, it may help to simplify verbal instructions. Often participants will take cues from how something sounds rather than from what is said. Consistency in voice tone, voice quality, and communication pattern is helpful. Keep directions brief and simple to increase the person's attention to the most important parts of the task. Use repetitious, slow, meaningful progression.

Implement rules and procedures, especially as related to health and safety, before the activity starts. Learning by example, repetition, reminders, verbal feedback and experience will foster an individual's comprehension of instructions. It can be helpful to vary activities and introduce new skills early in a session. Alternate active and quiet games so that a person is not overstimulated and the person's interest is maintained. Structure the environment so that all participants may become involved. The circle formation is an excellent leadership tool; clients are then able to take advantage of modeling, imitation, demonstration, and peer interaction.

Meet Calvin, Who Enjoys Playing Cards

One morning in 1990, Calvin awoke early as usual and swung his legs over the side of the bed. To his surprise, he fell to the floor, unable to speak or move. When his wife, Ruby, awoke, she assumed he had gone for his ritual walk. Not until his grandson came by two hours later did they find Calvin on the floor. The doctor told his family he had experienced a stroke.

After one month in a rehabilitation hospital, Calvin returned home and began a new phase in his life. Many of his favorite pastimes still gave him pleasure: listening to gospel music, enjoying his grandchildren and attending their Little League baseball games. Other activities were no longer pleasurable. He no longer enjoyed church due to the emotional arousal that brought on tears and embarrassment. He also had difficulty talking to acquaintances due to the impaired speech caused by the stroke. One of his greatest pleasures is playing cribbage with his wife and best friend, Charlie. For a long time, Calvin did not think he would ever be able to remember the rules and hold the cards, but with Charlie's patient tutoring and the help of an adaptive cardholder, Calvin is now the reigning cribbage champion of the neighborhood.

What are characteristics of a stroke?

A *stroke* or *cerebrovascular accident* (CVA) is a form of traumatic brain injury that originates inside the brain itself. A stroke occurs when a portion of the brain is deprived of blood. The incidence is higher for men than women and higher for African-Americans than other racial groups. Since long-standing hypertension (high-blood pressure) is a major cause of stroke, very few people under the age of 40 experience a stroke.

The most common form of stroke is a *cerebral thrombosis*, which occurs when a blood clot forms in an artery that supplies blood to the brain. A *cerebral embolism* occurs when a blood clot travels to the brain from another part of the body, often from the heart. In both instances, the brain is deprived of blood due to the clot and damage ensues. A *cerebral hemorrhage* is a stroke caused by a blood vessel bursting in the brain. Not only is the area beyond the burst deprived of blood but also the blood that spilled out puts pressure on the brain tissue in the area of the rupture. A cerebral hemorrhage is the most serious form of stroke, and frequently causes coma and death.

There may be no warning that a stroke will occur, although some individuals may be forewarned by a series of small strokes known as *transient ischemic attacks*—brief episodes of circulatory deficiency to the brain. These small strokes may cause sudden weakness or numbness on one side of the face, in one arm, or in one leg; sudden and sharp dizziness; dimness or loss of vision (especially in one eye); or loss of the ability to speak clearly or understand speech. The individual may not realize that a stroke has actually occurred. Transient ischemic attacks are a warning sign that a major stroke may occur if medical attention is not sought. They can occur days, weeks, or months before the major stroke.

The amount of injury caused by a stroke depends on the type and location of the damage. A right-brain stroke affects the left side of the body and may cause *hemiplegia*, which involves paralysis or weakness, memory loss, and impulsive behavior. Individuals who have had a right-brain stroke often experience inappropriate reflex crying, reflex laughter, or reflex anger. These reflexes occur when some emotion is triggered, and the area of the cerebral cortex that controls emotions has been damaged. A left-brain stroke causes right-side hemiplegia, memory loss, speech and language problems, and slow, cautious behavior. These patterns may be opposite for those who are left-handed.

The brain damage caused by stroke may suddenly alter every aspect of the person's life. In addition to paralysis, some individuals have a condition known as *hemianopsia*. This condition causes half of the visual field to disappear. The person may eat only the food on one side of the plate and may not be aware of the other food unless the plate is turned. Likewise, the person may only respond to people who approach on one side and seem to ignore those who are standing on the other side. It is helpful to guide an individual who has hemianopsia to a position in the room where he or she will be able to see the most. Take care when approaching the person from the affected side, since it may startle the person when you suddenly appear in the field of vision.

Aphasia is the term used to indicate difficulties in processing language. *Receptive aphasia* means that the person can no longer understand the messages received as either spoken or written language. *Expressive aphasia* describes the condition in which the person can understand what is said or written but cannot respond to it. Some people may be able to sing or count but not speak, or may be able to say only a few words such as "okay," "amen," or "bye." Families are often shocked when their relative is only able to say swear words, which were never used before the stroke.

What are considerations for inclusion of people with have had a stroke?

Give the Person Time to Respond

Treat the individual in an age-appropriate manner and do not to respond as though the person is a child. Encourage the individual to speak and to indicate personal preferences. Be patient and allow the person sufficient time to speak, rather than finishing sentences or thoughts for the person. Likewise, we should give the individual opportunities to do as much independently as possible. Enabling independence will enhance the dignity of the person.

Understand Reflexive Behaviors

One aspect of maintaining the participant's dignity relates to how we respond to reflex crying. Understand that crying does not necessarily reflect the mood of a person who has had a brain injury. If not clear how a person is feeling, ask the participant and respond appropriately. Reflex crying has a tendency to come and go suddenly and may look different than real crying. It can be helpful to speak with people who are reflexively crying when they are not crying to determine how they would like to be treated when an episode does occur. Similar steps can be taken with reflex anger and laughter as well.

Meet Thomas, Who Enjoys the Outdoors

Thomas likes taking long walks in the woods nearby his home. He often brings his binoculars so that he can identify birds and more closely observe other wildlife. Although many may enjoy such an activity, for Thomas it brings a sense of pride. It was not long ago when he had difficulty leaving his home because he experienced hallucinations due to his schizophrenia.

When his schizophrenia emerged during his early 30s, Thomas withdrew from his friends and family and from activities that brought him joy. He lost his job and finally sought psychiatric assistance. After actively participating in therapy sessions with mental health professionals and following a scheduled plan for taking medication, Thomas has returned to his community. He is now employed and takes advantage of many recreation programs within his community.

Thomas expresses concern about the prejudice he has experienced as a result of his clinical diagnosis of schizophrenia. He hopes that in the future people will keep an open mind about people and focus on them as individuals rather than labels.

What are characteristics of mental health problems?

Many people believe that individuals receiving a psychiatric diagnosis are dangerous and should be incarcerated. As a result of certain news reports and horror movies, many people harbor the misconception that people who are receiving psychiatric care are a menace to society. While it is true that a small minority of people with psychiatric diagnoses have a history of violence, the majority do not engage in violent behavior.

Unfortunately, some people believe that individuals with mental disorders do not really need help. People still have the general belief that others should be able to handle mental health problems by themselves. The view that people should "pull themselves up by the bootstraps" or "talk themselves out of it" closely relates to the belief that problems with mental health are shameful. There is a tendency to think that there is something weak or morally wrong with someone seeking help for a mental impairment. According to Michels (1985):

> The irony of this popular view is that growing evidence links cancer, heart disease and other "traditional" health problems to such personal behaviors as cigarette smoking or improper eating habits. In fact, as many as half the deaths from the 10 leading causes of death in our country can be traced to people's lifestyle. It would be fairer to attribute these diseases to "weak characters and poor decisions" than to make the same claim about the most familiar mental disorders, such as schizophrenia or depression which stem from causes that have little to do with voluntary choice.

Some mental disorders are identified as those associated with mood problems, such as depression and mania. *Clinical depression* is different than the temporary experience of "everyday" depression that results from such emotions as sadness, frustration, and discouragement, but tends not to significantly impair a person's ability to function over time. Depression becomes a psychiatric diagnoses based on the frequency of the depressed mood, the intensity of the depressed feelings, and the degree to which it impairs an individual's ability to participate in daily activities.

Diminished interest and pleasure with life, fatigue and a loss of energy, and a sense of worthlessness or guilt characterize clinical depression. It is also a common cause of memory loss. The loss of concentration that accompanies depression makes it difficult for the affected person to acquire new information. The slowed thinking process associated with clinical depression makes the retrieval of information more difficult and sometimes even impossible for certain periods of time. In addition, people experiencing clinical depression may reflect their feeling in changes in their weight (excessive losses or gains) or sleeping patterns (insomnia or oversleeping). At times, severe depression can result in thoughts of, or attempts at, suicide.

Extreme elevated, expansive, or irritable mood states characterize *manic episodes*, another type of mood disorder. During a manic episode the person may exhibit several of the following behaviors: inflated self-esteem, decreased sleep need, excessive talkativeness, racing thoughts, distractibility, physical activeness, and risk-taking. Individuals who shift between states of depression and mania are often diagnosed as having *bipolar disorder*.

Schizophrenia, a mental disorder familiar to many people, in truth affects less than one percent of the population and does not refer to someone who has multiple personalities. Schizophrenia is a psychotic disorder characterized by an individual who at various times departs from reality. The lack of awareness of reality can be manifested in a variety of ways.

Some individuals with schizophrenia experience hallucinations that involve the perception, through any of the senses, of objects or beings that are not actually there, such as hearing voices telling one what to do. *Delusions* are another symptom of schizophrenia, and involve false beliefs about self, others, or objects that persist despite presentation of facts to the contrary, such as the belief that one's thoughts are not their own, but imposed by some outside force. Individuals with schizophrenia may have disturbances in speech, motor activity and expression of emotion. One characteristic of schizophrenia strongly tied to leisure participation is disturbances associated with *volition*. People experience difficulty making a decision that often results in the absence of self-determination.

Anxiety disorders are associated with intense fear or panic of a situation, object or person that is not justified and should not result in fear. Many situations justify fear; however, a person experiencing an anxiety disorder will have continuous intense fears about something for no apparent reason, such as worrying about the welfare of a loved one. Physical symptoms include shortness of breath, accelerated heart rate, dizziness, abdominal distress, and chills or hot flashes. Anxiety disorders result in a decreased ability to function and relate to other people.

Closely linked to anxiety disorders is a category of mental disturbances identified as phobias. *Phobias* involve continuous, unrealistic fears and dominate a person's thinking, such as agoraphobia (fear of leaving one's house) or claustrophobia (fear of closed spaces). Other phobias include fear of speaking in public, fear of snakes, and fear of seeing blood. The most common phobia, social anxiety disorder, is characterized by an intense fear of being scrutinized and humiliated by others in social situations that results in trembling, sweating, and racing heartbeat (Meyer, 2000).

Obsessive-compulsive disorders result in people not being able to think clearly because of recurring thoughts and repetitive behaviors. Obsessions involve a persistent disturbing preoccupation with unreasonable ideas or feelings. Compulsions are irresistible impulses to perform irrational acts. The two conditions are linked in that a person may be obsessed with an idea (such as cleanliness) which may result in a compulsion (such as washing hands hundreds of times in a brief period of time).

What are considerations for inclusion of people with mental health problems?

See Similarities First

We view people who have problems related to mental health as different from us, so we are uncomfortable in interacting with them. If we view them as similar to us, we can interact with them more comfortably. With careful planning, activity inclusion can help to enhance self-esteem and provide a sense of well being for the individual. It is important to establish rapport with all program participants.

Demonstrate Respect When Speaking and Listening

To start a conversation, choose a topic you think the person may be interested in, something that has happened to them lately, or a "safe" topic like the weather or sports. If you receive no response, it may be that the person did not hear you or did not understand you. Repeat the question, point to what you are talking about, rephrase the question, and make eye contact. If there is still no response, try to put them at ease by telling about something that happened to you or make light conversation. As with anyone who may have difficulty holding a conversation, the person may still very much like to listen to others and be spoken to.

If we cannot understand people when they speak, we may ask them to repeat themselves or, if someone is talking about a topic we know nothing about, we may ask to change the subject or just listen politely. Even though we may feel awkward our listening is often appreciated and we may begin to understand some of the person's speech. It is acceptable to tell a person we do not understand or ask them to repeat something. If someone responds to us on a totally different topic, it is helpful if we are polite and either bring the topic back, or speak to the new topic. We could say, "That's interesting, but let me ask you again about your job." Or you could respond to the new topic.

If someone asks a personal or embarrassing question, honesty is the best way to handle this. A good response is, "That is not something I want to talk about. Let's talk about something else." The person can learn from you that some things are not to be asked. If someone is extending a conversation, honesty is the best policy. "I'm sorry, but I need to move on. Could we talk more another time? Right now I don't have time to listen further." If someone is rudely interrupting your conversation, you can say something like, "I'm talking with Mary now, come talk to me some other time."

Final Thoughts

People who meet individuals with cognitive impairments may have incorrect perceptions about their skills and abilities. For those whose brain-related impairment is acquired later in life, there are inevitable changes that people experience as they transition back into their families and communities. With the necessary assistance and support, people with cognitive impairments can live meaningful and often enjoyable lives.

It may be helpful when thinking how we might include people with conditions that affect their cognitive functioning to consider a report in the newsletter *Recreation: Access in the 90s* that described a situation with a child with Attention Deficit and Hyperactivity Disorder ("Oh, so this is the most integrated setting," 1997). This child chose to register for an after-school recreation program, instead of a separate after-school program for youth with disabilities. When the registrant displayed some disruptive behavior, an additional staff member with behavior management training was hired and assigned as a companion or aide to the child. The child's disruptive behavior diminished.

Unfortunately the additional assistance was soon terminated. The child's behavior deteriorated and his participation in the program was suspended. The family filed a complaint with the U. S. Department of the Interior, who ordered reinstatement. They decided that the additional one-to-one staff was not an undue burden and did not result in a fundamental alteration in the after-school program.

This is an example of how leisure service professionals initially responded to the spirit of the ADA and helped facilitate the inclusion of a youth with a cognitive impairment. The provision of an additional staff member to work with this person was an effective accommodation. However, this is also an instance when a family was required to assert their legal rights achieved by ADA to gain access to an inclusive program and to avoid segregation.

Discussion Questions

1. What are the characteristics of mental retardation?
2. What are considerations for the inclusion of people with mental retardation?
3. What is the difference between intelligence and IQ?
4. What are three factors that can affect IQ scores?
5. What are characteristics common to persons with autistic disorder?
6. What are considerations for the inclusion of people with autism?
7. What is the best way to assist a person having a grand mal epileptic seizure?
8. What are behaviors common to traumatic brain injury?
9. What are considerations for the inclusion of people with traumatic brain injuries?
10. How would you determine the best way to proceed with a participant who exhibits reflex crying?
11. What are difficulties in adjustment that may occur following acquisition of a brain-related disability during adulthood?

Photo by Lynda Greer

Kathy Sullivan, Jane Mazur, RoseBary Trammell, and Christine Eckman

Pictured from left to right are Kathy Sullivan, Jane Mazur, RoseBary Trammell, and Christine Eckman, who were born with various types of mental retardation. All are employed and live together with a resident manager in a house in Roswell, Georgia.

The Stories of
Kathy, Jane, RoseBary, and Christine

Kathy

My family . . . mother, stepfather, brother, and sister live near in Atlanta and I live at Barrington Landing. I really love the people here. We mostly get along really well. I'm supposed to move my room into the basement soon . . . and I'll have more privacy. I work at the Haynes Bridge Kroger where I make pizzas in the deli and help Chris [Eckman] in the bakery if I can. Right now we need more people to work at Kroger. I like to ride my exercise bike, listen to music—mostly rock and roll. At night I do what I need to to get dinner ready and clean up. Then I relax, watch TV.

Jane

My sister and brother live in Atlanta; I see them holidays, weekends, sometimes. The rest of the time I live with my friends. I love my friends here! I work at Herman Miller, where they make furniture. Now I am gluing furniture pieces together and I like that job a lot. When I'm not working, I love to look at *TV Guide.* And I like listening to music and coloring.

RoseBary

Mom and Dad live on E. Wesley Rd. in Atlanta. My brother lives near Atlanta. Whenever I can, I see my family, but we're very busy at Barrington Landing. It's almost three years since I moved here. I love Jane and Kathy and Chris. And I like this house a lot. I work at RRA [Resources for Retarded Adults], helping with the cleaning. I also go to the training center and do different things. This Christmas we're helping the homeless and the needy, giving food; and I took some pennies to school today. I like to read my encyclopedias, *Reader's Digest,* things like that. I ride my exercise bike sometimes, and when the weather is nice, I like to take walks and talk to the neighbors.

Christine

My parents live in Atlanta and I have a sister in New York. For three years I have lived at Barrington Landing with Sasha, the cat; RoseBary, Jane, Kathy, and now, Tanya [resident manager]. I'm happy here. I work at the Haynes Bridge Kroger. I bake cookies and some bread; I enjoy baking cookies the best. My friend, Kathy, works there, too. We eat lunch together when we can. At night I watch television, listen to music—many kinds of music. I like to sing, too. Every night I write in my diary about my day.

Chapter 18

People, Inclusion, and Sensory Limitations

Photo by Lynda Greer

Will and Robby Smith

Fraternal twins Will (left) and Robby Smith are high school students in Gainesville, Georgia. Born prematurely, they sustained severe hearing losses during neonatal care.

The Stories of Will and Robby Smith

Will

I was born in Augusta, GA. I have a brother who is named Robby Smith. My father is a doctor and my mother deals with art. When I was three years old, the whole family moved to Gainesville, GA. Now I go to a school called Gainesville Middle School. I have some friends named Chip and Justin, and a bunch of others that I cannot remember their names.

I am an editor and a movie reviewer for the Gainesville Middle School's newspaper,"The Mirror." I hate "The Mirror" but I always wanted to be an editor and a movie reviewer so I got no choice. I always get a feeling like I am a special guest of the newspaper and I try to take a break from it whenever possible.

I have a lot of hobbies. I am not sure exactly how many, but I got comic books, rockets, stamps, books, movie reviews, articles, posters, and role-playing games.

I have told you not all, but some parts of my life.

Robby

Hey! Well, my name is Robby Smith and I have a hearing loss and eyesight problem. I love reading books, and usually stake out the local bookstore when I hear that a good book has been published.

I enjoy living life to the fullest and relaxing. I like to go to the beach, the city, and the mountains. I'm going to be a freshman at high school. My favorite movies are the *Indiana Jones* trilogy, *Midnight Run,* and *Mr. North.*

My hearing/sight losses never bother me, and I really don't make a major deal out of it.

Detachment will not do . . . And there ought to be mutual respect, regard for each one's competence and integrity.
-M. Green

Orientation Activity: Silvia and Shavaun— What to do?

Directions Alone: Read the following scenarios and respond to the tasks posed.

- Silvia would like to use our cruise line to take a vacation with her husband. She has communicated to you that she has *diabetic retinopathy*, a disorder of the retina due to diabetes. As a member of the recreation department on the ship, identify some adaptations or considerations we may make when attempting to make this vacation one of the best Silvia has ever experienced.

- Shavaun, a teenager, would like to participate in the basketball league offered by the local parks and recreation department. Since Shavaun happens to have a *sensorineural hearing loss* caused by a childhood disease, identify some ways we may assist Shavaun in having a successful experience with the basketball league.

Directions with Others: Move about the room with your responses and share your thoughts with another person. After a specified time, discuss what you have learned with the entire group.

Debriefing: To permit Silvia to access the cruise line, we could provide her with an orientation to the ship and ask her for suggestions on how we could best serve her. The lighting is often a consideration: natural daylight varies from extremely bright sun that creates glare, to overcast skies that provide insufficient light. These conditions may make it difficult for individuals to see demonstrations, environmental obstructions, or signage. We can assist Silvia by checking the signs on the ship for compliance with the Americans with Disabilities Act regarding positioning, color, and use of raised letters or Braille. When making visual demonstrations, it can be helpful if we attempt to use an increased number of verbal instructions and directions. During the evening entertainment, we can reserve a place at one of the front tables for Silvia and her party so that she can enjoy the show. Since Silvia has diabetes we can work with her to have appropriate refreshments, such as sugar-free options.

To promote Shavaun's ability to play in the basketball league, we could determine the level of his residual hearing and learn how to maximize his hearing abilities on the basketball court. Many athletes with hearing impairments play successfully by using signs to represent verbal instructions. We could work with local basketball officials to educate them on accommodations required for compliance with the ADA. For example, it may help to have a light flash to signal Shavaun each time the whistle is blown. Shavaun's teammates will also be an important component in his successful participation. Identify a player to be an informer to ensure Shavaun understands verbal discussions. If desired, this person could go to Shavaun each time there is a break in the action and be available to clarify any situation. If Shavaun uses sign language, he may choose to teach the coach and his teammates a couple of signs a day to help with communication. Once some signs have been learned, it will help to always use the sign and the spoken word together. The American Athletic Association for the Deaf, headquartered at Gallaudet University in Washington, DC, provides additional information on sports for individuals with hearing impairments. Consider the following questions when thinking about the orientation activity:

- Why is lighting an important consideration when working with individuals with visual impairments?
- Why is it important to include Silvia's entire party at a front table if only she is visually impaired?
- What is the purpose of using an informer during activities?
- Why is it important to use sign language and the spoken word together when addressing individuals with deafness?

Introduction

Visual and hearing impairments can be congenital or acquired at any point across one's life span. These impairments can affect a person's ability to perform daily tasks at home and in their communities. Sensory impairments can also have an effect on the individual's leisure lifestyle. Without leisure options, the individual may eventually become isolated from other people. This chapter will present information on the causes and treatments for visual and hearing impairments and offer suggestions for inclusion into leisure services.

Meet Donna, Who Enjoys Nature

The following description is based on the testimony given by Donna Veno (1986) before the President's Commission on Americans Outdoors.

I still hear professionals in the recreation field tell me that they do not know why they should make their parks or programs accessible to blind people. "No blind people ever come here," they explain, while, to me, their attitude screams "Keep Out!" How little they know about blind people and our ability to see beauty around us. These professionals ask me why someone with no sight would be interested in seeing mountains, or watching the sun as it rises over the ocean. It is sad that they clearly believe life's beauty can only be experienced through the eyes.

One day I boarded a ski lift and went to the summit of Mount Wild Cat. On the way I leaned as far as I could out of my window (which, of course, is against the rules), and listened intently to the trees passing by me. This ride actually ascends the face of the mountain. That enabled me to sense the rock formations, smell the pines, hear the wind blowing through the trees, and listen to a stream descending the mountain, twisting and curving beneath me.

Then I arrived at the summit. As I moved about, I saw some areas thick with vegetation. The flowers felt beautiful and soft as I looked at them. How can I describe to professionals the joy I felt standing on the top of the mountain, listening to its silence and seeing it not with my eyes, but with every part of me!

Descending the mountain provided me with the opportunity to drop heavy stones from the ski lift's window and listen to them roll down, down, down. The trees rose up to greet me; the air became warmer, and soon I was at the base. I kept a stone from my mountain; it now sits in a dried arrangement I made for my living room. The stone and the cassette tape I made of the mountain's sounds are my photograph!

Those with sight admire the sun as it rises above the horizon; I listen to the sounds created by daybreak, feel the increase of light and warmth, and become part of the total experience. True, I do not see the beautiful colors; but what is color when you have a world of sounds, smells, and feelings around you to absorb?

According to Donna (Veno, 1986), a freelance writer who happens to be blind, people with visual impairments will be best served when service providers stop viewing blindness through their eyes. "Most of us do not feel restricted or disadvantaged; we lead normal, healthy and active lives. We work hard and want to play hard as well. While you who see stand at a distance and view the beauty of the mountain, I go to the top and become one with it."

Meet Alex, Who Likes to Plan His Strategy

Alex is faced with some tough decisions these days. The 17-year-old high school senior has to decide where to go to college next year—University of Pennsylvania, University of Michigan, or the University of California at Berkeley—whether to attend a conference, accept a scholarship he has been awarded, start guide dog training, or take a computer training class—all of which start at about the same time.

Not an easy set of decisions for any 17-year-old, but certainly not any less difficult for a teenager who is blind and about to start a new life away from home for the first time. Home for Alex is Staten Island. A town that is miles outside of Manhattan, Staten Island is far enough away to require his daily commute of a bus, a ferry, and a subway to Hunter College High School, one of Manhattan's public schools for children who are academically gifted.

But commutes do not seem to bother Alex. When he is not running uptown to complete his senior year internship, he is dashing downtown to meet with his chess teacher. Alex has won accolades in both areas. This year, he won a Class-C national chess championship and has garnered top scores in the New York state exams in Spanish.

Alex, who returned from a solo two-week trip to Spain in April, says he has always been interested in Spanish culture and language. "I plan to major in Spanish and other foreign languages, and then go on to law school where I will specialize in international law." Ambitions aside, Alex is not all that different from any other 17-year-old testing new waters as a young adult. Alex's mother would prefer a college closer to home and family, while Alex thinks otherwise. But mother and son are willing to compromise. Says his mother: "After all, this is the beginning of a new life."

What are characteristics of visual impairments?

Terms that Describe Visual Loss

The terms blind and blindness are typically reserved for persons who have no usable sight. The terms visually impaired, partially sighted, or low vision describe a host of conditions that indicate a serious loss of vision that cannot be corrected by medical or surgical procedures or with conventional eyeglasses.

In the early 1930s, the U.S. federal government developed a "legal" definition for blindness to determine whether individuals are eligible for special benefits. Because of this definition, there is often confusion between the terms blindness and visual impairment. The government adopted the same terms used by medical specialists to describe low vision acuity and visual field.

Acuity describes the amount of detail an individual sees compared to what a person with normal vision sees. It is the measurement taken of the best eye with the best correction to determine what the individual can see at 20 feet compared to what a person with unimpaired vision sees. For example, if a person has to be 20 feet away from an object that a person with normal vision can view from at least 70 feet away, the person would be said to have 20/70 vision. The larger the second number, the less vision a person has. The common phrase "20/20 vision" means the individual's sight is normal and needs no correction for distance.

Visual field refers to how great an area a person can see at one time with the fixed eye, measured in degrees (as an angle). The normal visual field is 180 degrees. If a person with normal vision looks straight ahead, that person should be able to see nearly all of the objects in a half-circle (180 degrees), with an equal area perceived on each side of the nose. Both eyes see the central one third of the visual field. A loss of visual field restricts either *central vision* (what is seen in the center of either eye) or *peripheral vision* (side vision). The definition of field used for legal blindness is 20 degrees.

A person is said to have *low vision* if he or she can only see a 20-degree to 40-degree field or less in their best eye. *Legal blindness* occurs when a person's visual acuity is 20/200 or less in the better eye (with the best possible correction) and/or the visual field is 20 degrees or less at the widest point. Seventy-two percent of people identified as legally blind are 65 or older. Eighty percent of people who are legally blind have some degree of usable vision, such as perception of light and dark.

Having low vision or a severe visual impairment means that a person's vision can range between 20/70 and 20/200 acuity or have 30 degrees or less visual field. There are five times as many individuals with low vision as people who are legally blind. People with low vision often encounter reading and mobility problems; however, with the aid of special devices, they are able to read and perform tasks requiring vision.

Causes of Visual Loss

Visual impairments can be *congenital* (present at birth) or *acquired*. *Rubella* (German measles) is an infectious disease that can cause multiple disabilities in the fetus, including blindness, if contracted during the first trimester of pregnancy. Although once common, rubella can now be prevented by immunizations that are mandatory in the United States and many industrialized nations. *Trachoma* is an infectious disease caused when a microorganism spread by flies enters the eye, producing infection and scarring the cornea or eyelid. Although rare in the United States, trachoma is the major cause of blindness in the world, found most often in areas with poor hygienic conditions.

Accidents are another common cause of visual impairments. Since pieces of flying metal from construction or home workshops cause many eye wounds, safety glasses are strongly recommended when doing projects that include these items. School-aged children sustain sports-related eye injuries that could be prevented with proper headgear and eyewear. For children of preschool age, cigarettes, cigars and pipes that dangle at eye level cause eye damage as well.

In addition to accidents that puncture, rupture, or burn the eye, two additional accidents are *retinopathy of prematurity* (ROP) and *detached retina*. ROP is blindness that occurs when premature infants are exposed to 100-percent oxygen for prolonged periods of time. There is often accompanying brain damage. Detached retina occurs when the retina (the sensory tissue upon which the lens image is formed) detaches and rips a hole in the outer wall. This creates a blind spot as the blood supply decreases. Detached retina can be surgically repaired, often using laser technology. The condition is often associated with trauma.

Diabetic retinopathy is a vascular disease that is a leading cause of blindness in United States for adults. Retinal blood vessels degenerate due to an imbalance of insulin, the hormone that the pancreas does not secrete in diabetes. There is no cure for this disorder; however, it is possible to slow the loss of sight through laser technology to coagulate and seal off leaking blood vessels.

Glaucoma is a blinding disease caused by increased pressure in the eye. The intraocular pressure is usually due to a malfunction in the system that controls the amount of fluid in the eye. If the pressure rises enough, it may damage structures in the back of the eye, particularly the optic nerve. Glaucoma may be *acute*, but is usually *progressive* (gradual peripheral sight loss) and unnoticed until peripheral vision is lost, causing a condition known as *tunnel vision*. Glaucoma is most often treated with eye drops or with surgery to drain the excess fluid in the eye to relieve pressure on the optic nerve.

Cataracts describe opacity (fogging) of the lens, and are found at the two extremes of the life span: infancy and advanced age. Cataracts are usually caused by a breakdown of the metabolic process that keeps the lens transparent. For older adults, vision decreases very gradually as the developing cataract blocks more and more of the light needed for vision. Cataracts can also be caused by external factors, such as electrical shock, wounds, or X-rays. Treatment ranges from the use of prescription eyeglasses and contact lenses to surgically implanted lenses to replace the opaque natural lens.

The macula is the region of the retina that is the most important for such activities as reading or sewing. *Macular degeneration*, a leading cause of new cases of legal blindness, is a malfunction of the pigment epithelium that removes waste from the inner fluid of the eye. This condition tends to run in families and is most common in people who have blue, gray, or green eyes. There is little treatment for macular degeneration; however, it usually does not result in total blindness.

Retinitis pigmentosa, another inherited disease, often leads to blindness in adolescence or young adulthood. The cause of the disease has not been fully established; however, the result is the failure of the normal process of rod and cone rejuvenation. Over time, the rods and cones (receptor cells) grow shorter, resulting in night blindness, tunnel vision, and loss of central vision.

What are considerations for inclusion of people with visual impairments?

Communicate with Participants

As always, it is best to ask program participants how best to meet their needs. The individual may disclose information regarding residual vision that will help us to maximize their participation and enjoyment. When first meeting an individual with visual impairments, it is helpful for us to introduce ourselves and let the person know we are speaking to them. Speak directly to the individual rather than through a companion, parent, or sibling. Speak in a normal tone of voice.

Someone who has a loss of vision probably does not also have a loss of hearing. We do not need to hesitate to use "sighted" terminology such as "look," and "see." People who are blind usually use such words themselves to help those who are sighted feel more relaxed. When others enter or leave the room, it is helpful to use their names when greeting them or saying good-bye to help the person who is visually impaired keep track of who is in the room. We must be careful to reduce the chances of loud, monotonous noises of prolonged duration because they can interfere with participants' ability to utilize auditory cues.

Include Participants in Planning

Including people with visual impairments in the planning process makes sense and can benefit everyone. Therefore, we can involve people with disabilities at all levels of recreation, from planning of services to participation in programs. In addition, we can discourage separate services, like segregated trails in parks, or specially designed tactual rooms in museums.

Though opportunities to enjoy services at parks and recreation areas have increased, there are still barriers that must be eliminated. A barrier may be physical (e.g., lack of materials in Braille or on tape) or attitudinal. Attitudinal barriers are by far the worst to encounter and the most difficult to break down. For both types of barriers planning teams including not only leisure services professionals but also participants with visual impairments are essential. Veno (1986) encouraged leisure services professionals to:

> Look at who we are and what we have, not at what you think we lack. Accept the reality that people with visual impairments are like others, except we do not see with our eyes. Be assured, however, we see with our hands, feet, ears and minds. Blindness allows me to use the gift of imagination. I create my own beauty in the space around me. You see your world as it is; I see the same world, as I want it to be in my own mind's eye. Who can tell, then, whose appreciation is greater? (p. 14)

Facilitate Inclusion

Many parks provide special trails with Braille signs guiding people with visual impairments along their way. It is helpful if we make a general trail usable by visitors with visual impairments rather than designing off-the-beaten-track trails with big signs indicating only people who are blind may use them. Most people with visual impairments are not asking for specialized services; rather, they are demanding an equal opportunity to use existing services and facilities.

Sometimes being placed in a large group of people in an unfamiliar context may overwhelm an individual with a visual impairment. For example, a young child beginning a playgroup, a teenager attending a social function, or an older adult joining a senior center may be reticent to interact with available materials or people. One approach to promote the inclusion of a person with visual impairments is to introduce the person to another individual and encourage their interaction by introducing an activity they might enjoy doing jointly. For instance, two young children might like to play together with puppets, teenagers might find it fun to help prepare the refreshments for a social function, and two older adults who were raised in the same area might enjoy reminiscing about their childhood with each other. In reference to young children, Rettig (1994, p. 417) stated:

> Even if young children with visual impairments and sighted children are served in the same setting, some intervention by adults will be required to ensure that the children interact with each other in positive ways. Any spontaneous interactions should be reinforced, and any discriminatory behaviors should be addressed immediately.

Meet Reba, Who Advocates for Rights

Nelson (1987) reported that like most pageant winners, Reba is talented, attractive, and articulate. She has used her status as a pageant winner to advocate for the rights of people with disabilities, especially those with hearing impairments. Reba has asked people she meets to help remove the communication and attitudinal barriers between people who hear and those who do not.

> I want people to learn that people with hearing impairments should not be looked upon as having a handicap that cannot be overcome. We must reciprocate the best way we can and overcome communication difficulties.

Reba was raised in a family with parents who are deaf and several brothers and sisters, some of whom hear and others who do not. In response to the varying hearing abilities of her family members, Reba is fluent in oral and manual communication. Reba herself has had a severe hearing impairment since birth.

Since her days as pageant winner, Reba has completed her degree in recreation and leisure studies and is a practicing Certified Therapeutic Recreation Specialist. She enjoys helping others, as she recognizes that others have helped her along the way. Reba is not only able to help people with disabilities develop meaningful leisure lifestyles, but also to serve as a role model for them. In addition, Reba continues to be a strong advocate for people with disabilities, educating all citizens regarding the ability of people with disabilities to be successful members of their communities.

Meet John, Who Has Signed His Way to the Top

John founded a high-tech computer company and turned it into a multimillion-dollar enterprise. What is interesting about his company is that more than 12% of the 375 employees have some form of hearing impairment and at least half of the employees without hearing impairments use sign language (Andersen, 1988). They do so because it is the most effective way to communicate with their boss, John, who is deaf.

John remembers when he was 10 and had just moved to a new community. The neighborhood children decided to test the newcomer by setting a firecracker off behind his back. Of course, he never heard the explosion. The humiliation drew tears. How did John cope with the cruelty? Did he fight back? "No, I made friends with them."

John continues to make friends wherever he goes. He enjoys the social contact and values his relationships. For relaxation, he spends time with his wife and their three children. John also feels it is important to advocate for the rights of people with disabilities. "I want the business world to understand that any person has capabilities. They can work and perform well if given the opportunity."

What are characteristics of hearing impairments?

Terms that Describe Hearing Loss

A *hearing impairment* is an invisible condition but one of the most prevalent disabilities. Hearing impairments include all losses of hearing, regardless of type or degree. *Deafness* can be defined as the state occurring when a person is unable to understand speech through the ear alone, either with or without a hearing aid. Hearing loss can range from *total congenital deafness* to *mild partial deafness*. Hearing losses are also experienced as people age—almost half of senior citizens have some hearing loss. Although hearing impairments are common, many people who are affected do not fully understand the problem. They may be unaware of the need for (or unwilling to seek) treatment. Those who have adjusted to a gradual loss of hearing through the years often do not realize that the sounds reaching them are greatly diminished.

Hearing impairment is categorized by the degree of hearing loss in one or both ears. *Mild hearing loss* is a loss of some sounds, while *moderate hearing loss* indicates a loss of enough sounds so that a person's ability to understand his or her surrounding environment is affected, including some speech sounds. When both ears have some hearing loss and the better ear has some difficulty hearing and understanding speech, the individual is said to have *significant bilateral loss*. *Severe loss* indicates that many sounds are not heard including most speech. Finally, *profound loss* indicates the inability to hear almost all sounds. These classifications and their audible ranges are listed in **Table 18.1**.

Total or partial impairment of hearing may result from a variety of causes. The onset can be either *insidious* (having a gradual and cumulative effect) or *acute* (having a sudden onset, sharp rise, and short course). People are said to be *hard-of-hearing* if they have mild to moderate hearing loss resulting in decreased perception of conversational speech, but sufficient hearing to permit understanding with optimal circumstances. These people have losses that can result in sound distortions or trouble interpreting sounds. Depending on the causes of the hearing loss, some people who are hard-of-hearing can benefit from the use of a hearing aid. Many people who are deaf prefer the term hard-of-hearing rather than the term hearing impaired; however, hearing impairment is the term of choice by the general public.

Ways of Measuring Hearing

Units of sound intensity called *decibels* (dB) are used to measure hearing (see **Table 18.2**, p. 360). Zero decibels is the softest intensity of sound or speech that can be heard by a person with normal hearing. People who can hear sounds from 0–25 dB and up are considered to have normal hearing.

Audible Range	Classification
0–25 dB +	Normal Hearing
25–40 dB +	Mild Loss
40–55 dB +	Moderate Loss
55–70 dB +	Severe Loss
90 dB +	Profound Loss (Deaf)

Table 18.1 Hearing loss classifications based on audible decibel levels

People who can only hear sounds starting at 25–40 dB are considered to have a mild hearing loss, whereas those who begin to hear at 40–55 dB are said to have a moderate loss. Moderately severe loss occurs when the individual cannot hear at volumes lower than 55–70 decibels. Severe loss refers to the inability to hear sounds and speech under 70–90 decibels. Not being able to hear until a sound is at least 90 decibels or above is termed a profound hearing loss. Beyond 90 decibels, many people would be called deaf, but with modern hearing devices some people can obtain usable sound. People with hearing in the normal range begin to experience discomfort at volume levels of 90–100 dB; danger to one's hearing increases with exposure.

Hertz (Hz), the unit of measurement of the frequency of sound waves, describes pitch. Persons who have difficulty understanding speech generally have losses of high or low pitch. Some people may find it easier to understand low (deeper) voices rather than high voices, or vice versa.

Learn about the Types of Hearing Loss

There are three basic types of hearing impairments: conductive, sensorineural, and central. With a *conductive loss*, sound waves are blocked as they travel through the auditory canal or middle ear and cannot reach the inner ear. Sounds seem muffled and an earache may be present. Both children and adults are often affected by conductive hearing loss caused by wax blocking the ear canal, infection, or a punctured eardrum. Another

Decibels	Example
20 dB	Whisper
50–60 dB	Typical conversational speech
80 dB	Alarm clock volume (at two feet)
90 dB	Lawn mower
100 dB	Chain saw or stereo headphones
120 dB	Music concert (in front of speakers)

Table 18.2 Examples of sounds at various decibels

cause of conductive-type loss is otosclerosis. In this disorder, the bones of the middle ear soften, do not vibrate well, and then calcify. This, and other conductive hearing problems, can often be treated successfully with surgery or other procedures.

A *sensorineural hearing loss*, commonly termed *nerve deafness*, involves the inner ear and is the result of damage to the hair cells, nerve fibers, or both. Sounds are distorted, high tones are usually inaudible, and *tinnitus* (ringing or buzzing sounds) may be present. Speech can be heard, but is not easily understood. This type of loss is permanent and irreversible. Infants are born with sensorineural hearing loss caused by genetics, birth injury (loss of oxygen during labor) or damage to the developing fetus because of maternal infection (rubella, herpes, or other viral diseases). Other causes include high fevers, excessive noise, heredity, adverse reactions to drugs, head injuries, the aging process, and diseases such as meningitis.

A third, although rare, form of hearing loss is *central hearing loss*. With this type of impairment, the pathways to the brain or the brain itself are damaged. Sound levels are not affected, but understanding of language becomes difficult. Central hearing loss results from excess exposure to loud noise, head injuries, high fever, or tumors.

What are considerations for inclusion of people with hearing impairments?

Consider Diversity of Skills

People who access leisure services possess many different types of hearing loss that result in varied skills, abilities, and experiences. For example, some people with hearing impairments may have cochlear implants and communicate orally, others may use an English-based sign system of American Sign Language, while other people may have additional disabilities or reside in a home where the spoken language is not English (Easterbrooks & Baker, 2001).

Use Meaningful Communication

When speaking to a person with a hearing impairment use a normal tone of voice and speak in complete sentences. We can speak slowly and distinctly, and enunciate clearly without "mouthing" the words. Overarticulation does not make it easier to read lips. Look at the person when speaking and maintain face-to-face contact while communicating.

Ensure that adequate lighting is available to facilitate reading the person's lips. When interacting with the person, watch their gestures and face to gain additional cues to understand them. Use demonstration when teaching skills or explaining activities, because demonstrations are often more meaningful to the person who is hearing impaired than lengthy explanations.

Individuals who have hearing impairments benefit from communication and information presented visually. For example, charts, graphs, simulations, demonstrations, models, and other forms of visual representations can enhance the chance that a person will learn and understand information that is presented (Easterbrooks & Baker, 2001).

Understand Methods of Assistance

Speech reading and sign language are other modalities available to persons with severe hearing loss. Speech reading is a virtual necessity in cases of severe or profound loss and can be self-taught to some extent; however, professional training may be needed for many persons. Depending upon the degree of impairment and individual needs, each person must decide what options offer the most advantages.

Know Classifications of Hearing Impairments

Consider when the onset of the hearing impairment occurred, if the individual chooses to disclose the information. People are identified as having *prelingual deafness* if deafness occurs before language skills have been acquired. The deafness can be congenital or acquired in infancy. The second category, *postlingual deafness* is deafness that occurs after language has been acquired. The most common known causes of postlingual hearing impairments are high fevers during childhood and certain childhood diseases, such as meningitis, encephalitis, measles, mumps, and influenza.

Facilitate Inclusion

Inclusion of people with hearing impairments has positive effects on people who do not have significant hearing loss. For example, Most, Weisel, and Tur-Kaspa (1999) asked 140 high school students without hearing impairments (half of whom had regular contact with youth with hearing impairments) to listen to the speech of youth with hearing impairments and rate the speakers personal qualities. Students who had regular contact with youth with hearing impairments reported more positive evaluations of personal qualities of speakers than students who did not have contact. This finding supports studies indicating that inclusion has positive effects on attitudes towards individuals with hearing impairments.

Meet Lisa, Who Tends the Garden

One look at the flower garden in Lisa's front yard tells you how much she enjoys beauty. Lisa has been blind since birth. She lost her hearing at age 5 from complications of meningitis. She tells all of the people she meets how fortunate she was to have learned to speak.

> I remember the sound of the piano—my mother was a music teacher when I was a girl. The fragrance of the flowers, the subtle ways they move with the breeze, the delicate, velvety texture of their petals, all remind me of the music that came from my mother's piano. One doesn't need to be able to see or hear to find beauty in the world. My flower garden gives me so much pleasure. I grow different flowers every season. Every type is unique in fragrance, shape, and texture. Of course, the gardenias are my favorite: simple, pungent, and yet delicate.

Another source of pleasure for Lisa is her imagination. She knows Braille and reads at least one new book a week that she receives from her public library's Talking Book program. Lisa provides us with some insight about her love of reading:

> The books I enjoy reading the most are the stories with rich descriptions about people and their environment, like Charles Dickens or John Steinbeck. I also love poetry, especially Maya Angelou. The written word can so eloquently convey beauty.

What are characteristics of deaf-blindness?

Most people who are deaf-blind are over 65 years of age, and most are women, due to the longer life span for women. However, many children who are deaf-blind are born each year due to accidents, diseases, and genetic problems. Prior to the advent of rubella vaccine, incidence of deaf-blindness was much higher. Although some conditions that cause deaf-blindness may cause other impairments, most children with deaf-blindness are just as intelligent as children without disabilities.

Infants who are deaf-blind require immediate and intense stimulation to the remaining senses to increase their awareness of the world around them. Without outside stimulation, infants with deaf-blindness withdraw and develop behaviors such as rocking, finger waving, and eye rubbing. Play and recreation activities are excellent forms of stimulation. Even though toddlers with deaf-blindness may have balance difficulties, it is important for them to walk frequently, rather than being carried, because by walking they can develop a clear perception of space and its relationship to their bodies.

People who deaf-blind can learn leisure skills; however they may learn in different ways and at different rates than people with hearing and vision. Providing educational and leisure services often requires perseverance of the family and professionals.

What are considerations for inclusion of people who are deaf-blind?

The family and the individual are the greatest resource for information on how to provide meaningful recreational opportunities for the person with deaf-blindness. We can learn how we can best communicate with the individual to discover their leisure preferences. The recommendations given for providing services to individuals with visual impairments (e.g., assuring a barrier-free environment), and those for individuals with hearing impairments (e.g., teaching through demonstration), are helpful when providing services for participants with deaf-blindness.

Final Thoughts

One goal of leisure services providers is to facilitate meaningful recreation opportunities for all participants. People who have sensory impairments can successfully participate in leisure services when offered appropriate support. When first meeting individuals with sensory impairments, avoid the assumption that they have limited skills and cognitive abilities; rather, consider that these participants may only have difficulty communicating their preferences and needs. It is our responsibility to discover the best way to communicate with each individual who happens to have a sensory impairment.

All participants with sensory impairments have the right to be served with dignity and respect. The National Federation of the Blind has published the following narrative to communicate courtesies to follow when interacting with people with visual impairments. Many of these recommendations are equally applicable to people with hearing impairments.

I am an ordinary person, just blind. You don't need to raise your voice or address me as if I were a child. Don't ask my spouse if I want cream in the coffee — ask me. I may use a long white cane or dog guide to walk independently, or I may ask to take your arm. Let me decide. And please don't grab my arm. Let me take yours. I'll keep a half-step behind to anticipate curbs and steps. I want to know who's in the room with me. Speak to me when you enter. And please introduce me to the others. Include the children and tell me if there's a cat or dog. A partially opened door to a room, cabinet or car can be a hazard to me. Please be considerate.

I have no trouble with ordinary table skills and can manage with no help. Don't avoid words like "see." I use them, too. I'm always glad to see you. Please don't talk about the "wonderful compensations" of blindness. My sense of smell, touch and hearing didn't improve when I became blind. I rely on them more and therefore may get more information through those senses, but that's all. If I'm your houseguest, show me the bathroom, closet, dresser, window and the light switch. I like to know whether the lights are on, so please tell me. I'll discuss blindness with you and answer all your questions if you're curious, but it's an old story to me. I have as many other interests as you do.

Don't think of me as just "a blind person." I'm just a person who happens to be blind. In all 50 states the law requires drivers to yield the right-of-way when they see my white cane. Only the blind may carry white canes. You see more blind persons today walking alone, not because there are more of us, but because more of us have learned to make our own way.

Discussion Questions

1. What is the difference between blindness and low vision?
2. What is acuity?
3. What is the visual field?
4. What are considerations for inclusion of individuals with visual impairments?
5. What are the differences among the terms deaf, hearing impairment, and hard-of-hearing?
6. What is the difference between prelingual deafness and postlingual deafness?
7. What are decibels? How are they related to each of the categories of hearing loss?
8. What are the three basic types of hearing impairments?
9. What is a hertz? How does it affect hearing?
10. What are considerations for inclusion of individuals with hearing impairments?

Photo by Lynda Greer

Mary Jane Owen

Mary Jane Owen lives in Washington, DC, where she is Executive Director of Disability Focus, Inc., as well as Executive Director of National Catholic Office for Persons with Disabilities. She also works as a freelance writer and public speaker. Mary Jane's loss of sight in 1972 was the result of a hereditary ophthalmic disorder. An inner ear dysfunction caused hearing impairment and severe loss of balance which requires her to use a wheelchair.

Mary Jane's Story

I'm a lot of things rolled into one package: laughter and tears; triumphs and defeats; dreams and disappointments; foolishness and wit; self-concern and willingness to sacrifice for others. Sometimes I wonder how I manage to balance so many differing abilities and disabilities. I'm proud of my American heritage and humble before those who have prevailed without my advantages.

I'm a strong, intelligent, principled, articulate, and very stubborn woman (who happens to be blind, partially hearing, and a wheelchair user) who will probably continue to fill roles I consider essential in the struggle to create opportunities and allow my species to fulfill its potential.

I started out with all the obvious gifts life had to offer. I was born to young parents who cared about racism and a religious life. I lived in small northern Illinois towns where my father published a small newspaper and both shared responsibilities for ministering to small congregations within the Rock River Conference of the Methodist Church. I gained my sense of women's roles when my mother assumed total responsibilities following the death of my father when I was six. From my family I gained an inquiring mind, a strong attractive body, a sense of moral obligation to others, an orientation toward art and literature, and a life-long interest in ideas and education.

With such unlimited possibilities I learned to be complacent. The miracles which life holds became apparent only as I personally began to explore the all too common experience of evolving flaws. The mysteries of human vulnerability and the strength of the human spirit to survive and thrive has been a fascinating puzzle for the last few decades of my life.

Several years ago it became evident to me that the risks and stresses of the living process itself bring assorted impairments but also awaken one of the evolving joys of life. Therefore, I recognize the power of experiences I would never have selected for myself. Through them I have gained a firm knowledge of the power of the human spirit and its drive toward self-determination. The weakest among us is empowered by a dream of possibilities and the gift of "being."

Chapter 19

People, Inclusion, and Assistive Technology

Photo by Lynda Greer

C. Anthony Cunningham

C. Anthony Cunningham is an attorney in Decatur, Georgia. Born with a detached retina and glaucoma, he was totally blind by the age of 23.

C. Anthony's Story

My eyesight was never any good, but nobody really knew for a long time. My mother worked in domestic and restaurant service; my father was a heavy equipment operator. They stayed busy, working and raising ten kids. Of course when I started to school, I had to deal with it. I developed certain "tricks of the trade" to compensate and conceal my poor vision. They worked pretty well most of the time. I went through school as a sighted person and graduated a quarter early. But by the time I was 17 I was legally blind in my left eye and had no vision in my right.

Between 1973 and 1978 my sight deteriorated rapidly, but after working for three years I was finally able to start college . . . while still working, in 1976. In 1978 I began to come to grips with the fact of my blindness. I quit working and took time off from school to do rehabilitation training. During this time I came to the realization that I'm me, blind or not blind, and that was fine. After the time in rehab training I had the confidence to go back to college full time.

Since I was young I've wanted to be in a helping profession, to do something socially responsible. I grew up hearing the cries of the sixties and seventies, aware of the need to create social change. So while in college I decided to become a criminal lawyer . . . to help those accused of crimes. I'm not talking about corporate types, rich people who hire big names for big money. I mean the little guy, usually not much money, no real understanding of the system, who is in trouble and scared. For 5 years after law school I worked on the civil side of poverty law practice for the Atlanta, Georgia, Legal Aid Society and now I'm practicing on my own. I opened my office in early 1990. It was a big step. There were no guarantees it will work out. But it was a step I had to take.

In Memory

After the publication of this text's first edition, C. Anthony Cunningham died. His photo and story are included in the second edition as a memorial.

Ability is of little account without opportunity.
-Napoleon Bonaparte

Orientation Activity: What's New?

Directions Alone: Read the following scenario and identify the technological advances that were not available to people just fifty years ago.

Carlos leaned back in his chair, took off his glasses, and rubbed his eyes. It had been a productive afternoon at the computer and time had slipped away. Gazing out the window, he was surprised to see that it was dusk and the streetlights were on. A glance at the digital clock confirmed the time as 6:06 p.m. and he had not started dinner. Carlos saved his document and then hurried to the kitchen. This would be a good night for the frozen gourmet dinners. Placing them in the microwave, he turned his attention to the remaining portion of the meal. By the time the aroma of chicken and rice filled the kitchen, Carlos had whipped an instant chocolate mousse in the blender, started the coffeemaker, and put a loaf of brown-and-serve French bread in the convection oven. Place mats and tableware were put into place just as he heard the automatic garage door begin to open. Carlos rolled his wheelchair into the living room to turn on the CD player and ignite the gas log. At 6:30 p.m. Jennifer walked in the house to find her smiling Carlos, a fire, her favorite music, and wonderful smells. It was good to be home!

Directions with Others: Move about the room with your list, find a person, and discuss your impression of the paragraph. Identify one technological advance that has occurred during your lifetime and explain its specific influence for you. Once the other person has done the same, move on to another person until you are given a signal to stop.

Debriefing: Innovations appear so rapidly that we quickly forget the way things used to be. Many people cannot remember televisions without remote controls, kitchens without a microwave oven, and music systems that played only records or eight-track tapes. The scenario above has many examples of inventions not available 50 years ago, including the computer, automatic streetlights, digital clock, frozen dinners, microwave oven, instant chocolate mousse, blender, automatic coffeemaker, brown-and-serve French bread, convection oven, automatic garage door opener, CD player, and gas log. Consider the following questions when reflecting on the orientation activity:

- What are some technological advances that may increase leisure opportunities for people with disabilities?
- Why is technology important to consider relative to leisure participation of people with disabilities?
- What is meant by the phrase "assistive technology?"

Introduction

Advances in computers and other technology have helped individuals with disabilities to be included into society by increasing their mobility, communication, and opportunities to learn (Siegel, 1999). Individuals with disabilities can be assisted by technology because in many cases programs are self-paced, provide opportunities for practice, and can be individualized (Siegel, Good & Moore, 1996). However, Baum (1998) warned us that since use of assistive technology is a very individual experience, service providers should think about differences in skills and interests of participants when considering the use of different assistive technologies.

Professionals who see the leisure-related potential of computers and adapted devices and who are also interested in advancing the independence of people they serve contribute to a growing interest in assistive technology (Coale, 1999). Although assistive technology can improve the lives of people with disabilities, Cooper (1998) pointed out that its cost is significant and probably many more people could benefit from assistive technology if they could afford it. Therefore, leisure service providers are encouraged to promote the use of assistive technology whenever possible and to seek ways to support acquisition of such devices, systems, and services. By incorporating technology into inclusive leisure services participants with disabilities can increase their independence, become more expressive and creative, make more choices, and improve their self-images.

What is meant by technology and assistive technology?

The variety of terms used to describe technology sometimes can create confusion. The following terms are described in this section:

- technology, and
- assistive technology.

Technology

Technological developments have made it possible for people with disabilities to participate in previously inaccessible leisure opportunities. *Technology* is the use of systematic procedures to produce outcomes that require less work and that are more uniform and predictable than can be produced by unassisted effort (Kipnis, 1991). According to Kipnis, technological changes enhance skills and talents, increase a sense of control, and broaden the scope of activities. Technology can help people overcome barriers by supporting independence and self-reliance and provide opportunities for them to do things for themselves. Many technological advances and conveniences have transformed the quality of life for people who have disabilities.

Assistive Technology

Assistive technology can help people with disabilities overcome limitations and perform tasks that might otherwise not be possible. Siegel (1999) identified *assistive technology* as devices and services used by people with disabilities to compensate for functional limitations and to enhance learning, independence, mobility, communication, environmental control, and choice. The use of assistive technology by individuals with disabilities should increase the likelihood that they will be included in community leisure pursuits. In addition, Cooper (1998) stated that assistive technologies are devices and techniques used to optimize human function by:

- enhancing existing skills (computers to help organize thoughts),
- replacing missing structures (prosthetic hand),
- substituting structures (wheelchairs for mobility instead of legs),
- providing alternative means of function (speech synthesizer to communicate), and
- minimizing environmental barriers (universal design of buildings).

Technological tools that restore or extend human functions are called *assistive technology devices* (Mann & Lane, 1991). Today many assistive devices exist to help people with disabilities learn more efficiently, communicate more effectively, live more independently, and experience leisure more easily. Assistive technology devices include adaptive toys, wheelchairs, augmentative communication systems, and many other items that have been modified, or customized to increase, maintain, or improve the function of individuals with disabilities (Broach, Dattilo & Deavours,

2000). Mann and Lane (1991, p. 7) offered the following description of assistive devices:

> New assistive devices for persons with disabilities are based on technologies from many fields. Computer-based devices (hard technology) come from the electronics industry, while applications (soft technology) come from health and education. Controls, switches, and robotics are based on advances in the industrial and aerospace programs. Commercial and military developments generate new composite materials useful for mobility devices. Advances in biotechnology will generate unimaginable devices and functions for persons with disabilities.

The next section will examine how assistive technology can enhance independence and promote interdependence and allow people with disabilities to:

- improve physiological functioning,
- enhance skills,
- control their environment,
- utilize animal assistance, and
- expand their experiences.

Meet the Six-Million-Dollar Family

A popular television program during the 1970s, *The Six-Million-Dollar Man*, portrayed a futuristic Air Force pilot whose shattered body had been rebuilt with artificial parts, giving him extraordinary powers of speed, strength, and vision. Bill likes to tell friends that his family is making the fantasy come true. When his rheumatoid arthritis finally became too painful, Bill had two artificial hip replacements. One year later, he is able to take his grandchildren fishing again. Bill's wife, Edna, is able to go with them now that she has a heart pacemaker implanted. Their oldest son, Rodney, is also enjoying better health since being fitted with an insulin pump to automatically monitor and treat his diabetes. Finally, Bill is happy that granddaughter Celeste has received permanent dental implants to replace the teeth she lost in a fall from her bicycle.

How can technology improve physiological functioning?

Devices implanted in or attached to the body to simulate more typical functioning may sound like science fiction, but they are real and making differences in the lives of individuals with disabilities. Since there are too many innovations to discuss them all and more are being developed rapidly, this section only provides an overview of only some of the many advances. Technology designed to improve physiological functioning can help to:

- manage health problems,
- control one's body,
- improve muscle tone, and
- promote hearing.

Manage Health Problems

Neuroimplantation is a procedure that implants electrodes on the spinal cord, in limbs, or directly in the brain. The electrical impulses generated help to alleviate dysfunctions (e.g., seizures and spasticity) found in individuals who have cerebral palsy, closed head injuries, spinal cord injuries, and multiple sclerosis.

To benefit people with heart problems, the *artificial pacemaker* is a small device permanently implanted under the skin of the chest wall. A pacemaker regulates the heart rate by sending out electrical impulses that force the heart to contract rhythmically.

Control One's Body

Technology has enabled people with disabilities to have more control over their bodies. Personal *cooling systems* help individuals with spinal cord injuries to regulate body temperature. Custom-made *gloves* assist those who use wheelchairs to experience less strain on their hands and wrists.

People with disabilities may need assistance with personal care, and welcome products that enable more privacy and independence. An instrument is available that uses completely external *ultrasound* to inform individuals who have no lower body sensation when it is appropriate to mechanically empty their bladder. Technological advances have made it possible for men with paralysis due to spinal cord injury to father children and for women with disabilities to conceive and carry pregnancies to term.

Improve Muscle Tone

Research continues on ways people with paralyzing disabilities might be able to walk. *Neurorehabilitation* is an experimental system of stimulating muscles to contract by sending electrical impulses to them through surface electrodes. In addition to enabling a few people with partial paraplegia to walk again, the technology has greater potential for the improvement of muscle tone and circulation in many people with paralysis. The alternate contracting and relaxing of the muscle via electrical impulse helps to build muscle mass, which improves the health of the skin, helps to build bone, and increases cardiovascular health.

Promote Hearing

Several instruments have been created to assist hearing processes. Approved by the U.S. Food and Drug Administration in 1985, *cochlear implants* are electrode devices that are surgically implanted in the mastoid bone behind the ear to stimulate the hearing nerve. Although they do not restore total hearing, they have helped people to gain some understanding of spoken words.

What are considerations for inclusion with technology that improves physiological functioning?

Biotechnology holds enormous potential for increasing leisure experiences for people with disabilities. Often we are unaware that participants are using biotechnological aids. The key is a willingness to work with individuals and facilitate their leisure involvement.

Meet Stephen, Who Enjoys a Joke and an Occasional Dance

Berger (1992) wrote about Stephen, possibly the world's most brilliant physicist and best known as the developer of the black hole theory.

Stephen, who has amyotrophic lateral sclerosis (Lou Gehrig's Disease), rolled noiselessly into the darkened conference room accompanied by two nurses. Fingering a control panel with the partial motion remaining in his left hand, he positioned himself at the back of the center aisle, quietly attended the lectures of his fellow physicists, and took in their illustrative slides. When he had a comment to interject, he fingered the same panel, triggering an artificial voice that emanated from somewhere beneath him.

Over lunch a friendly discussion ensued about why Americans often groan rather than laugh at puns. Was it back-handed appreciation or were they seriously offended? As the debate proceeded, Stephen began fingering his panel and gazed around the table, eyes sparkling mischievously, and a voice beneath him said, in elevated tones, "I am trying to get my synthesizer to groan."

During the last night of the conference, participants were bused to a flamenco club for dinner and entertainment. Guitarists, singers, and dancers took to the stage, gave an accomplished performance, and then invited the physicists to dance with them. When one of the dancers made her way through the tables to dance in front of Stephen, I thought it might cross that nebulous boundary into bad taste. Here was a young woman stomping her feet in front of a man who could barely move. Other physicists stood aside to make room. Grinning asymmetrically, Stephen programmed his chair to move back and forth in synchronicity with the dancer. As correctly as his fellow physicists, Stephen ended the conference by dancing flamenco.

The impact of assistive technology on an individual's life is immediately apparent when noting the accomplishments of this world-renowned physicist who uses a motorized wheelchair to help him with mobility and a computer and voice synthesizer to facilitate his communication. In covering one of his lectures, the following report was published in the *Athens Daily News* (1995, p. 2A):

Leave it to Stephen Hawking to pack a stadium with talk of quantum physics and black holes. A record 9,185 people flocked to the University of Utah's Huntsman arena Monday night to hear the physicist discuss those subjects and more. "It's a bit like a rock concert, and shows physics can be as popular as heavy metal," Hawking said at a reception.

How can technology enhance skills?

Stephen is able to continue his work because he has a combination of human and technological assistance. For a person with severe disabilities, no amount of computerized, robotic, or biomechanical equipment can completely substitute for human assistance with activities of daily living. People, not machines, make technological adaptations work for people with disabilities. The application of technology is especially meaningful for people with severe disabilities. Assistive technology can provide new ways to:

- move better,
- speak better,
- hear better, and
- see better.

Move Better

For people who cannot see, technological advances such as laser canes and other *electronic travel aids* help to lead the way. These instruments provide information about objects in the vicinity, including distance, direction, and surface characteristics. The electronic travel aids are most useful in unfamiliar areas but are not preferred in rainy, snowy, or noisy conditions.

Power wheelchairs have undergone major improvements since the first motor was attached to a manual chair. Lightweight materials, improved shock-absorbing features, better batteries, and other advances have created more reliable, customized chairs. Individuals who have cervical (high) spinal cord injuries, severe developmental disabilities, post-polio weakness syndrome, or other degenerative disease processes typically use power chairs. Power chairs have been developed that roll forward and back and raise the individual to a standing position, because periods of standing can have positive mental and physical effects. An individual with such a chair could stand to work at a drawing board, or stand facing others at a party. Manual and power chairs are not the only option for moving about the community. To illustrate the capacity of some power wheelchairs Claudia Paniagua (2000, p. 13) stated:

> Because of the severity of my disability (my bones break easily), I am unable to walk. So I use an assistive technology device, which is a power chair. This chair is not like you might think of a wheelchair. It has a neat feature which allows me to go up to five feet high and all the way down to the floor. It's a great help because

now I can reach for things that are up on a counter, and I can reach for things that I drop on the floor. I can also look people in the eye.

Individuals who have arthritis or multiple sclerosis often use *battery-powered scooters*. These compact scooters are often collapsible to fit into the trunk of a car. In addition, specialized *battery-operated cushions* are available that automatically shift the pressure points of the cushion at regular intervals to prevent skin ulcers.

To transport a power chair requires a van with specialized lifts and other equipment. Under the requirements of the ADA, most metropolitan areas are now purchasing power wheelchair accessible buses and vans, as the buses currently in use need replacement. Individuals with disabilities are also able to operate their cars and vans with adaptations. *Automobile hand controls* installed on the steering column can brake and accelerate the vehicle. For those who do not have the range of motion to turn a standard steering wheel, there are miniature wheels and joysticks as substitutes. There is a joystick-type invention that replaces the steering wheel, throttle, and brakes of a converted van. A person who can move a joystick only three inches is able to drive independently.

Speak Better

We communicate in a variety of ways including vocalizations, hand gestures, body movements, and facial expressions. Acquisition of speech allows people to join the community of language users who share conversation about objects, actions, and events (Adamson, 1996). When children fail to develop functional spoken language, their access to topics and partners may be severely limited (Romski, Sevcik & Adamson, 1999).

Freedom of expression is a highly prized right for many. However, many people with significant speech disabilities routinely experience isolation, discrimination, segregation, illiteracy, institutionalization, unemployment, poverty, and despair. Due to the lack of understandable speech, these individuals are perceived to be unable to direct their own lives—a perception that often leads to deprivation of their most basic civil rights and liberties.

Bryen, Slesaransky, and Baker (1995) suggested that this problem be addressed by providing persons with speech impairments access to augmentative and alternative communication devices, services, and supports. Since speech alone may not be a viable mode of communication for many people with disabilities, the use of these systems should be welcomed so that individuals can express preferences, make choices, and gain some control over their daily activities and events.

An *augmentative and alternative communication* (AAC) system describes the symbols, aids, strategies, and techniques that are used by individuals whose disabilities prevent typical communication. Systems can be simple paper charts or elaborate computers. Systems can utilize pictures in the form of simple line drawings, full-color photographs, or picture symbols. Information can be recorded into these systems via keyboard or by touching the display on the monitor. AAC systems are typically about the size and shape of a large computer keyboard and can be mounted on a wheelchair, desk, or table in front of the individual. Several models of AAC systems are the size of an electronic organizer and can fit into a person's pocket. Some units even come in a choice of colors. Once the device is selected, the communication options are customized to the needs of the person.

Some AAC systems operate as a simple *visual display format* projected when a person activates the system. The advantage of such a system is that it is silent and can be used anywhere. One disadvantage is the tendency of the listener to focus on the system, rather than the face of the person who is communicating. Another disadvantage is that the person cannot communicate with anyone who is not able to read the screen, such as a young child, someone in another room, a person who has a visual impairment, or one who is not literate.

Other AAC systems have auditory output in the form of *digitized speech* that converts the written message to sound. Manufacturers of AAC systems offer a choice of different male and female voices with some sounding like children and others like adults. Digitized speech can enable people to participate in discussions and to have a voice and speak for themselves. For active people, small, portable devices are available that can be used for both receptive and expressive communication.

Romski, Sevcik, and Wilkinson (1994) found that individuals with speech impairments eagerly integrated the use of AAC systems into their repertoire of vocalizations and gestures. Subsequently, Romski and colleagues (1999) reported that use of speech output communication systems had a positive effect on the communication of people with speech impairments. Statements of a man interviewed by Bryen and colleagues (1995, p. 85) who has a significant speech disability and began using an AAC system called a TouchTalker support this conclusion:

> I am very active in my church. Up until the time when I got my TouchTalker, most of the people in the church never interacted with me. I think they were intimidated because they had a very difficult time communicating with me. But now, everybody is very friendly with me.

Hear Better

Technology has drastically changed the way people with hearing impairments socialize and experience leisure. The ADA has helped support many advances in technology that have allowed people to hear better. Walker (2001, p. 4) spoke to this idea:

> The 1990 Americans with Disabilities Act, which outlawed discriminatory practices against the disabled, gave deaf people the legislative muscle to make headway as never before. A new "can-do" attitude and sense of pride soon emerged. Then, as the 1990s saw a virtual explosion of technological advances, deaf people finally had the tools to fully enter the mainstream.

Individuals who have natural speech but are not able to produce volume may be assisted with a *personal amplifier*, a small, portable, battery-powered device with adjustable volume. The amplifier enables the person to carry on conversations, speak up in class, or make public presentations. If the larynx, a person's voice box, is removed, speech is still possible with an electronic device held against the throat that converts vibrations into sound.

Another innovation, *computerized eyeglasses*, convert spoken language to print and display it at the bottom of the lens. This technology is most useful for individuals whose hearing loss occurred after their spoken language had developed.

The most common and best-known assistive hearing device, the *hearing aid*, improves hearing in many instances, but it does not correct hearing nor does it necessarily restore hearing to normal levels. A hearing aid will, however, lessen the degree of severity of hearing loss and enable the user to hear many previously inaudible sounds.

If a hearing aid is recommended, there are many types from which to choose. These range from tiny, all-in-the-ear models for mild to moderate losses to large body aids for profound impairments. Hearing aids may also be worn in eyeglasses or behind the ear. Some people require only one aid (*monaural*) while others gain the most benefit from two (*binaural*). Many hearing aids are equipped with a telephone switch, which enables the sound from the telephone to go directly into the hearing aid, greatly increasing clarity.

The *ear mold* is a vital component of any hearing aid. Some ear molds are made from a solid plastic material, others from a more pliable substance. Some are simple tubular inserts, while other molds fill the entire cavity of the outer ear. They are made in a manner similar to taking an impression for dentures. Like hearing aids, ear molds eventually need replacement. Danger signs are whistling noises (feedback), indicating the ear mold no longer fits snugly in the ear.

In various situations, and especially with a severe to profound loss, a hearing aid may not be enough. In addition, technology has been helpful for those who have hearing impairments but are not candidates for implants. While hearing aids are helpful for some individuals, others find the background noise that is picked up to be very distracting. *Amplification systems* consist of a wireless microphone worn by the speaker, and a headset or insert ear mold worn by the listener. This may be the ideal solution in an instructional situation, allowing the instructor to move about freely, all the while "broadcasting" to an audience of one.

Another instrument, an *electronic metronome device* worn outside the ear, has been successful in reducing stuttering for some individuals. Finally, a hearing-aid type device is available to mask the ringing of the ear caused by tinnitus. The device produces a soothing white noise, which makes the ringing less distracting for many individuals.

Modern technology has provided a variety of *assistive listening devices* for telephones, conference rooms, classrooms, theaters, and places of worship. They include portable and permanent telephone amplifiers, direct audio input devices, personal infrared systems, alarm systems, and telecaptioning devices. The many devices available for people with hearing impairments allow them to be included in interactions with other people. Three of the more common ones include alerting systems, text telephones, and telecaption decoders.

Alerting systems, also identified as "signalers," allow people with hearing impairments to be aware of audible sounds or warnings such as those generated from telephones, smoke alarms, and timers. For example, a flashing signaler can consist of a single lamp attached to a receiver or several lights strategically placed in a building that flash in response to an alarm. As another option, a vibrating signaler can be used to page a person.

Text telephones (TTYs), sometimes referred to as a TDDs or TTs, were invented in 1964 and enable people who have severe hearing impairments to use the telephone. The TTY resembles a small computer keyboard with a telephone modem and a small liquid crystal display (LCD) screen to transmit coded signals across the standard telephone network. To use the TTY a person dials the telephone and places the handset on a couple (modem) which then transmits an electronic signal across the phone line to another person who has a TTY. Once a connection is made the individuals type their messages to each other and the messages are displayed on the LCD panel. If a person who has a TTY wants to contact a person who does not have a TTY then the person dials a specific number that connects the person to an operator equipped with a TTY. The operator then contacts the person to be called and acts as a relay as the operator listens to the person who does not have a TTY and then types the message to the person using the TTY. The ADA stipulates that telephone companies provide telecommunication relay services 24 hours a day, seven days a week, at no additional charge.

Telecaption decoders (the size of a VCR) are connected to the television and allow people to view closed captions being transmitted that are not typically available for viewing.

See Better

Computers hold promise for people who have visual impairments. Characters can be displayed on the computer screen in very large type and with varying degrees of color and contrast to assist readers who have reduced vision. *Video magnifiers* can be used with computers but also are available in self-contained portable units that can be more easily transported than an entire computer system. Printers are also available that produce messages in braille or raised standard print.

A variety of assistive technology devices available do not necessarily help a person to see better but improve the ability of people with severe visual impairments to experience leisure. In addition to services that place books on to audiotapes, *reading scanners* can convert text to verbal output and allow individuals to acquire the information presented in books. *Pagers* that keep people in touch with their families and friends are available that vibrate to notify a person of a message and then present the message auditorily. Written material can be presented in alternative formats.

Videotapes and audiotapes can be used to present information to people that has typically only been presented in text. Videos on television and radio advertisements inform people who may not be able to read flyers and notices placed in the newspaper. In addition, Menacker and Batshaw (1997, p. 235) reported:

> Text can be converted to Braille using a machine called an Optacon that scans typed text and converts it into a tactile stimulus of vibrating pins. Another system, VersaBraille, converts material received by a computer into Braille. Computer printouts can also be converted into speech using a Kurzweil Reading Machine; and TotalTalk and other software programs provide speech capacity to a personal computer. There are also verbal note-taking devices and

talking calculators. In addition, books on tape are generally available from Recording for the Blind and Dyslexic and at bookstores and libraries.

What are considerations for inclusion with technology that enhances skills?

Many people with a significant hearing loss will not choose to participate in activities where conversation is an important element unless they know that there will be others who use the same communication mode with whom they can communicate. Oliva and Simonsen (2000; p. 85) offered the following suggestions to leisure service providers:

> For persons who are deaf and hard of hearing, the concepts of right to leisure, quality of life, and barrier removal involve much more than just removing the barriers between leader and follower, providing a TTY, or employing a person who signs at the community center. Instead of merely concentrating on making the facility accessible so that deaf and hard of hearing participants can recreate alongside their hearing counterparts, the recreation professional might also want to consider expending more energy in the area of social accessibility, that is encouraging, validating, and promoting recreation participation with others who share the same communication method.

People of all levels of cognitive ability have used technological systems with positive results. For example, Dattilo and Camarata (1991) demonstrated that an AAC system enabled a college student and a man with mental retardation to have synthetic speech that enhanced their quality of life. However, simply providing an individual with an AAC system, a mobility aid, or a sophisticated piece of sports equipment does not enable them to have a better quality of life if they have not learned how to use the device.

It is helpful for us to ask about the skills and interests of the participant who uses assistive technology. For example, if a participant enjoys playing video games on the computer, an AAC might be programmed to say, "I want to play computer games." Other words to include in an AAC system might be the names of the leisure services providers, activities the participant enjoys, rooms or spaces in recreation centers such as the pool and baseball field, and personal needs, such as going to the restroom. We can use computers to assess the preferences of program participants, such as the toy preferences of children with severe disabilities. Such information is useful in both the recreation setting and in the home to provide the individual with satisfying choices.

If people use assistive technology that results in them communicating in different ways, it is critical to give them adequate time to engage in meaningful dialogue. We must learn to give people our attention, wait for their contribution, listen to them, and respond accordingly. Often when people use alternative forms of communication there are times when silence occurs. We must resist the temptation to fill that silence with our words; rather, we should remain silent and allow the person adequate time to contribute. Joe, a person with cerebral palsy wrote that "some people have asked me questions and walked away before I point to a word or answer" (Crossley, 1999, p. 9).

Meet J. D., Who Makes His World Move

Hallem (1991) reported on J. D., who has quadriplegia and is unable to move his arms or legs, yet can walk his dachshunds, escape a house fire, answer the phone and set his burglar alarm—all without any assistance. These tasks are completed with the assistance of an electronic box the size of a clock radio.

The high-tech device rests on his bedroom dresser, lighting up in red. This environmental control unit is a sophisticated, centralized system that is connected to his wheelchair and almost every electronic device in his home—from his TV, VCR, and personal computer to the back door that swings open for his dogs. Using either a mouth stick or a sip-and-puff mechanical straw attached to his wheelchair, he can activate these systems and function without someone constantly at his side. That independence is important to J. D.

How can technology help to control the environment?

Environmental control units can increase independence and personal safety. Manufacturers advertise the following capabilities:

- control lights, electric beds, electric doors, appliances, and TVs,
- make and answer phone calls,
- detect intruders,
- activate an alarm to wake you in the morning, and
- awaken an attendant if you fall out of bed.

These services are controlled by the owner's voice in any language from up to 20 feet away. One manufacturer sums the advantages of their system with the words, "If you can move your head . . . you can move your world" (Prentke Romich Company, 1992).

Technology can help people to find their way around public buildings. One such system consists of small transmitters placed throughout public buildings such as shopping malls and museums. Individuals with visual or cognitive impairments obtain a pocket size receiver when they enter the building. As the person moves through the environment, the transmitter provides information (in multiple languages, as needed) on the location of the nearest exit, public phone, elevator, restroom, or office. A typical message might be, "Welcome to the City Hall Second Street entrance—nine steps up to double door entry, Verbal Landmark Directory to your right." The person may replay the message as often as desired and at the desired volume.

What are considerations for inclusion with technology that helps to control the environment?

Technological advances have greatly improved opportunities for individuals with disabilities to enjoy a wide range of recreational and leisure choices. For young participants, toys and games have been adapted to utilize switches and computers. Levin and Enselein (1990) provided clear, illustrated instructions on adapting toys for children as young as 2 or 3 years of age.

Interactive computer programs allow children to touch the computer screen and have immediate results. Popular children's books are available in interactive computer versions, complete with voice narration and sound effects. When the child touches the portion of the screen that shows a bird in the tree, for example, the bird chirps and flies away. Touching the mailbox causes it to open, allowing a frog to jump out one time, an ocean wave to roll out the next. The random display of these many interactive choices—and finding unexpected things in unexpected places—entertains and teaches young children.

Older children enjoy making popcorn, using a blender to make a milkshake, watching videos, and playing video games using electronic adaptations. Adult hobbies can be made more accessible by use of such devices as a battery-powered card shuffler for card enthusiasts who have some use of their hands. Poker, blackjack, bridge, and chess are also available in computer versions for one or more players to enjoy. For those who like to sew, electric scissors and chin-controlled sewing machine power units are a couple of the adaptations available.

Meet Kim and Her Best Friend Sophie

Kim and Sophie are a familiar sight around the university campus. Like other best friends, they share a dorm room, rely on each other, enjoy ice cream, and spend time together outdoors whenever possible. Sophie walks to class with Kim and waits quietly during the lecture. She always seems to know when Kim is feeling sad and does her best to let her know that she is there for her.

Kim is proud to be seen with Sophie, who always attracts admirers with her golden hair and big brown eyes. Kim likes to tease her boyfriend Lee by telling him that he only hangs around her because he has a crush on Sophie. Lee laughs and responds that he is not interested in younger females, especially the four-legged type who gets fleas. Kim's best friend, Sophie is a 5-year-old golden retriever trained as a dog guide for Kim, who is blind.

How can animals be of assistance?

In addition to the companionship that pets provide, animals can help people with disabilities in a variety of other ways. Animals can assist people with:

- visual impairments,
- hearing impairments,
- physical limitations, and
- mental health problems.

Assist People with Visual Impairments

Although dogs have aided humans for thousands of years as watchdogs and farm helpers, they have only recently been trained to guide owners who are blind. *Dog guides* for people with visual impairments have enabled thousands of individuals to move about their communities in confidence and safety. To qualify for a dog, an applicant must be between the ages of 16 and 55, be in good health, have good hearing and at least average intelligence, and possess the temperament, emotional stability, and responsibility to maintain a working relationship with the dog. The applicant must be totally blind or without any useful vision that might interfere with reliance on the dog and must also like dogs.

Dog guides require daily exercise and grooming. Generally, dogs are not suitable for children, who may lack the necessary maturity. The applicant and the dog must train together for 4 weeks at a dog guide school. For these reasons, only 1% of people who are blind actually use a dog.

Assist People with Hearing Impairments

Hearing-ear dogs are trained to assist people who have hearing impairments. Such dogs are often obtained from animal shelters and may be almost any breed. During a 6-month training program, hearing-ear dogs are taught to alert the owner to such sounds as the doorbell ringing, a pot boiling over on the stove, a baby crying, or a smoke detector alarm. The dogs respond to these noises by going to the owners and leading them to the cause of the sound. Hearing-ear dogs can be recognized by an orange collar and leash.

Assist People with Physical Limitations

Assistive dogs (also called *helper dogs* or *service dogs*) are trained to accompany individuals who have disabilities that affect their strength and balance, such as multiple sclerosis or spinal cord injury. Each dog is trained to help with the specific needs of its owner. The dogs may be fitted with backpacks to carry objects or trained to pick up dropped objects such as pencils and keys. They can turn light switches on and off and provide a stable support for the person when transferring from wheelchair to bed or car. Some dogs can answer the phone and bring it to the owner, change the television channel, push elevator buttons, and pull wheelchairs up the curb. Canine Companions for Independence of Santa Rosa, California, breeds dogs and trains them to respond to approximately 100 instructions before they are placed with the new owner (Maddox, 1988).

Lesser-known animal helpers are *simian aides*—capuchin monkeys that are trained to perform activities of daily living for owners with disabilities. The owner must be able to operate a motorized wheelchair and to operate the equipment needed to signal the monkey. Three-year-old female monkeys receive extensive training in the activities of daily living that are difficult for the owner. The 5-pound, 18-inch capuchins can retrieve a snack from the refrigerator, open it, feed it to the owner, wipe the owner's mouth, and put the dirty container in the sink. They can brush the owner's hair, hold up a mirror, and return the brush and mirror to the bathroom. The owner directs the monkey through verbal commands or by pointing with a light beam attached to a mouth stick. Fruit-flavored pellets are dispensed from a device attached to the owner's wheelchair to reward the monkey for tasks completed. Only the imagination and patience of the owner and trainer limit the possibilities for simian help. As an added bonus, the little monkeys are affectionate, playful, and fun to watch.

Assist People with Mental Health Problems

Dogs have been trained as companion animals, otherwise known as *therapy dogs*, for some people with depression and mental illness. The affection that an animal gives the person helps to enhance the self-esteem of the owner. Knowing that the dog depends on the owner for food, water, and care can be therapeutic and can encourage the owner to develop relationships (Maddox, 1988).

What are considerations for inclusion with people who use assistance animals?

The ADA guarantees the use of animal assistants in public. Leisure services providers are responsible to educate all participants about proper etiquette with animal aides. The owners can help everyone understand how their animals have been trained to respond in public. Most animal aides are very protective of their owners, but will enjoy a kind word and pat when they are not working—but only after the owner has given you permission to approach the animal.

Meet Calandra, Who Enjoys being Creative and Playing with her Friends

Calandra enjoys spending time at the recreation center with her friends. Often she makes her way to the computer lounge where she finds several of her friends playing computer games. They talk about various ways to improve their scores and succeed in the games. One particular game requires the operator to move through a series of mazes. Calandra has studied a magazine that explains strategies for this game. As a result of her preparation and practice Calandra is very skilled at this game and her friends seek her advice on ways to solve various problems.

 After some socializing and playing, Calandra begins using the Internet to complete a school project that requires her to report on birds of South

America. She visits several websites that provide her with ample information for her report. While she is on the Web she checks her e-mail and jots off a quick note to her new pen pal in Argentina.

Before she leaves the recreation center computer lounge Calandra tries the new painting program that was recently installed on the computers. She loves to use the computer to create artwork. She enjoys the new program and uses it to try a variety of techniques that resemble her favorite type of art, French Impressionism.

Calandra has worked with members of the recreation staff who have been very helpful in finding ways for her to access the computer. Because Calandra has quadriplegia and uses a motorized wheelchair, she is able to access some programs using a sensitive simple switch and other programs she operates more effectively using a joystick. She states that if it were not for the helpful staff she probably would not come to the recreation center and would go home to do her homework and watch television alone.

How can technology expand experiences?

Many positive experiences associated with leisure involvement have been influenced by technology. Most leisure pursuits contain an element of socialization. Since humans are social creatures, we tend to pursue activities that allow us to interact with other people. Many consider writing to be a form of leisure because it allows us to express ourselves and can bring meaning to our lives. The ability to be creative and engage in artistic endeavors is also considered to be leisure. Virtual reality may simulate various experiences that may not be available at a particular time or place. Finally, technology can help improve people's ability to engage in recreation activities and have fun. This section examines technology's influence on our ability to:

* socialize better,
* write better,
* create better,
* simulate better, and
* recreate better.

Socialize Better

A critical aspect of the inclusion of people with disabilities into community recreation programs is the chance to interact with other participants in a socially meaningful way. Computer-based activities can be used to facilitate positive interactions between participants, such as initiating and terminating turn-taking, attending to an object or person, and following instructions (Lau, 2000). Greenwood (1994) observed that social skills can be modeled and reacted to by computer simulations, and information can be recorded in portable computers and analyzed quickly for decision-making purposes. In another study, Howard, Greyrose, Espinosa, and Beckwith (1996) observed that computer activities facilitated by a practitioner enhanced the social play and positive affect of young children with disabilities.

In addition, Hutinger, Johanson, and Stoneburner (1996) conducted a case study of a child with multiple disabilities and found that the most notable benefits of using computers were associated with social interactions, cooperation, and exploratory play. Similarly, Margalit (1991) found that children with cognitive limitations who received instruction via the computer scored higher on classroom adjustment and social skills than their peers who did not receive such instruction. Lau (2000) suggested that practitioners who incorporate computers into their services could facilitate social interactions of participants by modeling social behaviors, praising positive social interactions, structuring cooperative activities, and establishing a system of peer tutoring.

Write Better

Computers enable people to write more rapidly and legibly than by hand. Individuals who have difficulty manipulating the letters on a keyboard can benefit from software that uses a *scanning system* to help a person write. With one such device installed, the computer displays the alphabet, numbers, and important symbols on the bottom of the screen and slowly moves the cursor across the display. The person hits the switch when the desired letter is highlighted and it is then pasted on the screen. By selecting one letter at a time, the person can type an entire document by pressing one switch. The switch could be placed under a person's hand, foot, chin, elbow, or against the cheek. Blowing air through a sip-and-puff control could also trigger the switch.

Computers are also able to respond to speech. People who cannot access a keyboard because of physical limitations, or people who have attention limitations, can enter their thoughts through speech. This allows participants another input option and can create situations that help the people express their thoughts through the written word.

Electronic notetakers allow people who have severe visual limitations to type in their notes. The notes are then converted to Braille or to speech that will allow individuals with limited sight to access their notes.

Create Better

Computers provide people with a way to experience leisure by offering an outlet for creative expression through the development of artwork. When computers are used, people with a variety of physical and cognitive limitations can participate. People of all ages can enjoy exploring the creative possibilities of a computer (McLeod, 1999).

After reviewing a series of articles describing the use of computers to facilitate artistic expression, Maichiodi (1999) concluded that the computer could help people with disabilities draw, paint, and sculpt, thereby promoting their inclusion. The time, energy, and expense associated with purchasing, setting up, and cleaning art materials can be significantly reduced if computers are incorporated into a person's artistic repertoire.

Simulate Better

Broida and Germann (1999) described a project where virtual reality was used to help people with extensive physical disabilities simulate experiences they may encounter when pursuing leisure opportunities in their community. The authors described virtual reality in the following way:

> Virtual reality refers to an alternative world filled with 3-D computer-generated images that respond to human movements. These simulated images can be enhanced through the use of stereoscopic goggles and fiber optic data gloves. Virtual reality integrates computer graphics, body-tracking devices, visual displays, and other sensory input devices to immerse a participant in a computer-generated environment. (p. 95)

The intent of the project described by Broida and Germann was to provide virtual reality situations so that participants' fears could be alleviated and their access enhanced. They reported that comments by participants indicated the value of the virtual reality project in helping them overcome their apprehension of new places.

Recreate Better

Wheeled sports are enjoyed by people of all ages. Bicycles have been adapted to allow individuals to pedal with the hands instead of the feet, and are available in three-wheel and tandem models. Wheelchair wheels with carbon fiber spokes offer less resistance and facilitate faster acceleration than conventional wheels. Throwing events such as discus, shot put, and javelin are benefiting from an anchor system that utilizes four strong suction pads to hold wheelchairs in place instead of the traditional ropes and rigging systems.

Sailors with disabilities are assisted by specialized systems to adapt racing boats. Those who prefer to spend their time on the water fishing, rather than racing, can do so with a push-button drive system to operate a fishing reel. Chesapeake Region Accessible Boating has developed a weatherproof, salt-water resistant portable lift device to transfer sailors from their wheelchairs on and off watercraft (Brady, 1993). Mono-skis, sit-skis, and bi-skis enable both water and snow enthusiasts who have physical limitations to enjoy skiing.

For those who want to participate in rigorous outdoor activities, all-terrain vehicles can be adapted. Golf, scuba diving, fencing, and archery— the list of activities being transformed by technology continues to grow.

What are considerations for inclusion with technology that expands experiences?

Technology contributes to the leisure experiences of all people. Computers are being used in a variety of ways that allow people to pursue leisure activities. Some agencies have labs containing computers available to the public on a drop-in basis and conduct different instructional classes.

The computer can be used a means to socialize through discussion via e-mail, chat rooms, and instant messages. Socialization can also be encouraged by having participants work jointly on projects completed with the computer. Specific software that allows people to create visual art as well as music can be used to allow participants to be creative and to socialize with one another. Technology can be acquired that allows people to simulate experiences through interaction with virtual reality hardware and software. Leisure services providers must work to use assistive technology to help people participate in recreation activities and enjoy themselves through active participation.

Most people have a limited awareness of assistive technology. A fundamental problem is the misconception that individuals with disabilities cannnot be productive and capable citizens. We must increase our awareness that people with disabilities have widely ranging skills and capabilities. The term *reasonable accommodation* suggests that there is an expanding array of options and resources available to integrate people with disabilities in our society. The role that assistive technology can play in inclusion of people into leisure opportunities needs to be more widely known and understood. Awareness directly impacts the delivery of assistive technology services.

Technological advances do not solve all problems for people with disabilities and are only as helpful as the people who design them for the user. Anyone who has used a computer knows that systems must be programmed, debugged, and updated. Some products just do not perform as advertised or do not work. Even the best advances are often a bit temperamental and will not always work the first time they are used.

Advanced technology can be costly. A device that looks as if it should cost hundreds of dollars usually costs thousands. The story of Max Frazier (Bradley, 2000, p. 10) illustrated this point:

> Max Frazier, 4, grabbed the Dyna Myte 3100 off the coffee table and punched a couple of pictures on the keyboard. "Hi, my name is Max," an electronic voice said, "and this is my talking device." His parents smiled. His parents said that the smile is worth the year-long fight they waged with their insurance company to get their son the speech-communication device.

The Assistive Technology Act of 1998, formerly known as the Technology-Related Assistance for Individuals with Disabilities Act, does not directly provide technological systems to individuals, but it does enable states to set up information and referral centers. In some states, for example, individuals have the opportunity to borrow a system for a 4-week trial period before making a decision to purchase it. Unsatisfactory systems can be returned and another tried until the best possible match is determined.

Technology can greatly enhance a person's abilities and may open new ways to explore his or her world. However, using these new technologies can be frustrating and difficult for some people with disabilities. For example, there are word processing systems that can be activated by merely sipping and puffing on a straw connected to a special switch. Such devices make it possible for people who are immobile and lack speech to communicate in ways that were not previously possible. Yet, sipping and puffing through the 2,000 characters of a short one-page letter is laborious and mentally demanding. For every other similar technological solution, there is a corresponding challenge.

Technology enables many people with disabilities to exercise control over their lives and to become more fully integrated into society. Assistive technology extends the same options commonly available for people without disabilities by offering tools necessary for access. Unfortunately, persistent misconceptions about assistive technology services and devices limit their use as a solution for people with disabilities. As a result, this great equalizer is underutilized despite the growing number of technology-related options currently available.

Technology can provide a means for people with disabilities to experience enjoyment facilitated through the leisure experience. Construction of a supportive environment responsive to people using assistive technology is needed in the area of leisure services delivery. Leisure services providers are encouraged to:

- develop a position statement on assistive technology devices and services,
- initiate forums and discussions of assistive technology issues as they relate to recreation participation,
- develop a public awareness campaign on assistive technology and describe its benefits to leisure involvement,
- conduct surveys on present levels of technology knowledge and availability of resources in homes, agencies, communities, and local businesses,
- establish a peer support network for sharing ideas and resources,
- document existing technology resources as they relate to enhancing recreation participation,
- identify needs of participants and develop a list of priorities for incorporating assistive technology,
- secure appropriate technology devices to meet priority needs,
- compile a "wish list" for additional devices and target potential funding groups, and
- become familiar with the needs of participants and the possibilities technology offers.

Final Thoughts

Assistive technology can make a considerable difference in the leisure participation of many people. Technology originally intended for other uses can support people with disabilities in their pursuit of leisure experiences. For example, personal computers can help people compensate for cognitive impairments that can impede independence, self-determination, and inclusion (Wehmeyer, 1998). Kaminker (1995, p. 47) noted:

Though not designed solely for recreational use, environmental control units, infrared remote devices and voice- or head- or eye-controlled computers all increase leisure options—both indirectly, by offering greater independence and privacy, and directly, by providing access to computer games, TVs, VCRs and CD players.

The following statement by Matt Boyer (Boyer, 2000) identifies the extent to which a person with a disability can use assistive technology and illustrates the impact that assistive technology can have on an individual's life:

> My current arsenal of tricks includes a Braille-n-Speak Classic (which is an electronic talking Braille note taker with a built-in calculator, clock, calendar, stopwatch, and countdown time); a MultiVoice (a device that takes the output of what I write on the Braille-n-Speak and speaks it in a more intelligible voice); an IBM-compatible computer with a variety of speech output programs, screen readers, and a Braille translator; and a Hewlett Packard 5200 scanner that reads print. I use the Braille-n-Speak to keep a diary, do my math more easily, keep an appointment calendar, keep track of names and e-mail addresses, write some of my programs on, and keep a log of what we're doing on trips. I use the MultiVoice to communicate with people who don't understand my speech or the Braille-n-Speak's speech.

Discussion Questions

1. What is meant by assistive technology?
2. What are some examples of assistive technology devices?
3. What are some ways that assistive technology can improve people's abilities to write, work, hear, communicate, speak, see, move, and participate in recreation activities?
4. What do the initials "AAC" represent?
5. What are two mobility aids for individuals who are visually impaired or blind?
6. What are four recreation activities available to people with disabilities through the use of assistive technology?
7. How could environmental control devices influence leisure participation for some people with disabilities?
8. How can animals be used to assist people with disabilities in participation in recreation activities?
9. What are some advantages and disadvantages for people with disabilities using assistive technology?
10. What can be done to encourage the use of technology that increases leisure participation for people with disabilities?

Photo by Lynda Greer

Paul Guest

Paul Guest lives in Fort Oglethorpe, Georgia, with his parents and younger brothers Chan, and Bo and Clay (pictured here). He is currently a sophomore in high school. When he was 11 he sustained a spinal cord injury in a bike accident.

Paul's Story

Several years ago, when I was hurt, the other kids didn't make a big deal of it when I went back to school. They still don't. I have some really great friends and we have great times together. But there are a number of things that I like about being in high school . . . this year I'm a sophomore. So . . . I'm on the editorial staff of our yearbook, THE WARRIOR. I'm one of the people responsible for the design of the yearbook; I also design motifs, do a little editing . . . whatever is needed.

The yearbook work is really good, but I especially like being on the Toss-Up Team . . . that's our academic competition team. We meet twice a week to practice, but mostly you just have to read a lot and keep up with current events to prepare for matches with other teams. We have to try out every year for Toss-Up. I hope I can make it every year until I graduate, and then I'd like to continue in college on a college bowl team. I guess I have to say that the competition is what I really love about it.

Another thing I really like is basketball . . . professional basketball. My teams are the Detroit Pistons and the Atlanta Hawks. I guess home state loyalty gives the Hawks an edge on the Pistons for me, but they're both great teams . . . very different teams.

When it comes to academics, the areas that interest me most are biological science and computer science. Working with computers seems to come easily to me most of the time; when it doesn't, I enjoy the challenge. Computer science is definitely a career choice I consider for the future. BUT my first love is writing . . . science fiction, fantasy. Right now I keep my stories to myself, but someday I want to be a published writer. I wouldn't mind a career like Stephen King's! Of course, I could do something in the field of computer science AND be a writer. Well, I've got a little while to think about it!

Attitude Survey about People with Disabilities

Directions: Please respond with only one answer that best describes your reaction to each statement.

SA = Strongly Agree   A = Agree   MA = Mildly Agree
MD = Mildly Disagree   D = Disagree SD = Strongly Disagree

1. People with disabilities have similar needs and desires as other people.
2. People with disabilities are entitled to the same rights as other people.
3. People with disabilities can experience pleasure as often as other people.
4. It is unlikely that a person with disabilities will lead a productive life.
5. People with disabilities do not possess the potential to acquire the skills needed to participate in meaningful leisure experiences.
6. Most people with disabilities should be admitted to a large residential institution.
7. You should not expect as much from a person with a disability as you do a person without a disability.
8. All people with disabilities require assistance to complete their daily activities.
9. Most people with disabilities prefer associating predominately with other people with disabilities.
10. People with disabilities are more aggressive than other people.
11. A person can be disabled physically, mentally, emotionally, and/or socially.
12. People with disabilities are entitled to experience meaningful leisure.
13. People with disabilities are more similar to other people than they are dissimilar from other people.
14. It is difficult to make generalizations about people with disabilities because every person is unique.

Debriefing: Statements that reaffirm similarities between people with and without disabilities (statements 1-3, and 13) are often identified as representative of a more positive attitude than those that emphasize differences (statement 7). In addition, statements we make that avoid making generalizations about any group of individuals and recognize differences within a group (such as statements 11 and 14) often reflect more positive attitudes than statements that tend to miss individual differences (statements 4, 5, and 8-10). Finally, statements that reflect support for the inclusion of people with disabilities into the mainstream of community life (statement 12) are often more positive than those focusing on segregation (statement 6).

- How did you feel about responding to these questions?
- How did you differ with the responses indicated in the debriefing?
- What are some actions you could take to improve your attitudes toward people with disabilities?

Attitude Survey about Recreation for People with Disabilities

Directions: Please respond with only one answer that best describes your reaction to each statement.

SA = Strongly Agree   A = Agree   MA = Mildly Agree
MD = Mildly Disagree   D = Disagree   SD = Strongly Disagree

1. People with disabilities should be prevented from attending an activity if you feel the disability will hinder the person's performance in the activity.
2. You should change the location of a recreation activity to accommodate people with disabilities, even if the new location is inferior to the original one.
3. You should promote interaction between people with and without disabilities during recreation participation.
4. Adaptation of activities should occur if the changes will make participation opportunities more equal.
5. Someone should be available to assist you in maximizing learning opportunities for people with disabilities.
6. You should be willing to spend extra time assisting a participant with a disability in a recreation program.
7. Providing aids and services is likely to impinge on your leadership freedom.
8. You should alter your leadership style to enhance communications with participants with disabilities.
9. You should integrate people with disabilities into the recreation programs you offer.
10. Each recreation agency should conduct meetings to increase service delivery to people with disabilities.
11. An interpreter for a person with a hearing impairment is a distraction in a recreation program.
12. You should design group activities in which people with disabilities can participate with other people.
13. People with disabilities can participate in team and individual sports with people without disabilities.

14. People with disabilities are able to make decisions about their leisure participation.
15. People with disabilities have more free time than people without disabilities.
16. The main purpose of recreation programs for people with disabilities is therapy.
17. Most people with disabilities prefer individual activities to group activities.
18. You should provide similar activity opportunities to people with and without disabilities.
19. Making arrangements for people with disabilities is likely to lower program objectives.
20. Background information concerning participants' disabilities would be useful.
21. You should help people with disabilities receive assistance for maximum recreation participation.
22. It may be better to exclude people with disabilities from participation if it is difficult to evaluate them.
23. You should consult with the person with disabilities concerning conditions for optimal participation.
24. People with disabilities are more likely to be injured in activities than people without disabilities.
25. Therapeutic recreation specialists are the only personnel who should provide recreation activities for people with disabilities.
26. Most people with disabilities would rather participate with other people with disabilities.
27. People with disabilities are unable to participate with other people in competitive recreation activities.
28. Segregated recreation programs should be provided for people with disabilities.
29. People with disabilities are more easily frustrated than other people.
30. People with disabilities should be allowed to participate in all public recreation programs.
31. All recreational facilities should be made accessible to people with disabilities.
32. People with disabilities need more supervision in activities than other people.
33. People with disabilities should not become highly excited in recreation activities.
34. Attendance in recreation programs will decline if people with disabilities attend the programs.

35. It is harmful to expose people with disabilities to ridicule by encouraging them to participate in community recreation programs.
36. Parents do not want their children without disabilities playing with children with disabilities.
37. People with disabilities are able to participate in selected high-risk activities.

Debriefing: Many people agree that treating people with disabilities in the same way you treat all participants is the best practice. Making accommodations without undue burden is stipulated in the Americans with Disabilities Act. Remember to think of each participant as an individual and take actions to include people in community recreation activities. Consider the following questions:

- How did you feel about responding to these questions?
- How did your responses differ from other people's responses?
- What are some actions you could take to improve your attitudes toward people with disabilities participating in recreation programs?

Glossary

access
freedom and ability to enter, approach, communicate with, or pass to and from a facility, agency, or individual

accessibility
degree to which a person with limitations can get to, enter and use a building or area surrounding a building

acuity
amount of detail an individual sees compared to what a person with normal vision sees

adaptive behavior
ability to meet standards of personal independence and social responsibility expected of their age and cultural group; includes maturation, learning, and social adjustment

advocate
to recommend, to be in favor of, to plead for a cause; a person who pleads the cause of another or gives support to a particular policy or proposal

affective predispositions
feelings or emotions that are fairly consistent and that set the stage for a pattern of behaviors

Americans with Disabilities Act (ADA)
law passed by Congress in 1990 that extends the federal mandate for access to public accommodations and programs to the private sector

amnesia
common type of memory loss whereby the person can only remember bits and pieces of events that occurred in the past

amputation
removal of all or a portion of a limb as the result of a trauma or infection

antecedent
condition that sets the stage for beliefs to develop

anxiety
intense fear or panic resulting from a situation, object, or person

aphasia
loss of the ability to speak, write, or comprehend spoken or written language due to injury or disease of the brain centers

architectural barrier
any feature of the physical environment constructed by humans that impedes or restricts the mobility of people to the full use of a facility

Architectural Barriers Act
law passed by Congress in 1968 that states all facilities receiving direct or indirect federal funds must provide access to all people

arthritis
group of conditions that involve an inflammation of joints, tissues, or bones

artificial pacemaker
small device permanently implanted under the skin of the chest wall that regulates the heart rate by sending electrical impulses that force the heart to contract rhythmically

assistive device
technological tool that restores or extends human functions

assistive dog
dog trained to accompany a person who has a disability that affects their strength and balance, such as multiple sclerosis or spinal cord injury

assistive listening device and system (ALDS)
equipment that includes portable and permanent telephone amplifiers, direct audio input devices, personal infrared systems, alarm systems, and telecaptioning devices designed to help people with disabilities

assistive technology
field concerned with research, development, and service on assistive devices

ataxia
subtle form of cerebral palsy that results in balance problems

athetosis
form of cerebral palsy in which individuals have worm-like movements
because of difficulty controlling affected muscles

attitude
learned predisposition to respond in a consistently favorable or unfavorable
manner with respect to a given object

attitudinal barrier
way of thinking about or perceiving a disability in a restrictive, condescending, or negative manner

auditory output
product of the conversion of written messages to synthetic (digitized)
speech

augmentative and alternative communication (AAC) system
symbols, strategies, and techniques used by individuals whose disabilities
prevent typical communication

autism
complex developmental disability of unknown etiology that typically
effects communication, social developmental, and behavior

autonomy
freedom and independence to manage one's life

barrier
any obstacle or obstruction, natural or manmade, that impedes progress but
is not necessarily impassable

behavioral predisposition
consistent desire to act in a particular way

behavior
any observable and measurable act, response, or movement by an individual

belief
what a person perceives to be true; composed of an individual's perception
of information that has been available in the form of antecedent conditions

bilateral hearing loss
hearing loss in both ears

binaural aid
hearing aid for both ears

blindness
condition in which a person has no usable sight

boredom
mental state that may result from the perception that activities are worthless, meaningless, frustrating, or monotonous

cataracts
opacity of the lens found at the two extremes of the lifespan: infancy and advanced age; usually caused by a breakdown of the metabolic process that keeps the lens transparent

central hearing loss
reduced ability to hear due to damage of the brain or pathways to the brain; sound levels are not affected, but the understanding of language becomes difficult; results from excess exposure to loud noise, head injuries, high fever, or tumors

cerebral embolism
stroke due to a blood clot traveling to the brain from another part of the body, often from the heart

cerebral hemorrhage
blood vessel bursting in the brain, frequently resulting in coma and death; most serious form of stroke

cerebral palsy
developmental disability caused by damage to the motor portions of the brain; results in an inability to control muscular and postural movements

cerebral thrombosis
stroke due to a blood clot (thrombus) that has formed in an artery that supplies blood to the brain

cerebrovascular accident
form of traumatic brain injury that originates inside the brain when a portion of the brain is deprived of blood; commonly called a stroke

childhood muscular dystrophy
most common type of muscular dystrophy that occurs prior to age 6 and
affects the pelvic musculature

choice
act of selecting one option, ideally a preferred one, from among others
simultaneously available

clinical depression
extended period where individuals experience diminished interest and
pleasure in life, fatigue, energy loss, and a sense of worthlessness or guilt

closed head injury
traumatic brain injury often caused by the brain being whipped back and
fourth in a quick motion

cochlear implant
electrode device that is surgically implanted in the mastoid bone behind the
ear to stimulate the hearing nerve

cognitive predisposition
consistent way that people think or develop ideas

conductive loss
type of hearing loss in which sound waves are blocked and cannot travel
through the auditory canal or middle ear to reach the inner ear

congenital anomaly
condition present at birth

congenital disability
condition present at birth that results in reduced ability

deafness
hearing loss that prevents understanding of conversational speech, even
with a hearing aid

decibel (db)
unit of measurement used to assess the volume of sound

detached retina
condition in which the retina detaches and rips a hole in the outer wall of
the eye, creating a blind spot as the blood supply decreases

developmental disability
severe, chronic mental and/or physical impairment manifested before age 22 that will likely continue indefinitely and results in substantial functional limitations

deviancy
straying from the majority of society, an established standard, or a highly regarded principle

diabetic retinopathy
vascular disease of the retina due to diabetes; leading cause of blindness in United States

direct competition
competition that involves pitting oneself against another

disability
condition resulting from a physical or mental impairment that substantially limits one or more major life activities; having a record of such impairment or being regarded as having such an impairment

discrimination
judgments made about people based on their affiliation with a group rather than on individual characteristics

dog guide
dog trained to guide a person with a visual impairment

ear mold
vital component of any hearing aid; made from a solid plastic or a more pliable substance

empower
to give power or authority to a person

enjoyment
experience derived from investing one's attention in intrinsically motivating action patterns; often assumed to be synonymous with fun; requires psychological involvement such as concentration, effort, and a sense of control and competence

epilepsy
seizure disorder in which a temporary chemical imbalance of the brain causes a disturbance of brain functioning

exacerbation
new outbreak of lesions with an increase in the severity of symptoms in multiple sclerosis

exclusion
barring of another person from oneself, resulting in the disregard of that person as a human presence in a face-to-face situation

expressive aphasia
condition in which a person can understand what is said or written but cannot respond

facio-scapulohumeral muscular dystrophy
form of muscular dystrophy that causes facial paralysis that spreads to the shoulders and upper arms

freedom
state of having personal independence and full rights of citizenship, including access to and unrestricted use of public and private facilities

free time
unobligated time not occupied by work or activities of daily living

glaucoma
blinding disease caused by increased intraocular tension (pressure) in the eye; may be acute or progressive

grand mal seizure
generalized epileptic seizure that consists of a convulsion accompanied by complete loss of consciousness

handicap
disadvantage caused by an interaction between environmental conditions and an individual

hard-of-hearing
mild to moderate hearing loss resulting in decreased perception of conversational speech but sufficient hearing to permit understanding under optimal circumstances; preferred term of the deaf community

head injury
traumatic insult to the brain that may cause physical, intellectual, emotional, or social changes

hearing aid
assistive device that improves hearing in many instances but does not correct hearing or necessarily restore it to normal levels

hearing ear dogs
dogs trained to assist people who have hearing impairments

hearing impairment
range of conditions that includes all losses of hearing regardless of type or degree; term preferred by the general public

hemianopsia
defective vision or blindness in half of the visual field

hemiplegia
paralysis of one side of the body

hertz (Hz)
unit of measurement of the frequency of sound waves; describes pitch

impairment
identifiable organic or functional condition that may be permanent (e.g., amputation) or temporary (e.g., sprain)

indirect competition
competition against one's own internal standards

integration
making activities, community resources, and facilities available to all people, including those with disabilities

intention
amount of effort a person plans to exert to perform a behavior

internalized oppression
tendency to accept negative stereotyping about oneself

intrinsic motivation
motivation (to complete an activity) based on one's own volition and free from expected results or external rewards

jacksonian seizure
partial epileptic seizure in which convulsions begin in one part of a limb (e.g., foot or hand) and quickly spread through that entire side of the body

legal blindness
condition that occurs when a person has visual acuity of 20/200 or less in the better eye (with the best possible correction) and/or a visual field of 20 or less at the widest point

leisure
experience that transcends time, environments, and situations; integrates elements of activity, time, and the perception of freedom to choose to participate in meaningful, enjoyable, and satisfying experiences

limb girdle muscular dystrophy
form of muscular dystrophy resulting in paralysis of the shoulder and pelvic musculature

low vision
severe visual impairment that results in a visual acuity range between 20/70 and 20/200 or a visual field of 30 degrees or less

macular degeneration
malfunction of the pigment epithelium that removes waste from the inner fluid of the eye

mania
extreme elevated mood state

manic episode
mood disorder characterized by extreme elevated, expansive, or irritable mood states

mental retardation
developmental disability manifested before age 18 characterized by significantly subaverage intellectual functioning resulting in or associated with concurrent impairments in at least two adaptive skill areas

mild hearing loss
loss of the ability to hear some sounds

mixed hearing loss
reduced ability to hear as a result of both conductive and sensorineural losses

mixed cerebral palsy
condition where an individual has more than one type of cerebral palsy

moderate hearing loss
reduction in the ability to hear sounds that limits one's ability to understand the surrounding environment as well as some speech sounds

monaural hearing aid
hearing aid for only one ear

monoplegia
paralysis of only one limb

multiple sclerosis
disease of the central nervous system in which lesions spontaneously appear at the nerve endings of the central nervous system and the protective nerve coverings disappear, impairing nervous impulses to the brain

muscular dystrophy
group of chronic, hereditary diseases characterized by the progressive degeneration and weakness of voluntary muscles

networking
establishing and maintaining connections with professionals and paraprofessionals from various disciplines and organizations

neuroimplantation
procedure that inserts implant electrodes on the spinal cord, in limbs, or directly in the brain

neurorehabilitation
experimental system of stimulating muscles to contract by sending electrical impulses to them through surface electrodes

obsessive-compulsive disorder
mental impairment resulting from the inability to think clearly because of
recurring thoughts and/or repetitive behaviors

open head injury
visible type of traumatic brain injury that results from an accident, gunshot
wound, fall, or other trauma, such as brain surgery to remove a clot or tumor

orthopedic impairment
limitation involving the locomotor components of the body, including the
bones, joints, and muscles

osteoarthritis
degenerative form of arthritis that creates stiffness, swelling, and pain in
he joints

overjustification effect
condition that occurs when intrinsic motivation is undermined by extrinsic
rewards

paraplegia
paralysis and/or loss of sensation of the lower body resulting from a variety
of conditions including injury to the spine and polio

partially sighted
severe visual impairment that results in a visual acuity range between 20/70
and 20.200 or 30 degrees or less visual field

partial participation
adaptations and assistance provided so that one may participate in the
leisure activity of choice without regard to degree of assistance required

peer tutoring
linking individuals without disabilities with individuals of a similar age
with disabilities to promote positive interactions and attitudes

perceived freedom
self-determined behavior or having the feeling of being the origin of the
activity

petit mal seizure
generalized epileptic seizure resulting in brief periods of fixation (absences) in which the individual appears to be staring into space and does not respond to external stimuli

phobia
unrealistic fear which dominates a person's thinking

postlingual hearing impairment
reduction in the ability to hear acquired after language development

preference
desire for an option following a comparison of that option against a continuum of other options

prejudice
judgment in disregard of a person's rights that results in that individual being injured or damaged in some way

prelingual hearing impairment
hearing limitation acquired before language acquisition; typically congenital or occurring in infancy

profound hearing loss
inability to hear almost all sounds

prosthesis
artificial body part

quadriplegia
paralysis and loss of sensation of the body below the neck resulting from a variety of conditions, including spinal cord injury, stroke, and multiple sclerosis

reasonable accommodation
action taken based on the premise that there is an expanding array of options and resources available to integrate people with disabilities in our society

receptive aphasia
inability to understand messages received as either spoken or written language

recreation
activity developed and accepted by a society designed for the primary
reasons of fun, enjoyment and satisfaction

Rehabilitation Act
law passed by Congress in 1973 that focused on the rights of all people to
have equal access to jobs, education, housing, transportation, and all
programs which directly or indirectly received federal funds

remission
healing of lesions and the relief of some symptoms in various medical
conditions, including multiple sclerosis

retinitis pigmentosa
disease in which the rods and cones (receptor cells) fail to rejuvenate,
resulting in night blindness, tunnel vision, and loss of central vision

retinopathy of prematurity (ROP)
blindness that occurs when premature infants are exposed to 100% oxygen
for prolonged periods of time

rheumatoid arthritis
progressive, profound form of arthritis resulting in severe inflammation
that primarily attacks the joints; can also affect other body tissues and
organs; characterized by unpredictable changes in pain and stiffness

rigidity
form of cerebral palsy causing individuals to be physically rigid and appear
stiff; neck, back, or limbs may be hyperextended

rubella
German measles; when passed from mother to child during the first trimester of pregnancy can cause a variety of disabling conditions, such as visual,
hearing, and cognitive impairments

schizophrenia
psychotic mental disorder characterized by departures from reality

segregation
separation or isolation of a group or individual in a restricted area by
discriminatory means; results in the group or individual receiving treatment
different from other people

self-advocacy
individuals and groups who have traditionally been powerless and largely voiceless speaking up on their own behalf to try to change their social status and situation

self-determination
feeling of being the origin of the activity; sometimes regarded as the basis of intrinsic motivation

self-fulfilling prophecy
expectations for another person's behavior that influence that person to such a degree that he or she exhibits the behaviors that were expected

sensorineural hearing loss
result of damage to the hair cells, nerve fibers, or both; commonly termed nerve deafness

severe hearing loss
loss of the ability to hear many sounds, including most speech

sighted guide
individual who guides a person with a visual impairment through subtle arm movements and verbal communications

simian aide
capuchin monkey trained to perform activities of daily living for owners who typically have quadriplegia

similarity
perception of a general likeness or having common characteristics

sip and puff
assistive device that allows individuals with quadriplegia to control their wheelchair and other electronic devices through a straw that signals the device to operate

spasticity
increased muscle stiffness (hypertonia) and immediate contraction when stretching the affected muscles

spina bifida
congenital disability of the spinal column that occurs early in prenatal development and results in incomplete formation of the vertebrae

spina bifida meningocele
moderate form of spina bifida in which the meninges, the protective covering around the spinal cord, protrudes through the vertebrae

spina bifida mylomeningocele
serious form of spina bifida in which a portion of the spinal cord itself protrudes through the back, sometimes exposing tissue and nerves

spina bifida occulta
mild variety of spina bifida in which no neural damage occurs

spinal cord injury
damage to the spinal cord resulting in the loss of function below the level of injury because of impaired transmission of neural impulses; severity is a result of the extent and location of the injury to the spinal column

spread phenomenon
association of additional imperfections to a person on the basis of an actual disabling condition

stereotype
standardized mental picture held in common by members of a group that represents an oversimplified opinion, attitude, or judgment

stigma
undesired differentness that separates a person from the rest of society

synthetic (digitized) speech
auditory output by an augmentative and alternative communication device that converts written messages to sound

therapy dog
dog trained as a companion for people experiencing mental health problems

thrombus
blood clot which forms in and obstructs a blood vessel

trachoma
infectious disease caused when a microorganism enters the eye producing infection and scarring the cornea or eyelid; major cause of blindness in the world but rare in the United States

transient ischemic attack (TIA)
brief episode of circulatory deficiency to the cerebrum

traumatic brain injury
physical insult to the brain resulting in changes to cognitive, physical, emotional, or social functioning

tremors
form of cerebral palsy where individuals exhibit frequent or constant involuntary shaking of body parts, especially the hands and arms

tunnel vision
loss of peripheral vision

visual field
area a person can see measured, in degrees; includes the entire area that can be seen at one time with the fixed eye; normal visual field is 180 degrees

visual impairment
condition in which a person experiences a loss of vision that cannot be corrected, but in which they retain some usable vision

References

Abery, B. (1994). A conceptual framework for enhancing self-determination. In M. Hayden and B. Abery (Eds.), *Challenges for a service system in transition: Ensuring quality community experience for persons with developmental disabilities.* Baltimore, MD: Paul H. Brookes.

Abu-Tahir, S. (1995). What is inclusion? Inclusion news. *Centre for Integrated Education and Community*, 1.

Adamson, L. B. (1996). *Communication development during infancy.* Boulder, CO: Westview.

Alderson, G. (1985). *Tips for tabs: Temporarily able bodied.* Altoona, PA: GHA Publications.

Algozzine, B., Mercer, C. D., and Countermine, T. (1977). The effects of labels and behavior on teacher expectations. *Exceptional Children*, 131–132.

Allport, G. W. (1954). *The nature of prejudice.* Reading, MA: Addison-Wesley.

Amado, A. N. (2000). Empowering agencies and staff in community inclusion. *AAMR News & Notes, 13*(5), 5–7.

American Association on Mental Retardation. (1992). *Mental retardation: Definition, classification, and systems of supports* (9th ed.). Washington, DC: Author.

Americans with Disabilities Act of 1990, PL 101-336, 104 Stat. 328 (1991).

Amir, Y. (1969). Contact hypothesis in ethnic relations. *Psychological Bulletin, 71*, 319–342.

Anderson, A. (1981). Exclusion: A study of depersonalization in health care. *Journal of Humanistic Psychology, 21*(3), 67–68.

Anderson, J. (1988, January). Success in a world of silence. *Parade Magazine, 31.*

Anderson, L. and Heyne, L. (2000). A statewide needs assessment using focus groups: Perceived challenges and goals in providing inclusive recreation service in rural communities. *Journal of Park and Recreation Administration, 18*(4), 17–37.

Anderson, S. C. and Allen, L. R. (1985). Effects of a leisure education program on activity involvement and social interaction of mentally retarded persons. *Adapted Physical Activity Quarterly, 2*(2), 107–116.

Antia, S. D. and Kreimeyer, K. (1992). Project Interest: Interventions for social integration of young hearing-impaired children. *OSERS: News in Print, 4*(4), 14–20.

Ahrweiler, M. (2000, May/June). Rooms to go: Making the most out of locker rooms and restrooms. *Recreation Management*, 12–15.

Ashton-Shaeffer, C. and Kleiber, D. A. (1990). The relationship between recreation participation and functional skill development in young people with mental retardation. *Annual in Therapeutic Recreation, 1*, 75–81.

Assistive Technology Act of 1998, PL 105-394, 112 Stat. 3662 (1999).

Austin, D. R., Powell, L. G., and Martin, D. W. (1981). Modifying attitudes toward handicapped individuals in a classroom setting. *The Journal for Special Educators, 17*(2), 135–141.

Baer, D. (1981). A hung jury and a Scottish verdict not proven. *Analysis and Intervention in Developmental Disabilities, 1*, 91–97.

Baker, E. T., Wang, M C., and Walberg, H. J. (1995). The effects of inclusion on learning. *Educational Leadership, 52*(4), 33–35.

Baker, M. J., Koegel, R. L., and Koegel, L. K. (1998). Increasing the social behavior of young children with autism using their obsessive behaviors. *Journal of the Association for Persons with Severe Handicaps, 23*(4), 300–308.

Bambara, L. M. and Ager, C. (1992). Using self-scheduling to promote self-directed leisure activity in home and community settings. *Journal of the Association for Persons with Severe Handicaps, 17*(2), 67–76.

Bambara, L. M., Cole, C. L., and Koger, F. (1998). Translating self-determination concepts into support for adults with severe disabilities. *JASH, 23*(1), 27–37.

Baroff, G. S. (1986). *Mental retardation: Nature, cause, and management.* (2nd ed.). Washington, DC: Hemisphere.

Barrera, I. and Kramer, L. (1997). From monologues to skilled dialogues: Teaching the process of crafting culturally competent early childhood environments. In P. J. Winton, J. A. McCullum, and C. Catlet (Eds.). *Reforming personnel preparation in early intervention* (pp. 217–251). Baltimore, MD: Paul H. Brookes.

Barry, V. (1997). *The dog ate my homework. Personal responsibility: How we avoid it and what to do about it.* Kansas City, MO: Andrews and McMeel.

Baum, C. M. (1998). Achieving effectiveness with a client-centered approach. In D.B. Gray, L.A. Quatrano, and M. L. Lieberman (Eds.), *Designing and using assistive technology: The human perspective* (pp. 137–147). Baltimore, MD: Paul H. Brookes.

Baumgart, D., Brown, L., Pumpian, I., Nisbet, J., Ford, A., Sweet, M., Messina, R., and Schroeder, J. (1982). The principle of partial participation and individualized adaptations in educational programs for severely handicapped students. *Journal of the Association for the Developmentally Handicapped, 7,* 17–27.

Baylor, J. (1996). Accommodation or inclusion. *New Mobility, 7*(28), 14.

Beck, A. R. and Dennis, M. (1996). Attitudes of children toward a similar-aged child who uses augmentative communication. *Augmentative and Alternative Communication, 12,* 78–87.

Beckwith, J. and Matthews, J. M. (1995). Measurement of attitudes of trainee professionals to people with disabilities. *Journal of Intellectual Disability Research, 39*(4), 255–262.

Bedini, L. A. (1992). Encouraging change in attitudes toward people with disabilities through undergraduate leisure studies and recreation courses. *Schole, 7,* 44–54.

Bedini, L. A. (2000). "Just sit down so we can talk": Perceived stigma and community recreation pursuits of people with disabilities. *Therapeutic Recreation Journal, 34,* 55–68.

Bedini, L. A., Bullock, C. C., and Driscoll, L. B. (1993). The effects of leisure education to the successful transition of students with mental retardation from school to adult life. *Therapeutic Recreation Journal, 26*(2), 70–82.

Beland, R. M. (1993). Outdoor recreation for everyone. *Parks and Recreation Magazine, 28*(8), 62–63.

Belgrave, F. Z. and Mills, J. (1981). Effect upon desire for social interaction with a physically disabled person of mentioning the disability in different contexts. *Journal of Applied Social Psychology, 11,* 44–57.

Berger, A. (1994). Inclusion: Not an ideology, but a way of life. *TASH Newsletter, 20*(3), 4–5.

Berger, B. (1992). Dancing with time. *American Way,* February 15th, 40, 44, 89.

Bieler, R. B. (2000). Inclusion and universal cooperation. *TASH Newsletter, 26*(2/3), 18–20.

Biklen, D. (1989). Making difference ordinary. In S. Stainback, W. Stainback, and M. Forest (Eds.), *Educating all students in the mainstream of regular education* (pp. 235–248). Baltimore, MD: Paul H. Brookes.

"Black holes figured in time." (1988, June). *Insight.*

Blatt, B. (1982). *The conquest of mental retardation.* Austin, TX: Pro-ed.

Bleecker, T. (2000). The new paradigm of disability: Implications for research and policy. *Consumer Choice News, 4,* 1–3.

Block, M. and Malloy, M. (1998). Attitudes on inclusion of a player with disabilities in a regular softball league. *Mental Retardation 36*(2), 137–144.

Bloom, M. (1997). Tuesdays with Morrie: An old man, a young man, and life's greatest lesson. New York, NY: Doubleday.

Blue-Banning, M. J., Turnbull, A. P., and Pereira, L. (2000). Group action planning as a support strategy for Hispanic families: Parent and professional perspectives. *Mental Retardation, 38*(3), 262–275.

Bogdan, R. and Taylor, S. J. (1992). The social construction of humanness. In P. M. Ferguson, D. L. Ferguson, and S. J. Taylor (Eds.), *Interpreting disability* (pp. 169–171). New York, NY: Teachers College Press.

Bogdan, W. K. (2000). Celebrating our diversity in the new millennium. *Teaching Exceptional Children, 32*(3), 4–5.

Boling, R. (1995, September/October). Move it or lose it. *Modern Maturity,* 22.

Boyer, M. (2000). Freedom. *TASH Newsletter, 26*(10), 11–12.

Braddock, D., Hemp, R., and Fujiura, G. (1987). National study of public spending for mental retardation and developmental disabilities. *American Journal on Mental Deficiency, 92,* 121–133.

Bradley, D. (2000, October 15). Parents, insurers battle over kids' special needs. *Atlanta Journal Constitution,* F10.

Brady, J. (1995, Summer). Speech by James Brady highlights Shepherd Center day. *Spinal Column, 54,* 4–5.

Brady, M. (1993, July 23). Governor William Donald Schaefer announces recreation grants for Marylanders with disabilities. *Press Release.* Annapolis, MD: Governor's Press Office.

Brawn, G. (1995). (1995, March/April). New reality. *New Mobility, 13.*

Bregha. F. J. (1985). Leisure and freedom re-examined. In T. A. Goodale and P. A. Witt (Eds.), *Recreation and leisure: Issues in an era of change* (2nd ed., pp. 35–43). State College, PA: Venture Publishing, Inc.

Brehm, J. (1977). *A theory of psychological reactance.* New York, NY: Academic Press.

Bricker, D. (1995). The challenge of inclusion. *Journal of Early Intervention, 19*(3), 179–194.

Brickman, P., Coates, D., and Janoff-Bulman, R. (1978). Lottery winners and accident victims: Is happiness relative? *Journal of Personality and Social Psychology, 36*(8), 917–927.

Broach, E., Dattilo, J., and Deavours, M. (2000). Assistive technology. In J. Dattilo (Ed.), *Facilitation techniques in therapeutic recreation* (pp. 99–132). State College, PA: Venture Publishing, Inc.

Broida, L. P. and Germann, C. (1999). Enhancing accessibility through virtual environments. *Parks and Recreation, 34*(5), 94–97.

Brown, D. S. (1992). Empowerment through peer counseling. *OSERS: News in Print, 5*(2), 27–29.

Brown, F., Gothelf, C. R., Guess, D., and Lehr, D. H. (1998). Self-determination for individuals with the most severe disabilities: Moving beyond Chimera. *JASH, 23*(10), 17–26.

Brown, L., Long, E., Udvari-Solner, A., Davis, L., Van Deventer, P., Ahlgren, C., Johnson, F., Gruenewald, L., and Jorgensen, J. (1989). The home school: Why students with severe intellectual disabilities must attend the schools of their brothers, sisters, friends, and neighbors. *Journal of the Association for Persons with Severe Handicaps, 14*(1), 1–7.

Brown v. Board of Education, 347 US 483 (1954).

Brown, W. H., Fox, J. J., and Brady, M. P. (1987). Effects of spatial density on three- and four-year-old children's socially directed behavior during freeplay: An investigation of setting factor. *Education and Treatment of Children, 10,* 247–258.

Bruno, R. L. (1997). Who pitches the goods? *New Mobility, 40*(3), 58–59. the disabled person in Nicaragua. In B. Ingstad and Whyte, S. R. (Eds.), *Disability and culture* (pp. 196–209). Berkeley, CA: University of California Press.

Bruun, F. J. (1995). Hero, beggar, or sports star: Negotiating the identity of the disabled person in Nicaragua. In B. Ingstad and S. R. Whyte (Eds.), *Disability and culture* (pp. 196–209). Berkeley, CA: University of California Press.

Bryen, D. N., Slesaransky, G., and Baker, D. B. (1995). Augmentative communication and empowerment supports: A look at outcomes. *AAC Augmentative and Alternative Communication, 11*, 79–88.

Burstein, E. (1999, January/February). When they're standing and you are not: Putting them at ease is the first move. *On the Level: The Newsletter of the League of Human Dignity*, p. 9.

Byrd, K., Crews, B., and Ebener, D. (1991). A study of appropriate use of language when making reference to persons with disabilities. *Journal of Applied Rehabilitation Counseling, 22*(2), 40–41.

Caldwell, L. L., Darling, N., Payne, L. L., and Dowdy, B. (1999). "Why are you bored?": An explanation of psychological and social control causes of boredom among adolescents. *Journal of Leisure Research, 31*(2), 103–121.

Caldwell, L. L. and Smith, E. A. (1998). Health behavior of leisure alienated youth. *Leisure and Society, 18,* 143–156.

Calhoun, C. (1994). *Social theory and the politics of identity*. Cambridge, MA: Blackwell.

Calhoun, M. L. and Calhoun, L. G. (1993). Age-appropriate activities: Effects on the social perception of adults with mental retardation. *Education and Training in Mental Retardation, 28*(2), 143–148.

Cangemi, P., Williams, W., and Gaskell, P. (1992). Going to the source for accessibility assessment. *Parks and Recreation, 27*(10), 66–69.

Carson, C. (1998). *The autobiography of Martin Luther King, Jr.* New York, NY: Warner Books.

Cartledge, G., Kea, C. D., and Ida, D. J. (2000). Anticipating differences: Celebrating strength. *Teaching Exceptional Children, 32*(3), 30–37.

Chadsey-Rusch, J. (1992). Toward defining and measuring social skills in employment settings. *American Journal on Mental Retardation, 96*, 405–416.

Chandler, L. K., Fowler, S. A., and Lubeck, R. C. (1992). An analysis of the effects of multiple setting events on the social behavior of preschool children with special needs. *Journal of Applied Behavior Analysis, 25*(2), 249–263.

Cipriano, R. E. (1998). An individualized person-centered approach to therapeutic recreation services. *TASH Newsletter, 24*(4), 6–7.

Clements, J. (1998). Development, cognition and performance. In E. Emerson, C. Hatton, J. Bromley, and A. Caine (Eds.), *Clinical psychology and people with intellectual disabilities* (pp. 39–53). New York, NY: John Wiley.

Clemetson, L. (1999, July 5). A sharper image of bias. *Time*, 27.

Coale, P. J. (1999). Greetings from Camp Technology. *Parks and Recreation, 34*(5), 78–81.

Cobb, S. (1976). Social support as a moderator of life stress. *Psychosomatic Medicine, 38*, 300–314.

Cole, M. and Meyer, L. H. (1991). Social integration and severe disabilities: A longitudinal analysis of child outcomes. *Journal of Special Education, 25*, 340–351.

Coleman, D. and Iso-Ahola, S. E. (1993). Leisure and health: The role of social support and self-determination. *Journal of Leisure Research, 25*(2), 11–128.

Cone, A. A. (2001). Self-reported training needs and training issues of advisors of self-advocacy groups for people with mental retardation. *Mental Retardation, 39*(1), 1–10.

Cook, S. and Makas, E. (1979). Why, some of my best friends are disabled! A study of the interaction between disabled people and nondisabled rehabilitation professionals. Unpublished manuscript, George Washington University.

Cooper, R. A. (1998). Incorporating human needs into assistive technology design. In D. B. Gray, L. A. Quatrano, and M. L. Lieberman (Eds.), *Designing and using assistive technology: The human perspective* (pp. 137–147). Baltimore, MD: Paul H. Brookes.

Coulter, D. L. (1992). An ecology of prevention for the future. *Mental Retardation, 30*(6), 363–369.

Crabtree, M. (1994, May/June). Overcoming adversity: Judy Clouston has turned her loss into poetry. *Independent Living*, 34–36.

Craig, S., Hull, K., Haggart, A. G., and Perez-Selles, M. (2000). Promoting cultural competence through teacher assistance teams. *Teaching Exceptional Children, 32*(3), 6–13.

Crossley, R. (1999). Talking politics: Empowering communication aid users. *TASH Newsletter, 25*(7/8), 8–11.

Crouser, M. D. (1999). Mental retardation: Should the term be changed? *AAMR News & Notes, 12*(6), 2–9.

Csikszentmihalyi, M. (1990). *Flow: The psychology of optimal experience.* New York, NY: Harper & Row, Publishers.

Csikszentmihalyi, M. (1997). *Finding flow: The psychology of engagement with everyday life.* New York: Basic Books.

Curulla, M. A. and Strong, J. (2000). Community partnerships for inclusive challenge course development. *Parks and Recreation, 35*(5), 48–55.

Dattilo, J. (1999). *Leisure education program planning: A systematic approach* (2nd edition). State College, PA: Venture Publishing, Inc.

Dattilo, J., Caldwell, L., Lee, Y., and Kleiber, D. (1998). Returning to the community with a spinal cord injury: Implications for therapeutic recreation specialists. *Therapeutic Recreation Journal, 32*(1), 13–27.

Dattilo, J. and Camarata, S. (1991). Facilitating conversation through self-initiated augmentative communication treatment. *Journal of Applied Behavior Analysis, 24*(2), 369–378.

Deci, E. L. (1971). Effects of externally mediated rewards on intrinsic motivation. *Journal of Personality and Social Psychology, 18*, 105–115.

Deci, E. L. (1980). *The psychology of self-determination.* Lexington, MA: Lexington Books.

Deci, E. L. (1995). *Why we do what we do: Understanding self-motivation.* New York, NY: Penguin Books.

Deci, E. L. Betley, G., Kahle, J., Abrams, L., and Porac, J. (1981). When trying to win: Competition and intrinsic motivation. *Personality and Social Psychology Bulletin, 7*, 79–83.

Deci, E. L. and Olsen, B. C. (1989). Motivation and competition: Their role in sports. In J. Goldstein (Ed.), *Sports, games, and play: Social and psychological viewpoints* (pp. 83–110). Mahwah, NJ: Lawrence Erlbaum Associates.

Deci, E. L. and Ryan, W. (1985). *Intrinsic motivation and self-determination in human behavior*. New York, NY: Plenum Press.

Demchak, M. (1994). Helping individuals with severe disabilities find leisure activities. *Teaching Exceptional Children, 26*(3), 49–53.

Deutsch, M. (1969). Socially relevant science: Reflections on some studies of interpersonal conflict. *American Psychologist, 24*, 1076–1092.

de Villiers, P. (1987). Choice in concurrent schedules and a quantitative formulation of the law of effect. In W. K. Honig and J. E. R. Staddon (Eds.), *Handbook of operant behavior* (pp. 233–287). Englewood Cliffs, NJ: Prentice-Hall.

Devine, M. A. (1999). Inclusion . . . An update: Results of a national survey. *NTRS Report, 23*(3), 8–9.

Devine, M. A. and Kotowski, L. (1998). It's all in an attitude. *Recreation . . . Access in the 90s, 5*(3), 7.

Devine, M. A. and Kotowski, L. (1999). Inclusive leisure services: Results of a national survey of park and recreation departments. *Journal of Park and Recreation Administration, 17*(4), 56–72.

Devine, M. A., McGovern, J. N., and Hermann, P. (1998). Inclusion in youth sports. *Parks and Recreation, 33*(7), 68–76.

Dieser, R. B. and Peregoy, J. J. (1999). A multicultural critique of three therapeutic recreation service models. *Annual in Therapeutic Recreation, 8*, 56–69.

Dietl, D. (1988). They won the roles with talent. *Worklife, 1*, 4–5.

Dolnick, E. (1993). Deafness as culture. *The Atlantic Monthly, 272*(3), 37–53.

Donaldson, J. (1980). Changing attitudes toward handicapped persons: A review and analysis of research. *Exceptional Children, 46*, 504–515.

Dreimanus, M., Sobsey, D., Gray, S., Hamaha, B., Uditsky, B., and Wells, D. (1992). Annotated bibliography reveals strategies for education integration. *Edmonton Autism Society Update, 8*(1), 25–26. (Reprinted from Edmonton, AB: University of Alberta Severe Disabilities Program, 1990.)

Dunn, R. (2001, Jan 21). Treating discrimination with silence only strengthens it. *Athens Daily News/Athens Banner Herald*, p. 7A.

Dunn, S. L. (1994). Determinants of attitudes toward people with disabilities. *Journal of Social Behavior and Personality, 9*(5), 43–64.

Easterbrooks, S. R. and Baker, S. K. (2001). Enter the matrix: Considering the communication needs of students who are deaf and hard of hearing. *Teaching Exceptional Children, 33*(3), 70–76.

Edgar, E. (1992). Secondary options for students with mild intellectual disabilities: Facing the issues of tracking. *Education and Training in Mental Retardation, 27*(2), 101–111.

Eichmiller, S. (1990). Wheelchairs: Simulating is believing. *Penn State Journalist, 1*(1).

Eisenberg, M. G. (1982). Disability as stigma. In M. B. Eisenberg, C. Griggins, and R. J. Duval, (Eds.), *Disabled people as second-class citizens* (pp. 3–12). New York, NY: Springer.

Evans, J. H. (1976). Changing attitudes toward disabled persons: An experiemental study. *Rehabilitation Counseling Bulletin, 19*, 572–579.

Evans, D. W., Hodapp, R. M., and Zigler, E. (1995). Mental and chronological age as predictors of age-appropriate leisure activity in children with mental retardation. *Mental Retardation, 33*(2), 120–127.

Fabbri, P. (1991). You just can't keep Chuck down. *Sports Illustrated.*

Fairclough, A. (1995). *Martin Luther King, Jr.* Athens, GA: The University of Georgia Press.

Favazza, P. C., Phillipsen, L., and Kumar, P. (2000). Measuring and promoting acceptance of young children with disabilities. *Exceptional Children, 66*(4), 491–508.

Fawley, K. (1999, September). Supreme Court limits rights of people with diabetes. *Diabetes Interview: The News Magazine for the Diabetes Community Since 1991*, 12.

Ferguson, D. L. and Baumgart, D. (1991). Partial participation revisited. *Journal of the Association for Persons with Severe Handicaps, 16*(4), 218–227.

Fernald, C. D. (1995). When in London . . .: Differences in disability language preferences among English-speaking countries. *Mental Retardation, 33*(2), 99–103.

Fink, D. (1988). *School-age children with special needs. What do they do when school is out?* Boston, MA: Exceptional Parent Press.

Fishbein, M. and Ajzen, I. (1975). Belief, attitude, intention and behavior: An introduction to theory and research. Reading, MA: Addison-Wesley.

Fisher, D., Pupian, I., and Sax, C. (1998). High school students attitudes about and recommendation for their peers with significant disabilities. *JASH, 23*(2), 272–282.

Folsom-Meek, S. L., Hearing, R. J., Groteluschen, W., and Krampf, H. (1999). *Adapted Physical Education Quarterly, 16*, 389–402.

Ford, J. A. (2001). The culture of disability. *The Newsletter on Alcohol, Drugs, and Disability, 4*(1), 3.

Forest, M. and Pearpoint, J. (1995). *Inclusion! The bigger picture*. Toronto, ON: Inclusion Press.

Foster, G. G., Ysseldyke, J. E., and Reese, J. H. (1975). I wouldn't have seen it if I hadn't believed it. *Exceptional Children, 41*, 469–473.

Frankl, V. E. (1984). *Man's search for meaning*. New York, NY: Pocket Books.

Fredricks, B. (1987). Tim becomes an Eagle Scout. *The Exceptional Parent, 17*, 22–27.

Fulghum, R. (1989). *It was on fire when I lay down on it*. New York, NY: Ivy Books.

Galambos, L., Lee, R., Rahn, P., and Williams, B. (1994). The ADA: Getting beyond the door. *Parks and Recreation,29*(4) 66–71.

Gallaher, H. G. (1994). *FDR's splendid deception*. Arlington, VA: Vandamere Press.

Garber, J. and Seligman, M. (1980). *Human Helplessness*. New York, NY: Academic Press.

Gardner, H. (1995). *Leading minds: An anatomy of leadership*. New York, NY: Basic Books.

Georgia Advocacy Office. (1992). *Promoting inclusion*. Atlanta, GA: Author.

Germ, P. A. and Schleien, S. J. (1997). Inclusive community leisure services: Responsibilities of key players. *Therapeutic Recreation Journal, 31*(1), 22–37.

~ething, L. (1992). *Person to person*. Baltimore, MD: Paul H. Brookes.

Gilbert, A., MacCauley, M. I., and Smale, B. J. (1997). Newspaper portrayal of persons with disabilities over a decade. *Therapeutic Recreation Journal, 31*, 108–120.

Gilhool, M. (1976). Changing public policies. In M. Reynolds (Ed.), *Mainstreaming* (pp. 8–13). Reston, VA: Council for Exceptional Children.

Gill, C. (1994). Disability and the family. *Mainstream, 18*(5), 30–35.

Gleick, E. (1997, May 19). Mental adjustment. *Time*, 62–63.

Glozier, K. (2000). Keynote remarks. *TASH Newsletter, 26*, 2–14.

Goffman, E. (1963). *Stigma: Notes on the management of spoiled identity.* Englewood Cliffs, NJ: Prentice-Hall.

Goffman, E. (1974). *Stigma*. New York, NY: Jason Aronson.

Goldstein, H., Kaczmarek, L., Pennington, R., and Schafer, K. (1992) Peer-mediated interventions: Attending to, commenting on, and acknowledging the behavior of preschoolers with autism. *Journal of Applied Behavior Analysis, 25*(2), 289–305.

Goodale, T. (1992). Roger Mannell, social psychology of leisure researcher, receives 1991 Roosevelt Award. *Parks and Recreation, 27*(4), 18–21, 82.

Gore, A. (1999). Americans with Disabilities Act Ninth Anniversary Event. *ADA Pipeline, 8*(3), 15.

Green, F. P. and DeCoux, V. (1994). A procedure for evaluating the effectiveness of a community recreation integration program. *Therapeutic Recreation Journal, 28*(1), 41–47.

Greenwood, C. (1994). Advances in technology-based assessment with special education. *Exceptional Children, 61*(2), 102–104.

Grenot-Scheyer, M., Schwartz, I. S., and Meyer, L. H. (1997). Blending best practices for young children: Inclusive early childhood programs. *TASH Newsletter, 23*(4), 8–10.

Grizzle, J. (1994, Fall). On the move! *Spinal Column*, 4–5.

Guralnick, M. J. and Groom, J. M. (1988). Peer interactions in mainstreamed and specialized classrooms: A comparative analysis. *Specialized Children, 54*, 415–426.

Hagan, L. P., Green, F. P., and Starling, S. (1998). Addressing stress in caregivers of older adults through leisure education. *Annual in Therapeutic Recreation, 7*, 42–51.

Hallem, J. (1991). J. D. controls his environment. *Spinal Column*, 49.

Handy, T. (1999). Beyond public playground safety standards. *Parks and Recreation*, 34(4), 84–97.

Hale, G. (1979). *The source book for the disabled*. New York, NY: Bantam Books.

Hanline, M. F. (1993). Inclusion of preschoolers with profound disabilities: An analysis of children's interactions. *JASH, 18*(1), 28–35.

Hanline, M. F. and Fox, L. (1993). Learning within the context of play: Providing typical early childhood experiences for children with severe disabilities. *The Journal of the Association for Persons with Severe Handicaps, 18*(2), 121–129.

Hanson, M. J. (1998). Ethnic, cultural, and language diversity in intervention settings. In E. W. Lynch and M. J. Hanson (Eds.), *Developing cross-cultural competence* (2nd ed., pp. 3–22). Baltimore, MD: Paul H. Brookes.

Hanson, M. J., Lynch, E. W., and Wayman, K. I. (1990). Honoring the cultural diversity of families when gathering data. *Topics in Early Childhood Special education, 10*(1), 112–131.

Hartman, T. S. (1998). Media advocacy and empowerment. *TASH Newsletter, 24*(10), 8–10.

Hasazi, S. B., Johnston, P. Ligget, A. M., and Schattman, R. A. (1994). A qualitative policy study of the least restrictive environment provision of the Individuals with Disabilities Education Act. *Exceptional Children, 60*, 491–507.

Hatton, C. (1998). Intellectual disabilities—epidemiology and causes. In E. Emerson, C. Hatton, J. Bromley, and A. Caine (Eds.), *Clinical psychology and people with intellectual disabilities* (pp. 20–38). New York, NY: John Wiley.

Hauser, S. (2001, May 6). He's a hero on wheels. *Parade Magazine*, 18–20.

Hayes, G. A. (1977). Professional preparation and leisure counseling. *Journal of Physical Education and Recreation, 48*(4), 36–38.

Helff, C. A. and Glidden, L. M. (1998). More positive or less negative? Trends in research on adjustment of families rearing children with developmental disabilities. *Mental Retardation, 36*, 457–464.

Heller, T., Miller, A. B., Hsieh, K., and Sterns, H. (2000). Later-life planning: Promoting knowledge of options and choice-making. *Mental Retardation, 38*(4), 395–406.

Helmstetter, E., Peck, C. A., and Giangreco, M. F. (1994). Outcomes of interactions with peers with moderate or severe disabilities: A statewide survey of high school students. *JASH, 19*(4), 263–276.

Henderson, K. (1997). Diversity, differences, and leisure services. *Parks and Recreation, 32*(11), 24–35.

Hendy, T. (2001). The Americans with Disabilities Act insures the right of every child to play. *Parks and Recreation, 35*(4), 109–117.

Henry, D., Keys, C., Jopp, D., and Balcazar, F. (1996). The Community Living Attitudes Scale, Mental Retardation Form: Development and psychometric properties. *Mental Retardation, 34*(3), 149–158.

Herbert, J. Y. (2000). Director and staff views on including persons with severe disabilities in therapeutic adventure. *Therapeutic Recreation Journal, 34*, 16–32.

Herman, S. and Hazel, K. L. (1991). Evaluation of family support services: Changes in availability and accessibility. *Mental Retardation, 29*(6), 351–357.

Hernandez, M., Isaacs, M. R., Nesman, T., and Burns, D. (1998). Perspective on culturally competent systems of care. In M. Hernandez and M. R. Isaacs (Eds.), Promoting cultural competencein children's mental health services. (pp. 1–25). Baltimore, MD: Paul H. Brookes.

Hersch, H. (1991). Ace of the Angels. *Sports Illustrated*, 22–29.

Heyne, L. A., and Schleien, S. J. (1997). Teaming up with parents to support inclusive recreation. *Parks and Recreation, 32*(5), 76–81.

Heyne, L. A., Schleien, S. J., and McEvoy, L. H. (Eds.). (1993). *Making friends: Using recreation activities to promote friendship between children with and without disabilities*. Minneapolis, MN: Institute on Community Integration (UAP).

Hintermair, M. (2000). Children who are hearing impaired with additional disabilities and related aspects of parental stress. *Exceptional Children, 66*(3), 327–332.

Hockenberry, J. (1994, November/December). A place called disability. *Modern Maturity*, 33.

Hockenberry, J. (1995). *Moving violations: A memoir*. New York, NY: Hyperion.

Hoenk, A. H. and Mobily, K. E. (1987). Mainstreaming the play environment: Effects of previous exposure and salience of disability. *Therapeutic Recreation Journal, 21*(4), 23–31.

Hoge, G., Dattilo, J., Schneider, S., and Bemisderfer, K. (1997). Transition through recreation and integration for life. In S. Schleien, M. Ray, and F. Green (Eds.), *Community recreation and people with disabilities: Strategies for inclusion* (pp. 180–185). Baltimore, MD: Paul H. Brookes.

Holland, J. (1997, May). Enhancing multicultural sensitivity through teaching multiculturally in recreation. *Parks and Recreation,32*(5), 42–50.

Howard, J., Greyrose, E., Kehr, K., Espinosa, M., Beckwith, L. (1996). Teacher facilitated microcomputer activities: Enhancing social play and affect in young children with disabilities. *Journal of Special Education Technology, 13*(1), 16–35.

Howe-Murphy, R. and Charboneau, B. G. (1987). *Therapeutic recreation intervention: An ecological perspective*. Englewood Cliffs, NJ: Prentice-Hall.

Hughes, C. and Agran, M. (1998). Introduction to the special section. Self-determination: Signaling a systems change? *JASH, 23*(1), 1–4.

Hughes, C., Eisenman, L. T., Hwang, B., Kim, J., Killian, D. J., and Scott, S. V. (1997). Transition from secondary special education to adult life: A review of analysis of empirical measures. *Education and Training in Mental Retardation and Developmental Disabilities, 32*(2), 85–104.

Hultsman, W. Z. (1993). The influence of others as a barrier to recreation participation among early adolescents. *Journal of Leisure Research, 25*, 150–164.

Hunt, P. and Goetz, L. (1997). Research on inclusive educational programs: Practices and outcomes for students with severe disabilities. *The Journal of Special Education, 31*(1), 3–29.

Hutchison, P. (1990). *Making friends: Developing relationships between people with a disability and other members of the community*. Toronto, ON: G. Allan Roeher Institute.

Hutchison, P. and McGill, J. (1992). *Leisure, integration and community*. Concord, ON: Leisurability Publications, Inc.

Hutchinson, S. and Dattilo, J. (2001). Processing in therapeutic settings: Possibilities for therapeutic recreation. *Therapeutic Recreation Journal, 35*, 43–56.

Hutinger, P., Johanson, J., and Stoneburner, R. (1996). Assistive technology applications in educational program of children with multiple disabilities: A case study report of the state of practice. *Journal of Special Education Technology, 13*(1), 16–35.

Ingstad, B. (1995). Mpho ya Modimo—A gift from God: Perspectives on "attitudes." In B. Ingstad and Whyte, S. R. (Eds.), *Disability and culture* (pp. 246–266). Berkeley, CA: University of California Press.

Ivory, J. J. and McCollum, J. A. (1999). Effects of social and isolate toys on social play in an inclusive setting. *The Journal of Special Education, 32*(4), 238–243.

Jackson, L. T., Dunne, J., Lanham, G., Heitkamp, K., and Dailey, S. (1993). Age-appropriate activities: Establishing guidelines. *Activities, Adaptations, & Aging, 17*(4), 1–9.

Jenkinson, J. (1999). Factors affecting decision-making by young adults with intellectual disabilities. *American Journal on Mental Retardation, 104*(4), 320–329.

Jesiolowski, J. (1988). Attitudes toward disabilities discussed. *The Daily Collegian*, p. 2.

Johnson, D. E., Bullock, C. C., and Ashton-Shaeffer, C. (1997, November/December). Families and leisure: A context for learning. *Teaching Exceptional Children*, 30–34.

Johnson, D. W. and Johnson, R. T. (1984). *Cooperation in the classroom.* Edina, MN: Interaction Book Company.

Jones, W. J., Sowell, V. M., Jones, J. K., and Butler, L. G. (1981). Changing children's perceptions of handicapped people. *Exceptional Children, 47*, 365–368.

Joswiak, K. F. (1979). Leisure counseling program materials for the developmentally disabled. Washington, DC: Hawkins & Associates.

Kalyanpur, M. and Harry, B. (1999). *Culture in special education: Building reciprocal family-professional relationships.* Baltimore, MD: Paul H. Brookes.

Kaminker, L. (1995, May). Quads take the plunge. *New Mobility*, 44–47.

Karagiannis, A., Stainback, S., and Stainback W. (1996). Concluding remarks. In S. Stainback and W. Stainback (Eds.), *Inclusion: A guide for educators* (pp. 383–385). Baltimore, MD: Paul H. Brookes.

Karlis, G. (1998). Social cohesion, social closure, and recreation: The ethnic experience in multicultural societies. *Journal of Applied Recreation Research, 23*(1), 3–22.

Karlis, G. and Kartakoullis, N. (1996). Recreation and the preservation of ethnic cultural identity in multicultural Canada. *Journal of Business and Society, 5*(1), 153–161.

Karnilowicz, W., Sparrow, W. A., and Shinkfield, A. J. (1994). High school students' attitudes toward performing social behaviors and mentally retarded and physically disabled peers. *Journal of Social Behavior and Personality, 9*(5), 65–80.

Kaufman-Broida, J. and Wenzel, K. (1994). Shaping our future through advocacy. *Parks and Recreation, 29*(4), 72–77.

Kaye, S. (1998, May). Is the status of people with disabilities improving? *Disability Statistics Abstract, 21*, 1–4.

Kemp, J. (1994). Growing up with inclusion. *Exceptional Parent 26*(6), 24–28.

Kennedy, T., Jr. (1986, November 23). Our right to independence. *Parade Magazine*, pp. 4–6.

Kipnis, D. (1991). The technological perspective. *Psychological Science, 2*(2), 62–69.

Kisabeth, K. L. and Richardson, D. B. (1985). Changing attitudes toward disabled individuals: The effect of one disabled person. *Therapeutic Recreation Journal, 19*(2), 24–33.

Kivel, B. (2000). Leisure experience and identity: What difference does difference make? *Journal of Leisure Research, 32*(1), 79–81.

Kleiber, D. A. and Rickards, M. (1985). Leisure and recreation in adolescence: Limitations and potential. In M. G. Wade (Ed.), *Constraints on leisure* (pp. 289–317). Springfield, IL: C.C. Thomas.

Kliewer, C. (1998). The meaning of inclusion. *Mental Retardation, 36*(4), 317–321.

Kliewer, C. (1999). Seeking the functional. *Mental Retardation, 37*(2), 151–154,

Kloeze, J. W. (1999). Family and leisure: Between harmony and conflict. *World Leisure and Recreation, 41*(4), 4–10.

Kowalski, E. M. and Rizzo, T. L. (1996). Factors influencing preservice student attitudes toward individuals with disabilities. *Adapted Physical Activity Quarterly, 13*, 180–196.

Kozlowski, J. C. (2000). "Fore" the love of the game: Pro golfer's cart "reasonable accommodation" under ADA. *Parks and Recreation, 35*(5), 36–43.

Kozub, F. M. and Poretta, D. L. (1998). Interscholastic coaches' attitudes toward integration of adolescents with disabilities. *Adapted Physical Activity Quarterly, 15*, 328–344.

Krajewski, J. and Flaherty, T. (2000). Attitudes of high school students toward individuals with mental retardation. *Mental Retardation, 18*(2), 154–162.

Kunen, J. S. (1996). The end of integration. *Time, 147*(18), 39–45.

Laird, R. (1992, Winter). Access—It's a matter of attitude. *Integrare*, 7–8.

Lama, D. and Cutler, H. C. (1998). *The art of happiness*. New York, NY: Penguin Putnam.

LaMaster, K., Gall, K., Kinchin, G., and Siedentop, D. (1998). Inclusion practices of effective elementary specialists. *Adapted Physical Activity Quarterly, 15*, 64–81.

Lamplia, L. (1998). Special athletes in "normal" athletics. *AAMR News and Notes, 11*(3), 3–9.

Larson, R. (1994). Youth organizations, hobbies, and sport developmental contexts. In R. K. Sibereisen and E. Todt (Eds.). *Adolescence in context: The interplay of family, school, peers and work adjustment*. New York, NY: Springer.

Larson, R., Mannell, R., and Zuzanek, J. (1986). Daily well-being of older adults with friends and family. *Journal of Psychology and Aging, 1*, 117–126.

Larson, R., Zuzanek, J., and Mannell, R. (1985). Being alone versus being with people: Disengagement in the daily experience of older adults. *Journal of Gerontology, 40*, 375–381.

Lashua, B. B., Widmer, M. A., and Munson, W. W. (2000). Some well deserved R & R. *Parks and Recreation, 35*(5), 57–63.

Laski, F. (1997). Upfront. *TASH Newsletter, 23*(6), 2.

Lau, C. (2000). I learned how to take turns, and other important early childhood lessons helped along by computers. *Teaching Exceptional Children, 32*(4), 8–13.

LeConey, S., Devine, M. A., Bunker, H., and Montgomery, S. (2000). Utilizing the therapeutic recreation process in community settings: The case of Sue. *Parks and Recreation, 35*(5), 70–77.

Ledman, S. M., Thompson, B., and Hill, J. W. (1992). The every buddy program: An integrated after-school program. *Children Today, 20*(2), 17–20.

Lee, Y., Dattilo, J., Kleiber, D. A., and Caldwell, L. (1996). Exploring the meaning of continuity of recreation activity in the early stages of adjustment for people with spinal cord injury. *Leisure Sciences, 18*, 209–225.

Lee, Y., Mittelstaedt, R., and Askins, J. (1999). Predicting free time boredom of people with spinal cord injury. *Therapeutic Recreation Journal, 33*, 122–134.

Lehman, J. P. and Baker, C. (1995, March). Mother's expectations for their adolescent children: A comparison between families with disabled adolescents and those with non-disabled adolescents. *Education and Training in Mental Retardation and Developmental Disabilities*, 27–40.

Lemonick, M. D. (1998, September 28). Arthritis under arrest. *Time*, 75.

Lepper, M. R. and Greene, D. (1978). *The hidden costs of rewards*. Mahwah, NJ: Lawrence Erlbaum Associates.

Levin, J. and Enselein, K. (1990). *Fun for everyone: A guide to adapted leisure activities for children with disabilities*. Minneapolis, MN: Able Net.

Levy, J. M., Jessop, D. J., Rimmerman, A., and Levy, P. H. (1992). Attitudes of Fortune 500 corporate executives toward the employability of persons with severe disabilities: A national study. *Mental Retardation, 30*(2), 67–75.

Lin, S. (2000). Coping and adaptation in families of children with cerebral palsy. *Exceptional Children, 66*(2), 201–218.

Lord, J. (1981). Opening doors, opening minds! *Recreation Canada Special Issue*, 4–5.

Lord, M. A. (1997). Leisure's role in enhancing social competencies of individuals with developmental disabilities. *Parks and Recreation, 32*(4), 35–39.

Lott, B. and Maluso, D. (1995a). Introduction: Framing the questions. In B. Lott and D. Maluso (Eds.), *The social psychology of interpersonal discrimination* (pp. 1–11). New York, NY: Guilford.

Lott, B. and Maluso, D. (1995b). *The social psychology of interpersonal discrimination*. New York, NY: Guilford.

Lovell, J. and Lovell, J. (1993, August 15). I am not defined by my disorder. *Parade Magazine*, 6.

Luckasson, R. and Reeve, A. (2001). Naming, defining, and classifying in mental retardation. *Mental Retardation, 39*(1), 47–52.

Luckner, J. L. and Nadler, R. S. (1997). *Processing the experience: Strategies to enhance and generalize learning* (2nd ed.). Dubuque, IO: Kendall/Hunt.

Luken, K. (1993, April). Reintegration through recreation. *Parks and Recreation*, 54–57.

Lynch, E. W. and Hanson, M. J. (1998). *Developing cross-cultural competence* (2nd ed.). Baltimore, MD: Paul H. Brookes.

MacNeil, R. D. and Anderson, S. C. (1999). Leisure and persons with developmental disabilities: Empowering self-determination through inclusion. In P. Retish and S. Reiter (Eds.), *Adults with disabilities: International perspectives in the community* (pp. 125–143). Mahwah, NJ: Lawrence Erlbaum Associates.

Maddox, S. (Ed.). (1988). *Spinal Network*. Boulder, CO: Spinal Network.

Mahon, M. J. and Goatcher, S. (1999). Later-life planning for older adults with mental retardation: A field experiment. *Mental Retardation, 37*(5), 371–382.

Mahon, M. J., Mactavish, J., and Bockstael, E. (2000). Social integration, leisure, and individuals with intellectual disability. *Parks and Recreation, 35*, 25–40.

Mahon, M. J., Mactavish, J. B., and Rodrigue, M. M. (1998). Islands of social integration: Perspectives on social integration and leisure for persons with mental disabilities. *Abstracts from the 1998 Symposium on Leisure Research*. Ashburn, VA: National Recreation and Park Association.

Mahon, M. J., and Martens, C. (1996). Planning for the future: The impact of leisure education for adults with developmental disabilities is supported employment settings. *Journal of Applied Recreation Research, 21*, 283–312.

Maichiodi, C. A. (1999). Inclusive or exclusive. *Art Therapy, 16*(4), 178–179.

Makas, E. (1988). Positive attitudes toward disabled people: Disabled and nondisabled persons' perspectives. *Journal of Social Sciences, 44*(1), 49–61.

Mann, W. and Lane, J. (1991). *Assistive technology for persons with disabilities: The role of occupational therapy.* Rockville, MD: The American Occupational Therapy Association.

Margalit, M. (1991). Promoting classroom adjustment and social skills for students with mental retardation within an experimental and control group design. *Exceptionality, 2*(4), 195–204.

Martens, R., Vealey, R. S., and Burton, D. (1990). *Competitive anxiety in sport.* Champaign, IL: Human Kinetics Press.

Maughan, M. and Ellis, G. D. (1991). Effect of efficacy information during recreation participation on efficacy judgments of depressed adolescents. *Therapeutic Recreation Journal, 25*(1), 50–59.

McCarty, K. S. (1991). *Complying with the ADA.* Washington, DC: National League of Cities.

McFadden, D. L. and Burke, E. P. (1991). Developmental disabilities and the new paradigm: Directions for the 1990s. *Mental Retardation, 29*(1), iii–vi.

McGill, J. (1984). Training for integration: Are blindfolds really enough? *Journal of Leisurability, 11*(2), 12–15.

McGill, L. B. and Holden, H. (1995, Spring). Out of the wilderness. *Spinal Column,* 10–11.

McGovern, J. (1992). The Americans with disabilities act: How will this law be enforced and what is its impact on recreation programming. *Impact,* 21–23.

McGovern, J. N. (1996). The ADA is a tremendous . . . opportunity! *Parks and Recreation, 31*(11), 34–35.

McLean, M. and Hanline, M. F. (1990). Providing early intervention services in integrated environments: Challenges and opportunities for the future. *Topics in Early Childhood Special Education, 10*(2), 62–77.

McLeod, C. (1999). Empowering creativity and computer-assisted art therapy: An introduction to available programs and techniques. *Art Therapy, 16*(4), 201–205.

Medgyesi, V. (1988). Media watch: How the press reports on disability issues. *Habilitation News, 8*(5), 10–11.

Menacker, S. J. and Batshaw, M. L. (1997). Vision: Our window to the world. In M. L. Batshaw (Ed.), *Children with disabilities* (4th ed., pp. 211–240). Baltimore, MD: Paul H. Brookes.

Meyer, L. H. (1994). Quality inclusive schooling: How to know it, when to see it. *TASH Newsletter, 20*(10), 18–20.

Meyer, M. (2000, December 17). There's help for social phobia. *Parade Magazine*, 10–11.

Michels, R. (1985, January 27). Greater research necessary into mental ills, addictions. *Sunday Journal-Star*.

Miller, E. (1991, July 1). The rabbi of roundball. *Sports Illustrated*, pp. 5–6.

Miller, H., Rynders, J. E., and Schleien, S. J. (1993). Drama: A medium to enhance social interaction between students with and without mental retardation. *Mental Retardation, 31*(4), 228–233.

Miller, N. B. and Sammons, C. C. (1999). *Everybody's different: Understanding and changing our reactions to disabilities*. Baltimore, MD: Paul H. Brookes.

Minke, K. M., Baer, G. G., Deemer, S.A., and Griffin, S. M. (1996). Teachers' experiences with inclusive classrooms: Implications for special education reform. *The Journal of Special Education, 30*(2), 152–186.

Minkoff, B. A. (1997). Surf chairs benefit a variety of individuals. *Parks and Recreation, 36*(2), 22.

Minnes, P. (1998). Mental retardation: The impact upon the family. In J. A. Burack, R. M. Hodapp, and E. Zigler (Eds.). *Handbook of mental retardation and development* (pp. 693–712). New York, NY: Cambridge University Press.

Minors, A. (1996). From uni-versity to poly-versity: Organizations in transition to anti-racism. In C. James (Ed.), *Perspectives on racism and the human services sector* (pp. 196–208). Toronto, ON: University of Toronto Press.

Minow, M. (1990). *Making all the difference: Inclusion, exclusion, and the American law*. Ithaca, NY: Cornell University Press.

Mobily, K. E., Lemke, J. H., and Gisin, G. J. (1991). The idea of leisure repertoire. *Journal of Applied Gerontology, 10*, 208–223.

Mobily, K., Mobily, P. R., Lessard, K. A., and Berkenpas, M. S. (2000). Case comparison of response to aquatic exercise: Acute versus chronic conditions. *Therapeutic Recreation Journal, 34*, 103–119.

Modell, S. J., Rider, R. A., and Menchetti, B. M. (1997). An exploration of the influence of educational placement on the community recreation and leisure patterns of children with developmental disabilities. *Perceptual Motor Skills, 85*, 695–714.

Moes, D. R. (1998). Integrating choice-making opportunities within teacher-assigned academic tasks to facilitate the performance of children with autism. *JASH, 23*, 319–328.

Montgomery, R. (1992, November). First encounters. *Parenting*, 261–262.

Moon, M. S., Hart, D., Komissar, C., and Freidlander, R. (1995). Making sports and recreation activities accessible: Assistive technology and other accommodations. In K. F. Flippo, K. J. Inge, and J. M. Barcus (Eds.), *Assistive technology: A resource for school, work and community* (pp. 187–198). Baltimore, MD: Paul H. Brookes.

Moss, K. (Ed.). (1993). *P.S. News, 5*(1).

Most, T., Weisel, A., and Tur-Kaspa, H. (1999). Contact with students with hearing impairments and the evaluation of speech intelligibility and personal qualities. *The Journal of Special Education, 33*(2), 103–111, 124.

Murphy, J. F. (1975). *Recreation and leisure service: A humanistic perspective*. Dubuque, IA: W. C. Brown.

Murphy, R. F. (1990). *The silent body*. New York, NY: W. W. Norton & Co.

National Easter Seals Society. (1981). Portraying persons with disabilities in print. *Rehabilitation Literature, 42*, 284–285.

Nelson, M. (1987, November, 20). Miss deaf Pennsylvania breaks barriers. *Bloomsburg Press-Enterprise*.

Newton, J. S., Horner, R. H., and Lund, L. (1991). Honoring activity preferences in individualized plan development: A descriptive analysis. *Journal of the Association of Severe Handicaps, 16*(4), 207–221.

National Office of Disability. (2000). NOD/Harris survey of Americans with disabilities. Washington, DC: Author.

NIH Consensus Development Panel on Rehabilitation of Persons with Traumatic Brain Injury (1999). Rehabilitation of persons with traumatic brain injury. *Journal of the American Medical Association, 282*(10), 972–983.

Nissen, S. J. and Newman, W. P. (1992). Factors influencing reintegration to normal living after amputation. *Archives of Physical Medicine and Rehabilitation, 73*, 548–551.

O'Brien, J. and O'Brien, C. L. (1992). Members of each other: Perspective on social support for people with severe disabilities. In J. Nisbet (Ed.), *Natural supports in school, work, and in the community for people with severe disabilities* (pp. 17–64). Baltimore, MD: Paul H. Brookes.

O'Dell, C. (2001, March). First aid for seizures. *Exceptional Parent Magazine*, 86–89.

Oestreicher, M. (1990). Accessible recreation: 20 years behind the times. *Parks and Recreation Magazine, 25*(8), 52–55.

"Oh, so this is the most integrated setting." (1997). *Recreation...Access in the 90s, 5*(1), 8–9.

Oliva, G. A. and Simonsen, A. (2000). Re-thinking leisure services for deaf and hard of hearing persons: A new paradigm. *Parks and Recreation, 35*(5), 79–85.

Oliver, M. (1996). *Understanding disability: From theory to practice*. London: Macmillan.

Orlick, T. D. and Mosher, R. (1978). Extrinsic rewards and participant motivation in a sport related task. *International Journal of Sport Psychology, 9*, 27–39.

Owens, K. (2001, January/February). The final rules: The latest and last (probably) accessibility guidelines for play areas. *Recreation Management*, 6–7.

Palus, C. J. (1993). Transformative experiences of adulthood: A new look at the seasons of life. In J. Demeck, K. Bursik, and R. Dibiase (Eds.), *Parental development* (pp. 39–58). Hillsdale, NJ: Lawrence Erlbaum Associates.

Paniagua, C. (2000). Life is good. *TASH Newsletter, 26*(10), 13–14.

Parette, H. P., Huer, M.B., and Brotherson, M. J. (2001). Related service personnel perceptions of team AAC decision-making across cultures. *Education and Training in Mental Retardation and Developmental Disabilities, 36*(1), 69–82.

Parker, L. (1998). The sandbox. In J. Canfield, M. V. Hansen, P. Hansen, and I. Dunlap. *Chicken soup for the kid's soul* (p. 250). Deerfield Beach, FL: Health Communications.

Parks, R. (1992). *Rosa Parks: My story*. New York, NY: Puffin Books.

Passentino, E. and Cranfield, P. (1994, Fall). Inclusion at recess: A foundation for friendship. *Palaestra*, 45–48.

Paul, P. V. (1998). Radical heart, moderate mind: A perspective on inclusion. *TASH Newsletter, 24*, 11–19.

Payne, L., Orsega-Smith, E., Spangler, K. J., and Godbey, G. (1999). Local parks and recreation for the health of it. *Parks and Recreation, 34*(10), 72–77.

Pedlar, A., Haworth, L., Hutchison, P., Taylor, A., and Dunn, P. (1999). *A textured life: Empowerment and adults with developmental disabilities*. Waterloo: Wilfrid Laurier University Press.

Peniston, L. C. (1996). Hotel accessibility and accommodations for people with disabilities. *Parks and Recreation, 31*(12), 24–29.

Peniston, L. C. (1998). *Developing recreation skills in persons with learning disabilities*. Champaign, IL: Sagamore Publishing.

Perez, T. (2000). The Olmstead decision and the states. *AAMR News & Notes, 13*(2), 1, 11.

Perlin, L. I., Mullan, J. T., Semple, S. J., and Skaff, M. M. (1990). Caregiving and the stress process: An overview of concepts and their measures. *The Gerontologist, 30*(5), 583–594.

Perlman, I. (1987, March). To help the handicapped, talk to them. *Glamour*, p. 64

Perry, K. (1995). In high gear: Dennis Walters. *Sports 'n Spokes, 21*(3), 65.

Pomeranz, T. E. (1997). I am somebody: Beyond inclusion. *AAMR News & Notes, 10*(3), 4.

Prentke Romich Company. (1992). *Changing Lives*. Wooster, OH: Author.

Pumpian, I. (1996). Foreword. In D. J. Sands and M. L. Wehmeyer, (Eds.), *Self-determination across the life span: Independence and choice for people with disabilities*. Baltimore, MD: Paul H. Brookes.

"Rag Time." (1989, February). *TASH Newsletter, 15*, 6, 8.

Rankin, D., Hallick, A., Ban, S., Hartley, P., Bost, C., and Uggla, N. (1994). Who's dreaming?: A general education perspective on inclusion. *JASH, 19*(3), 235–237.

Ray, M. T. and Meidl, D. (1991). *Fun futures: Community recreation and developmental disabilities*. St. Paul, MN: SCOLA of Arc Ramsey County.

Rees, L., Spreen, O., and Harnadek, M. (1991). Do attitudes toward persons with handicaps really shift over time? *Mental Retardation, 29*(2), 81–86.

Reiter, S. (1999). Conclusion: Cross-cultural perspectives—Diversity and universalism. In P. Retish and S. Reiter (Eds.), *Adults with disabilities: International perspectives in the community* (pp. 325–335). Mahwah, NJ: Lawrence Erlbaum Associates.

Rettig, M. (1994). The play of young children with visual impairments: Characteristics and interventions. *Journal of Visual Impairment & Blindness, 88*, 410–420.

Retzinger, J. (1990). Chair image. *Spinal Network Extra*, 6.

Reyes, K. W. (1995, September/October). The many faces of arthritis. *Modern Maturity*, 19.

Risisky, D., Caldwell, L. L., and Fors, S. W. (1997). The prevention of HIV among adolescents: A leisure education intervention. *Journal of Health Education, 28*(6), 350–356.

Rizzo, T. L., Bishop, P., and Tobar, D. (1997). Attitudes of soccer coaches toward youth players with mild mental retardation: A pilot study. *Adapted Physical Activity Quarterly, 14*, 238–251.

Rizzo, T. L. and Vispoel, W. P. (1991). Physical educators' attributes and attitudes toward teaching students with handicaps. *Adapted Physical Activity Quarterly, 8*, 4–11.

Rizzo, T. L. and Vispoel, W. P. (1992). Changing attitudes about teaching students with handicaps. *Adapted Physical Activity Quarterly, 9*, 54–63.

Rizzo, T. L. and Wright, R. G. (1987). Secondary school physical educators' attitudes toward teaching students with handicaps. *American Corrective Therapy Journal, 41*(2), 52–55.

Roach, M. A., Orsmond, G. I., and Barratt, M. S. (1999). Mothers and fathers of children with Down syndrome: Parental stress and involvement in childcare. *American Journal of Mental Retardation, 104*(5), 422–436.

"Roaming the Cosmos." (1988, February). *Time*.

Roberts, G., Becker, H., and Seay, P. (1997). A process for measuring adoption of innovation within the supports paradigm. *JASH, 22*(2), 109–119.

Rock, M. L. (2000). Parents as equal partners. *Teaching Exceptional Children, 32*(6), 30–37.

Rogers, D. (2000). To the top: Future challenge courses offer access for persons with disabilities. *Parks & Recreation, 35*(3), 76–87.

Romski, M. A., Sevcik, R. A., and Adamson, L. B. (1999). Communication patterns of youth with mental retardation with and without their speech-output communication devices. *American Journal on Mental Retardation, 104*(3), 249–259.

Romski, M. A., Sevcik, R. A., and Wilkinson, K. (1994). Peer-directed communicative interactions of augmented language learners with mental retardation. *American Journal on Mental Retardation, 98*, 527–538.

Rook, K. S. (1987). Social support versus companionship: Effects on life stress, loneliness, and evaluations by others. *Journal of Personality and Social Psychology, 52*, 1132–1147.

Roper, P. A. (1990). Special Olympics volunteers' perceptions of people with mental retardation. *Education and Training in Mental Retardation, 25*(2), 164–175.

Rosenthal, R. and Jacobson, L. (1968). *Pygmalion in the classroom*. New York, NY: Holt, Rinehart & Winston.

Rowe, J. and Stutts, R. M. (1987). Effects of practical type, experience, and gender on attitudes of undergraduate physical education majors toward disabled persons. *Adapted Physical Activity Quarterly, 4*, 268–277.

Rowitz, L. (1992). A family affair. *Mental Retardation, 30*(2), iii–iv.

Rugg, M. E. and Weber, J. (1995, Winter). Riding with Mad Dog. *Update*. Athens, GA: The University of Georgia's University Affiliated Program.

Rush, W. L. (November/December, 1999). The making of a square hole: On the level: *The Newsletter of the League of Human Dignity*, 1, 4.

Russell, R. (1996). *Pastimes: The context of contemporary leisure*. Chicago, IL: Brown & Benchmark.

Ryndak, D. L., Downing, J. E., Jacqueline, L. R., and Morrison, A. P. (1995). Parents' perceptions after inclusion of their children with moderate or severe disabilities. *JASH, 20*(2), 147–157.

Ryndak, D. L. and Kennedy, C. H. (2000). Meeting the needs of students with severe disabilities: Issues and practices in teacher education. *JASH, 25*(2), 69–71.

Rynders, J. and Schleien, S. (1991). *Together successfully: Creating recreational and educational programs that integrate people with and without disabilities*. Arlington, TX: Association for Retarded Citizens-United State, National 4-H, and the Institute on Community Integration, University of Minnesota.

Sable, J. (1992). Collaborating to create an integrated camping program: Design and evaluation. *Therapeutic Recreation Journal, 26*(3), 38–48.

Sadowsky, D. (1997, Fall). No limits. *Spinal Column, 56*, 18–20.

Saetermoe, C., Wideman, K. and Borthwick-Duffy, S. (1991). Validation of the parenting style survey for parents of children with mental retardation. *Mental Retardation, 29*, 149–157.

Salisbury, C. and Chambers, A. (1994). Instructional costs of inclusive schooling. *JASH, 19*(3), 215–222.

"Salt Lake City: Leave it to Stephen Hawking." (1995, July 19). Athens Daily News p. 2A.

Sands, D. J. and Doll, B. (1996). Fostering self-determination is a developmental task. *Journal of Special Education, 30*(1), 58–76.

Sanford, M. E. and Petajan, J. H. (1990). Effects of multiple sclerosis on daily living. In S. M. Rao (Ed.), *Neurobehavioral aspects of multiple sclerosis* (pp. 251–265). New York, NY: Oxford University Press, Inc.

Sapon-Shevin, M. and Smith, R. (1999). Disability humor: Moving beyond, "That's not funny!" *TASH Newsletter, 25*(3), 25–27.

Sayeed, Z. (1999). A 1998 TASH Conference Keynote Address: Zuhy Sayeeed. *TASH Newsletter, 25*(1/2), 12–14.

Sayne T. (1996). Ability awareness day. *Parks and Recreation, 31*(5), 24–25.

Schacht, R. M. (1999, Spring). Is "cultural sensitivity" enough? *American Indian Rehabilitation*, 9.

Schleien, S. J. (1993). Access and inclusion in community leisure services. *Parks and Recreation, 28*(4), 66–72.

Schleien, S. J., Germ, P. A., and McAvoy, L. H. (1996). Inclusive community leisure services: Recommended professional practices and barriers encountered. *Therapeutic Recreation Journal, 30*(4), 260–273.

Schleien, S. J. and Green, F. P. (1992). Three approaches for integrating persons with disabilities into community recreation. *Journal of Parks and Recreation Administration, 10*(2), 51–66.

Schleien, S. J., Ray, M. T., Soderman-Olson, M., and McMahon, K. T. (1987). Integrating children with moderate to severe cognitive deficits into a community museum program. *Education and Training in Mental Retardation, 22*(2), 112–120.

Schleien, S. J. and Werder, J. (1985). Perceived responsibilities of special recreation services in Minnesota. *Therapeutic Recreation Journal, 19*(3), 51–62.

Schuman, D. and Olufs, D. (1995). *Diversity on campus.* Boston, MA: Allyn & Bacon.

Scorgie, K. and Sobsey, D. (2000). Transformational outcomes associated with parenting children who have disabilities. *Mental Retardation, 38*(3), 195–206.

Seligman, M. (1975). *Helplessness: On depression, development, and death.* San Francisco, CA: W. H. Freeman.

Shamir, B. (1992). Some correlates of leisure identity salience: Three exploratory studies. *Journal of Leisure Research, 24*(4), 301–323.

Shapiro, J. P. (1993). *No pity: People with disabilities forging a new civil rights movement.* New York, NY: Times Books.

Shapiro, J. P. (1994). The mothers of invention. *U.S. News & World Report, 116* (1), 38–42.

Shaw, B. (1994, November/December). The cost of modification. *Modern Maturity,* 30.

Shaw, S. M. (1992). Family leisure and leisure services. *Parks and Recreation, 27*(12), 13–16, 66.

Sherrid, P. (1988). The prison of paralysis, the freedom of words. *U.S. News & World Report,* 60.

Siegel, J. (1999). Utilizing technology for the inclusion of individuals with mental retardation. In P. Retish and S. Reiter (Eds.), *Adults with disabilities: International perspective in the community* (pp. 287–508). Mahwah, NJ: Lawrence Erlbaum Associates.

Siegel, J., Good, K., and Moore, J. (1996). Integrating technology into educating preservice special education teachers. *Action in Teacher Education, 17*(4), 53–63.

Sigafoos, J. (1998). Choice making and personal selection strategies. In J. K. Luiselli and M. J. Cameron (Eds.), *Antecedent control: Innovative approaches to behavioral support* (pp. 187–221). Baltimore, MD: Paul H. Brookes.

Skellenger, A., McEvoy, M., McConnell, S., and Odom, S. (1991). *Environmental arrangements intervention manual.* Unpublished manuscript, George Peabody College, Vanderbilt University, Nashville, TN.

Smith, M. R. (1992). Semeiotics and the coverage of people with disabilities. *Disability Studies Quarterly, 12*(1), 1–4.

Smith, R. (1993). Sport and physical activity for people with physical disabilities. *Parks and Recreation, 28*(2), 22–27.

Smith, J. (1995, May). Double jeopardy. *New Mobility*, 58.

Smith, J. D. (1997). Mental retardation as an educational construct: Time for a new shared view? *Education and Training in Mental Retardation and Developmental Disabilities, 32*(3), 167–173.

Smith, J. D. (2000). The power of mental retardation: Reflections on the value of people with disabilities. *Mental Retardation, 38*(1), 70–72.

Smith, J. D. and Hilton, A. (1997). The preparation and training of the educational community for the inclusion of students with developmental disabilities: The MRDD Position. *Education and Training in Mental Retardation and Developmental Disabilities, 32*(1), 3–10.

Smolowe, J. (1995, July 31). Noble aims, mixed results. *Time, 146*(5), 54–55.

Snell, M. E. (1988). Curriculum and methodology for individuals with severe disabilities. *Education and Training in Mental Retardation, 23*, 302–314.

Snow, K. (1998). To achieve inclusion, community, and freedom for people with disabilities we must use people first language. *TASH Newsletter, 24*(10), 14–16.

Sobsey, R. (1998). Community inclusion and personal safety. *TASH Newsletter, 24*(9), 8.

Soodak, L, C., Podell, D. M., Lehman, L. R. (1998). Teacher, student, and school attributes as predictors of teachers' response to inclusion. *The Journal of Special Education, 31*(4), 480–497.

Soto, G. and Goetz, L. (1998). Self-efficacy beliefs and the education of students with severe disabilities. *JASH, 23*(2), 134–143.

Speigel-McGill, P., Bambara, L. M., Shores, R. E., and Fox, J. J. (1984). The effects of proximity on socially oriented behaviors of severely multiply handicapped children. *Education and Treatment of Children, 7*, 365–378.

Spirit of ADA. (2000). *ADA Pipeline, 9*(2), 1, 6, 15.

Stainback, S. and Stainback, W. (1996). *Inclusion: A guide for educators*. Baltimore, MD: Paul H. Brookes.

Stainback, S., Stainback, W., East, K., and Sapon-Shevin, M. (1996). Inclusion and the development of positive self-identity by persons with disabilities. In S. Stainback and W. Stainback (Eds.), *Inclusion: A guide for educators* (pp. 361–366). Baltimore, MD: Paul H. Brookes.

Stainback, S., Stainback, W., Strathe, M., and Dedrick, C. (1983). Preparing regular classroom teachers for the integration of severely retarded students: An experimental study. *Education and Training of the Mentally Retarded*, 204–209.

Stainback, W. and Stainback, S. (1987). Facilitating friendships. *Education and Training in Mental Retardation, 22*, 18–25.

Stainback, W., Stainback, S., and Stefanich, G. (1996). Learning together in inclusive classrooms. *Teaching Exceptional Children*, 14–19.

Stancliffe, R. J., Abery, B. H., and Smith, J. (2000). Personal control and the ecology of community living settings: Beyond living-unit size and type. *American Journal on Mental Retardation, 105*(6), 431–454.

Stancliffe, R. J., Abery, B. H., Springborg, H., and Elkin, S. (2000). Substitute decision-making and personal control: Implications for self-determination. *Mental Retardation, 38*(4), 407–421.

Stern-Larosa, C. and Bettman, E. H. (2000). Hate hurts: How children learn and unlearn prejudice. New York, NY: Antidefamation League.

Stewart, C. C. (1988). Modification of student attitudes toward disabled peers. *Adapted Physical Activity Quarterly, 5*, 44–48.

Stodolska, M. and Jackson, E. L. (1998). Discrimination in leisure and work experienced by a white ethnic minority group. *Journal of Leisure Research, 30*(1), 23–46.

Storey, K., Stern, R., and Parker, R. (1991). A comparison of attitudes toward typical recreational activities versus the Special Olympics. *Education and Training in Mental Retardation, 25*, 94–99.

Strully, J. L. and Strully, C. F. (1989). Friendships as an educational goal. In S. Stainback, W. Stainback, and Forest, M. (Ed.), *Educating all students in the mainstream of regular education* (pp. 59–68). Baltimore, MD: Paul H. Brookes.

Stumbo, N. (1995). Social skills instruction through commercially available resources. *Therapeutic Recreation Journal, 29*, 30–55.

Talle, A. (1995). A child is a child: Disability and equality among the Kenya Maasai. In B. Ingstad and Whyte, S. R. (Eds.), *Disability and culture* (pp. 56–72). Berkeley, CA: University of California Press.

Technology-Related Assistance for Individuals with Disabilities Act of 1988, Pub. L. No. 100–407, 102 Stat. 1044 (1990).

Terrill, C. F. (1992). What's in a name? *AAMR: News and Notes, 5*(5), 8.

"The results are in!" (1986, March/April). *The Disability Rag*, 33.

Thompson, A. and Vierno, P. (1991, November 13). Wheelchairs change the way people react. *The Daily Collegian*, 4.

Thousand, J. S., Villa, R. A., and Falvey, M. A. (1995). Introduction. In M. A. Falvey (Ed.), *Inclusive and heterogeneous schooling* (pp. 1–6). Baltimore, MD: Paul H. Brookes.

Tiersten, T. (1994, October). Two ADA cases serve notice: Disabled access means more than ramps and elevators. *Meeting News*. Miller Freeman, Inc.

Tinsley, H. E. A. and Tinsley, D. J. (1982). A holistic model of leisure counseling. *Journal of Leisure Research, 2*, 100–116.

Tomlinson, C. A., Callahan, C. M., Tomchin, E. M., Eiss, N., Imgeau, M., and Landrum, M. (1997). Becoming architects of communities of learning: Addressing academic diversity in contemporary classrooms. *Exceptional Children, 63*(2), 269–282.

Trace Center. (1995). *The principles of universal design*. Madison, WI: Author.

Tripp, A., French, R., and Sherrill, C. (1995). Contact theory and attitudes of children in physical education programs toward peers with disabilities. *Adapted Physical Activity Quarterly, 12*, 323–332.

Tripp, A. and Sherrill, C. (1991). Attitude theories of relevance to adapted physical education. *Adapted Physical Activity Quarterly, 8*, 12–27.

Turnbull, A. P., Blue-Banning, M., and Pereira, L. (2000). Successful friendships of Hispanic children and youth with disabilities: An exploratory study. *Mental Retardation, 38*(2), 138–153.

Turnbull, A. P. and Ruef, M. (1997). Family perspectives on inclusion lifestyles issues for people with problem behavior. *Exceptional Children, 63*(2), 221–227.

Turnbull, A. P. and Turnbull, H. R. (1996). Group action planning as a strategy for providing comprehensive family support. In L. K. Koegel, R. L. Koegel, and G. Dunlap (Eds.), *Positive behavioral support: Including people with difficult behavior in the community* (pp. 99–114). Baltimore, MD: Paul H. Brookes.

Umstead, S., Boyd, K., and Dunst, C. (1995, July). Building community resources. *Exceptional Parent*, 36–37.

U. S. Architectural and Transportation Barriers Compliance Board. (1992). Equal access to meetings, information. *Access America, 2*(2), 10.

U. S. Department of Health and Human Services Administration for Children and Families. (1994). The national reform agenda and citizens with mental retardation: A journey of renewal for all Americans. Report to the President. Washington, DC: U. S. Government Printing Office.

Valerius, L., Hodges, J. S., and Perez, M. A. (1997). Cultural tunnel syndrome: A disabling condition. *Parks and Recreation, 32*(5), 60–67.

Vallerand, R. J., Gauvin, L. I., and Halliwell, W. R. (1986). Negative effects of competition on children's intrinsic motivation. *Journal of Social Psychology, 126*, 649–657.

Vandercook, T., York, J., and Forest, M. (1989). The McGill Action Planning System (MAPS): A strategy for building the vision. *Journal of the Association for Persons with Severe Handicaps, 14*(3), 205–215.

Veno, D. (1986). Wild mountains and errant attitudes: Taming them requires mainstreamed planning. *Disabled U.S.A., 1-2,* 13–14.

Walker, L. A. (2001, May 13). They're breaking the sound barrier. *Parade Magazine*, 4–5.

Walker, P. (1999). From community presence to sense of place: Community experiences of adults with developmental disabilities. *JASH, 24*(1), 23–32.

Wall, M. and Dattilo, J. (1995). Creating option-rich learning environments: Facilitating self-determination. *Journal of Special Education, 29*(3), 276–294.

Ward, M. J. (1988). The many facets of self-determination. National Information Center for Children and Youth with Disabilities. *Transition Summary, 5*, 2–3.

Ward, M. J. and Meyer, R. N. (1999). Self-determination for people with developmental disabilities and autism: Two self-advocates' perspectives. *Focus on Autism and other Developmental Disabilities, 14*(3), 133–139.

Warren, S. F. (2000). Mental retardation: Curse, characteristics, or coin of the realm? *AAMR News & Notes, 13*(2), 1–11.

Wehman, P. (1993). *The ADA mandate for social change.* Baltimore, MD: Paul H. Brookes.

Wehmeyer, M. I. (1994). Perception of self-determination and psychological empowerment of adolescents with mental retardation. *Education and Training in Mental Retardation, 29*(1), 9–21.

Wehmeyer, M. L. (1996). Self-determination as an educational-outcome: Why is it important to children, youth and adults with disabilities? In D. J. Sands and M. L. Wehmeyer (Eds.), *Self-determination across the life span: Independence and choice for people with disabilities* (pp. 15–34). Baltimore, MD: Paul H. Brookes.

Wehmeyer, M. L. (1998). National survey of the use of assistive technology by adults with mental retardation. *Mental Retardation, 36*(1), 44–51.

Wehmeyer, M. L. and Bolding, N. (1999). Self-determination across living and working environments: A matched-samples of adults with mental retardation. *Mental Retardation, 37*(5), 353–363.

Wehmeyer, M. L., Palmer, S. B., Agran, M., Mithaug, D. E., and Martin, J. E. (2000). Promoting causal agency: The self-determined learning model of instruction. *Exceptional Children, 66*(4), 439–453.

Wehmeyer, M. and Schwartz, M. (1998). The relationship between self-determination and quality of life of adults with mental retardation. *Education and Training in Mental Retardation and Developmental Disabilities, 33*(1), 3–12.

Weicker, L. (1988, July). The Americans with Disabilities Act. *DC Update*, 1.

Weinberg, R. S. and Ragan, J. (1979). Effects of competition, success/failure, and sex on intrinsic motivation. *Research Quarterly, 50*, 503–510.

Weinum, T. C. and Mitchell, M. L. (1997). Inclusion: Are you ready, willing and able? *Recreation Access in the 90s, 5*(1), 7–8.

Weirs, P. (1988, October 28). Integrated recreation activities set for today. *The Daily Collegian*, 8.

West, M. and Parent, W. S. (1992). Consumer choice and empowerment in supported employment services: Issues and strategies. *The Journal of the Association for Persons with Severe Handicaps, 17*(1), 47–52.

Wheat, A. (2000). Running the rapids of risk. *Parks and Recreation, 35*(7), 78–83.

Whyte, S. R. and Ingstad, B. (1995). Disability and culture: An overview. In B. Ingstad and Whyte, S. R. (Eds.), *Disability and culture* (pp. 3–34). Berkeley, CA: University of California Press.

Wilhite, B., Devine, M. A., and Goldenberg, L. (1999). Perception of youth with and without disabilities: Implication for inclusive leisure programs and services. *Therapeutic Recreation Journal, 33*, 15–28.

Williams, R. (1991). Choices, communication, and control—A call for expanding them in the lives of people with severe disabilities. In L. H. Meyer, C. A. Peck, and L. Brown (Eds.), *Critical issues in the lives of people with severe disabilities* (pp. 543–544). Baltimore, MD: Paul H. Brookes.

Wolfensberger, W. (1995). An "If this, then that" formulation of decisions related to social role valorization as a better way of interpreting it to people. *Mental Retardation, 33*(3), 163–169.

Wolfensberger, W. (2000). A brief overview of social role valorization. *Mental Retardation, 38*(2), 105–123.

Wolfensberger, W. and Thomas, S. (1983). *PASSING (Program Analysis of Service Systems' Implementation of Normalization Goals: Normalization Criteria and Ratings Manual)* (2nd ed.). Toronto, ON: National Institute on Mental Retardation.

Wright, B. A. (1988). Attitudes and the fundamental negative bias: Conditions and corrections. In H. E. Yuker (Ed.), *Attitudes toward people with disabilities* (pp. 3–21). New York, NY: Springer.

Yates, J. and Brooks, G. (1993). *Standing outside the fire*. Criterion Music Corp./Escudilla Music/Bob Music Co., Inc./No Fences Music, Adm. by Major Bob Music Co., Inc., ASCAP.

York, J. (1994). A shared agenda for educational change. *Newsletter: The Association for Persons with Severe Handicaps 20*(2), 10–11.

Young, L. W. (1990). Being temporarily disabled is an eye-opening experience. *Centre Daily Times*.

Yuker, H. E. (1988). *Attitudes of the general public toward handicapped individuals*. Washington, DC: White House Conference on Handicapped Individuals.

Zeltin, A. G. and Morrison, G. M. (1998). Adaptation through the life span. In J.A. Burack, R.M., Hodapp and E. Zigler (Eds.), *Handbook of mental retardation and development* (pp. 481–503). New York, NY: Cambridge University Press.

Zoerink, D. A. (1988). Effects of a short-term leisure education program upon the leisure functioning of young people with spina bifida. *Therapeutic Recreation Journal, 22*(3), 44–52.

Index

M

Macular degeneration 353
Mainstream/mainstreaming 106, 226
Manic episodes 339
Manual chair 378
Martin, Casey 159
Mastery orientation 133–134
Mental health problem(s) 259, 337–338
Mental illness 9, 145
Mental retardation 9, 13, 95, 98, 259, 318–319, 321–324
Mild hearing loss 358
Mild partial deafness 358
Mixed cerebral palsy 327
Mobility/mobility aids 180, 260, 262, 296, 305, 354, 401
Moderate hearing loss 358–359
Monoplegia 327
Multiple disabilities 391
Multiple sclerosis 10, 167, 294–295, 311, 375, 388
Muscular dystrophy 10, 95, 291, 306
Mylomeningocele (spina bifida) 296

N

Natural proportions 79, 84–85
Negative attitude(s) 34, 37, 45, 50, 61, 74
Negative feedback 136
Nerve deafness 361
Neuroimplantation 375
Neurological disorder 257
Neurorehabilitation 376
Noncompliance 151
Nondirective approach 202

O

Objectives 264
Observations 251–252
Obsessive-compulsive disorder 339
Olmstead case 151
Open head injury 332
Optimal experience 197

S

U

V

W

Other Books by Venture Publishing

The A•B•Cs of Behavior Change: Skills for Working With Behavior Problems in Nursing Homes
by Margaret D. Cohn, Michael A. Smyer, and Ann L. Horgas

Activity Experiences and Programming Within Long-Term Care
by Ted Tedrick and Elaine R. Green

The Activity Gourmet
by Peggy Powers

Advanced Concepts for Geriatric Nursing Assistants
by Carolyn A. McDonald

Adventure Programming
edited by John C. Miles and Simon Priest

Aerobics of the Mind: Keeping the Mind Active in Aging—A New Perspective on Programming for Older Adults
by Marge Engelman

Assessment: The Cornerstone of Activity Programs
by Ruth Perschbacher

Behavior Modification in Therapeutic Recreation: An Introductory Manual
by John Datillo and William D. Murphy

Benefits of Leisure
edited by B. L. Driver, Perry J. Brown, and George L. Peterson

Benefits of Recreation Research Update
by Judy M. Sefton and W. Kerry Mummery

Beyond Bingo: Innovative Programs for the New Senior
by Sal Arrigo, Jr., Ann Lewis, and Hank Mattimore

Beyond Bingo 2: More Innovative Programs for the New Senior
by Sal Arrigo, Jr.

Both Gains and Gaps: Feminist Perspectives on Women's Leisure
by Karla Henderson, M. Deborah Bialeschki, Susan M. Shaw, and Valeria J. Freysinger

Dimensions of Choice: A Qualitative Approach to Recreation, Parks, and Leisure Research
by Karla A. Henderson

Diversity and the Recreation Profession: Organizational Perspectives
edited by Maria T. Allison and Ingrid E. Schneider

Effective Management in Therapeutic Recreation Service
by Gerald S. O'Morrow and Marcia Jean Carter

Evaluating Leisure Services: Making Enlightened Decisions, Second Edition
By Karla A. Henderson and M. Deborah Bialeschki

Leadership in Leisure Services: Making a Difference, Second Edition
   by Debra J. Jordan

Leisure and Leisure Services in the 21st Century
   by Geoffrey Godbey

The Leisure Diagnostic Battery: Users Manual and Sample Forms
   by Peter A. Witt and Gary Ellis

Leisure Education: A Manual of Activities and Resources, Second Edition
   by Norma J. Stumbo and Steven R. Thompson

Leisure Education II: More Activities and Resources, Second Edition
   by Norma J. Stumbo

Leisure Education III: More Goal-Oriented Activities
   by Norma J. Stumbo

*Leisure Education IV: Activities for
Individuals with Substance Addictions*
   by Norma J. Stumbo

Leisure Education Program Planning: A Systematic Approach, Second Edition
   by John Dattilo

Leisure Education Specific Programs
   by John Dattilo

Leisure in Your Life: An Exploration, Fifth Edition
   by Geoffrey Godbey

Leisure Services in Canada: An Introduction, Second Edition
   by Mark S. Searle and Russell E. Brayley

Leisure Studies: Prospects for the Twenty-First Century
   edited by Edgar L. Jackson and Thomas L. Burton

The Lifestory Re-Play Circle: A Manual of Activities and Techniques
   by Rosilyn Wilder

*Models of Change in Municipal Parks and Recreation: A Book of Innovative Case
Studies*
   edited by Mark E. Havitz

More Than a Game: A New Focus on Senior Activity Services
   by Brenda Corbett

Nature and the Human Spirit: Toward an Expanded Land Management Ethic
   edited by B. L. Driver, Daniel Dustin, Tony Baltic, Gary Elsner, and George
      Peterson

Outdoor Recreation Management: Theory and Application, Third Edition
   by Alan Jubenville and Ben Twight

Planning Parks for People, Second Edition
   by John Hultsman, Richard L. Cottrell, and Wendy Z. Hultsman

The Process of Recreation Programming Theory and Technique, Third Edition
   by Patricia Farrell and Herberta M. Lundegren

Therapeutic Recreation Protocol for Treatment of Substance Addictions
  by Rozanne W. Faulkner

Tourism and Society: A Guide to Problems and Issues
  by Robert W. Wyllie

A Training Manual for Americans with Disabilities Act Compliance in Parks and Recreation Settings
  by Carol Stensrud

Venture Publishing, Inc.
1999 Cato Avenue
State College, PA 16801
phone: 814–234–4561
fax: 814–234–1651